LIBRARY OF NEW TESTAMENT STUDIES
579

Formerly the Journal for the Study of the New Testament Supplement Series

Editor
Chris Keith

Editorial Board
Dale C. Allison, John M. G. Barclay, Lynn H. Cohick, R. Alan Culpepper,
Craig A. Evans, Robert Fowler, Simon J. Gathercole, Juan Hernandez Jr.,
John S. Kloppenborg, Michael Labahn, Love L. Sechrest, Robert Wall,
Catrin H. Williams

Methodology in the Use of the Old Testament in the New

Context and Criteria

Edited by
David Allen and Steve Smith

t&tclark

LONDON • NEW YORK • OXFORD • NEW DELHI • SYDNEY

T&T CLARK
Bloomsbury Publishing Plc
50 Bedford Square, London, WC1B 3DP, UK
1385 Broadway, New York, NY 10018, USA
29 Earlsfort Terrace, Dublin 2, Ireland

BLOOMSBURY, T&T CLARK and the T&T Clark logo are trademarks of
Bloomsbury Publishing Plc

First published in Great Britain 2020
This paperback edition published in 2021

Copyright © David Allen, Steve Smith and contributors, 2020

David Allen and Steve Smith have asserted their right under the Copyright, Designs
and Patents Act, 1988, to be identified as Editors of this work.

All rights reserved. No part of this publication may be reproduced or transmitted in any
form or by any means, electronic or mechanical, including photocopying, recording, or
any information storage or retrieval system, without prior permission in writing from
the publishers.

Bloomsbury Publishing Plc does not have any control over, or responsibility for, any
third-party websites referred to or in this book. All internet addresses given in this
book were correct at the time of going to press. The author and publisher regret any
inconvenience caused if addresses have changed or sites have ceased to exist, but
can accept no responsibility for any such changes.

A catalogue record for this book is available from the British Library.

Library of Congress Cataloging-in-Publication Data
Names: Allen, David (David H.), editor.
Title: Methodology in the use of the Old Testament in the new:
context and criteria/edited by David Allen and Steve Smith.
Description: 1 [edition]. | New York: T&T Clark, 2019. | Series: Library of New Testament
studies; volume 597 | Includes bibliographical references and index.
Identifiers: LCCN 2019016130 | ISBN 9780567678041 (hardback) |
ISBN 9780567678058 (epdf)
Subjects: LCSH: Bible. New Testament–Relation to the Old Testament. |
Bible–Hermeneutics.
Classification: LCC BS2387 .M48 2019 | DDC 225.6–dc23
LC record available at https://lccn.loc.gov/2019016130

ISBN: HB: 978-0-5676-7804-1
PB: 978-0-5677-0068-1
ePDF: 978-0-5676-7805-8
ePUB: 978-0-5676-9121-7

Series: Library of New Testament Studies, 2513-8790X, volume 579

Typeset by Deanta Global Publishing Services, Chennai, India

To find out more about our authors and books visit www.bloomsbury.com
and sign up for our newsletters.

Contents

Foreword to the Hawarden anniversary volume *Susan Docherty* — vii
List of contributors — x
List of abbreviations — xi

Introduction *David Allen and Steve Smith* — 1

Section A Methodological insights for OT/NT studies from outside the NT

1. Crossing testamentary borders: Methodological insights for OT/NT study from contemporary Hebrew Bible scholarship *Susan Docherty* — 11
2. Scriptural reuse in ancient Jewish literature: Comments and reflections on the state of the art *William A. Tooman* — 23
3. Genre versus intertextuality: Linking wisdom texts, themes and contexts with the wider Old Testament and with the sayings of Jesus *Katharine J. Dell* — 40
4. How Scripture 'speaks': Insights from the study of ancient media culture *Catrin H. Williams* — 53

Section B The role of OT context in OT/NT studies

5. The meaning and place of Old Testament context in OT/NT methodology *Arthur Keefer* — 73
6. Selective versus contextual allusions: Reconsidering technical terms of intertextuality *Beate Kowalski* — 86
7. Old Testament context: Insights from Philo *Kenneth Schenck* — 103
8. Old Testament context: Insights from the Dead Sea Scrolls *Benjamin Wold* — 115

Section C The role of criteria for OT/NT studies

9. The use of criteria: The state of the question *David Allen* — 129
10. The use of criteria: A proposal from relevance theory *Steve Smith* — 142

Section D Responses

11 Rethinking context in the relationship of Israel's Scriptures to the NT: Character, agency and the possibility of genuine change *Rikk Watts* — 157
12 Concluding reflection *Steve Moyise* — 178

Bibliography — 187
Author index — 211
Index of references — 216

This forty-year period does not evoke for members of the Hawarden Seminar connotations of desert times or of journeys that only lead towards a promised goal. For us, these years have been a real experience of learning and fellowship, enrichment and progress. The conversations, both personal and professional, around the papers and over meals and coffee have been fundamental to our success and endurance. When we marked our anniversary at our meeting on 22 to 24 March 2018, I highlighted some of the most significant ways in which the seminar has contributed to developing the field of the use of the OT in the NT within Britain and internationally, including:

- providing a regular opportunity for focused scholarly investigation and discussion of the use of the OT in the NT;
- creating a network which offers professional and personal support to those of us who work in this area and which also provides a clear reference point for editors, publishers and other biblical commentators;
- nurturing a new generation of OT/NT scholars;
- linking British New Testament study with the wider academic world;
- moving the sub-discipline forward, particularly through the major publications that have emerged from within the seminar, such as the series on the *New Testament and the Scriptures* of Israel edited by Steve Moyise and Maarten Menken between 2004 and 2012; the 2015 special edition of *JSNT* devoted to the use of the OT in the NT edited by David Allen and I; and this publication, which addresses some of the most pressing current methodological questions within OT/NT study.

It is in a spirit of pride in these achievements, gratitude towards those who have built up the seminar since its beginnings, and hope for a long and productive future, then, that we offer this volume and look forward *ad multos annos*.

Susan Docherty, Newman University Birmingham
Chair, Annual Seminar on the Use of the OT in the NT

Contributors

David Allen is Academic Dean at the Queen's Foundation for Ecumenical Theological Education, Birmingham.

Katharine J. Dell is Reader in Old Testament Literature and Theology in the Faculty of Divinity, University of Cambridge, and a Fellow of St Catharine's College, Cambridge.

Susan Docherty is Professor of New Testament and Early Judaism at Newman University, Birmingham.

Arthur Keefer is Chaplain and Teacher of Theology at Eton College, Windsor.

Beate Kowalski is Chair of Exegesis and Theology of the New Testament at TU Dortmund University, Germany.

Steve Moyise is Visiting Professor at Newman University, Birmingham.

Kenneth Schenck is Professor of New Testament and Christian Ministry, Wesley Seminary at Indiana Wesleyan University, Marion, IN.

Steve Smith is Tutor and Lecturer in New Testament Studies at St Mellitus College, London.

William A. Tooman is Senior Lecturer in Hebrew Bible/Old Testament at the University of St. Andrews, Scotland.

Rikk Watts is Dean of Faculty of Theology at Alphacrucis College, Parramatta, Australia.

Catrin H. Williams is Reader in New Testament Studies at the University of Wales Trinity Saint David, and Research Fellow in the Department of Old and New Testament Studies at University of the Free State, Bloemfontein.

Benjamin Wold is Lecturer in New Testament Studies at Trinity College, Dublin.

Abbreviations

AB	Anchor Bible
ABS	Approaches to Biblical Studies
AIL	Ancient Israel and its Literature
AJSR	*Association for Jewish Studies Review*
ArB	The Aramaic Bible
ASTI	Annual of the Swedish Theological Institute
AUSDDS	Andrews University Seminary Doctoral Dissertation Series
AUSS	*Andrews University Seminary Studies*
BBRSup	Bulletin for Biblical Research Supplement
Bib	*Biblica*
BiR	*Biblical Research*
BIS	Biblical Interpretation Series
BJS	Brown Judaic Studies
BTB	*Biblical Theology Bulletin*
BZAW	Beihefte zur Zeitschrift für die alttestamentliche Wissenschaft
CBET	Contributions to Biblical Exegesis and Theology
CBQ	*Catholic Biblical Quarterly*
CBQMS	*Catholic Biblical Quarterly*, Monograph Series
CBR	*Currents in Biblical Research*
CRINT	Compendia rerum iudaicarum ad Novum Testamentum
CurBS	*Currents in Research: Biblical Studies*
DSD	*Dead Sea Discoveries*
ECL	Early Christianity and Its Literature
EvQ	*Evangelical Quarterly*
FAT	Forschungen zum Alten Testament
FAT II	Forschungen zum Alten Testament. 2. Reihe
FB	Forschung zur Bibel
FJB	*Frankfurter Judaistische Beiträge*
FRLANT	Forschungen zur Religion und Literatur des Alten und Neuen Testaments
HUCA	*Hebrew Union College Annual*
IDS	In die Skriflig
JAC	*Jahrbuch für Antike und Christentum*
JAOS	*Journal of the American Oriental Society*
JBL	*Journal of Biblical Literature*
JETS	*Journal of the Evangelical Theological Society*
JLS	Journal of Literary Semantics
JNSL	*Journal of Northwest Semitic Languages*

JPOS	*Journal of the Palestine Oriental Society*
JQR	*Jewish Quarterly Review*
JSJ	*Journal for the Study of Judaism in the Persian, Hellenistic and Roman Periods*
JSJSup	Supplements to the Journal for the Study of Judaism
JSNT	*Journal for the Study of the New Testament*
JSNTSup	*Journal for the Study of the New Testament*, Supplement Series
JSOTSup	*Journal for the Study of the Old Testament*, Supplement Series
JSS	*Journal of Semitic Studies*
JSSSup	*Journal of Semitic Studies*, Supplements
JTS	*Journal of Theological Studies*
LHBOTS	The Library of Hebrew Bible/Old Testament Studies
LSTS	Library of Second Temple Studies
MNTS	Mcmaster New Testament Studies
Neot	*Neotestamentica*
NET	New Explorations in Theology
NIGTC	The New International Greek Testament Commentary
NovT	*Novum Testamentum*
NovTSup	Supplements to Novum Testamentum
NTC	The New Testament in Context
NTM	New Testament Monographs
NTR	New Testament Readings
NTS	*New Testament Studies*
OBO	Orbis biblicus et orientalis
OTL	Old Testament Library
OTG	Old Testament Guide
OTM	Oxford Theological Monographs
OTS	Oudtestamentische Stüdien
PAAJR	*Proceedings of the American Academy of Jewish Research*
PBNS	Pragmatics and Beyond New Series
PTMS	Princeton Theological Monograph Series
PzB	*Protokolle zur Bibel*
RHPR	*Revue d'histoire et de philosophie religieuses*
RevQ	*Revue de Qumran*
SBL	Studies in Biblical Literature
SBLEJL	Society of Biblical Literature Early Judaism and Its Literature
SBLMS	SBL Monograph Series
SBLSS	Society of Biblical Literature Symposium Series
SBLRBS	SBL Resources for Biblical Study
SBS	Stuttgarter Bibelstudien
SBT	Studies in Biblical Theology
SDSSRL	Studies in the Dead Sea Scrolls and Related Literature
SEÅ	Svensk exegetisk årsbok
Sem	*Semitica*
SJSJ	Supplements to the Journal for the Study of Judaism

SNTSMS	Society for New Testament Studies Monograph Series
SPhA	*Studia Philonica Annual*
ST	Studica theologica
STDJ	Studies on the Texts of the Desert of Judah
SVT	*Supplements to Vetus Testamentum*
SWBA	Social World of Biblical Antiquity
TSAJ	Texte und Studien zum antiken Judentum
TynBul	*Tyndale Bulletin*
UTB.W	Uni-Taschenbücher
VT	*Vetus Testamentum*
VTSup	*Vetus Testamentum*, Supplements
WBC	Word Biblical Commentary
WMANT	Wissenschaftliche Monographien zum Alten und Neuen Testament
WUNT	Wissenschaftliche Untersuchungen zum Neuen Testament
ZAW	*Zeitschrift für die alttestamentliche Wissenschaft*

Introduction

David Allen and Steve Smith

As Susan Docherty notes in her foreword to this volume, the Old Testament in the New Testament (OT/NT) annual seminar has recently celebrated its fortieth birthday. Just as with a ruby wedding anniversary, such a landmark would traditionally warrant or occasion some form of celebration or reflection, and this would seem particularly appropriate for biblical scholars for whom the resonance of forty years/days ripples across both testamentary discourses. As the seminar has emerged from this period of 'wilderness' reflections, one of the suggestions from its members was to mark the anniversary with a volume of essays focused upon matters with which the seminar has recently grappled (and with which it continues so to do). In recent years, a core issue in this regard has been questions of methodology – seeking to determine and/or explore the different lenses, methods and approaches that are used to assess how the NT writers went about using the Jewish Scriptures. Since such matters get to the very heart of what might define or distinguish OT/NT discourse, seminar members were invited to contribute papers engaging with the question, and the volume presented here is comprised of such submissions, along with some other formally requested papers from interested parties and critical friends. The papers are presented within three thematic sections, along with some final reflection and evaluation.

It is well recognized that OT/NT discourse owes much to many different disciplines, historical, literary, text critical and linguistic – for example, Richard Hays's engagement with the work of John Hollander[1] or the indebtedness that OT/NT research has to the work of OT exegetes. However, its engagement with some disciplines has been less than what might be thought. There has not been as much dialogue with OT study on inner-biblical allusion, particularly their methodology, as one would have thought;[2] in addition, other sub-disciplines in NT studies deserve greater attention in OT/NT methodology, especially social memory theory

---

[1] Richard B. Hays, *Echoes of Scripture in the Letters of Paul* (New Haven; London: Yale University Press, 1989), 18–21; John Hollander, *Figure of Echo: A Mode of Allusion in Milton and After* (Berkeley: University of California Press, 1981).

[2] Some texts have received attention like Michael Fishbane, *Biblical Interpretation in Ancient Israel* (Oxford: Clarendon, 1985); Benjamin D. Sommer, *A Prophet Reads Scripture: Allusion in Isaiah 40-66* (Stanford: Stanford University Press, 1998); but the discipline is full of helpful research that is less likely to be engaged with, for example, Ziony Zevit, ed., *Subtle Citation, Allusion, and Translation in the Hebrew Bible* (Sheffield: Equinox Publishing, 2017).

and theories about first-century media.³ The first section of this volume opens up discussion with these areas in a series of four chapters.

Opening up, Susan Docherty gives an overview of the significant contributions of OT inner-biblical allusions research from the perspective of NT scholarship, noting the great degree of overlap in interest with OT/NT methodology. She begins with the contributions of Michael Fishbane, who demonstrated both that there is a continuity between later forms of Jewish scriptural interpretation and those of the Hebrew Bible, and that OT scriptural exegesis is typically driven more by exegetical concern for understanding the older text than it is with examining the text of the author. This second issue is particularly relevant in NT scholarship, and while Docherty thinks Fishbane overstates his case, she notes that the idea does have some scholarly support in recent scholarship. Docherty then discusses how OT scholars have approached the question of identifying allusions, where much of their discussion is not known to NT scholarship, despite active investigation of the same problem. A significant difference between citation methods in the two testaments is the relative lack of introductory formulae in the OT, but there are places in the NT where citation is similarly unannounced (Revelation and paraenetic sections, for example), suggesting that genre has a role in signalling allusions. Overall, OT research on unsignalled citation, apparent inaccuracy in citation and rhetorical effects add interesting insights to NT scholarship, for example by drawing attention to ideas of 'pastiche' in Revelation.

In the second chapter, Bill Tooman reviews some recent contributions of scholarship on inner-biblical exegesis, beginning by noting the growing acknowledgement among scholars that most books of the Hebrew Bible were written or edited late, taking on more of the characteristics of Second Temple literature than was previously accepted. This means two things: First, because they were composed later than previously assumed, there is often no clear path of literary dependence from one text to another; rather, the rewriting leads to mutual influence between texts. Secondly, just as Second Temple texts like apocalyptic can contain an amalgamation of prior texts, so books of the Hebrew Bible can also contain an amalgamation of diverse material, typically linked through common content or context. When it comes to the amount of context of the original text that is utilized in textual reuse, Tooman notes that the Hebrew Bible (HB) can be atomistic in its interpretation, but its exegesis is not characterized by this; as evidence for this, he notes examples from Psalms and Daniel where a wider context from Isaiah is assumed. Considering the diversity of ways that the OT presents textual reuse, from allusion to parody, it is notable that Tooman finds that there is a standard stock of exegetical operations that underlie these diverse presentations of other texts. He finishes the overview of OT textual reuse with a discussion of polysemy, the surplus of meaning that the rabbinic writers found in the OT as divine communication; he proposes that this is more frequent in the HB than often assumed, as texts interact with each other through allusion. In this way, he proposes that HB writers may not be demanding a particular interpretive choice of their reader but exploiting the different perspectives that polysemy offers.

---

³ Anthony Le Donne and Tom Thatcher, eds, *The Fourth Gospel in First-Century Media Culture* (LNTS 426; London: T&T Clark, 2011).

The third chapter deals with OT textual reuse, where Katherine Dell takes a different approach by evaluating textual reuse involving the wisdom tradition, comparing the method of intertextuality to older genre-based methods. Intertextuality has the advantage of focusing on the text and it gives an interesting new approach to textual relationships, but it does not always contribute something beyond older methods. In order to demonstrate this, Dell surveys ways that a genre-orientated approach has been used to identify both the proverbial form in prophets and similarities in content between the books. When she turns to intertextuality, she notes that it can focus on thematic links where textual relationships are more allusive and where there are no clear verbal similarities; as such, she questions whether the thematic links identified by intertextuality are similar to those which older methods would have identified. The chapter then explores this by examining links between wisdom texts and other OT texts: with Psalms and Job, Dell notes that intertextuality does seem to be more robust as a method, but with other texts (Ecclesiastes and Genesis or Proverbs and Ruth), the case is less clear and thematic links are found by both methods, meaning that both potentially have their place. Finally, turning to Jesus's sayings and the wisdom tradition, Dell notes that the few intertextual links that are identified are typically thematic, meaning that older methods are just as fruitful in practice.

The fourth chapter moves the discussion to a second area of interdisciplinary discussion. Much of the discourse of OT/NT study focuses around the discussion of written texts, for obvious reasons, but this can marginalize how texts were written and used in the predominantly oral world of the first century. This raises significant issues including how writers recalled the texts they alluded to and how those who heard the texts being read remembered and processed those same texts. Catrin Williams explores such issues by detailing how advances in ancient media studies can contribute to our understanding of how the NT uses OT Scriptures. First, she examines the interaction between orality and the written text in the ancient world, because these were closely linked, especially because the written texts were read in public. In this way, the ancient audience made use of additional oral traditions that are not limited to the written text alone. Secondly, Williams evaluates the strategies and techniques used in the public performance of these texts, noting how they draw attention to the OT texts for their audiences, requiring them to draw on their common cultural memory associated with these OT texts. Finally, the chapter addresses the important area of memory. Theories of cultural or social memory have an important contribution to make as they articulate how groups of people remember the past and interpret it in the light of their present experience. Bearing this in mind, one is able to appreciate more significantly how writers articulate the significance of the past for their present writing purposes, using the OT not just as allusions but parts of the group memory of the Christian community.

One of the fundamental questions that permeates OT/NT discourse is the extent to which the original 'context' of an OT citation impacts upon or shapes its reception into the NT.[4] Particularly since the work of C. H. Dodd, though equally evident in

---

[4] D. M. Allen, 'Introduction: The Study of the Use of the Old Testament in the New', *JSNT* 38 (2015): 3–16 (3).

subsequent landmark works by Anthony Hanson or Barnabas Lindars,[5] scholars within the sub-discipline have grappled with the degree to which the original 'context' – however defined – is transferred along with the cited OT text. The second section of the volume considers such matters, reviewing both contemporary and historical scholarship accordingly.

The two opening discourses grapple theoretically with the concept. Arthur Keefer begins by considering the 'context' theme, appraising the differing scholarly perceptions as to how the NT writers might have respected (or otherwise) the cited OT text's original context. Reviewing a number of different contributors to the topic, and the methodologies they have utilized in respect of considering 'context', Keefer draws attention to the contested definition of 'context' and concludes that the heart of the question is essentially a 'semantic problem'. For context is interpreted as operative in a variety of ways – historical circumstance, literary or grammatical location, or theological impact – and its breadth or scope is viewed in similarly multivalent terms: 'a dozen verses, a group of texts, the entire OT canon, a theological concept, or a single theme'. Such definitional variation inevitably impacts the methodological approach respective commentators adopt, thereby leading to different – sometimes conflicting – assessments as to the NT writer's respect for context. To evidence this, Keefer offers three case studies (Hab. 2.4 in Rom. 1.17, Hos 11.1 in Mt 2.15; Exod 3.6 in Lk 20.37) to illustrate how 'context' is variously interpreted (e.g. whether Habbakuk's could be potentially understood as the Minor Prophets scroll or the whole OT canon). As such, he concludes that attending to the semantic variations of context makes for more robust OT/NT theological methodology and scholarly precision.

Beate Kowalski assumes a complementary approach to the context question, paying attention instead to the role that context takes in recognizing and evaluating intertextual allusions. She advocates for the importance of taking context seriously, both for the potential interpretative benefits it so yields within OT/NT discourse but also for the wider intertextual engagement it encourages and enables. After a brief review of intertextual discussion within OT/NT discourse, she turns, more specifically, to its function within Revelation and the varying ways in which scholars have recognized or addressed the theme. In particular, she rejects the notion of atomistic or 'selective' allusions, ones that don't in some way bring a context with them. Instead, she avers that 'a critical evaluation of the intertextual method reveals a high sensitivity for the context and the avoidance of an atomistic view on texts'.[6] Developing her argument outside of Revelation, Kowalski argues for a widening of the contextual remit of an allusion and the interpretative fruit this might achieve. Addressing the relationship between Luke 15 and the book of Ruth, and the associations with the Abraham narrative (Gen. 12.1), she proposes that Ruth may be seen as offering an intratextual model for faithful following, and by extension (cf. Luke 15) a window onto NT motifs of discipleship (particularly the notion of 'following').

---

[5] C. H. Dodd, *According to the Scriptures: The Sub-Structure of New Testament Theology* (London: Nisbet, 1952); Anthony Tyrrell Hanson, *The Living Utterances of God: The New Testament Exegesis of the Old* (London: Darton, Longman & Todd, 1983); Barnabas Lindars, *New Testament Apologetic* (London: SCM, 1961).

[6] Kowalski, 94.

The other two chapters remain focused on the 'context' question, but echo the approach taken in the previous section, namely to investigate what OT/NT discourse might learn from other related areas in terms of contextual awareness. First up, Kenneth Schenck considers Philo's contribution in this regard. To set the scene, Schenck attends to several aspects of Philonic scriptural engagement – what he conceived of as 'Scripture', what hermeneutical approaches informed such engagement and the degree to which Philo embraced a literal and/or allegorical interpretative lens. Assessing both Philo's application of the 'meaning' of words and the way in which he attended to the grammatical nuance within scriptural texts, Schenck subsequently turns to Philonic attention to literary and historical context, and the degree to which they influenced his scriptural interpretation. Schenck thus contrasts Philo's hermeneutic with that of the modern exegete – both are attentive to textual detail but are driven by different agendas or goals. Hence he concludes:

> Philo paid a great deal of attention to various details of the immediate literary context of passages in the Jewish Scriptures. However, his keen eye in this regard more often than not served non-contextual goals. That is to say, his eye for details in the context more typically served to find figural meanings rather than contextual ones.[7]

Benjamin Wold pursues similar questions in respect of the contextual awareness of the Qumran interpreters. Building on the prior analysis of such matters by Joseph Fitzmyer in respect of the supposed Yaḥad texts, Wold extends Fitzmyer's analysis to include more ('previously unknown')[8] non-Yaḥad material. Unlike Kowalski, he focuses on explicit citations as the primary locus for assessing contextual sensitivity but equally recognizes the implications of such comparatively infrequent usage/citation. As such, he observes that 'when asking about how and if OT contexts carry over when Scripture is cited in their new contexts, the dominance of non-explicit usages already indicate a lack of interest into original context(s)'.[9] Wold utilizes Fitzmyer's four categories by which to classify interpretative, contextual awareness (literary/historical; modernization; accommodation; eschatological) and (re)applies them to both the Yaḥad and non-Yaḥad texts. In so doing, he discerns relatively little interest in the original historical or literary setting; instead the 'context' tends to be accommodated to the needs/situation of the community and/or reshaped to justify or support particular theological views or positions. In sum, 'the use of OT in its many varieties ... as represented in Qumran discoveries reflects little interest in original contexts'.[10]

The final section examines how allusions to or echoes of the OT in the NT may be detected. It is now thirty years since the publication of Richard Hays's seminal *Echoes of Scripture in the Letters of Paul*,[11] and perhaps no part of this book has affected scholarship more than his criteria for the detection of allusions. While his criteria are

---

[7] Schenck, 103.
[8] That is, to exclude Rewritten Bible or similar texts.
[9] Wold, 116.
[10] Ibid., 125.
[11] Hays, *Echoes*.

not the only discussion of how allusions may be detected, many scholars explicitly or tacitly adopt them; while this adoption is not always uncritical, they still form the most commonly used basis for identifying allusions. This is a critical issue for methodology in OT/NT studies, and as the criticisms of Hays make clear, it is important that his criteria are re-assessed. David Allen does just this in his chapter. He reviews the scholarship on criteria for identifying echoes and allusions, beginning with a review of the criteria themselves and their adaptation by other scholars. In reviewing the criticisms of Hays's criteria, Allen notes that there is no clear scholarly consensus against them, but he calls for a more drastic re-evaluation. The scholarly discussion since Hays has not moved things very far beyond the criteria that he described, and most of the discussion is about which of the criteria are required. Allen argues that the re-evaluation should be more fundamental than that – 'It may be that we need to offer a different lens to the allusion discourse, one no longer predicated in terms of criteria, or "criteria" utilized or understood in a different way.'[12] He goes on to suggest an approach orientated around social memory theory as described by Tom Thatcher (and which, in several ways, picks up on the themes raised in Catrin Williams's chapter).

Finally, Steve Smith proposes another approach for identifying allusions. Rather than adopting the criteria to measure the likelihood of an allusion, Smith utilizes Sperber and Wilson's relevance theory, a cognitive linguistic approach which its proponents argue lies behind all human communication. Relevance helps the interpreter to understand the subconscious and often instantaneous intellectual processes that readers/hearers go through in searching for the correct interpretive context (and which writers also use to ensure clear communication). The identification of echoes is a subjective process, both for the reader of a text and for the biblical interpreter, and Smith proposes a series of guides drawn from relevance theory which permit the interpreter to focus on the significant stages of the process of identifying allusions; he argues that this provides the biblical interpreter with 'a framework for understanding how readers approach texts', thereby permitting the scholar to think their thoughts after them. It is not simply that the reader accesses the most obvious text, instead the reader's selection of texts is a complex interaction directed by how much the NT text encourages a sustained exploration of OT context. As such the theory helps to articulate the different readings that occur on first reading a text and on repeated readings or study.

This volume's final two chapters are more self-standing. Rather than then comprising a discrete section, each one – albeit in different fashion – engages with the various ways in which the volume seeks to move forward debates around methodological approaches in OT/NT discourse. First up, Rikk Watts sets forth a wide-ranging proposal on how one might assess fundamental aspects of the NT authors' appeal to the Jewish Scriptures. Rather than beginning with the NT writers' usage and 'reading back' into the OT accordingly, Watts advocates for beginning with how the Scriptures were already viewed as opening up the faithful character of Israel's God. In effect, he traces a methodological path that reads *forwards* rather than backwards, so venturing: 'Given the historical and contextual priority of the Scriptures, it makes better sense methodologically to begin, not with the NT use of the OT, but with Israel's Scriptures

---

[12] Allen, 141.

normative shaping of the NT.'[13] Effectively, therefore, Watts advocates for adopting a theological as much as a literary lens when considering OT/NT methodology. This has implications, for example, for questions of context; the NT writers, he avers, believed they were working with scriptural texts, and thus the context of those texts *as Scripture* is foundational. It also necessitates, as Watts suggests, taking more serious account of authorial intention than literary approaches traditionally embrace.

In the concluding chapter, Steve Moyise engages with the previous entries, and the material/ground they seek to cover, so offering some reflections on how the volume might be able to progress scholarly thinking on OT/NT methodologies. Moyise does not interact with the fine details of each chapter, but instead seeks to tease out some themes and issues that emerge within the constituent sections. In so doing, he draws particularly on Michelle Fletcher's recent work on the use of the OT in Revelation, as one recent monograph that similarly grapples with the questions of context and the identification of scriptural allusions.[14] Moyise is not convinced by all the respective proposals of the individual contributors but concludes nonetheless that the volume is 'a rich collection of essays that shows that many traditional questions are being rethought, as well new avenues of research opening up'.[15] As editors, we trust that other readers will conclude likewise.

---

[13] Watts, 165.
[14] Michelle Fletcher, *Reading Revelation as Pastiche: Imitating the Past* (LNTS 571, London: Bloomsbury T&T Clark, 2017).
[15] Moyise, 186.

Section A

Methodological insights for OT/NT studies from outside the NT

1

Crossing testamentary borders: Methodological insights for OT/NT study from contemporary Hebrew Bible scholarship

Susan Docherty

Introduction: Disciplinary borders

The investigation of the use of the Old Testament in the New (OT/NT) is of necessity a cross-disciplinary activity, both making use of and contributing much to the wider study of the NT, Septuagint, Qumran Scrolls, Second Temple Judaism and early Christianity. It might be assumed that the relationship of this sub-discipline of NT studies to Hebrew Bible scholarship would be particularly strong and yet, in his introduction to the 2015 OT/NT special issue of *JSNT*, David Allen felt compelled to conclude, 'Whilst, of course, OT in the NT draws heavily on Hebrew Bible scholarship, one senses that the direction of travel has tended to be only one-way; i.e. Hebrew Bible scholars have generally been less interested in the findings of OT in the NT scholarship such that it informs … their scholarly output.'[1] This relative lack of wider impact of the advances made in the last four decades in understanding the early Christian interpretation of Scripture is rather surprising, given the shared interest of commentators on both sides of the testamentary divide in questions about the textual transmission of the scriptural writings, their reception history and the quotation within them of earlier authoritative sources. One of the aims of this volume – and of the current Hawarden Seminar itself – is, therefore, to begin to bridge this gap.

This chapter starts from the premise that those working on *both* sides of this disciplinary border would benefit from greater engagement across it, for it is as difficult for NT scholars to keep fully abreast of developments in the study of the Hebrew Bible as vice versa. In what follows, therefore, I propose to highlight current trends in research into the specific area of inner-biblical exegesis that have implications for the methods employed to analyse the use of Scripture in the NT. The starting point for any

---

[1] D. M. Allen, 'Introduction: The Study of the Use of the Old Testament in the New', *JSNT* 38 (2015): 3–16 (3).

survey of this field is the publication in 1985 of Michael Fishbane's groundbreaking *Biblical Interpretation in Ancient Israel*.[2] This volume has been influential across biblical studies as a whole, but there has not been a similarly wide reception within NT circles of subsequent attempts to build on the foundations laid by Fishbane. The constraints of this chapter do not allow for anything like a comprehensive treatment of the work of later commentators such as Richard Schultz, Benjamin Sommer or Bill Tooman, but key aspects of their approaches and conclusions that have particular relevance for the sub-discipline of OT/NT will be explored.

It is essential to acknowledge at the outset that there are important differences between the phenomenon of inner-biblical quotation and early Christian uses of Scripture. Unlike the NT, the writings that make up the Hebrew Bible do not operate within a context in which an authoritative collection of 'scriptures' has been established, and they contain very few clear examples of formal citation. Their complex transmission history also provides a particular methodological challenge, raising issues of dating and the need to agree on criteria for assessing the direction of dependence of any perceived literary borrowing. This is a task with which Fishbane did not engage in any great detail but to which some of his successors have brought a high degree of sophistication. David Carr, for example, argues cogently that in Israel, as in other Ancient Near Eastern cultures, memory and oral repetition played a central role in the passing on of valued traditions, even after these had started to be preserved in writing.[3] This helps to explain the presence within the OT of differing forms of the same material. No direct equivalence is being suggested between the reuse of older traditions within the books of the Hebrew Bible and the interpretation of the Scriptures in the NT, then, but the methodological tools currently being applied to the analysis of the former may still yield insights useful for those investigating the latter.

1 Inner-biblical exegesis: Methodological insights and implications

1.1 Exegetical tradition

One of Fishbane's major contributions to the field is his persuasive demonstration of the fundamental continuity between the interpretative traditions and techniques present within the Hebrew Bible and those employed in later forms of Jewish scriptural

---

[2] M. Fishbane, *Biblical Interpretation in Ancient Israel* (Oxford: Clarendon Press, 1985).
[3] See D. M. Carr, *Writing on the Tablet of the Heart: Origins of Scripture and Literature* (New York: Oxford University Press, 2005). In his *The Formation of the Hebrew Bible: A New Reconstruction* (New York: Oxford University Press, 2011) he also provides a particularly useful summary of his methodology for establishing the presence of intertextual relationships and the direction of dependence (425–8). For a much earlier article arguing similarly that oral and written transmission are complementary rather than mutually exclusive, see H. Ringgren, 'Oral and Written Transmission in the OT: Some Observations', *ST* 3 (1949): 34–59.

exposition.⁴ The publication of more of the Qumran manuscripts in the decades immediately following the publication of Fishbane's work has provided further information about this shared hermeneutical framework and has also revealed some interesting correspondences between these scrolls and the NT writings, in terms of both the selection of scriptural texts and the methods used to interpret them.⁵ Contemporary approaches to OT/NT study have been profoundly influenced by the growing appreciation of the significance of this exegetical heritage, which clearly shaped the ways in which the first followers of Jesus read their Scriptures. Methodologically, then, it has now become axiomatic to situate the NT interpretation of Scripture firmly within this early Jewish context.⁶

1.2 Exegetical motivation

Fishbane's second major conclusion is that the use of older material within a scriptural writing is generally prompted by exegetical reflection on this tradition rather than by any external theological or sociological concern: 'For inner-biblical exegesis there is no merely literary or theological playfulness. Exegesis arises out of a practical crisis of some sort – the incomprehensibility of a word or rule, or the failure of the covenantal tradition to engage its audience.'⁷ He supports this judgement by pointing to examples of the clarification of legal ambiguities (e.g. Jer. 17.21-2; cf. Deut. 5.12-14) and the updating of earlier prophecies when they are not fulfilled as expected (e.g. Isa. 16.11-14; Dan. 9.2, 24-7; cf. Jer. 25.11-14). It is difficult to maintain consistently the kind of rigid distinction between 'pure' exegesis and ideologically motivated interpretation that Fishbane seems to envisage, so his position is not entirely convincing.⁸ His former student Bernard Levinson, for instance, argues that the wholesale reworking of tradition evident in some parts of the Hebrew Bible goes far beyond the elucidation of a challenging text: 'Neither "interpretation" nor "exegesis" adequately suggests the

---

⁴ See especially Fishbane, *Biblical Interpretation*, 23–88; cf. his *The Garments of Torah: Essays in Biblical Hermeneutics* (Bloomington and Indianapolis: Indiana University Press, 1989), 4–16. Other commentators also emphasize the importance of engaging with the long history of Jewish biblical interpretation; see, for example, G. Vermes, *Scripture and Tradition in Judaism: Haggadic Studies* (SB 4; Leiden: Brill, 1983); J. L. Kugel, *In Potiphar's House: The Interpretive Lives of Biblical Texts* (Cambridge: Harvard University Press, 1994); and, for an earlier example of this approach, L. Ginzberg, *Legends of the Jews* (Philadelphia: Jewish Publication Society, 1909).

⁵ For further detail, see, for example, G. J. Brooke, '"The Canon within the Canon" at Qumran and in the New Testament', in *The Scrolls and the Scriptures: Qumran Fifty Years After* (ed. S. E. Porter and C. A. Evans; Sheffield: Sheffield Academic Press, 1997), 242–66; J. A. Fitzmyer, 'The Use of Explicit Old Testament Quotations in Qumran Literature and in the New Testament', *NTS* 7 (1960-1): 297–333; and T. H. Lim, *Holy Scripture in the Qumran Commentaries and Pauline Letters* (Oxford: Clarendon Press, 1997).

⁶ For a fuller treatment of this point, see S. E. Docherty, 'New Testament Scriptural Interpretation in its Early Jewish Context: Reflections on the *Status Quaestionis* and Future Directions', *NovT* 57 (2015): 1–19.

⁷ Fishbane, *Garments of Torah*, 16; cf. *Biblical Interpretation*, 282.

⁸ Geza Vermes coined the terms 'pure' and 'applied' exegesis to cover this distinction in 'Bible and Midrash: Early Old Testament Exegesis', in *The Cambridge History of the Bible Vol. 1: From the Beginnings to Rome* (ed. P. R. Ackroyd and C. F. Evans; Cambridge: Cambridge University Press, 1970), 199–231 (202).

extent to which Deuteronomy radically transforms literary and legal history [referring particularly to the Covenant Code in Exodus] in order to forge a new vision of religion and the state.'[9]

Nevertheless, the question Fishbane raises about how closely a later interpretation is related to the scriptural text generating it remains central to the disciplines of both Hebrew Bible and the NT. Steve Moyise, for example, points to the importance of seeking to understand 'whether Paul derives his interpretations mainly through "inner-biblical exegesis" or from the rhetorical exigencies of his and his reader's situation'.[10] A significant development in this ongoing debate is that leading figures in contemporary Jewish studies, such as Daniel Boyarin and Alexander Samely, now stress that the roots of rabbinic exegesis lie principally in attempts to deal with perceived problems in the underlying biblical texts. Their conclusions mirror Fishbane's, then, and they pose a clear challenge to earlier characterizations of rabbinic literature as a largely ideological enterprise in which later theological beliefs were read back into the Scriptures.[11] This shift towards a fuller recognition of the often genuinely exegetical motivation of early Jewish interpreters has methodological implications for the field of OT/NT study. In particular, it requires serious consideration of the possibility that the selection and interpretation of scriptural texts by the first Christians was governed not only – perhaps not even primarily – by their christological convictions but also reflects their engagement with textual difficulties of the kind that exercised other ancient Jewish readers.[12]

This claim may be illustrated by Hebrews chs 3–4. The author's definition of 'rest' here as specifically 'sabbath rest' (Heb. 4.9) reflects his understanding of Jesus and of salvation, but it also serves to resolve an apparent contradiction in Scripture, between the divine declaration made in the Psalms that the wilderness generation would *not* enter God's rest (Ps. 95.11) and the report in the book of Numbers that some of them *did* achieve the 'rest' of entry into the promised land (Num. 14.24, 30). Similar exegetical *cruces* also appear to underlie passages in the Gospels and Acts, such as the discussions about resurrection (Mk 12.24-7 and parallels; cf. Deut. 25.5) and the existence of two 'lords' (Mk 12.35-7 and parallels; cf. Ps. 110.1), or the questions put to Philip by the Ethiopian eunuch about the identity of the 'suffering servant' (Acts 8.34; Isa. 53.7-8).[13] It is not, of course, the case that the NT writers

---

[9] B. Levinson, *Deuteronomy and the Hermeneutics of Legal Innovation* (New York: Oxford University Press, 1997), 15. For a similar view, see, for example, J. Stackert, *Rewriting the Torah: Literary Revision in Deuteronomy and the Holiness Legislation* (FAT 52; Tübingen: Mohr Siebeck, 2007).

[10] S. Moyise, 'Does Paul Respect the Context of His Quotations?' in *Paul and Scripture: Extending the Conversation* (ed. C. D. Stanley; Atlanta: Society of Biblical Literature Press, 2012), 97–114 (101).

[11] See especially D. Boyarin, *Intertextuality and the Reading of Midrash* (Bloomington and Indianapolis: Indiana University Press, 1990), where he explains the questions underpinning his study of midrash as follows: 'What in the Bible's text might have motivated this gloss on this verse? Can I explain this text in such a way that this gloss makes sense as an interpretation of this verse?' (ix). See also A. Samely, *The Interpretation of Speech in the Pentateuch Targums: A Study of Method and Presentation in Targumic Exegesis* (Tübingen: Mohr Siebeck, 1992), 3, 162, 165–73, 180–1.

[12] On the shared hermeneutical stance (but differing conclusions) of the NT writings and the Qumran scrolls, see further T. H. Lim, 'Qumran Scholarship and the Study of the Old Testament in the New Testament', *JSNT* 38 (2015): 68–80.

[13] These examples are treated at greater length in Docherty, 'New Testament Scriptural Interpretation', 10–18.

always reached the same conclusions as other early Jews about the meaning of a scriptural passage, nor that they always drew from their texts an interpretation which can be regarded as closely linked to their 'plain sense' or original context, for their readings certainly were shaped by their convictions about Jesus's messiahship and by the needs of their particular audiences.[14] Contemporary Hebrew Bible scholarship does, however, point to the methodological value of exploring the extent to which specific phrases or potential ambiguities within a scriptural passage made it a suitable 'target' for exegesis and so played some part in stimulating the interpretation it receives in the NT.

1.3 Identifying quotations and allusions

The formulation of agreed criteria for identifying both citations and allusions is a further key methodological focus of OT/NT research. This is no less pressing an issue for the investigation of inner-biblical exegesis, so there is clear potential for valuable cross-disciplinary engagement in this area. In fact, however, recent attempts within Hebrew Bible scholarship to bring greater precision to this task have not been widely disseminated in NT circles. Similarly, beyond limited recognition of the work of Richard Hays on scriptural 'echoes',[15] Hebrew Bible commentators seem largely to have remained unaffected by important developments in the application to the NT writings of various theories of intertextuality.

Since citation within the OT is largely implicit rather than explicit,[16] so that most examples of it are neither formally marked nor follow their assumed source exactly (see further below, sections 1.4. and 1.5.), considerable care has to be taken to distinguish between an intentional *quotation* of an older scriptural text and a *verbal parallel*, which may have been introduced unconsciously or for purely stylistic reasons. Fishbane recognizes this problem and regards both 'volume' (the extent of lexical overlap with a proposed source text) and a level of exegetical engagement (as opposed to simple restatement) as essential to the classification of a citation.[17] This aspect of his methodology has been further refined by subsequent commentators. Sommer, for instance, draws directly on Hays's seven 'tests' in his attempt to identify the allusions to earlier scriptural texts in Deutero-Isaiah. He suggests the addition of an eighth criterion to exclude correspondences which may reflect the use of a well-known Israelite or

---

[14] For further discussion of this issue, see, for example, S. Moyise, *Evoking Scripture: Seeing the Old Testament in the New* (London: T&T Clark, 2008), 125–41; and, for an opposing view, G. K. Beale, *Handbook on the New Testament Use of the Old Testament: Exegesis and Interpretation* (Grand Rapids: Baker Academic, 2012).

[15] R. B. Hays, *Echoes of Scripture in the Letters of Paul* (New Haven: Yale University Press, 1989).

[16] See, for example, Fishbane, *Biblical Interpretation*, 284–5; R. Schultz, *Search for Quotation: Verbal Parallels in the Prophets* (JSOTSup 180; Sheffield: Sheffield Academic Press, 1999), 218–19.

[17] 'The identification of aggadic exegesis where external objective criteria are lacking is proportionally increased to the extent that multiple and sustained lexical linkages between two texts can be recognized, and where the second text (the putative *traditio*) uses a segment of the first (the putative *traditum*) in a lexically reorganized and topically rethematized way' (Fishbane, *Biblical Interpretation*, 285; cf. 287).

Ancient Near Eastern *topos* rather than a deliberate literary borrowing.[18] He therefore anticipates a criticism which has been levelled against some post-Haysian approaches to the detection of scriptural allusions in the NT, which do not take sufficient account of the possibility that a phrase may have been circulating in common parlance, quite independently of any connection to its original scriptural location.[19]

Among contemporary Hebrew Bible scholars, it is perhaps Bill Tooman who has most helpfully taken forward this quest for greater accuracy in determining cases of inner-biblical citation. Following the literary theorist Stefan Morawski, he argues that 'quotations' involve both a degree of literal or word-for-word agreement between the evoking text and its original source, and a certain discreteness between the cited material and its surrounding frame.[20] According to this definition, only a segment that is clearly separable from its new context can be classified as a quotation 'proper', making this a rare phenomenon in the Hebrew Bible.[21] Nevertheless, there are numerous passages throughout the OT in which older scriptural material is apparently being reused, even if not formally quoted. Tooman proposes a set of five criteria for identifying examples of such inner-biblical allusion or literary borrowing: uniqueness, distinctiveness, multiplicity (or volume), thematic correspondence and inversion.[22] In other words, the lemma in question should occur only in the proposed source text or else be distinctive of it (e.g. the phrase 'to dwell securely', which is characteristic of the Holiness Code, see, for example, Lev. 25.18, 19; 26.5, but occurs only infrequently in other scriptural books); there should be multiple references to it in close proximity; it is likely to share some element of theme or argument with the evoking text; and components of it may be inverted when it is reproduced (see further below, section 1.5.). There is clear overlap between these principles and Hays's seven tests, although Tooman refers only very briefly to the influence of Hays on his list.[23]

Tooman's efforts to define inner-biblical quotations more rigorously are less relevant for the NT, where scriptural citations are often clearly introduced as such, but they may well contribute to the ongoing debate within OT/NT research around the detection of allusions. His approach reinforces the value of criteria such as uniqueness and distinctiveness, which are widely accepted in theory but which may not have been given sufficient weight in practice by all commentators post-Hays, leading some to

---

[18] B. Sommer, *A Prophet Reads Scripture: Allusion in Isaiah 40-66* (Stanford: Stanford University Press, 1988), 219–20, and, for a more general discussion of this problem, 7–33; see also Schultz, *Search for Quotation*, 18–114, 223; M. A. Lyons, *From Law to Prophecy: Ezekiel's Use of the Holiness Code* (New York and London: T&T Clark, 2009), 73; and P. Ackroyd, 'The Vitality of the Word of God in the Old Testament: A Contribution to the Study of the Transmission of Old Testament Material', *ASTI* 1 (1962): 7–23 (9).

[19] See, for example, P. Foster, 'Echoes without Resonance: Critiquing Certain Aspects of Recent Scholarly Trends in the Study of the Jewish Scriptures in the New Testament', *JSNT* 38 (2015): 96–111 (98).

[20] W. Tooman, *Gog of Magog: Reuse of Scripture and Compositional Technique in Ezekiel 38-39* (FAT 2/52; Tübingen: Mohr Siebeck, 2011), 5; S. Morawski, 'The Basic Functions of Quotation', in *Sign, Language, Culture* (ed. A. J. Greimas; The Hague: Mouton 1970), 690–705.

[21] Tooman, *Gog of Magog*, 5.

[22] Ibid., 27–31. See also the similar four criteria proposed by Michael Lyons: frequency and distribution; awareness of context; availability of options to express the idea; interaction with the source text (*From Law to Prophecy*, 68–73).

[23] Tooman, *Gog of Magog*, 8–9.

perhaps overstate both the number and the theological significance of the scriptural 'echoes' employed in some NT writings.[24]

1.4 Introducing citations

Not only are there very few marked quotations within the Hebrew Bible, as has been observed above, but even where an introduction of some kind is provided, the information given about the source is usually only rather vague: '... which you commanded by your servants the prophets, saying ...' (Ezra 9.10), for instance, or '... according to what is written in the book of the law of Moses, where the Lord commanded ...' (2 Kgs 14.6). In his thorough examination of this aspect of inner-biblical citation, Schultz compares it to the practices evident in the surviving literature from ancient Egypt and Mesopotamia, concluding that although the reuse of earlier material was very widespread in those literary cultures, formally drawing attention to the presence of quotations was not.[25]

By the time of the later apocryphal books and the Qumran texts, however, citations are formally introduced far more frequently,[26] and this development within early Judaism is clearly reflected in the NT. It is doubtless connected to the process of canon formation, by which certain writings acquired a particular status, so that they were commonly appealed to in theological argument, and the distinction between these authoritative traditions and their later interpretation became more clearly emphasized. Even so, the use of imprecise (e.g. Mt. 2.5, 23; Lk. 1.70; Acts 3.22; Heb. 2.6) or even inaccurate (e.g. Mt. 27.9-10; cf. Zech. 11.12-13; Mk 1.2; cf. Mal. 3.1) introductory formulae does not appear to have been regarded as problematic by the early Christian authors or their audiences, as long as the presence of a quotation was signalled. There are, however, interesting exceptions within the NT to this general tendency to explicitly cite Scripture: most obviously, the one example of an apocalyptic work, Revelation, lacks any direct quotations, although the author is clearly drawing on the Jewish Scriptures throughout for his imagery and expression. Similar embedded use of unmarked allusions is also common in paraenetical sections of the NT that draw on teaching from Proverbs, Psalms or other wisdom writings (see, for example, Rom. 12.15; 2 Cor. 9.6, 7; Heb. 13.15). Genre may have been a significant factor, then, in determining the ways in which later authors reused scriptural material, affecting the extent to which both quotation marking and exact reproduction was expected. This is an area of OT/NT study which could fruitfully be further explored.

1.5 Literal accuracy of quotation

One of the most interesting emphases to emerge from recent study of the Hebrew Bible is that inner-scriptural quotations and allusions do not generally re-present the original with absolute accuracy. In a detailed examination of the reuse of the Pentateuchal Laws in Ezra-Nehemiah, for instance, Juha Pakkala concludes that 'in

---

[24] See the examples cited by Foster in 'Echoes without Resonance'.
[25] Schultz, *Search for Quotation*, 116-43.
[26] Ibid., 170. See also Fitzmyer, 'Use of Explicit Old Testament Quotations', 299-305.

no single case does the quotation or purported quotation correspond exactly to a known Pentateuchal text'.[27] Sources can be adapted through the employment of various techniques, such as abbreviation, expansion, omission, reordering, conflation with another scriptural passage, or by making any grammatical or stylistic changes demanded by the new textual frame. The verses from Nehemiah set out below, for example, follow a section of Deuteronomy closely, but reproduce it selectively rather than identically:

On that day they read from the book of Moses in the hearing of the people; and in it was found written that no Ammonite or Moabite should ever enter the assembly of God, because they did not meet the Israelites with bread and water, but hired Balaam against them to curse them – yet our God turned the curse into a blessing. (Neh. 13.1-2)[28]	No Ammonite or Moabite shall be admitted to the assembly of the Lord. Even to the tenth generation, none of their descendants shall be admitted to the assembly of the Lord, because they did not meet you with food and water on your journey out of Egypt, and because they hired against you Balaam son of Beor, from Pethor of Mesopotamia, to curse you. (Yet the Lord your God refused to heed Balaam; the Lord your God turned the curse into a blessing for you, because the Lord your God loved you.) (Deut. 23.3-5)

The same level of apparently deliberate alteration is also evident when non-scriptural sources are repeated within the Hebrew Bible.[29] In just one of many such examples, Abraham's servant quotes his master's instructions to him about finding a wife for Isaac from among his kin, but with notable differences from the original speech.

But he [Abraham] said to me, 'The Lord, before whom I walk, will send his angel with you and make your way successful. You shall get a wife for my son from my kindred, from my father's house. Then you will be free from my oath, when you come to my kindred; even if they will not give her to you, you will be free from my oath.' (Gen. 24.40-1)	Abraham said to him [his servant] … 'The Lord, the God of heaven, who took me from my father's house and from the land of my birth, and who spoke to me and swore to me, "To your offspring I will give this land", he will send his angel before you; you shall take a wife for my son from there. But if the woman is not willing to follow you, then you will be free from this oath of mine; only you must not take my son back there.' (Gen. 24.6-8)

---

[27] J. Pakkala, 'The Quotations and References of the Pentateuchal Laws in Ezra-Nehemiah', in *Changes in Scripture: Rewriting and Interpreting Authoritative Traditions in the Second Temple Period* (ed. H. von Weissenberg, J. Pakkala and M. Marttila; BZAW 419; Berlin and New York: De Gruyter, 2011), 193–221 (214); cf. R. Mason, 'The Use of Earlier Biblical Material in Zechariah 9-14: A Study in Inner-Biblical Exegesis', in *Bringing Out the Treasure: Inner-Biblical Allusion in Zechariah 9-14* (ed. M. J. Boda and M. H. Floyd; JSOTSup 203; Sheffield: Sheffield Academic Press, 2003), 3–207 (201).
[28] All English translations of the Bible used in this chapter follow the NRSV.
[29] For a full study of quotation and repetition of non-scriptural material in biblical narrative see G. Savran, *Telling and Retelling: Quotation in Biblical Narrative* (Bloomington and Indianapolis: Indiana University Press, 1988).

Like the lack of citation markers, this tendency to avoid verbatim reproduction probably reflects contemporary literary practices and cultural expectations. Schultz concludes, for instance, that across Ancient Near Eastern literature 'a large degree of verbal divergence can be tolerated as long as the quotation is still recognizable'.[30] Modern conventions have conditioned us to expect exact citation, but such literal agreement is not an absolute requirement for a quotation to serve its rhetorical or didactic purpose, as long as the readers can recognize where it begins and ends. Tooman draws particular attention to the employment in the Hebrew Bible of the technique of inversion as one means of signalling to the audience that an older authoritative text is being reused.[31] In Ezekiel, for example, the prophet's inaugural vision (Ezek. 1.26-8) is clearly being recalled later (in Ezek. 8.2), but elements in the description of the supernatural figure are given in a different order:[32]

And seated above the likeness of a throne was something that seemed like a human form. *Upwards* from what appeared like the loins I saw something like *gleaming amber*, something that looked like fire enclosed all round; and *downwards* from what looked like the loins I saw something that looked like *fire*, and there was splendour all round. (Ezek. 1.26-7)	I looked, and there was a figure that looked like a human being; *below* what appeared to be its loins it was *fire*, and *above* the loins it was like the appearance of brightness, like *gleaming amber*. (Ezek. 8.2)

As has been stated throughout this chapter, the findings of commentators like Schultz and Tooman are not all directly applicable to the NT, in which both formally marked and completely accurate citations do regularly occur. They also have to be considered in the light of other significant factors: the role of memory in the formation of the Hebrew Bible, for instance; the probable existence of multiple versions (both oral and written) of Israel's laws and narrative traditions for many centuries; and the tolerance of a degree of scribal intervention in the copying and transmission of authoritative texts during the Second Temple period, resulting in a situation of considerable textual pluriformity.[33] Nevertheless, their work does open up some potentially useful fresh lines of enquiry into early Christian quotation of Scripture. First, one of Tooman's specific conclusions about the employment of older material within the Gog and Magog oracles (Ezekiel 38–9) may have implications for some sections of the NT. He regards these chapters as an example of a pastiche-like genre that is relatively common in Second Temple Jewish literature, in which phrases, images and themes drawn from a wide range of scriptural passages are reworked into a new composition marked by a

---

[30] Schultz, *Search for Quotation*, 143.
[31] Moshe Seidel first pointed to this technique over sixty years ago in his 'Parallels between Isaiah and Psalms', *Sinai* 38 (1955–6): 149–72, 229–40, 271–80, 335–55; cf. P. C. Beentjes, 'Inverted Quotations in the Bible: A Neglected Stylistic Pattern', *Bib* 63 (1982): 506–23. Levinson also points to several instances of this phenomenon in *Deuteronomy*, 18–19, 35, 90, 100, 119.
[32] See Tooman, *Gog of Magog*, 27–31.
[33] On these issues, in addition to the earlier references to Carr, *Writing on the Tablet of the Heart*, and *Formation of the Hebrew Bible*, see, for example, S. Talmon, *Text and Canon of the Hebrew Bible: Collected Studies* (Winona Lake: Eisenbrauns, 2010); and, most recently, S. White Crawford, 'Textual Growth and the Activity of Scribes', *SEÅ* 82 (2017): 6–27.

clearly biblical style.³⁴ This may enable commentators to situate the book of Revelation more precisely within the early Jewish literary and textual culture, and in particular to explain its use of Scripture, as this author, too, combines an extensive array of texts and motifs without explicit or exact citation. This new thinking helpfully informs two recently published monographs on Revelation by Garrick Allen and Michelle Fletcher, for example.³⁵ Second, the work of these Hebrew Bible scholars invites deeper reflection on the reasons for any differences between a quotation in the NT and its original scriptural expression. The evidence of practices such as inversion does imply that ancient exegetes intentionally employed dissimilarity when reproducing earlier material, perhaps to draw the attention of their audience to particularly significant phrases. This is an aspect of the cultural background of the early Christian authors which should be considered, then, although it has to be balanced with due awareness also of the availability to them of variant textual forms.

1.6 Rhetorical purposes of quotation

The discussion in section 1.5. connects with a final area of shared interest across Hebrew Bible and NT study: the investigation of the rhetorical or theological purposes for which the scriptural authors employed citations. Several of those who first took up Fishbane's ideas, including Sommer, Levinson and Schultz, go further than him in exploring the reasons for the extensive appeal to earlier material within the Hebrew Bible, pointing to possible factors like a perceived need to provide 'authority and legitimacy for a new work'.³⁶ Contemporary commentators like Tooman and Lyons also pay close attention to the question of the communicative strategy underlying the selection, quotation and modification of Israel's laws in the writings of the later prophets.³⁷ The commandment prohibiting work on the sabbath (see Deut. 5.12-14) is restated in Jeremiah (Jer. 17.21-2), for instance, but reinterpreted to include a specific warning against 'carrying a burden', presumably a reference to the transportation of goods to storehouses or to market on the sabbath. This expansion is, therefore, a concrete response to a practical concern of many Second Temple Jews (cf. Neh. 13.15-16; *Jub.* 2.29-30; 50.8; *CD* 11.7-9) which is not addressed directly in the Decalogue. The version of this law in Jeremiah is presented

---

34 For further examples of this form of composition, see, for example, the throne vision in *1 En.* 14.8-25; the Qumran *Thanksgiving Hymns* (especially 1QH 11.6-19); other Qumran texts such as the *Temple Scroll* and the *Songs of the Sabbath Sacrifice*; and late biblical and post-scriptural prayers like Dan. 9.4b-19. For a fuller discussion of this kind of composition, see Tooman, *Gog of Magog*, 200–24; and S. Kaufman, 'The Temple Scroll and Higher Criticism', *HUCA* 53 (1982): 29–43.
35 G. V. Allen, *The Book of Revelation and Early Jewish Textual Culture* (SNTSMS 168; Cambridge: Cambridge University Press, 2017) specifically references Tooman's work on Ezekiel in considering the relationship between Revelation and the Jewish Scriptures; and in *Reading Revelation as Pastiche: Imitating the Past* (LNTS 571; London and New York: Bloomsbury T&T Clark, 2017), Fletcher considers the implications of reading the book as an example of the genre of pastiche, taking into account both early Jewish and Graeco-Roman parallels.
36 See, for example, Sommer, *A Prophet Reads Scripture*, 152–9; Levinson, *Deuteronomy*, 144–57; Schultz, *Search for Quotation*, 60, 206–7, 213, 229, 335–6.
37 See, for example, M. A. Lyons, 'Transformation of Law: Ezekiel's Use of the Holiness Code (Leviticus 17-26)', in *Transforming Visions: Transformations of Text, Tradition, and Theology in Ezekiel* (ed. W. A. Tooman and M. A. Lyons; PTMS 127; Eugene: Wipf and Stock, 2010), 1–32.

as embedded in a divine oracle, so that it can take on the authority of both God and the Sinai revelation, and thus effectively persuade its audience to adopt a certain behaviour.

Within NT scholarship, Christopher Stanley stands out for his insistence on the importance of interrogating the rhetorical significance of scriptural citations, arguing that this aspect of OT/NT research has been somewhat neglected in the past.[38] He draws on the disciplines of philosophy and linguistics in seeking to explain more precisely how scriptural quotations function in the NT, raising important questions such as why an author makes a choice to refer to Scripture at a particular point in his composition; why he then decides to employ a direct citation rather than a paraphrase or an allusion; and how far the audience's recognition of an appeal to an authoritative source is necessary to its rhetorical effectiveness.[39] Stanley thus demonstrates how the Scriptures can be used to create a sense of solidarity between the writer and his community, for example, or to convince the hearers of the truth and urgency of the Christian message. This approach is particularly useful in establishing the presence of allusions within the NT, as it goes beyond the simple counting of the number of shared words to probe how far the proposed scriptural reference actually contributes to the overall argument of the passage in which it appears. Stanley's work could profitably be applied to the analysis of inner-scriptural quotation, and so provides a clear example of the possible benefits to Hebrew Bible commentators of closer engagement with contemporary NT studies.

Conclusions: Implications of contemporary Hebrew Bible scholarship for OT/NT study

This survey of significant recent trends in Hebrew Bible scholarship has highlighted the extent of the overlap in the methodological issues faced by those investigating inner-biblical quotation and the use of the OT in the NT. Shared concerns include the formulation of precise criteria for identifying allusions and citations, the evaluation of the purposes and rhetorical effects of the re-presentation of older authoritative texts, and the proper location of these quotation practices within the wider literary and cultural matrix of the ancient world. Several specific insights have also been identified here as having potential implications for the NT, notably the need for a reappraisal of the book of Revelation as a possible example of the early Jewish literary form of scripturally inspired 'pastiche' and the recognition that the presence of a quotation can be signalled by means other than the use of an explicit introductory formula, such as through inversion of elements of the source text. Furthermore, it is clear that there is scope for

---

[38] See especially C. D. Stanley, *Arguing with Scripture: The Rhetoric of Quotations in the Letters of Paul* (New York: T&T Clark, 2004); and 'The Rhetoric of Quotations: An Essay on Method', in *Early Christian Interpretation of the Scriptures of Israel: Investigations and Proposals* (ed. C. A. Evans and J. A. Sanders; JSNTSup 148; Sheffield: Sheffield Academic Press, 1997), 44–58. See also J. P. Heil, *The Rhetorical Role of Scripture in 1 Corinthians* (SBLMS 15; Atlanta: Society of Biblical Literature, 2005).

[39] See further Stanley, 'The Rhetoric of Quotations', 54–6.

a fresh exploration of the impact of genre on the ways in which Scripture is reused, given the variations in the level of verbal accuracy in quotation and formal marking evident across the NT writings. Conversely, this chapter has indicated ways in which the efforts of Hebrew Bible commentators to better understand how inner-scriptural quotations functioned for their original audiences could be further strengthened by the application to their texts of the tools of literary theory and rhetorical criticism that have been employed so successfully within NT studies. Scholars on both sides of the sub-disciplinary border stand to gain much, then, by a willingness to venture forth across it more frequently and more openly.

2

Scriptural reuse in ancient Jewish literature: Comments and reflections on the state of the art

William A. Tooman

This chapter has a simple objective: to describe some of the findings and research horizons in the study of scriptural reuse from the fields of Hebrew Bible (HB) and early Jewish literature. Before doing so, though, some dutiful, preliminary comments are in order regarding my chosen terminology: *scripture, reuse* and *ancient Jewish literature*. The appropriateness of all three is contested and the referent of each indeterminate.

Current historical scholarship has an understandable aversion to the use of terms like 'canon', 'bible', and 'scripture' for any of the literatures of the Second Temple period. Nonetheless, most of Second Temple Jewish literature that was not included in the eventual HB adopted a subordinate posture to most of the literature that did.[1] Non-biblical Second Temple texts commented on the biblical texts, evoked them as authorities, referred to their special status, alluded to them and imitated them.[2] Even Eugene Ulrich, who has for decades cautioned biblical scholars against the thoughtless use of anachronistic terms for sacred texts, argues that in the Second Temple period Judaism had a 'canon-in-process' functioning as a *norma normans*.[3] This in-between

---

[1] Shani Tzoref, 'Qumran Pesharim and the Pentateuch: Explicit Citation, Overt Typologies, and Implicit Interpretive Traditions', *DSD* 16 (2009): 192.

[2] See, for example, Armin Lange, 'Pre-Macabean Literature from the Qumran Library and the Hebrew Bible', *DSD* 14 (2006): 277–305; M. Fishbane, 'Use, Authority, and Interpretation of Mikra at Qumran', in *Mikra: Text, Translation, Reading and Interpretation of the Hebrew Bible in Ancient Judaism and Early Christianity* (ed. M. J. Mulder and H. Sysling; Assen: Van Gorcum, 1988), 339–77; William Tooman, 'Between Imitation and Interpretation: Reuse of Scripture and Composition in *Hodayot* (1QHa) 11.6-19', *DSD* 18 (2011): 54–73. Reference to the Mosaic, prophetic or Davidic authorship of the Torah, Prophets and Psalms indicate the special status of those biblical materials (e.g. 4QD 5.8; 7.10; 8.14-15; 4QDb 19.7; 1QM 10.6; 4Q174 1-2 i 16; 11QPsa 27.11; 11Q13 2.10); Katell Bertholet, 'Les titres des livres bibliques: Le témoignage de la bibliothèque de Qumrân', in *Flores Florentino: Dead Sea Scolls and Other Early Jewish Studies in Honour of Florentino García Martínez* (ed. A. Hilhorst, É. Puech and E. J. C. Tigchelaar; Leiden: Brill, 2007), 127–40; Daniel R. Schwartz, 'Special People or Special Books?: On Qumran and New Testament Notions of Canon', in *Text, Thought, and Practice in Qumran and Early Christianity* (ed. D. R. Schwartz and R. A. Clements; Leiden: Brill, 2009), 49–60.

[3] Eugene Ulrich, 'The Qumran Biblical Scrolls', in *The Dead Sea Scrolls in their Historical Context* (ed. Timothy Lim; Edinburgh: T&T Clark, 2000), 85.

state of the biblical literature in the Second Temple period, sacred but not yet canonized, is what I have in mind when I use the term 'scripture'.

'Reuse', in my personal lexicon, is an umbrella. It covers every variety of textual dependency, whether overt or covert, intentional or unintentional, atomistic or expansive, exegetical or ornamental. It includes all manifestations of textual dependency – quotation, allusion, mimicry, commentary, satire and so forth – and it is deliberately indeterminate as to the purpose or function of the reuse. But it is not an entirely shapeless word. *Re*-use, as opposed to *use*, signals diachrony. The study of scriptural reuse is a historical discipline, requiring some effort to correlate one's results with the history of literature, historical criticism and literary biography. One can, of course, adopt an ahistorical approach, in which the chronology of compositions does not figure at all. All that matters in such a case is the order in which the reader encounters works of literature. Such readerly approaches, rich as they can be, are outside of the domain of 'scriptural *reuse*'.

Finally, the reason that I have chosen the phrase *ancient Jewish literature*, as opposed to 'Hebrew Bible', 'Old Testament', 'ancient Israelite literature', 'Second Testament' or any other moniker, turns on my thesis. For the study of scriptural reuse in ancient Judaism, the frontier has been and continues to be the religious literature of Second Temple Judaism. Second Temple literature provides our oldest exemplars of scriptural reuse outside of the HB itself, and it does so in circumstances where directionality is seldom obscure. Second Temple literature is not only the most contemporaneous empirical evidence that we possess, but increasingly we find that techniques employed in Second Temple literature not only persisted into the rabbinic period, but they had precursors in the HB or even earlier in Ancient Near Eastern literature. Many of the techniques of scriptural reuse witnessed in Second Temple literature are extensions and developments of techniques already deployed within the pages of the HB. Familiar Second Temple phenomena like rewriting, typology, chronological schematization, analogical reasoning, conflation and assimilation, harmonization, and referential exegesis can be observed in the HB and are still at work in rabbinic *midrash*.[4] For these

---

[4] See, for example, Geza Vermes, *Scripture and Tradition in Judaism: Haggadic Studies* (Leiden: Brill, 1961); Thomas Willi, *Die Chronik als Auslegung: Untersuchungen zur literarischen Gestaltung der historischen Überlieferung Israels* (FRLANT 106; Göttingen: Vandenhoeck & Ruprecht, 1972); Brevard Childs, 'Psalm Titles and Midrashic Exegesis', *JSS* 16 (1971): 137–50; Michael Fishbane, *Biblical Myth and Rabbinic Mythmaking* (Oxford and New York: Oxford Universty Press, 2003); Daniel Boyarin, 'Inner-biblical Ambiguity, Intertextuality and the Dialectic of Midrash: The Waters of Marah', *Prooftexts* 10 (1990): 29–48; Michael Stone and Esther Chazon, eds, *Biblical Perspectives Early Use and Interpretation of the Bible in Light of the Dead Sea Scrolls Proceedings of the First International Symposium of the Orion Center, 12–14 May, 1996* (STDJ 28; Leiden: Brill, 1998); Paul Mandel, *Origins of Midrash: From Teaching to Text* (Leiden and Boston: Brill, 2017); Moshe Bernstein, 'The Contribution of the Qumran Discoveries to the History of Early Biblical Interpretation', in *The Idea of Biblical Interpretation: Essays in Honor of James L. Kugel* (ed. Hindy Najman and Judith Newman; SJSJ 83; Leiden and Boston: Brill, 2004), 215–38; Moshe Bernstein and Shlomo Koyfman, 'The Interpretation of Biblical Law in the Dead Sea Scrolls: Forms and Methods', in *Biblical Interpretation at Qumran* (ed. Matthias Henze; SDSSRL; Grand Rapids: Eerdmans, 2005), 61–87; David Halivni, 'Aspects of Classical Jewish Hermeneutics', in *Holy Scriptures in Judaism, Christianity and Islam: Hermeneutics, Values and Society* (ed. H. M. Vroom and J. D. Gort; Amsterdam: Rodopi, 1997), 77–97; Alexander Samely, *Rabbinic Interpretation of Scripture in the Mishna* (Oxford: Oxford University Press, 2002); Lieve Teugels, *Bible and Midrash: The Story of the 'Wooing of Rebecca' (Gen 24)* (Leiden: Peeters, 2004). These examples were chosen, somewhat randomly, from those I have on file. Many hundreds of additional studies could have been selected.

reasons, much of what I have to say touches on literatures that developed alongside and after the HB, up to and including the literature of the Amoraic period (c. 500 CE).

My thesis is hardly new or insightful. For decades, scholars in NT, HB, and Second Temple studies have been stressing the importance of Second Temple literature for understanding early Jewish exegesis.[5] Nonetheless, for HB scholarship, there are two unique reasons that Second Temple literature has become central and those reasons deserve some comment. They are (1) the relative ages of the two corpora and (2) the locatedness of the HB and the extra-biblical Second Temple compositions.

Regarding the relative ages of the HB and the corpus of Second Temple literature, there is ever-growing acceptance that much of the HB was still being written, edited and revised in the Hellenistic period (a stance that was viewed as extreme just forty years ago[6]). Included in this claim are not just those portions of the Ketuvim like Ezra-Nehemiah and Daniel that are obviously located after the neo-Babylonian period; much of the Torah and Prophets are included as well. That the HB had a long composition history is irrefutable. At many turns, it openly acknowledges this reality (e.g. Jeremiah 26). Erhard Blum has stressed that revision never stops. To be sure, it is carried on in less overt ways after communities crystalize a particular iteration of their sacred texts and identify that text form (or forms) with 'scripture', but the process of revision cannot be fully arrested.[7] Moreover, while the Ancient Near Eastern literatures continue to provide important comparative evidence for certain genres (e.g. casuistic laws and aphorisms), the kinds of large-scale compositions that we find in the HB, like the Primary History, only have analogues in the Hellenistic age.[8] The HB as a whole is increasingly appreciated as not just an ancient Israelite document but as an ancient Jewish document.

Archival discoveries have cast a new light on the locatedness of the HB, discoveries that *also* orient it towards the Second Temple period. Traditionally, Hebrew biblical literature has been conceptualized as an accumulating body of ancient Israelite and Judahite traditions that initially underwent oral and written transmission by scribal

---

[5] For example, Vermes, *Scripture and Tradition*; James Kugel, *In Potiphar's House: The Interpretive Life of Biblical Texts* (San Francisco: Harper, 1990); *The Bible as It Was* (Cambridge: Harvard University Press, 1997); George Brooke, 'Biblical Interpretation in the Qumran Scrolls and the New Testament', in *The Dead Sea Scrolls Fifty Years after their Discovery: Proceedings of the Jerusalem Congress, July 20-25, 1997* (ed. Lawrence Schiffman, Emanuel Tov and James Vanderkam; Jerusalem: Israel Exploration Society, in collaboration with The Shrine of the Book, Israel Museum, 2000), 60–73; idem., 'Shared Intertextual Interpretations in the Dead Sea Scrolls and the New Testament', in *Biblical Perspectives Early Use and Interpretation of the Bible in Light of the Dead Sea Scrolls Proceedings of the First International Symposium of the Orion Center, 12–14 May, 1996* (STDJ 28; ed. Michael Stome and Esther Chazon; Leiden: Brill, 1998); Reinhard Kratz, '"Denn dein ist das Reich": Das Judentum in persischer und hellenistisch-jüdischer Zeit', in *Götterbilder-Gottesbilder-Weltbilder. Polytheismus und Monotheismus in der Welt der Antike* (ed. R. G. Kratz and H. Spieckermann; Tübingen: Mohr Siebeck, 2006), 347–74.

[6] For example, Charles Cutler Torrey, *Pseudo-Ezekiel and the Original Prophecy* (New York: KTAV, 1970).

[7] Erhard Blum, 'Formgeschichte – ein irreführender Begirff?' in *Lesarten der Bibel: Untersuchungen zu einer Theorie der Exegese des Alten Testaments* (ed. Helmut Utzschneider and Erhard Blum; Stuttgaart: Kohlhammer, 2006), 85–96; cf. Andrew Teeter, 'The Hebrew Bible and/as Second Temple Literature', *DSD* 20 (2013): 349–77 (quote at 360–1).

[8] For example, Berossus, Mentho. Other biblical compositions, most notably the prophetic *books* (Isaiah, Jeremiah, and Ezekiel and the Twelve), have no known analogues in other ancient Near Eastern cultures.

elites at official institutions like the first temple, the royal court and the schools of the prophets. In this view, it was the exile in Babylon and, to a lesser degree, Egypt that provided the great push, spawning a great deal of redaction and causing the Hebrew Scriptures to coalesce into the books and collections that we know today.[9] Though venerable, the traditional view is complicated by recent archival finds. Jewish archives in Egypt, Babylon and Palestine have yielded up distinct collections that, when considered all together, call for a reconsideration of the traditional view.[10] The deposits of texts from Elephantine in Egypt (c. 400 BCE) and from the Judean colony of Al-Yahudu in Babylon (c. 570–470 BCE) have returned an abundance of information on the daily lives of Jews in the neo-Babylonian and Persian periods.[11] What they have not yielded is biblical material. No biblical manuscripts, para-biblical manuscripts or even allusions to biblical texts have been identified in these collections.[12] The archives from Egypt and Babylon contrast with those from Palestine. Palestine possesses rich deposits of biblical and para-biblical literature, most famously the scrolls from Khirbet Qumran (from the third century BCE to first century CE) and the Samaritan literature (by third century BCE). The 'biblical Judaism' of Palestine is distinct, even into the Persian period. This, of course, raises many questions for the traditional view. For the purposes of this chapter, it underlines the close relationship between Palestinian Judaism of the Second Temple period and the biblical materials themselves, not just chronologically, as I have argued, but geographically.

These considerations, when combined, identify Palestine of the Second Temple period as the probable context of the HB, and they direct our attention to the extra-biblical literature of the Second Temple period as the best correlate to the literature of the HB and its literary conventions, including scriptural reuse.[13]

---

[9] This is such a common view that it hardly requires citation. For an articulation of it in the context of a discussion of ancient Jewish interpretation, including scriptural reuse, see James Kugel and Rowan Greer, *Early Biblical Interpretation* (Philadelphia: Westminster, 1986), 13–102, esp. 13–26 and 52–63.

[10] The appropriateness of terms like 'archive', 'collection' and 'library' for the textual deposits discussed here is disputed. I am using them in a non-technical way to refer to nothing more than bodies of texts of (arguably) Jewish origin. On the appropriate vocabulary, see Jaqueline Du Toit, *Textual Memory: Archives, Libraries, and the Hebrew Bible* (SWBA 2/6; Sheffield: Phoenix, 2011).

[11] We might also mention the Jewish settlement at Kition on Cyprus. Michael Heltzer, 'Epigraphic Evidence Concerning a Jewish Settlement in Kition (Larnaca, Cyprus) in the Achaemenid Period (IV cent. BCE)', *Aula Orientalis* 7 (1989): 133–71.

[12] For analysis and discussion see Reinhard Gregor Kratz, *Historical and Biblical Israel: The History, Tradition, and Archives of Israel and Judah* (Oxford: Oxford University Press, 2015), 133–96. Papyrus Amhurst 63, a fragmentary collection of cultic hymns in Aramaic from the fourth century BCE, is sometimes compared to the biblical psalms, but none of its poems are identifiably biblical. See, for example, Sven P. Vleeming and Jan W. Wesselius, *Studies in Papyrus Amherst 63: Essays on the Aramaic/demotic Papyrus Amherst 63* (vol. 1; Amsterdam: Juda Palache Instituut, 1985); Martin Rösel, 'Israels Psalmen in Ägypten? Papyrus Amherst 63 und die Psalmen XX und LXXV', *VT* 50 (2000): 81–99; Raik Heckl, 'Inside the Canon and Out: The Relationship between Psalm 20 and Papyrus Amherst 63', *Sem* 56 (2014): 359–79.

[13] So Michael Fishbane, *Biblical Interpretation in Ancient Israel* (Oxford: Clarendon Press, 1985), 19, 134–5; idem., *The Garments of Torah: Essays in Biblical Hermeneutics* (Bloomington: Indiana University Press, 1989), 1–13; Michael Segal, 'Identifying Biblical Interpretation in Parabiblical Texts', in *The Dead Sea Scrolls in Context: Integrating the Dead Sea Scrolls in the Study of Ancient Texts, Languages, and Cultures* (ed. Armin Lange et al.; Leiden and Boston: Brill, 2011), 295–308. James Kugel and John Barton, to cite just two examples, dispute this claim. Kugel acknowledges modest exegesis within the HB but (suddenly) finds 'biblical interpretation in full flower' in the Second Temple literature

Returning our focus to our main topic, scriptural reuse in ancient Jewish literature, I have chosen to highlight five key findings from recent scholarship that have important implications for our understanding of scriptural reuse in Jewish antiquity. I will address them individually, and in no particular order.

1 Assimilation

As the texts of the HB are pressed forward chronologically, closer and closer to the year zero, more and more time is gained for their evolution. Likewise, as more and more books are implicated in this process, more time is given for them to mutually affect one another's development. The phenomenon of 'reverse assimilation', once acknowledged only occasionally, now appears to be a systemic feature of the Hebrew Scriptures.[14] That is, as new texts were written that evoked antecedent Scriptures, there was ample time for those younger texts to then affect the redaction of the older texts. As scriptural texts were written and rewritten, often many times over, they were linked backwards and forwards across the scriptural corpus. The book of Isaiah, for example, was once conceived as three books, First, Second and Third Isaiah, written in that sequence and attached, one to the other, in that order. In recent decades, stress has fallen on the ways that Second Isaiah both provided an expansion of First Isaiah and also reworked and interpreted portions of First Isaiah to craft a more coherent whole. Third Isaiah, in turn, did the same for First and Second Isaiah, further enriching and complicating the final product.[15] The book of Ezekiel is a similar case. One of the most well-recognized features of the book of Ezekiel is its close relationship to the Holiness Code (H). Traditionally, Ezekiel scholars have been divided into three camps: those who concluded that Ezekiel was the borrowing text, those who concluded that H was the borrowing text and those who concluded that both borrowed from a third lost source. The current debate, however, circles not around which was first but how the two books mutually influenced one another.[16] The increased recognition of reverse assimilation

---

('The Beginnings of Biblical Interpretation', in *A Companion to Biblical Interpretation in Early Judaism* [ed. Matthias Henze; Grand Rapids: Eerdmans, 2012], 11). Barton believes that there is a deep fissure between the practice of scriptural interpretation before and after the Second Temple period: 'The theology and thought-forms of Second Temple Judaism are not just slightly different from the theology and thought-forms of the Old Testament, they represent a radically different system articulated on quite fresh lines. ... Anyone who thinks Enoch, or even Daniel, is anything like Isaiah or Amos must be living in a quite different world of thought' (*Oracles of God: Perceptions of Ancient Prophecy in Israel after the Exile* [London: Darton, Longman & Todd, 1986], 151).

[14] Yair Zakovitch, 'Assimilation in Biblical Narratives', in *Empirical Models for Biblical Criticism* (ed. Jeffery Tigay; Philadelphia: University of Philadelphia Press, 1985), 175–96.

[15] Hugh Williamson, *The Book Called Isaiah: Deutero-Isaiah's Role in Composition and Redaction* (Oxford: Clarendon Press, 1994); Jacob Stromberg, *Isaiah After Exile: The Author of Third Isaiah as Reader and Redactor of the Book* (OTM; Oxford: Oxford University Press, 2011).

[16] Michael Lyons, 'How Have We Changed? Older and Newer Arguments about the Relationship of Ezekiel and the Holiness Code', in *The Formation of the Pentateuch: Bridging the Academic Cultures of Israel, Europe, and North America* (FAT 111; ed. Jan C. Gertz, Bernard M. Levinson, Dalit Rom-Shiloni and Konrad Schmid; Tübingen: Mohr Siebeck, 2016), 1055–74; Christophe Nihan, 'Ezekiel and the Holiness Legislation – A Plea for Nonlinear Models', in *The Formation of the Pentateuch*, 1015–40; idem., 'Ezekiel 34–37 and Leviticus 26: A Reevaluation', in *Ezekiel: Current Debates and Future Directions* (FAT 112; ed. William Tooman and Penelope Barter; Tübingen: Mohr Siebeck, 2017), 153–78.

has obvious and profound effects for literary history, but its significance for scriptural reuse is no less profound. No separation can be made between redaction, reception and reuse. Redaction is predicated on the scribes' reception of the redacted text; redaction is an act of reception. Likewise, redaction often entails acts of multidirectional reuse. Elements of older texts are reused in the composition of younger ones and elements of those younger texts in the revision and rewriting of the older. The turning of the wheel, naturally, does not stop there. Younger texts are then revised in light of the newly redacted older sources and so on.[17]

The scipturalization of the biblical books did not arrest the process of assimilation as scholars once supposed but accelerated and extended it (as is easily observable in textual transmission), making the protean Bible into an evermore elaborate web of words. *Any* of its parts, eventually, lead a reader to *all* its parts. In this way, all the biblical genres, books and collections are mutually evoking and mutually interpreting. This poses *major* challenges for any student of scriptural reuse. Synchronic and diachronic reading processes become blurred; the diachrony of literary influence moves in multiple directions; and the discipline of scriptural reuse becomes evermore inseparable from historical criticism, textual criticism and reception history.

2 Amalgamation

The Second Temple period was, above all, a period of interpretation 'and its major project was amalgamating, through interpretation, concepts from diverse biblical strata'.[18] The Temple Scroll famously amalgamates and coordinates laws from all of the legal corpora. The Genesis Apocryphon, though replicating doublets like the wife–sister stories (Genesis 12, 20, 26), conflates details from each with the others. More obviously, the so-called 'thematic commentaries' – such as 4QTestamonia and 4QFlorilegium – excerpt biblical sources, aggregating them as new compositions. All this is well documented.[19]

---

[17] Reinhard Kratz, 'Innerbiblische Exegese und Redaktionsgeschichte im Lichte empirischer Evidenz', in *Das Judentum im Zeitalter des Zweiten Tempels* (FAT 42; Tübingen: Mohr Siebeck, 2004; 2nd edn, 2013), 126–56; idem., 'Die Redaktion der Prophetenbücher', in *Rezeption und Auslegung im Alten Testament und in seinem Umfeld: Ein Symposion aus Anlass des 60. Geburts- tags von Odil Hannes Steck* (OBO 153; ed. Reinhard G. Kratz and Thomas Krüger: Freiburg: Universitätsverlag; Göttingen: Vandenhoeck & Ruprecht, 1997), 9–27.

[18] Menahem Kister, 'Wisdom Literature and Its Relation to Other Genres: From Ben Sira to Mysteries', in *Sapiential Perspectives: Wisdom Literature in Light of the Dead Sea Scrolls: Proceedings of the Sixth International Symposium of the Orion Center for the Study of the Dead Sea Scrolls and Associated Literature, 20-22 May, 2001* (STDJ 51; ed. John J. Collins, Gregory E. Sterling and Ruth A. Clements; Leiden and Boston: Brill, 2004), 13–47, quote at 19.

[19] Yigel Yadin, *The Temple Scroll* (3 vols.; Jerusalem: Israel Exploration Society, The Institute of Archaeology of the Hebrew University and The Shrine of the Book, 1983); Joseph A. Fitzmyer, *The Genesis Apocryphon of Qumran Cave 1 (1Q20): A Commentary* (3rd edn; Rome: Pontificio Istituto Biblico, 2004); Moshe Bernstein, 'Re-arrangement, Anticipation, and Harmonization as Exegetical Features in the Genesis Apocryphon', *DSD* 3 (1996): 37–57; George Brooke, *Exegesis at Qumran: 4QFlorilegium in Its Jewish Context* (JSOTSup 29; Sheffield: JSOT Press, 1985). More broadly: Zakovitch, 'Assimilation'; J. Carmignac, 'Le Document de Qumrân sur Melkisédeq', *RevQ* 7 (1969–71): 343–78; George Brooke, 'Thematic Commentaries on Prophetic Scriptures', in *Biblical Interpretation at Qumran* (ed. Henze; Grand Rapids: Eerdmans, 2005), 134–57. It should be stressed that Second Temple literature does not limit its attention to biblical sources, but draws on other literatures as well, a point stressed by, for example, Kister, 'Wisdom Literature', and Segal, 'Identifying'.

As far as I can tell, the Second Temple habit of amalgamation is well recognized at the micro-level, that is, on the level of individual clauses, sentences and couplets. When Ezra quotes the 'prophets' in defence of his ban on intermarriage in Ezra 9.11b-12, he amalgamates the marriage laws in Deut. 7.1-3 and 23.7. When *2 Enoch* (30.15) describes Adam's error in the garden, equating the knowledge of good and evil with love or abhorrence of God, it conflates the language of Gen. 2.9b with that of the Levitical covenant (Leviticus 26, esp. v. 15) and the *Shema* (Deut. 6.5). When Jesus is baptized in Luke, a voice from heaven proclaims, 'You are my Son, the beloved one; with you I am well pleased' (3.22), conflating poetic lines about the Davidic monarch (Ps. 2.7) and the Suffering Servant (Isa. 42.1).

Likewise, the amalgamated nature of whole texts is appreciated in select cases (e.g. 11QT). What is less well appreciated in the biblical disciplines generally is the *extent* and *volume* of admixture. There is no limit to the volume or kinds of material that can be amalgamated. Indeed, material from a wide array of genres, arguments and stocks of vocabulary and imagery are routinely mingled in Second Temple literature. 4Q*Mysteries*, though presented as a wisdom text, borrows from narrative, law, prophecy, apocalyptic and wisdom, from biblical and extra-biblical sources. The *Hodayot* routinely mix locutions and images from across the Psalms, prophets, wisdom literature and Torah to create new psalms and hymns.[20] *Tobit*, notionally an uncomplicated story, is in fact a rich matrix of allusions and narrative mimicry, crafted as a complex engagement with (at least) the patriarchal stories, the poems of Deuteronomy (chs 31-2) and the book of Job.[21] Books like *1 Enoch* and *Baruch* make use of the greater part of the biblical corpus, gleaning from the Torah, Prophets and Writings alike, arranging, combining and coordinating to create complex compositions that participate with the whole Hebrew canon. Pressing the point further, I would suggest that amalgamation is the norm for Second Temple literature. *Most* texts are a complex of diverse scriptural materials. This is most obvious for the various types of commentaries and rewritten scriptural texts, but it extends to all genres: prayers, hymns, *halakic* texts, sectarian regulations, sapiential texts, apocalypses, novellas, testaments and ritual texts. Going beyond the Second Temple literature, Arnold Goldberg and Alexander Samely have provided numerous examples of the pastiche or *bricolage* technique at work in rabbinic texts.[22]

Such capacious amalgamation, though, was not an invention of post-biblical writers. Similar examples can be identified within the HB, too, occurring more frequently than was appreciated just a few decades ago. In some cases, the locutions,

---

[20] Svend Holm-Nielsen, *Hodayot: Psalms from Qumran* (Aarhus: Universitets-forlaget I Aarhus, 1960); Julie A. Hughes, *Scriptural Allusions and Exegesis in the Hodayot* (Leiden: Brill, 2006); Tooman, 'Between Imitation and Interpretation'.

[21] See, for example, George W. E. Nickelsburg, 'The Search for Tobit's Mixed Ancestry: A Historical and Hermeneutical Odyssey', *RevQ* 17 (1996): 339-49; Lothar Ruppert, 'Das Buch Tobias – ein Modellfall nachgestaltender Erzählung', in *Wort, Lied und Gottesspruch: Beiträge zur Septuaginta Festschrift für Joseph Ziegler* (ed. Josef Schreiner; FB 1, Würsburg: Echter Verlag, 1972), 113-17; Daniel A. Bertrand, 'Le chevreau d'Anna: La signification de l'anecdotique dans le livre de Tobit', *RHPR* 68 (1988): 269-74; Steven Weitzman, 'Allusion, Artifice, and Exile in the Hymn of Tobit', *JBL* 115 (1996): 49-61; Irene Nowell, 'The Book of Tobit: An Ancestral Story', in *Intertextual Studies in Ben Sira and Tobit: Essays in Honor of Alexander A. Di Leila, O. F. M.* (CBQMS 38; ed. Jeremy Corley and Vincent Skemp; Washington DC: Catholic Biblical Association of America, 2005), 3-13; Tzvi Novick, 'Biblicized Narrative: On Tobit and Genesis 22', *JBL* 127 (2007): 755-64.

[22] 'Die funktionale Form Midrasch', *FJB* 10 (1982): 1-45, esp. 3-5; Samely, *Rabbinic Interpretation*.

images and arguments that are amalgamated are obviously *related by context*. In 1 Samuel 25, for example, Abigail rushes to meet the bandit David to dissuade him aside from murdering her household. For the reader who is already familiar with the book, her words have a familiar ring. The resonance is easily understood when we realize that many of her phrases and clauses appeared in the book before ch. 25. Many of the remaining phrases and clauses foreshadow words yet to come, most notably in the Davidic covenant. Appropriating Abigail's voice, the writer has crafted what might be considered the first theology of the house of David, constructing it by aggregating elements from within the book of Samuel.[23]

In other biblical texts, locutions, images and arguments are combined that are, in one way or another, *topically related* to one another. Ezra 9 is a classic example. Soon after celebrating the festival of Succoth, certain officials among the returnees informed Ezra that 'the people of Israel', including members of the Levites, priests and political leadership, had not separated themselves from the inhabitants of the land (9.1-2). The officials' accusation is a conflation of locutions and ideas from legal texts like Exodus 23, Exodus 34, Deuteronomy 7 and Deuteronomy 23, supplemented by verbiage and ideas from the holiness tradition.[24] All four source texts are concerned with interactions between Israelites and Canaanites, combined, conflated and reapplied in the service of their xenophobic ideology. Ezra responds with an act of personal confession and mourning (9.4-15), from which we learn that he accepts the officials' complaint. His confession is also a pastiche of legal extracts, drawn, in this case, from the Deuteronomic exogamy laws and Holiness Code (esp. Deut. 7.1-3; 23.6-7; Lev. 18.19-30). Whatever we think of the officials' and Ezra's *halakic* exegesis, it is not difficult to discern how their sources were selected, in large part because they share a common topic.

Still other biblical pericopae are constructed from a potpourri of locutions, images and arguments that are drawn from such a wide array of texts and genres that it is not immediately obvious how they might be related to one another. I have written extensively about one of these, the Gog oracles in Ezekiel 38–9.[25] Another example is the so-called 'little apocalypse' of Isaiah 24–7. Unlike the other oracles in First Isaiah, chs 24–7 do not make reference to any historical situation but describe the judgement of the world at the end of days. These chapters are assembled, in *bricolage* style, from a truly astonishing collection of linguistic elements, derived from the book of Isaiah itself and from many other biblical books. Law, poetry, prophecy and narrative are all

---

[23] Jon Levenson, '1 Samuel 25 as Literature and as History', *CBQ* 10 (1978): 12–28; Michael Avioz, *Nathan's Oracle (2 Sam 7) and Its Interpreters* (Bern: Peter Lang, 2005), 56–9.

[24] The allusions in Ezra 9 to the laws of the Torah have been discussed by, most notably, Fishbane, *Biblical Interpretation*, 114–21; Saul Olyan, 'Purity Ideology in Ezra-Nehemiah as a Tool to Reconstitute the Community', *JSJ* 35 (2004): 1–16; Jonathan Klawans, *Impurity and Sin in Ancient Judaism* (Oxford: Oxford University Press, 2004), 43–4; J. Milgrom, *Leviticus 1-16* (AB 3; New York: Doubleday, 1991), 359–61; and Christine Hayes, *Gentile Impurities and Jewish Identities: Intermarriage and Conversion from the Bible to the Talmud* (Oxford: Oxford University Press, 2002), 19–33. For a survey of older views, see Ulrich Kellermann, 'Erwägungen zum Esragesetz', *ZAW* 80 (1968): 373–85.

[25] William Tooman, *Gog of Magog: Reuse of Scripture and Compositional Technique in Ezekiel 38-39* (FAT II/52; Tübingen: Mohr Siebeck 2011).

represented.²⁶ The same could be said about the prayer of Daniel in ch. 9 of the book that bears his name.²⁷

In short, the kind of relentless evocation of Scripture that we commonly identify with select genres (e.g. apocalyptic) and with post-biblical literature is more common than was once appreciated. Furthermore, the practice of assimilation appears to have originated *within* the scriptural compositions themselves, growing evermore expansive and elaborate with time.²⁸

3 Atomistic interpretation?

To my knowledge, the first person to characterize ancient Jewish interpretation as 'atomistic' was George Foote Moore in 1927. In his words, Jewish interpretation in the first centuries of the Common Era was 'atomistic exegesis which interprets sentences, clauses, phrases and even single words independently of the context or the historical situation'.²⁹ Henry Cadbury seconded this claim, but, in his case, it was applied to early Christian interpretation.³⁰ Whether or not the term 'atomistic' is applied, the claim has been repeated frequently, for the NT interpretation of the HB, for rabbinic exegesis and even for Cuneiform commentaries from the Sumerian to the Persian periods.³¹

---

[26] Isaiah 24–27 evokes and engages with elements from Genesis 7–9, 11; Exodus 24; Leviticus 26; Deuteronomy 28; Jeremiah 48; Hosea 4, 13–14; Amos 5; Micah 1; Psalm 74, 89, 117, 118; Job 26; and, from Isaiah itself (esp. chs 2; 5; 11; 17; 21; 24; 52; 54; 60; 66); and from several notional 'collections' like the enthronement Psalms. (This list is not exhaustive.) See, for example, Marvin Sweeney, 'Textual Citations in Isaiah 24-27: Rhetoric and Redaction in Trito-Isaiah: The Structure, Growth, and Authorship of Isaiah 56-66', *JBL* 107 (1988): 39–52; Todd Hibbard, *Intertextuality in Isaiah: The Ruse and Evocation of Earlier Texts and Traditions* (FAT II/16; Tübingen: Mohr Siebeck, 2006).

[27] Michael Segal, *Dreams, Riddles, and Visions: Textual, Contextual, and Intertextual Approaches to the Book of Daniel* (BZAW 455; Berlin: de Gruyter, 2016), 155–79; Paul Redditt, 'Daniel 9: Its Structure and Meaning', *CBQ* 62 (2000): 236–49; P. M. Venter, 'Intertekstualiteit, kontekstualiteit en Daniël 9', *IDS* 31 (1997): 327–46; Gerald Wilson, 'The Prayer of Daniel: Reflection on Jeremiah 29', *JSOT* 48 (1990): 91–9; Fishbane, *Biblical Interpretation*, 487–9.

[28] There is an additional implication of the amalgamation habit for the reuse of scripture that deserves comment before moving on. Namely, genre does not appear to be a reliable diagnostic tool for validating scriptural reuse. Writers who work in a particular genre do not appear to be more likely to evoke pre-existing works in the same genre. Indeed, there are good historical reasons to think that genre was not a significant consideration when it came to selecting sources in the acts of reuse and rewriting. In the words of John Barton, 'The concept of genre, though theoretically available, was not in practice able to gain a foothold where the interpretation of Scripture was concerned' (Barton, *Oracles of God*, 141–9, quote at 143).

[29] George F. Moore, *Judaism of the First Centuries of the Christian Era: The Age of the Tannaim* (3 vols.; Cambridge: Harvard University Press, 1927-30), 1: 248.

[30] Henry J. Cadbury, 'The Titles of Jesus in Acts', in *The Beginnings of Christianity*, part 1: *The Acts of the Apostles*, vol. 5: *Additional Notes to the Commentary* (ed. K. Lake and H. J. Cadbury; London: McMillian, 1933), 369–70.

[31] Examples are legion. The following are a small selection. On NT, see Donald Juel, *Messianic Exegesis* (Philadelphia: Fortress, 1988); Lidija Novakic, 'Matthew's Atomistic use of Scripture: Messianic Interpretation of Isaiah 53.4 in Matthew 8.17', in *Biblical Interpretation in Early Christian Gospels, vol. 2: The Gospel of Mathew* (LNTS 310; ed. Thomas Hatina; London: T&T Clark, 2008), 147–62; Robert Foster, *Renaming Abraham's Children: Election, Ethnicity, and the Interpretation of Scripture in Romans 9* (WUNT 421; Tübingen: Mohr Siebeck, 2016). On Rabbinic literature, see S. J. Lieberman, 'A Mesopotamian Background for the So-Called Aggadic "Measures" of Biblical

In HB and Second Temple scholarship, two of the most prominent proponents of this view have been John Barton and James Kugel. In his 1986 monograph, *Oracles of God*, Barton claimed:

> A reading which tries to treat a large and complex book such as Isaiah as forming a closed, unitary whole bears little resemblance at all to the way scriptural books were read in ancient times, and owes much more to modern literary criticism than to ancient modes of understanding Scripture.[32]

James Kugel's approach to ancient biblical interpretation, inside and outside of the HB, is similar.

> It should be noted that ancient biblical interpretation is an interpretation of verses ... their comments are usually framed by a particular verse or even a phrase within a verse: 'and he was not, for God took him' meant Enoch ascended to heaven; 'walked with God after the birth of Methuselah' meant Enoch repented; and so forth. ... These little explanations of phrase or verse are called exegetical motifs. Such motifs travelled. They were passed on by word of mouth, or from one text to another, sometimes being modified on the way. ... Thus, in studying ancient biblical interpretation, it is best to break down such a running text into its constituent motifs.[33]

For Kugel, such an approach flows naturally from the origins of interpretation, which was required, in the first instance, to update unknown words and to tease out the practical implications of *halakah*.[34] It was given fresh energy and urgency by the exile and return. The return required fresh thinking about Israel's history, to learn from her past failures.[35] Nonetheless, ancient biblical interpretation, then and later, remained 'an interpretation of verses, not stories'.[36]

I have no objection in principle to the claim that early Jewish interpretation *can be* 'atomistic'. There are, to be sure, thousands of examples from all types of ancient Jewish literature of interpretations that focus attention on individual clauses, phrases, words and even parts of words with little consideration of wider literary context.[37] My

---

Hermeneutics?' *HUCA* 58 (1987): 157–225; John Barton, 'Intertextuality and the "Final Form" of the Text', in *Congress Volume: Oslo 1998* (ed. Andre Lemaire and Magne Sæbø; Leiden and Boston, Brill: 2000), 35. On ancient Near Eastern commentaries, see Jeffery Tigay, 'An Early Technique of Aggadic Exegesis', in *History, Historiography, and Interpretation: Studies in Biblical and Cuneiform Literatures* (ed. H. Tadmor and M. Weinfeld; Jerusalem: Magnes Press, 1983), 169–89; Ellery Frahm, *Babylonian and Assyrian Text Commentaries: Origins of Interpretation* (Münster: Ugarit-Verlag, 2011); Uri Gabbay, 'Akkadian Commentaries from Ancient Mesopotamia and Their Relation to Early Hebrew Exegesis', *DSD* 19 (2012): 267–312.

[32] Barton, *Oracles of God*, 150.
[33] 'The Beginnings of Biblical Interpretation', 21–2; Kugel's approach is articulated more fully in *In Potiphar's House*, 3–9, and it is robustly illustrated in *The Bible as It Was*.
[34] As was argued by, for example, Isaac Heinemann, *Darkhe ha-Aggadah* (Jerusalem: Magnes, 1948) and Simon Rawidowicz, 'On Interpretation', *PAAJR* 26 (1957): 83–126.
[35] Kugel and Greer, *Early Biblical Interpretation*, 27–39.
[36] James L. Kugel, *Traditions of the Bible: A Guide to the Bible as It Was at the Start of the Common Era* (Cambridge: Harvard University Press, 1998), 24.
[37] The most robust and fine grained analysis of the kinds of 'operations' ancient interpreters did undertake on such a small scale is that of Samely, *Rabbinic Interpretation*.

objection is to any claim, like those of Barton and Kugel, that 'atomism' *characterizes* early Jewish interpretation, that wider ways of reading are *alien* to the literature of the HB, to say nothing of the Second Temple and rabbinic periods. Corrections to such claims have come from several quarters. More wholistic descriptions of rabbinic exegesis have been offered by Jacob Neusner, Daniel Boyarin, Philip Alexander and, most pointedly, Devorah Steinmetz.[38] In the Second Temple literature, Reinhard Kratz, Shani Tzoref, Michael Segal, Christophe Berner and many others have charted complex, large-scale interpretive operations.[39] In keeping with the main theme of this chapter, I want to focus on scriptural reuse within the HB itself.

In 2015, Michael Lyons published an article on the reuse of Isaiah's Servant passages in Psalm 22. Many have noted the lexical parallels between Psalm 22 and the so-called Servant Songs. What Lyons showed is that Psalm 22 has contextualized the borrowed elements of Isaiah 40–55 in a way that has been influenced by the arguments of chs 54 and 56–66. Those chapters introduce a righteous community, the 'servants', who suffer and are vindicated like the individual servant. He argues:

> The shift from suffering to vindication to description of the eschatological rule of Yhwh in Psalm 22 is to be explained not as a simple transformation of the suffering and vindication of the individual servant ... but as an argument shaped in light of the already collective suffering and vindication of the servants (Isa 54:14-17; 57:1; 66:5-6) and the eschatological rule of Yhwh (Isaiah 65-66) in the latter part of the Book of Isaiah. In other words, Psalm 22 is not creating a new argument from Isaiah 53, or 'collectivizing' Isaiah 53, but is simply following a pattern that already exists in the larger context of the Book of Isaiah.[40]

He goes on to confirm his reading by showing that several other texts from the HB, Second Temple period and the NT (e.g. Psalms 69 and 102, Daniel, Wisdom of Solomon, Mk 10.45; Lk. 2.30-2, 3.22, 22.37; Acts 26.23) show a similar recognition of the wider argument about the servant and the servants in Isaiah. Many of these are well recognized, but Lyons brings them together to show that wholistic ways of reading are neither rare nor extraordinary.[41]

This example points to the dangers of failing to consider wider contextual arguments when assessing scriptural reuse. A similar caution should be sounded

---

[38] Daniel Boyarin, *Intertextuality and the Reading of Midrash* (Bloomington and Indianapolis: Indiana University Press, 1990); Jacob Neusner, *What is Midrash?* (Philadelphia: Fortress, 1987); idem., *Midrash as Literature* (Philadelphia: University Press of America, 1987); Philip Alexander adopts a mediating view between Vermes and Kugel, on the one hand, and Neusner, on the other, in 'Midrash' *A Dictionary of Biblical Interpretation* (ed. C. J. Coggins and T. L. Houlden; London: SCM & Trinity, 1990), 452–9; Devorah Steinmetz stresses that the *darshanim* engaged not just with individual lemmata but also with larger phenomena like narrative structure, repeating or echoing words, common or contrasting motifs, and so forth. Devorah Steinmetz, 'Beyond the Verse: Midrash Aggada as Interpretation of Biblical Narrative', *AJSR* 30 (2006): 325–45.

[39] See bibliography.

[40] 'Psalm 22 and the "Servants" of Isaiah 54; 56-66', *CBQ* 77 (2015): 640–56, quote at 651.

[41] For a similar example, see D. Andrew Teeter, 'Isaiah and the King of As/Syria in Daniel's Final Vision: On the Rhetoric of Inner-scriptural Allusion and the Hermeneutics of "Mantological Exegesis"', in *A Teacher for All Generations: Essays in Honor of James C. VanderKam* (JSJSup 153/1; ed. Eric Mason, Samuel Thomas, et al.; Leiden: Brill, 2012), 1: 169–99.

with respect to structural patterns. Genesis 1–11 has a well-recognized recurrence pattern.[42] The configuration of stories and genealogies in Gen. 2.1–6.4 is repeated in Gen. 6.5–11.9. A creation story (Gen. 1.1–2.24) is followed by a fall story, leading to exile (Gen. 3.1-23). Then comes a story of familial strife, stressing the progressive impact of sin on humanity (Gen. 4.3-16). The pattern concludes with a story of transgressed boundaries, a breach between the celestial and terrestrial realms (Gen. 6.1-4). The elements of this pattern are separated by intruding genealogical information (Gen. 2.4; 4.1-2; 4.17-26; 5.1-32). The same configuration of stories recurs in Gen. 6.5–11.9. A recreation story (Gen. 6.5–9.17) is followed by a story of a fall and familial strife (Gen. 9.20-7) and culminates in a story of an incursion of the terrestrial into the celestial realm (Gen. 11.1-9). The parts separated, once again, by bits of genealogy (Gen. 6.9-10; 9.18-19, 28; 10.1-32; 11.10-30). As I have said, this pattern is well recognized. What is less well recognized is that subsequent narratives make use of this same pattern, sometimes using it exactly as encountered in Genesis 1–11 and sometimes reordering the elements. At the beginning of the Jacob cycle, for example, we encounter a story in which Jacob steals Esau's blessing from Isaac, their father – a story punctuated by allusions to Genesis 3 (esp. 27.8, 10, 12, 16). This is followed by a story of family strife, in which Esau threatens his brother with fratricide (27.30-41), leading to Jacob's exile from Canaan (27.42–28.5). The segment culminates in Jacob's vision of celestial beings descending to and ascending from the terrestrial world (28.10-22). In this example, it is the pattern of content, which is shared by the stories of the early humans and Jacob, that establishes the connection between the texts. Under these conditions, the writers do not have to provide much in the way of explicit allusions to confirm the connection. In such a case, explicit allusions fade in importance, occurring in just enough density to confirm the link at a close reading. More importantly still, by this technique whole series of stories can be intertextually aligned. In this one example, thirteen chapters of Genesis are brought into a threefold alignment, encouraging readers to read backwards and forwards, comparing and contrasting.

The implications of these findings for the study of scriptural reuse are profound. The ways that we validate the presence of scriptural reuse, in particular, looking for explicit citations or density of rare and unique words and phrases, tends to focus our attention on very small text segments, individual lines or verses, or pericopae. Perhaps because of this, there is an understandable tendency to miss wider arguments or patterns when they are evoked. In some cases, scholars simply find it impossible to believe that ancient readers and writers could or would work in such ways. This, it seems to me, is a failure of imagination. Surely not all readers and all writers in antiquity, any more than today, had identical (and limited) habits and skills.

---

[42] Umberto Cassuto, *A Commentary on the Book of Genesis*, vol. 2: *From Noah to Abraham* (Jerusalem: Magnes Press, 1964), 30–3; idem., 'The Sequence and Arrangement of the Biblical Sections', in *World Congress of Jewish Studies 1947* (Jerusalem: Magnes, 1954), 165–9; Gary Rendsburg, *The Redaction of Genesis* (Winona Lake: Eisenbrauns, 1986), 7–25; Jerome Walsh, *Style and Structure in Biblical Hebrew Narrative* (Collegeville: Michael Glazier, 2001), 111–13.

4 Presentation versus operation

The multitude ways that scriptural reuse can be presented are well established. Writers can engage with antecedent literature directly or indirectly, overtly or covertly. In the act of *direct* engagement, writers can quote, allude, rewrite, redact or gloss their sources.[43] *Indirectly*, they can mimic in different ways – by satire, polemic, parody or by structural replication. Likewise, they can construct elaborate analogies between items, plots, characters, institutions or circumstances, which may be overt or covert. Each of these types of engagement is presented in a different way. Quotations are explicitly marked as acts of text replication, discrete from their contexts. Allusions are implicit and covert but anticipate readerly recognition. Rewritten scriptural texts follow a base text closely but expand, change, rework and interpret it at many turns. And the list goes on.

Naturally, each of these presentation possibilities imposes certain limitations on and presents certain possibilities to the writers who choose them. Presentation features, though, should be kept distinct from operational features. The term 'Operations', in the way that I am using it, indicates two things. In the first instance, it indicates *writing operations*, the mechanical writing techniques by which writers engage with their sources. It considers the visible similarities and differences between source and target: replication, expansion, subtraction and substitution. I also use the term 'operations' to indicate the interpretive choices made by ancient writers, *exegetical operations*. 'Operations', in the first sense, are represented in a text's graphemes; 'operations' in the second sense are indicated in its semantics.[44]

Although the presentation features of scriptural reuse can differ widely, the *exegetical operations* employed appear to transcend presentation features. That is, writers can make use of the same stock of interpretive possibilities regardless of whether they are quoting, alluding, rewriting, redacting or glossing. Presentation choices do place certain limitations on authors with respect to their *writing operations*. If an author alludes, for example, she cannot include a citation formula that identifies the source. Nonetheless, *most* writing techniques can and do appear in *most* presentation forms.[45]

The scholarly habit of distinguishing genres and presentation forms from one another is important, of course, for understanding many literary conventions: the projection of a text-world, *mimesis*, even syntax and semantics. It is less significant, though, for an understanding of ancient Jewish interpretation and scriptural reuse. The operations of ancient Jewish interpretation are a stock of behaviours that writers can apply in almost any literary environment. The results of the study of any one

---

[43] This includes marginal glosses as well as the traditional 'lemma + comment' commentary format.
[44] For the Second Temple and rabbinic literatures, these two features – presentation and operation – are described with great precision by Alexander Samely in, respectively, *Profiling Jewish Literature in Antiquity: An Inventory, from Second Temple Texts to the Talmuds* (Oxford: Oxford University Press, 2013) and *Rabbinic Interpretation*.
[45] Even quotations have this potentiality, despite the modern scholarly assumption that quotations must be verbatim replications from the source text. This is discussed in William Tooman, 'Authenticating Oral and Memory Variants in Ancient Hebrew Literature', *JSS* 64 (2019): 91–114.

presentation type are applicable to others. There is a related historical point. Judaism seems to have accumulated writing techniques and exegetical operations over the centuries, only rarely shedding them. This is one of the reasons that we can detect essential lines of continuity from Ancient Near Eastern literature, through the HB and deep into the rabbinic period. This complicates and undermines attempts to chart the historical development of exegetical traditions, but it does create rich opportunities for comparative research.

5 Polysemy

Polysemy is the facility of any sign, word, phrase, sentence or text to bear multiple meanings in a single context. All language cultures have the capacity for polysemy, and ancient Hebrew literature is richly endowed with techniques of polysemy.[46] Polysemy serves a wide range of functions. It can demonstrate erudition, serve mnemonic and organizational functions, or acquire hermeneutic functions.[47] Polysemy also can be deployed for purposes of power. Scott Noegel and Stephan Schorch have proposed that 'some forms of polysemy are mechanisms for unleashing or harnessing the illocutionary power of words, especially when employed in prophetic or ritually empowered contexts'.[48]

The type of polysemy that interests me here is something more expansive than the specific polysemic conventions like entendre, *gematria*, *haphak* or *atbash*. In some of the literatures and times of ancient Judaism, divine communication was assumed to possess a surplus of meaning, to be intrinsically multivalent. In rabbinic studies, this has long has been appreciated, and there is a long-standing and robust debate in *midrashic* scholarship about the precise contours, effects and limits of this

---

[46] Scott Noegel provides descriptions and examples of fifteen types of polysemy in the HB: contronymic polysemy, double entendre, antanaclasis, unidirectional polysemy, Janus parallelism, double polysemy, bilingual polysemy, polysemy clusters, numerical polysemy, *gematria*, *notariqon*, acronymy, acrostics, *atbash*, and amphiboly. 'Polysemy', *Encyclopedia of Hebrew Language and Linguistics* (vol. 3: P-Z; ed. Geoffrey Kahn; Leiden: Brill, 2013), 178–86.

[47] See, for example, F. Bohl, 'Wortspiele im Alten Testament', *JPOS* 6 (1926): 196-212; Walter Herzberg, 'Polysemy in the Hebrew Bible' (PhD diss., New York University, 1979); Michael Fishbane, 'The Qumran Pesher and Traits of Ancient Hermeneutics', in *Proceedings of the Sixth World Congress of Jewish Studies: Hebrew University of Jerusalem, 13–19 August, 1973* (ed. Malka Jagendorf and Avigdor Shinan; Jerusalem: World Union of Jewish Studies, 1977), 97–114; Moshe Garsiel, 'Punning upon the Names of the Letters of the Alphabet in Biblical Acrostics', *Beth Miqra* 139 (1994): 313–34; Robert Gordis, 'Studies in Hebrew Roots of Contrasted Meaning', *JQR* 27 (1936-7): 33–58; Daniel Grossberg, 'Pivotal Polysemy in Jeremiah XXV 10–11a', *VT* 36 (1986): 481–5.

[48] Noegel, 'Polysemy', 178; idem., '"Sign, Sign, Everywhere a Sign": Script, Power, and Interpretation in the Ancient Near East', in *Science and Superstition: Interpretation of Signs in the Ancient World: The Fifth Annual University of Chicago Oriental Institute Seminar* (ed. Amar Annus; Chicago: Oriental Institute of the University of Chicago, 2010), 143–62; Stefan Schorch, 'Between Science and Magic: The Function and Roots of Paronomasia in the Prophetic Books of the Hebrew Bible', in *Puns and Pundits: Wordplay in the Hebrew Bible and Ancient Near Eastern Literature* (ed. Scott B. Noegel; Bethesda: CDL, 2000), 205–22. Also Walter Farber, 'Associative Magic: Some Rituals, Word Plays, and Philology', *JAOS* 106 (1986): 447–9.

assumption.[49] This is only natural, of course, since one purpose of *midrash* is to realize the potentialities of Scripture.[50] So, this is hardly a new 'finding', and yet, its implications are just beginning to adumbrate into biblical and Second Temple studies. There are two reasons that the subject is beginning to garner increased attention by biblicists. First, the growing awareness (and acceptance) of the connections between rabbinic interpretation and the interpretation of earlier Judaisms raises significant questions about the origins of the belief that Scripture may possess a plenitude of meaning.[51] From the opposite chronological direction, recent research into the Akkadian omen texts and commentary tradition has revealed similar beliefs about the power of sacred words.[52] In the light of these two observations, it would be surprising if the HB were somehow an outlier. To date, the issue has been most openly discussed in the fields of textual criticism and Second Temple studies.[53] Nonetheless, a movement in this direction has been detected within the HB itself.[54]

Any text has the potentiality to bear one meaning in its local literary context and to still be 'coded' so-to-speak (by its allusions) to participate in another literary context. It may be that, when viewed from one or the other of its contexts, that text plays a different semantic or theological role. For example, Gen. 12.10-20 – the story of Sarah being taken into the household of Pharaoh – is a famously gapped text, omitting many salient details: Did Abram lie? Did Sarai endorse Abram's plan? What happened to Sarai while in the house of Pharaoh? How did God afflict Pharaoh? How did Pharaoh connect his possession of Sarai with the afflictions he was enduring? How did Pharaoh discover she was married? Was God's judgement just, if Pharaoh was ignorant? Was the affliction ever lifted? Genesis 20 tells a very similar tale, this time with Avimelek, king of Gerar. In the Genesis 20 story, though, all the gaps in Genesis 12 are filled.

---

[49] Arnold Goldberg, 'Entwurf einer formanalytischen Method für die Exegese der rabbinischen Traditionsliteratur', *FJB* 5 (1977): 1–14; Teugels, *Bible and Midrash*; Alexander, 'Midrash', 452–9; idem., 'The Bible in Qumran and Early Judaism', in *The Text in Context* (ed. A. D. H. Mayes; Oxford: Oxford University Press, 2000), 35–62; D. Weiss Halivni, *Peshat and Derash: Plain and Applied Meaning in Rabbinic Exegesis* (Oxford: Oxford University Press, 1998); Moshe Halbertal, *Commentary Revolutions in the Making: Values as Interpretative Considerations in Midrashei Halakhah* (Jerusalem: Magnes Press, 2010); Azzan Yadin-Israel, *Scripture as Logos: Rabbi Ishmael and the Origins of Midrash* (Philadelphia: University of Pennsylvania Press, 2011); idem., *Scripture and Tradition: Rabbi Akiva and the Triumph of Midrash* (Philadelphia: University of Pennsylvania Press, 2014); Steven Fraade, 'Response to Azzan Yadin-Israel on Rabbinic Polysemy: Do they "Preach" What they Practice?' *AJSR* 38 (2014): 339–61; Mandel, *The Origins of Midrash*. Many other sources could be cited.

[50] Philip Alexander, 'Why no Textual Criticism in Rabbinic Midrash? Reflections on the Textual Culture of the Rabbis', in *Jewish Ways of Reading the Bible* (ed. George Brooke; JSSSup 11; Oxford: Oxford University Press, 2000), 90–175.

[51] This question is raised, explicitly, by James Kugel in Kugel and Greer, *Early Biblical Interpretation*, 17.

[52] See, for example, Tigay, 'An Early Technique of Aggadic Exegesis', 169–89; Lieberman, 'A Mesopotamian Background for the so-called *Aggadic*', 179–83; Gabbay, 'Akkadian Commentaries from Ancient Mesopotamia', 267–312; idem., 'Levels of Meaning and Textual Polysemy in Akkadian and Hebrew Exegetical Texts', in *Jewish Cultural Encounters in the Ancient Mediterranean and Near Eastern World* (ed. M. Popović, M. Schoonover and M. Vandenberghe; Leiden and Boston: Brill, 2017), 76–95.

[53] David Andrew Teeter, *Scribal Laws: Exegetical Variation in the Textual Transmission of Biblical Law in the Late Second Temple Period* (FAT 92; Tübingen: Mohr Siebeck, 2014); A. Shemesh and C. Werman, 'Hidden Things and Their Revelation', *RevQ* 18 (1998): 409–27.

[54] See n. 48.

Now, Genesis 20 does not 'replace' Genesis 12 for the two texts are different events in the *diegesis* of the patriarchal stories. Nor are we meant to 'fill in' the gaps in Genesis 12 with information from Genesis 20, because it cannot be done seamlessly, and it would, once again, shatter the *diegesis*. So, each story has a meaning and role in its local literary context. And yet, when read as intertexts (which they surely are), they provide a play of perspectives on similar events. Genesis 20 does not 'fill in' Genesis 12, but it does provide an example of one way that the gaps *might* be filled. It highlights and underlines those gaps, while guiding the reader to acknowledge that it is possible to interpret Genesis 12 in a way that allows for the providential protection of the matriarch. But it still leaves room for the alternative interpretation that Abram allowed his wife to be taken into the house of Pharaoh in the fullest sense.

These two interpretive possibilities are complicated, once more, by the Exodus story. Genesis 12 also participates with the Exodus story in some rather obvious ways: Israelites go to Egypt to avoid a famine; Sarai is taken captive by Pharaoh; she is only freed when the Egyptians are plagued by God; and the Israelites go out of the land again, laden with plunder. As Yair Zakovitch has argued, the parallels between Genesis 12 and the Exodus story open up a new interpretive possibility: Israel's slavery in Egypt is a consequence of Abram's sin in Genesis 12. Genesis 12, then, is balanced between two possible interpretations in two different ways: one in which the matriarch enjoys divine protection, one in which she does not; one in which Abram's claim 'she is my sister' is a lie, and one in which it is not.[55]

Thus, Genesis 20 informs the reading of Genesis 12 in a way that Genesis 12 does not do for Genesis 20, and, simultaneously, Genesis 12 informs the reading of Exodus 1–13 in a way that Exodus 1–13 does not do for Genesis 12. Moreover, each does so without dictating how the intertext must be read. Thus, Genesis 20 alters the *possibilities* of meaning for Genesis 12, and Genesis 12 alters the *possibilities* of meaning for Exodus 1–13. The events are not collapsed, nor are they 'about' the same things, but the density of each text's meaning and its possible meanings are dramatically altered when read in light of its intertexts.

In light of the *possibility* that polysemy may be a more regular feature of biblical literature than has been assumed, I suggest that the ancient Hebrew writers may not be pressing us to make a choice. It may be, in fact, that neither is right and neither is wrong. In such a case, this constellation of stories presents us with multiple perspectives on the age-old Jewish problem of living in diaspora, under Gentile rulers. Sometimes those rulers are benevolent, and sometimes not; sometimes the Jewish community is innocent in their dealings with those rulers, and sometimes not.

* * *

The set of topics considered in this chapter are not exhaustive. Some scholars of scriptural reuse barely consider the issues that I have raised, and yet, they produce excellent work on scriptural reuse. I hope, nonetheless, that they present a tolerably

---

[55] Yair Zakovitch, *And You Shall Tell Your Son: The Concept of the Exodus in the Bible* (Jerusalem: Magnes, 1991), 18–26; Avigdor Shinan and Yair Zakovitch, *Abraham and Sarah in Egypt* (Research Projects of the Institute of Jewish Studies Monograph Studies 2; Jerusalem: Magnes, 1983), 133–8.

clear précis of some of the new directions the field is taking in the study of ancient Jewish literature and their potentialities for fresh research.

Throughout this essay, I have been hinting at a single idea, that ancient Jewish writers were free. They were free to use the literary works and conventions at their disposal to achieve whatever literary effects they could imagine, free to assimilate and amalgamate, free to coordinate texts of virtually any size and shape. Put differently, if my theme is freedom then my thesis lies in the 'Proteus Principle' – 'the many-to-many correspondences between linguistic form and representational function'.[56] According to the Proteus Principle, no compositional technique is enslaved to a single function. Representation, whether of ostensive reality, or ideas, or images, can be accomplished by any number of techniques. Ancient texts can be segmented or unified by means of a whole host of conventions. Literary structures – whether aural, graphic, diegetic or ideational – can be crafted, overlayed and amalgamated, and the techniques used to achieve these structural patterns are as unpredictable and numerous as the number of forms that those patterns can take.

The understandable scholarly desire to catalogue techniques, genres and literary features, and to assign likely functions to each blinkers our vision and clouds our perceptions. We have been, perhaps, too bound by our allegiance to distinction and validation. We distinguish genres from one another in form and function. We isolate individual meaning in individual texts. We insist on the replication of multiple lexemes (preferably rare ones) before we are ready to recognize textual reuse, limiting both the volume and scope of reuse that we are capable to observe. It goes without saying that ancient readers and writers did not share our modern scholarly allegiances, and I would suggest that the horizon of research into scriptural reuse lies in a new allegiance, an adherence to the omnipresent effects of the Proteus Principle in ancient Jewish literature.

---

[56] Meir Sternberg, 'Proteus in Quotation-Land: Mimesis and the Forms of Reported Discourse', *Poetics Today* 3 (1982): 112.

3

Genre versus intertextuality: Linking wisdom texts, themes and contexts with the wider Old Testament and with the sayings of Jesus

Katharine J. Dell

Since the rise of form criticism in the early twentieth century, scholars have tended to classify biblical material into 'genres' using three key criteria of form, content and context.[1] This genre classification has in turn led to the Old Testament (OT) groupings of 'wisdom literature', 'prophecy', 'law', 'historiography', 'narrative' and then, within the wisdom literature, to proverb, riddle, autobiographical story, numerical listing and onto New Testament (NT) groupings of saying, parable and so on.[2] Key aspects of this approach are (a) the link to author – the idea that an author, or oral material eventually given concretization by an author, generated the text and (b) the link to social context – the idea that a particular author or group at a given time were generating these 'genres' of material that were personal to their world view. Hence the wisdom literature was traditionally seen as the product of sages or wise men to be found at the courts of kings or at administrative levels in the national infrastructure.[3] They were the ones who had the time to write, reflect, archive and collect the kind of material, probably much of it oral, that characterizes wisdom literature and to educate the young using this same material.[4] The book of Proverbs represents such a collection of earlier wisdom genres largely made up of one, two or three-lined sayings,[5] or proverbs as they are more normally known, with Job and Ecclesiastes

---

[1] Following H. Gunkel, *The Psalms: A Form-Critical Introduction* (trans. Thomas Horner; Philadelphia: Fortress, 1967). See also E. Gerstenberger, 'Psalms', in *Old Testament Form Criticism* (ed. J. H. Hayes; San Antonio: Trinity University Press, 1974), 179–221.
[2] R. E. Murphy, *Wisdom Literature, The Forms of the Old Testament Literature* (Vol. XIII; ed. R. Knierim and G. M. Tucker; Grand Rapids: Eerdmans, 1981). Also J. L. Crenshaw, 'Wisdom', in *Old Testament Form Criticism* (ed. J. Hayes; San Antonio: Trinity University Press, 1974), 225–64.
[3] See W. L. Humphreys, 'The Motif of the Wise Courtier in the Book of Proverbs', in *Israelite Wisdom* (ed. J. G. Gammie et al.; Missoula: Scholars Press, 1978), 177–90.
[4] See E. W. Heaton, *The School Tradition in the Old Testament* (Oxford: Oxford University Press, 1994).
[5] W. McKane, *Proverbs: A New Approach* (Old Testament Library; London: SCM Press, 1970).

regarded as a more detailed exploration of wisdom themes using some similar, but other often quite different, genres.[6]

Some of these assumptions about the link between genre and authorial and social context in particular are currently under question in the wisdom field and this feeling is probably spreading.[7] It is generally felt that we have been too tied to these genre categories and that we should be breaking down the barriers between them. Many genres did not easily fit the strictures of form that were laid down – for example one might isolate the 'form' structure of a psalm of the 'hymn' genre (of which there are about thirty-five in the Psalter) with elements A, B and C as Gunkel did.[8] Element A was an invitation to song or hymnic introduction usually opened by a series of imperatives directed to those to whom the invitation is extended (form); a summons to praise the great god Yahweh (content): with the addressees usually people in the forecourt of the temple on some ceremonial occasion and the presenter leading the praise (context). Element B was a short transitional passage introducing the theme of the hymn, usually introduced by 'for' (form); it is a thematic sentence giving reasons for praise God who is trustworthy and unrivalled in power and sphere of activity (content); it is linked to the invitation to song (context). Element C was the enumeration of God's deeds in a longer list (form). This was a varied list comprising not only the salvation history of Israel and God's power over nature and the fate of the individual but also the primeval event of Yahweh's accession to the throne, by which he originally became king (content). The wider situation in life of the whole is the cult (context).

But the reality was that each psalm was slightly different and so failed the structural 'form' test and often tested the boundaries of the content criterion as well.[9] In fact, content – in this case, hymnic praise in enumeration of God's deeds – was often the main criterion for grouping, rather than form.[10] When it came to context, that too could vary from personal to communal, from private to cultic lament, for example – the categories were generally too broad. And it was always difficult when a genre from one walk of life turned up from another – what were wisdom elements doing in certain psalms? Psalm 1, for example, follows wisdom categories of the righteous and the wicked (especially in vv. 1, 4-6) but then brings in a focus on the law of

---

[6] Job and Ecclesiastes are often put together as a kind of 'wisdom in revolt' (as per L. G. Perdue's book title *Wisdom in Revolt* [Sheffield: Almond Press, 1991]), but I disagree with this assessment, seeing Ecclesiastes as closer to Proverbs in its wisdom character – see Katharine J. Dell, 'Ecclesiastes as Mainstream Wisdom (without Job)', in *Goochem in Mokum/Wisdom in Amsterdam: Papers on Biblical and Related Wisdom Read at the Fifteenth Joint Meeting of The Society of Old Testament Study and the Oudtestamentisch Werkgezelschap, Amsterdam July 2012* (ed. George J. Brooke and Pierre Van Hecke; OTS 68; Leiden: Brill, 2016), 43–52.

[7] Mark Sneed, 'Is the "Wisdom Tradition" a Tradition?' *CBQ* 73 (2011): 50–71. See my response in Katharine J. Dell, 'Deciding the Boundaries of Wisdom: Applying the Concept of Family Resemblance', in *Was there a Wisdom Tradition?: New Prospects in Israelite Wisdom Studies* (ed. Mark R. Sneed; Ancient Israel and Its Literature; Atlanta: SBL Press, 2015), 145–60.

[8] Examples were used from Psalms 47, 135 and 146.

[9] For a critique of the use of form in this way, see Erhard Blum, 'Formgeschichte – A Misleading Category? Some Critical Remarks', in *The Changing Face of Form Criticism for the Twenty-First Century* (ed. Marvin A Sweeney and Ehud Ben Zvi; Grand Rapids: Eerdmans, 2003), 32–45.

[10] Wisdom psalms were also aligned on the basis of common content with other wisdom books rather than on strict grounds of form.

the Lord that is not the usual stress in Proverbs. Did we need then a new 'wisdom psalms' category?[11] How much watering down of one genre could take place before its definition became too strained? On a wider level, how could we contain the categories of wisdom, prophecy, narrative and so on when they often bled into one another? How, for example, could woman wisdom in Prov. 1.20-33; 3.13-20 and Proverbs 8 look and sound so like a prophet and yet belong to a completely different tradition? Were prophets aware of proverbs and of those groups who coined and preserved them? How much of another 'genre' could be tolerated before it changed the grounding genre itself? This was particularly problematic in regard to psalms study where many psalms were found to be of mixed genre, where the majority seemed to fit the temple context but many did not, where there was material from many periods and redactions and where 'wisdom', or 'didactic', psalms could be regarded as non-cultic.[12] There were also psalms very like the prophetic oracles of, say, Deutero-Isaiah – the language of praise seemed too interchangeable at times (as, for example, when praising God as creator of the world – Isa. 42.4; 45.12; Ps. 19.1, 4; 33.6; 102.25).[13] In genre terms, Deutero-Isaiah's oracles could well be added to psalms of lament as reversing oracles of salvation and one would hardly notice the join. Did this similarity put Deutero-Isaiah in the cult? Or was this just an expression of known genres of the time? Questions abounded and answers seemed to be thin on the ground.

I would say that the sea change that is emerging in addressing these questions is largely inspired by the interest in intertextuality and inner-biblical citation that has grown up in biblical studies in the last few years.[14] Intertextuality shifts the focus from texts of the same 'genre' to texts that share features following Kristeva's principle that 'any text is the absorption and transformation of another'.[15] It is often seen as the 'new kid on the block', solving many of the above problems.[16] The difficulty, though, in intertextuality studies has been how to define the criteria for intertexts. How much overlap between texts makes one a citation of the other? Are we dealing simply with vocabulary? How many similar words make a link – a quotation (whether explicit or implicit),[17] a shared phrase, an

---

[11] Gunkel, *The Psalms*, had such a category, although he believed these psalms to be late and non-cultic. The category has been discussed at length since, for example, R. E. Murphy, 'A Consideration of the Classification "Wisdom Psalms"', *SVT* 9 (1962): 156–67. There are almost as many scholarly suggestions as to which the wisdom psalms are as there are scholars working on this topic. See the chart in Simon Cheung, *Wisdom Intoned: A Reappraisal of the Genre 'Wisdom Psalms'* (LHBOTS 613; London: Bloomsbury T&T Clark, 2015), 188–90.

[12] I find myself in disagreement with this conclusion – see Katharine J. Dell, '"I Will Solve My Riddle to the Music of the Lyre" (Psalm XLIX 4 [5]): A Cultic Setting for Wisdom Psalms?' *VT* 54 (2003): 445–58.

[13] See overview in R. N. Whybray, *The Second Isaiah* (Old Testament Guide; Sheffield: Sheffield Academic Press, 1983).

[14] Beth Tanner, *The Book of Psalms Through the Lens of Intertextuality* (Studies in Biblical Literature 26; New York: Lang, 2001); Michael Stead, *The Intertextuality of Zechariah 1-8* (LHBOTS 506; New York: T&T Clark International, 2009).

[15] Julia Kristeva, 'Word, Dialogue and Novel', in *Desire in Language: A Semiotic Approach to Literature and Art* (ed. Leon S. Roudiez; Oxford: Basil Blackwell, 1980), 64–91 (66).

[16] For a recent work on intertextuality and Deutero-Isaiah, see Benjamin D. Sommer, *A Prophet Reads Scripture: Allusion in Isaiah 40-66* (Contraversions; Stanford: Stanford University Press, 1998).

[17] Yair Hoffman, 'The Technique of Quotation and Citation as an Interpretive Device', in *Creative Biblical Exegesis: Christian and Jewish Hermeneutics through the Centuries* (ed. Benjamin Uffenheimer and Henning Graf Reventlow; JSOTSup 59; Sheffield: JSOT Press, 1988).

allusion, an echo?[18] Or is there a sense of theological intertext without strict vocabulary links – perhaps better named 'theological criticism'[19] or simply thematic links? How does an intertext function – on a strictly diachronic level with one text citing an older one (production-orientated)? Or do we need to move to wider synchronic connections which may never have been authorially intended but seem to us, as readers, to exist (reception-orientated)? Should we speak of hard or soft intertextuality?[20] Or just simply see it as 'a sort of umbrella term' designed 'to describe any kind of relationship between texts'.[21] The field is already saturated by theory.[22] In biblical studies, however, intertextuality has come to have a particular definition as textual citation and echo, usually on a diachronic model. Some have preferred the term 'inner biblical' since we are mainly speaking in biblical studies of texts within the one 'canon' of Scripture. This also avoids a discussion of the complexity of the transfer of an essentially French philosophical scheme onto literary studies and then into biblical studies itself.

In this article, I wish to look at the relative merits of these approaches with a few examples from the wisdom literature of the OT, while also dipping into the wider OT canon and ending with a scholarly example that compares Ecclesiastes with some of Jesus's sayings in the NT.

When the form critics turned to Proverbs and applied the concept of genre, great strides were made in the isolation of different proverb types and other genres:[23] first and foremost according to 'form' criteria, but in fact, as with the psalms, much of the real linkage was in terms of content and theological theme. Authorial and social context(s) were more difficult to reconstruct, but nevertheless great efforts were made. While Solomonic authorship was seen as honorary, the sages at the courts of kings were thought to have 'authored' the material in the sense that they probably collected and collated much older material.[24] Even if there were oral stages of sayings over long time periods, sayings that might have circulated in families, tribes or around the campfire, eventually an author(s) in a context(s) was responsible for the writing down and preservation of the sayings.[25] The key stage was their collection and placement in the book of Proverbs.[26] The difficulties of genre classification really came when trying to take the genre outside Proverbs, first into the so-called 'wisdom literature'[27] and

---

[18] Richard B. Hays, *Echoes of Scripture in the Letters of Paul* (New Haven; London: Yale University Press, 1989). These are taken up and adapted by Will Kynes in *My Psalm Has Turned into Weeping: Job's Dialogue with the Psalms* (BZAW 437; Berlin: Walter de Gruyter, 2012).

[19] William H. Anderson, 'The Curse of Work in Qoheleth: An Exposé of Genesis 3:17-19 in Ecclesiastes', *EvQ* 70 (1998): 99–113.

[20] John Barton, 'Déjà Lu: Intertextuality, Method or Theory?' in *Reading Job Intertextually* (ed. Katharine Dell and Will Kynes; LHBOTS 574; London: Bloomsbury, 2013), 1–16.

[21] Kynes, *My Psalm Has Turned into Weeping*, 20.

[22] For a survey of intertextual methods and disagreements, see Geoffrey D. Miller, 'Intertextuality in Old Testament Research', *CBR* 9 (June 2011): 283–309.

[23] Katharine J. Dell, *Get Wisdom, Get Insight: An Introduction to Israel's Wisdom Literature* (London: Darton, Longman, and Todd, 2000).

[24] E. W. Heaton, *Solomon's New Men* (London and New York: Pica Press, 1974).

[25] This two-stage (oral to written or written to written) model is the most persuasive in my view.

[26] Intertextual method emphasizes final form and this is the trend too in recent biblical scholarship.

[27] See Will Kynes, 'The Wisdom Literature Category: An Obituary', *JTS* 69 (2018): 1–24 and recent questioning of the category, by Stuart Weeks, *An Introduction to Wisdom Literature* (ABS; London: T&T Clark, 2010), who sees 'wisdom literature' as 'our category, not one bequeathed to us by the biblical writers themselves' (142).

second, beyond that, to evaluate influence on other texts, and that is where the water became muddy.[28] Even when applied to, for example, Job, a book normally seen as mainstream wisdom literature, the proverbial form is found to be essentially lacking and the dialogue form dominates, a dialogue that often contained, at least in the mouth of Job himself, largely psalmic sentiments of lament and disputation.[29] And outside the wisdom literature, it was hard to know what material to include – if a court context was posited for wisdom, then possibly the Joseph narrative,[30] Succession narrative[31] or the stories of Daniel 1–7 should be included.[32] If the context was more familial, then these would not fit. If one element of form, content or similar context could be found, how far was that a link with the main wisdom genre?

For example, the proverbial form is rarely found in the prophetic material. Perhaps the most famous example of a proverb in this literature is when both Jeremiah and Ezekiel both cite the sour grapes proverb (Jer. 31.29-30; Ezek. 18.2-3): 'In those days they shall no longer say: "The parents have eaten sour grapes, and the children's teeth are set on edge."' This is clearly delineated as a proverb, as mentioned specifically in Ezekiel: 'What do you mean by repeating this proverb concerning the land of Israel' (18.2a) is his prelude to the citation (often used when he is citing the views of others, not strictly when a proverb is in view) coined by the people, and it uses the distinctive parallelism of the proverbial form and imagery of the everyday. It is cited in order to be rebutted in the new context of a disputation. The only disappointment is that this proverb does not appear in the book of Proverbs! This might suggest that there was a wider store of proverbs around in society than actually got written down in Proverbs. Amos, the eighth-century prophet, is often cited as one who knew proverbs, but he reshaped them into rhetorical questions also in the context of a disputation – Amos 3.3-8, for example.[33] This seems to have happened in Isaiah, too, and he was even styled a sage by some.[34] The form and its content are thus changed in the light of reuse in a new context, normally that of a prophetic oracle.[35] So, in fact, we find few strictly proverbial forms in the prophets and all we can probably speak of, in a traditional contextual context, is that wisdom might have afforded some kind of training to the educated in a court setting, but somehow it did not go on to influence their styles in a profound way.

But turning from 'form' to the more general ground of 'content', even if the proverbial forms are not there in prophecy, there are undoubtedly oracles that overlap

---

[28] D. F. Morgan, *Wisdom in the Old Testament Traditions* (Atlanta: John Knox, 1981) stressed the breadth of wisdom influence on the canon.
[29] See discussion in Katharine J. Dell, *The Book of Job as Sceptical Literature* (BZAW 197; Berlin: Walter de Gruyter, 1991).
[30] Gerhard Von Rad, 'The Joseph Narrative and Ancient Wisdom', in *The Problem of the Hexateuch and Other Essays* (trans. E. W. Trueman Dicken; Edinburgh: Oliver & Boyd, 1966), 292–300.
[31] R. N. Whybray, *The Succession Narrative* (SBT Second Series 9; London: SCM, 1968).
[32] See John Goldingay, *Daniel* (WBC 50; Dallas: Word, 1989).
[33] A thorough study of wisdom influence on Amos was conducted by H. W. Wolff, *Joel and Amos* (translated from the German by W. Janzen, Fortress Press: Philadelphia, 1977). The numerical sequence of Amos 1–2 would seem to be a particularly good example (cf. Prov. 30.18-19). Not all scholars are in agreement that there is any definitive wisdom influence on Amos, notably J. L. Crenshaw, 'The Influence of the Wise Upon Amos: The "Doxologies of Amos" and Job 5.9-16; 9.5-10', *ZAW* 79 (1967): 42–52.
[34] By J. W. Whedbee, *Isaiah and Wisdom* (Nashville: Abingdon, 1971).
[35] G. Fohrer, *Introduction to the Old Testament* (Revised edn; Nashville: Abingdon Press 1968).

thematically, for example, 'justice and righteousness' – a key wise trait in Prov. 1.3 and repeated many times in the prophets (e.g. Isa. 33.5; Jer. 9.24; 22.3, 15; Jer. 23.5; 33.15). The divine quality of wisdom is attributed to God in Isa. 28.29; 31.2 and Jer. 10.12.

Then in terms of context, there is clearly awareness in the prophet Jeremiah of societal groups that are pursuing wisdom: 'instruction shall not perish from the priest, nor counsel from the wise, nor the word from the prophet' (Jer. 18.18).[36] This might suggest some cohesion among different genres and the groups responsible for them – perhaps we have tended to divide them up too much. When we notice some prophetic styling in the portrayal of woman wisdom in Prov 1.20-33; 3.13-20 and Proverbs 8 we might start to posit links between the two, running in both directions.[37] She stands on a street corner calling to young men (8.2-3), and in doing so, she perverts the usual feminine passivity and home-orientation; she is a woman in contrast to the main prophetic players who are all men, and like prophets, she breaks the usual boundaries in her high-sounding promises.

However, if we turn to an intertextual approach to any of these links, we would need more solid ground of citation, allusion, echo and so on. If we follow the more diachronic model of intertextuality, where the possibility of one work citing another is mooted and where questions of chronological contact therefore have a place, questions from the form-critical model are not irrelevant. And yet, intertextuality seeks to take the focus away from authorial intention and redactional stages to textual reality – that is, the text as it stands in its final form. The directions of borrowing are of less importance than the fact of connections. Speculation about the minds of ancient authors is avoided, chronological priority, riven with similar speculation, is also by-passed (at least on any kind of detailed level) and the question of redactional layers (or not) becomes irrelevant.[38]

On the other side of the coin, intertextuality has some disadvantages – for example, as mentioned, how many allusions are needed for an intertext to be spotted? Once we enter the world of 'echo' alone, we start to enter a similar area of speculation as that which dogged more traditional authorial and contextual approaches. As Richard Hays himself wrote, 'Quotation, allusion, and echo may be seen as points along a spectrum of intertextual reference, moving from the explicit to the subliminal. ... As we near the vanishing point of the echo, it inevitably become difficult to decide whether we are really hearing an echo at all, or whether we are only conjuring things out of the murmurings of our own imaginations.'[39] I find myself in some agreement with this view that we are in danger of finding what are essentially thematic links between texts, which is not very different from a thematic 'content-based' form-critical approach – I will test this theory in a minute. Yet, for some scholars, this more subjective end of

---

[36] J. Lindblom, 'Wisdom in the Old Testament Prophets', in *Wisdom in Israel and in the Ancient Near East* (ed. Martin Noth and D. Winton Thomas; VTSup 3; Leiden: Brill, 1955), 192–204. Lindblom argued this mainly based on Jer. 18.18. See also W. McKane, *Prophets and Wise Men* (SBT 44; London: SCM Press), 1965.

[37] C. Kayatz, *Studien zu Proverbien 1-9: Eine form- und motivgeschichtliche Untersuchung unter Einbeziehung ägyptischen Vergleichmaterials* (WMANT 22; Neukirchen-Vluyn: Neukirchener Verlag, 1966) argued that close common features between Wisdom and Yahweh in Proverbs 1–9 influenced the prophets rather than the other way around which is the more common view.

[38] Miller, 'Intertextuality in Old Testament Research'.

[39] Hays, *Echoes of Scripture in the Letters of Paul*, 23.

the spectrum is not a problem – as Spellman writes, 'The effects that intertextuality generates in the writing and reading of biblical texts is no less intended because it is understated.'[40] Paulien also writes, 'Echoes are not of lower value than allusions in interpretation, they simply need to be handled differently.'[41]

I have elsewhere coined the phrase 'didactic intertextuality' to describe the way that proverbs or their general thrust are often used in the context of teaching.[42] This is, of course, the inherent nature of a proverb – it features an observation, often of unlike phenomena, brought together to make an ethical point, and most significantly many proverbs use images of nature, animals and the everyday (e.g. Prov. 6.6, an illustration of laziness using the ant). Discussing Proverbs and Ruth using a synchronic intertextual method, I showed how proverbial material is hinted at in the narrative text for explicit didactic purposes. Didactic exemplars from the text of Proverbs are illustrated in the character of Ruth and in the wider story in that tale. For example, Prov. 21.21 states, 'Whoever pursues righteousness and kindness will find life and honour' – a maxim that characterizes much of Ruth's acts of kindness in the tale. This kind of textual linkage (whether or not an author intended it or not) is an exciting new approach.[43] But in this chapter, I am more in the realm of echo than allusion and of a kind of functional use of one text by another – in this case a didactic function, designed to teach the reader. I might have made use (although I did not) of Ziva Ben-Porat's definition of 'allusion' as a 'device for the simultaneous activation of two texts' which specifies function (i.e. simultaneous activation) alongside location (two texts) but which avoids judgements about form, authorial intention or social context.[44] But much of what I did find was thematic links between the texts, so could I have arrived at similar conclusions through a purely thematic route rather as in the content part of the old 'genre' scheme? Is this actual intertextuality or are these simply thematic links – a didactic intent, but little actual intertext if we are being strict about that definition?

When we turn to a kind of 'thematic intertextuality', then it seems to me that whichever method we are following tends to yield very similar results. So, for example, one can see on the level of genre that the character of Job is using traditional sentiments of the psalmists and turning them on their head (what I have called parody).[45] In my own view (as stated in 1991), it is not the citation of any specific psalms that matters (except that we have a prime example of citation of Job 7 and 14 in Ps. 8.4), it is simply that a genre (e.g. lament) or praise of God as creator was

---

[40] Ched Spellman, *Toward a Canon-Conscious Reading of the Bible: Exploring the History and Hermeneutics of the Canon* (NTM 34; Sheffield: Sheffield Phoenix Press, 2014), 160–1.

[41] Jon Paulien, 'Elusive Allusions in the Apocalypse: Two Decades of Research into John's Use of the Old Testament', in *The Intertextuality of the Epistles: Explorations of Theory and Practice* (ed. Thomas L. Brodie et al.; NTM 16; Sheffield: Sheffield Phoenix Press, 2006), 63.

[42] Katharine Dell, 'Didactic Intertextuality: Proverbial Wisdom as Illustrated in Ruth', in *Reading Proverbs Intertextuality* (ed. K. Dell and W. Kynes; LHBOTS 634; London: Bloomsbury, 2019), 103–14.

[43] Katharine Dell and Will Kynes, eds, *Reading Job Intertextually* (LHBOTS 574; London: Bloomsbury, 2012). Katharine Dell and Will Kynes, eds, *Reading Ecclesiastes Intertextually* (LHBOTS 587; London: Bloomsbury, 2014). Katharine Dell and Will Kynes, eds, *Reading Proverbs Intertextually* (LHBOTS 634; London: Bloomsbury, 2019).

[44] Ziva Ben-Porat, 'The Poetics of Literary Allusion', *PTL: A Journal for Descriptive Poetics and Theory of Literature* 1 (1976): 105–28 (107).

[45] Cf. Dell, *The Book of Job as Sceptical Literature*, 109–57.

being used rather differently in Job, notably by the protesting character of Job as portrayed by a sceptical author. For example, Job 23.8-9 parodies a hymn *such as* Psalm 23 – this passage speaks of being unable to find God, in comparison with Psalm 23 which rejoices in God's shepherding care for humans. However, building on these insights but using an 'intertextual' approach, my student Will Kynes found intertextual criteria for citation of psalms in Job that showed a more compact set of intertexts between the two works Job and Psalms. His starting point was the actual quotation of Ps. 8.4, but for Job 23.8-9, for example, he argues that it is an actual intertextual parody of Ps. 139.5, 7-10. The language of behind and before, of forwards or backwards, provides linguistic and thematic links. But the parody is in the fact that Psalm 139's note of praise at God's constant presence becomes, for Job, a total absence, as Mettinger writes, 'an ironic contrast to the psalmists' imaginary flight from God in Ps. 139.7-12' (Mettinger being another scholar who has been an early proponent of the application of intertextual method in Job).[46] Not only that, but Kynes also found a rich tapestry of citation of particular psalms in the friends' speeches – so Zophar also cites these verses from Psalm 139 in Job 11.7-9, both using rhetorical questions and the language of searching as well as referring to heaven, Sheol and the sea's limits. Kynes writes of the comparison: 'Whereas the psalmist used this imagery to emphasize the inescapable intimacy of a God who is with him no matter where he goes, Zophar uses it to depict God's omnipresent eye of judgement.'[47] These kinds of finding seemed to indicate that the intertextual method worked on a firmer footing than the old methods, at least in this case, although the case can only be a cumulative one because the evidence is of varying strength and relies on the difficult problems of defining links that I mentioned above.

In similar vein, but with intertextuality having the opposite effect, when working on Ecclesiastes, I found many commentators trotting off the links with Genesis, and big thematic connections can certainly be found.[48] But when I studied the so-called 'intertexts' closely, it seemed that the links were not so promising as at first thought.[49] How far were thematic links a product of links of thought-world; if intertexts were few and far between, were we not simply in the realm of echo or suggestion rather than on stronger ground? Maybe this is equally valid, but then why do we need to make such methodological distinctions in the first place? What then is the difference between seeking intertexts that are not really there except on a loose thematic level and using the 'content' criterion of the quest for genres to make the same link?

Another example is the book of Ecclesiastes (notably chapter 11) and Lamentations 5 in relation to the 'genre' of city lament. Here, a genre has been identified in Lamentations and then there is a question as to whether there is an 'intertext' in Ecclesiastes.[50] The

---

[46] T. N. D. Mettinger, 'The Enigma of Job: The Deconstruction of God in Intertextual Perspective', *JNSL* 23 (1997): 1-19.
[47] Kynes, *My Psalm Has Turned into Weeping*, 114.
[48] Given classic expression in C. C. Forman, 'Qoheleth's Use of Genesis', *JSS* 5 (1960): 256-63.
[49] Katharine J. Dell, 'Exploring Intertextual Links between Ecclesiastes and Genesis 1-11', in *Reading Ecclesiastes Intertextually*, 3-14.
[50] See Katharine J. Dell, 'All Is Decay: Intertextual Links between Lamentations 5 and Ecclesiastes 12:1-7', in *Reading Lamentations Intertextually* (ed. Heath Thomas and Brittany Melton; LHBOTS; London: Bloomsbury, forthcoming). See also Jennie Barbour, *The Story of Israel in the Book of Qohelet: Ecclesiastes as Cultural Memory* (Oxford: Oxford University Press, 2012).

result is partial intertext, with some overtones of vocabulary, but strong thematic links too. The dying city is likened to the human body dying through old age (e.g. Lam. 5.15/ Eccl. 12.5). Literary dependence between the two texts is unlikely on any traditional reading, but thematic resonance and awareness one of another in a contextual sense is strong. But how are these conclusions dictated by intertextuality, or by a general sense that there is a thematic overlap that needs to be investigated?

What I am suggesting here, though, is that while intertexuality can work well for many texts, the case for genre connections – notably on the level of content – can also function well to link texts together that don't have an obvious set of intertexts. It seems to me that questions of authorial purpose and possible social context(s) have led us into thinking that the two methods are further apart than in fact they actually are. A focus on theme is a uniting factor in both methods, but do we need such a complex statement of methodology to come to this rather obvious conclusion?

What I want to look at now is a few examples from a NT context. Perhaps this debate can help us with classifying the sayings of Jesus, which are, after all, the closest we have in the NT to proverbial wisdom. In a more traditional mode, questions were asked about the context of Jesus's relationship to wisdom sayings – was Jesus essentially a sage?[51] In Mt. 13.54, the people ask, 'Where did this man get this wisdom and these deeds of power?' Clearly Jesus's wisdom was recognized by those around him and there is little doubt that he said many wise things. After all, his words had a didactic intent – he was a teacher, and he gave, both to his disciples and to larger groups, instruction in how to live their lives in a meaningful way in the light of the new revelation that he came to bring. Was Jesus's context the same as the wise men (namely, teaching the young or uninitiated about all aspects of life, using clever sayings and comparisons)? On an intertextual level, much citation of the OT is found in the New, but when we come to the sayings of Jesus, that is not where the bulk of intertexts on the level of deliberate allusion and echo lie.

Form-critical studies based on genre tended to ask the question: Did Jesus use wisdom genres in his sayings? This does not mean that he had to cite anything specific from the OT, but rather it asked whether the way he formulated his sayings had any connection with known ways of doing so, notably in the Proverbs. On the level of content, was what he had to say of the same order as the content of Proverbs, with its reflection on human relationships? Leo Perdue did a definitive study of the various different types of proverbs in the book of Proverbs and their relationship to the sayings of Jesus.[52] On the level of form, he points to various categories of proverbs paralleled in Proverbs and the Gospels, including 'synonymous', which aligns two related sentiments (e.g. Mt. 10.24; Lk. 6.40a; Jn 13.16; 15.20, cf. Prov. 24.5), 'antithetical', involving a contrast (e.g. Mt. 8.20; Lk. 9.59; cf. Prov. 10.31) and 'synthetical', where the two halves of a verse agree (e.g. Lk. 6.38; Mt. 7.2; cf. Prov. 15.31). He also finds three types of comparative proverb, the first of which uses 'like' or 'as' (e.g. Mt. 13.52, cf. Prov. 26.11); a second type that uses the idea of less and more (e.g. Lk. 16.10, cf Prov. 15.11); and a

---

[51] Given definitive expression in B. Witherington III, *Jesus the Sage: The Pilgrimage of Wisdom* (Edinburgh: T&T Clark, 1994).

[52] L. G. Perdue, 'The Wisdom Sayings of Jesus', *A Journal of the Foundations and Facets of Western Culture* 2 (1986): 3–35.

third comparative type of 'better' saying (e.g. Mk 10.25, Mt. 19.24; Lk. 18.25, cf. Prov. 16.8). He also considers numerical sayings and rhetorical questions, known genres from Proverbs, of which there are a few parallels in the gospel tradition. Perdue was essentially looking here at the forms of the sayings in both traditions and finding some similar patterns.[53] But Perdue found no exact parallels or citations as one might be wanting to explore in an 'intertextual' methodology, and this underlines the 'fuzzy edges' of a genre approach.

When we turn to content as the second form-critical criterion, the results are more piecemeal. While some topics are found in common, as Ben Witherington III points out, when we turn to consider thematic parallels we cannot but notice that many of the wise sayings of Jesus do not cover the same subjects as proverbial wisdom; for example, proverbs about hard work and warnings about loose women are totally absent from Jesus's words. Rather, he is concerned with ethical behaviour, but this is always in the context of the coming kingdom, thus giving his ethics an eschatological spin. So what Witherington argues is that, in the sayings of Jesus, there is a new eschatological stance that coloured all his sayings and took attention away from their ethical thrust. Jesus was not simply commenting on human relationships and their ethical ramifications, but rather on such relationships as they would be changed by the fresh revelations of God to come imminently. Jesus speaks of his own person and significance using wisdom formulations, for example, Mk 8.35 (cf. Mt. 10.39, Lk. 17.37 and Jn 12.25): 'For whoever would save his life will lose it; and whoever loses his life for my sake and the gospel's will save it.' This has the character of an antithetical saying, but is formulated in a new way that speaks of eternal life and, in a veiled way, of his eschatological significance (cf. Mk 2.27-8). Jesus also speaks by use of this kind of wisdom saying about the coming of the kingdom, for example, Lk. 6.2b: 'Blessed are you who are poor, for yours is the kingdom of God' – a 'blessed are' saying (used in Ecclesiastes frequently, for example, in chapter 7) but shaped with an eschatological perspective.[54] This individual character of Jesus's sayings stands out – he asserts a counter order to the status quo, a vision of a new world order beyond traditional wisdom understandings.

Then there is the question of context – was Jesus's context one in which sayings were key? Traditional form-critical studies posited that many of the sayings of Jesus, since they were found mainly in Matthew and Luke, may have come from a shared sayings source 'Q' and might not have come from the mouth of Jesus himself. The ones shared by Mark's gospel possibly added to the case for the historicity of a sayings tradition going back to Jesus himself, but whether sayings were from Mark or Q, they had the feel of a common source material. Did this mean that Jesus was a kind of wise man standing in a common wisdom tradition as these many sayings indicate? Or was there some kind of imposition of this picture upon him or, more charitably, an enhancement of what was already the case? This is not to say that Q (or, if you prefer, shared Matthaean/Lukan) material was not potentially genuine but that the gospel writers chose to enhance this aspect of Jesus's character and ministry. This

---

[53] We might also look at parallels between maxims and beatitudes in Ben Sira and the maxims and beatitudes of Jesus and indeed at the parables of Jesus.

[54] By the time of Qumran, it is interesting that wisdom and eschatology became combined, so maybe Jesus is the product of his time more than is often realized.

incorporation of sayings material might have been an attempt to shift the focus away from Jesus being an apocalyptic visionary in the light of the fact that his predictions about the end time had not yet come about. To place the emphasis on Jesus's ethical teaching instead would ground his teaching in the universally applicable, in the 'here and now', rather than pointing towards a future in which such ethical admonition would be of little use. The Epistle of James is a good example of a letter containing a strong wisdom element (e.g. 1.5-6) retaining a practical reality about the present and distancing the emphasis on the end time.[55]

Another contextual point, traditionally raised, is how educated Jesus was in relation to the kind of education received by professional wise men. On the assumption that many of the wisdom writers were highly educated and that there are strong connections between wise men and royal courts, Jesus was clearly not in this category. He was educated, but probably not in a formal sense. He knew his Bible, the OT (Lk. 2.46), and no doubt the wisdom contained within it, but he also had a new message of his own to convey in language that people could understand. He was no wise man in any traditional sense – perhaps, he was a wise radical who used traditional ideas but essentially challenged the tradition with new ideas. As B. B. Scott writes, 'The construct of the voice of Jesus's aphorisms or parables embodies a distinctive, individual voice whose patterns, accents, styles, themes and even ideology are recognizable. This is to be distinguished from other proverbs and parables whose voice, being "anonymous" is the projection of common wisdom.'[56] There may have been temple schools or synagogues in this later period in which Jesus may have been educated at some point – there is the story of him listening and asking questions in the temple at Jerusalem (Lk. 2.46) – but his precise educational context is unknown and probably unknowable. The more important point, which Scott brings out, is the way that he used wisdom for his own purposes in his teaching.

This form-critical approach then has limited results and tends to generate more questions than we have answers. On a more intertextual reading, however, we would be looking for more direct citation of proverbial or other didactic material than traditional approaches such as this one afford. Authorship and contextual issues take a back seat in the quest for thematic connection. My hunch is that this approach would at first glance be less fruitful than a genre analysis because actual citation from proverbs or other wisdom material is not there. While intertextual studies, especially of St Paul, have shown that much citation of the OT is found in the New, when we come to the sayings of Jesus, that is not where the bulk of intertexts on the level of deliberate allusion and echo seem to lie. In a rare article combining intertextuality, wisdom and the NT, Craig Bartholomew[57] argues for a possible direct quotation from Eccl. 7.20 ('Surely there is

---

[55] James's characterization as wisdom is well established within NT scholarship – see, for example, Richard Bauckham, *James: Wisdom of James, Disciple of Jesus the Sage* (New Testament Readings; London: Routledge, 1999); also Robert W. Wall, *Community of the Wise: The Letter of James* (NTC; Valley Forge: Trinity Press International, 1997).

[56] B. B. Scott, 'Jesus as Sage: An Innovating Voice in Common Wisdom', in *The Sage in Israel and the Ancient Near East* (ed. J. G. Gammie and L. G. Perdue; Winona Lake: Eisenbrauns, 1990), 319–416 (407).

[57] Craig Bartholomew, 'The Intertextuality of Ecclesiastes and the New Testament', in *Reading Ecclesiastes Intertextually*, 226–39.

no one on earth so righteous as to do good without ever sinning') in Rom. 3.10 ('For there is not a righteous person on the earth who does good and does not sin'). The link of 'sin' is essentially a thematic one, but it is, of course, possible that the NT is citing the Old here; that this is more than a thematic link is indicated by the similar vocabulary.[58] Bartholomew argues that this intertext opens up the conversation of possible links between Ecclesiastes and the NT. I will outline his article here as a possible pointer towards future study in this neglected area.

Bartholomew also finds some broad thematic connections between Ecclesiastes and Romans 8 in terms of a common emphasis on 'futility' and then beyond into the broader NT. He notes some shared vocabulary between Ecclesiastes and the Gospels, for example, 'eye' and 'ear' in Ecclesiastes 1, bodily metaphors that are also used by Jesus (e.g. Mt. 6.22-3). But this kind of language is hardly enough to establish a specific link between these books, in my view, as bodily imagery is widespread in the OT (especially in Proverbs).[59] He also points to the theme of wealth in both Ecclesiastes and the Sermon on the Mount, but this is a very general thematic link. For the sayings and parables of Jesus in the Gospels, there is little intertextual fodder. In Mt. 11.16-19, Jesus relates his eating and drinking to wisdom. Bartholomew makes the point that just as Ecclesiastes affirms that eating and drinking and feasting is to be commended, so Jesus often attends parties and is described as eating and drinking at various times, including providing wine at a wedding and bread and fish at the end of a day of teaching. Jesus also relativizes eating and drinking when he compares them to more important things in life in Mt. 6.25-32: 'Therefore I tell you, do not worry about your life, what you will eat or what you will drink … is not life more than food' (Mt. 6.25). This point about thematic links with wisdom concerns had been made, though, long before intertextuality as a method was devised; Hubbard wrote in a rather overstated way in 1966: 'Christ was not only master of the wise man's techniques. He was steeped in the wise man's message. He not only personifies wisdom, after the manner of Proverbs 8, but He virtually identifies Himself with it. Surely it is His wisdom that will be justified by her deeds (Mt. 11.19).'[60] The link between Jesus and wisdom was well established by Hubbard and Witherington according to older methods – we do not need intertextuality to establish this point.

Bartholomew points out that the Sermon on the Mount is where Jesus is best seen as a wisdom teacher. The Sermon ends with the wise man and the fool building their houses (Mt. 7.24-7), and one can compare this to the two houses built by Wisdom and Folly, respectively, in Prov. 9.1, 14/Prov. 7.6, 8, 27. He writes, 'In Proverbs 9, the challenge is to enter the house of wisdom, whereas in Matthew 7 it is to build wisely.'[61] He also suggests that Eccl. 12.13 might be in mind when fearing God and keeping

---

[58] At the Hawarden conference on 'The Use of the Old Testament in the New' (2018) at which I presented a shorter version of this chapter, one delegate suggested to me that LXX Ecclesiastes was probably not formed at the time of Paul, so making an actual citation within a historical context unlikely. I would like to thank Susan Docherty for her kind invitation to speak at and attend this enjoyable event.

[59] Bodily language in Proverbs abounds – for example, Prov. 6.2; 8.7; 10.32 all mention lips and mouth in the context of communication. The body, as a complete psychosomatic unity, features in Prov. 15.20; 16.24; 18.8.

[60] David A. Hubbard, 'The Wisdom Movement and Israel's Covenant Faith', *TynBul* 17 (1966): 3-33 (28).

[61] Bartholomew, 'The Intertextuality of Ecclesiastes and the New Testament', 235.

his commandments is advocated, given that the stress on obedience to the will of the Father and Jesus as wise man are linked in the Mt. 7.21-9 passage. These are interesting connections, but they seem a far cry from definite intertexts and even quite a long way from an echo. Again, apart from his opening example from Romans, it is only really in the thematic connections that we can find links, and so we are back to the kind of outline done by Witherington and others when they outlined wisdom elements in the words of Jesus. I cannot but question Bartholomew's conclusion that his article 'demonstrates the fecundity of intertextual interpretation in opening up rich veins of exploration that have previously been ignored'.[62] This may be true in some areas of study, but it does not open up much for him in this article in Ecclesiastes or in the NT. Perhaps future work will emerge with more mileage.

So my feelings about the value of this new kid on the block – intertextuality – as a method are mixed. Intertextuality is not so interested in reconstructing 'authorial' or 'contextual' scenarios and so, in contrast to older approaches, would not be so interested in reconstructing Jesus's own authorial credentials or in reconstructing his educational context as the earlier writers have done. This is its strength – it goes back to the text, its language, themes and key concern – and so this might provide an interesting new approach. In its focus on final form, also, intertextuality as a method simply *receives* connections, rather than asking these historical questions that are ultimately unknowable and over which so much scholarly ink has been spilt in the past. I have argued in this article, then, that there is significant overlap of this method with form-critical or 'genre' method in the area of theme or content and, on this ticket at least, the two methods may be successfully aligned.

---

[62] Ibid., 238.

4

How Scripture 'speaks': Insights from the study of ancient media culture

Catrin H. Williams

It is unquestionably the case that most contributions to the field of OT/NT studies presuppose and work with literary models in their investigations of the composition, transmission and reception of ancient texts. The scholarly discourse, conducted by those 'born into the Gutenberg galaxy',[1] continues to be dominated by references to *written* texts and sources and to possible *readers* of the textual artefacts in question. John Miles Foley, one of the leading voices in twentieth-century orality studies, commented as follows on the literary presuppositions guiding what is arguably the most prevalent theoretical approach to 'the use of the Old Testament in the New':

> Even in an age learning to prize 'intertextuality', we can observe that the very etymology of that critical term denominates two or more formally bounded, complete items that interact – so that their separate contexts are more or less sharply defined, and the individual text maintains an absolute status uniquely its own. Even though the field of interpretation is enlarged and deepened, textual heuristics tacitly demands that we privilege the individual document above all else.[2]

Intertextual perspectives on the use and reception of Israel's Scriptures in the New Testament (NT) writings may largely be underpinned by print-based assumptions and are reliant on comparative analyses of discrete texts, but scholars are now increasingly coming to terms with the highly oral–aural environment in which those texts were produced and received by Jews and Christians in antiquity. Literacy rates were relatively low in the first-century CE Mediterranean world,[3] particularly if 'literacy' is defined as skilful competence in reading literary documents, although the rates decrease further if

---

[1] Anthony Le Donne and Tom Thatcher, *The Fourth Gospel and First-Century Media Culture* (LNTS, 296; London; New York: T&T Clark Continuum, 2011), 3.
[2] John Miles Foley, *The Singer of Tales in Performance* (Voices in Performance and Text; Bloomington: Indiana University Press, 1995), xi.
[3] See especially William V. Harris, *Ancient Literacy* (Cambridge: Harvard University Press, 1989). On the degrees and distribution of literacy in Jewish Palestine, see Catherine Hezser, *Jewish Literacy in Roman Palestine* (TSAJ, 81; Tübingen: Mohr Siebeck, 2001), 496–504.

the definition includes the writing and (scribal) copying of literary and religious texts.[4] Moreover, the unwieldy character of ancient scrolls made it difficult for those who could read to navigate their way through texts when searching for specific passages for the purpose of consultation and comparison; and the use of *scriptio continua* in literary texts – with no spaces between words, no section divisions and no punctuation – would have further hindered the reading process.[5] In performative contexts, such practical difficulties would undoubtedly have prompted lectors to familiarize themselves thoroughly, beforehand, with the content of texts. Whether scrolls functioned as visual aids for memorized delivery through oral acts of communication,[6] or were the basis of word-for-word recitation directly from the written sources,[7] texts during the Hellenistic and Roman periods were primarily, though not exclusively, read aloud for the benefit of a listening audience.[8]

NT authors and early Christian communities operated within a comparable ancient media environment and this included their reception of the Jewish Scriptures. It is, admittedly, difficult to determine whether, or when, Paul or the authors of the Gospels, for instance, were quoting directly from written scriptural sources or citing them from memory.[9] And despite the fact that public readings of Scripture are not included in Paul's references to corporate worship (1 Cor. 11.17-34; 14.1-40; cf. Eph. 5.19-20),[10] the NT writings do provide evidence that texts, including themselves (1 Thess. 5.27; Col. 4.16; Rev. 1.3) together with scriptural sources (Lk. 4.16-21; Acts 15.21; cf. Acts 8.28, 30; Justin, *1 Apol.* 67.3), were more typically read aloud in a group setting. The vocalization of scriptural readings in communal gatherings also supports the view that many Jews and early Christians would have aurally encountered and gained familiarity with the contents of Israel's sacred texts regardless of whether they were able to read the texts in question, thus acquiring what Dale Allison has labelled as 'oral literacy' as opposed to 'visual literacy'.[11]

---

[4] For example, Martin S. Jaffee, *Torah in the Mouth: Writing and Oral Tradition in Palestinian Judaism, 200 BCE–400 CE* (New York; Oxford: Oxford University Press, 2001), 16, refers to the 'socially stratified character of literacy' in Second Temple Judaism.

[5] On these cultural factors, see the oft-quoted study of Paul J. Achtemeier, '*Omne Verbum Sonat*: The New Testament and the Oral Environment of Late Western Antiquity', *JBL* 103 (1990): 3–27. Cf. Carol Harrison, *The Art of Listening in the Early Church* (Oxford: Oxford University Press, 2013), 1–14.

[6] Alan Kirk, 'Manuscript Tradition as a *Tertium Quid*: Orality and Memory in Scribal Practices', in *Jesus, the Voice, and the Text: Beyond the Oral and the Written Gospel* (ed. Tom Thatcher; Waco: Baylor University Press, 2008), 218: 'Memorative control of a written artefact was requisite for its practical utilization'. See also Jaffee, *Torah in the Mouth*, 16–17.

[7] For a recent debate on this and related issues, see Larry W. Hurtado, 'Oral Fixation and New Testament Studies? "Orality", "Performance" and Reading Texts in Early Christianity', *NTS* 60 (2014): 321–40; Kelly R. Iverson, 'Oral Fixation or Oral Corrective? A Response to Larry Hurtado', *NTS* 62 (2016): 183–200; and especially Larry W. Hurtado, 'Correcting Iverson's "Correction"', *NTS* 62 (2016): 201–6.

[8] For example, Plato, *Phaed.* 97c: ἀκούσας μέν ποτε ἐκ βιβλίου; *Theat.* 143bc; Theon, *Progymnasmata* 61; Pliny, *Ep.* 36.

[9] Although, see section 3.

[10] See Joanna Dewey, 'Textuality in an Oral Culture: A Survey of the Pauline Traditions', in *Orality and Textuality in Early Christian Literature* (ed. Joanna Dewey; Semeia, 65; Atlanta: SBL, 1995), 51–2, but this amounts to an argument from silence.

[11] Dale C. Allison, 'The Old Testament in the New Testament', in *The New Cambridge History of the Bible: From the Beginnings to 600* (ed. James Carleton Paget and Joachim Schaper; Cambridge: Cambridge University Press, 2013), 497.

These preliminary remarks offer no more than a snapshot of pertinent issues when OT/NT studies are brought into conversation with recent interdisciplinary developments in the field of ancient media studies. Investigating the first-century media culture in which Jews and early Christians lived, and in which their writings were produced, calls for an examination of the phenomena of orality,[12] textuality,[13] performance and memory, and, in particular, the intricate and multilayered relationship that existed between them.

The aim of this chapter is to consider the methodological issues and interpretative insights that can emerge when the study of the use and reception of the Jewish Scriptures in NT texts is probed from the perspective of ancient media cultural dynamics. In what ways has the complex oral–textual matrix of the first-century media world left its mark on how the NT authors cite and interpretatively interact with the authoritative Scriptures of Judaism in their own writings? What was the likely impact of the widespread oral communication of texts on the ways in which Israel's Scriptures were encountered, both with reference to author-centred (composition) and audience-centred (reception) questions? And what role did memory play in how Scripture 'speaks' and how it was 'heard' when mediated through a process of 'secondary orality'?[14] These questions will guide the discussion that follows, focusing on three central, often overlapping, topics: the ongoing interaction between orality and textuality in the composition and interpretation of texts; the dynamics of oral performance and audience reception; and the multifaceted processes and practices of memory. The chapter will examine how each of these three topics can inform the study of 'the use of the Old Testament in the New', highlighting some of the significant scholarly work that has already been undertaken in this area as well as seeking to identify how focusing on ancient media culture can open up other possibilities for future investigation.

1 The interface of orality and textuality

Earlier scholarship has tended to place oral and written modes of expression at opposite ends of the media spectrum, defining them as wholly distinct methods of communication belonging to 'the Great Divide'.[15] More recent studies, however, recognize the close symbiotic relationship between the spoken word and the written word in the ancient world.[16] Orality and textuality, as already intimated in the introduction to this study, could interact with each other in a variety of ways during the Hellenistic and Roman

---

[12] For a helpful survey of the impact of orality studies on the study of the New Testament, see Kelly R. Iverson, 'Orality and the Gospels: A Survey of Recent Research', *CBR* 8 (2009): 71–106.

[13] The term 'textuality' embraces the notion that even those who are illiterate can have direct access to textual artefacts (through recitation and performance) and also hold those artefacts in high esteem. See further Chris Keith, 'Literacy', in *The Dictionary of the Bible and Ancient Media* (ed. Tom Thatcher et al.; London: Bloomsbury, 2017), 209.

[14] The term 'secondary orality' was first applied in New Testament studies by Werner Kelber to describe how a written text 'enters the world of hearers by being read aloud'. See *The Oral and the Written Gospel: The Hermeneutics of Speaking and Writing in the Synoptic Tradition, Mark, Paul, and Q* (Philadelphia: Fortress Press, 1983), 217.

[15] See, for example, Nicholas A. Elder, 'New Testament Media Criticism', *CBR* 15 (2017): 316–17.

[16] See especially Rafael Rodríguez, 'Reading and Hearing in Ancient Contexts', *JSNT* 32 (2009): 154–61.

periods: written texts can offer glimpses into their intended oral–rhetorical effect within the setting of oral delivery,[17] but, at the same time, they are themselves the products of oral–aural cultural dynamics. For the purpose of exploring the use of the Jewish Scriptures in the NT, I will focus on two particular aspects that exhibit this close interrelation between speech and writing, between orality and textuality.

First, NT texts frequently draw attention to the *writtenness* of 'Scripture' (ἡ γραφή), although the repeated formulaic references to what is 'written' (γέγραπται, ἐστιν γεγραμμένον) are not necessarily intended as an indication that the scriptural citations can be accessed directly in a physical copy (rather than an orally memorized form) of the text; rather, the expression 'it is written' represents an appeal to the undisputed authoritative status of the text in question.[18] Regardless of whether people were able to read and/or gain direct access to scriptural sources, the texts were afforded the kind of 'authority and significance [that] are not limited to the actual words they contain'.[19] This can also extend to interpretative manoeuvres emerging from what is 'written' in Scripture,[20] from conflated quotations for which there is no identical or even comparable version in a single written text (e.g. Mk 1.2-3: καθὼς γέγραπται) to the interpretative opening of 'the scriptures' (αἱ γραφαί) in a manner that transcends what is actually inscribed in any single passage or even collection of texts (e.g. Lk. 24.27, 32, 44-5, 46: οὕτως γέγραπται). More overt representations of oral–textual interplay are attested in numerous references to scriptural *speech* (e.g. Rom. 4.3; 9.17; 11.2; Gal. 3.8; 4.30; 1 Tim. 5.18; Jas 2.23).[21] This is a characteristic feature of the letter to the Hebrews, whose scriptural quotations function as (predominantly divine) speech acts (e.g. Heb. 1.5-14; 2.12-13; 3.7-9; 8.8-12),[22] and it is also prevalent in the Gospel of John (cf. 7.38, 42; [19.24]; 19.37) where the Scriptures are distinctively presented as both a written and speaking authority. Michael Labahn has persuasively argued in this respect that the fourth evangelist calls attention to the 'oral enactment' of the written Scripture(s), because 'Scripture' – as an active, divinely given, character within the text – testifies persuasively on Jesus's behalf, even speaking directly to the audience of the gospel when it is recited in oral performance.[23]

---

[17] As discussed in section 2.
[18] See, for example, Richard A. Horsley, 'Oral Performance and Mark: Some Implications of *The Oral and the Written Gospel*, Twenty-Five Years Later', in *Jesus, the Voice, and the Text*, 61–2; Holly Hearon, 'Mapping Written and Spoken Word in the Gospel of Mark', in *The Interface of Orality and Writing: Speaking, Seeing, Writing in the Shaping of New Genres* (ed. Annette Weissenrieder and Robert B. Coote; Biblical Performance Criticism, 11; Eugene: Cascade Books, 2015), 382–3.
[19] Rafael Rodríguez, *Structuring Early Christian Memory: Jesus in Tradition, Performance and Text* (LNTS, 407; London: T&T Clark, 2010), 165–6.
[20] See further below in this section on 'text-interpretative traditions'.
[21] Cf. also the spoken words attributed to scriptural figures like Moses (Rom. 10.19), David (Rom. 4.6; 11.9) and Isaiah (John 1.23; 12.38-9; Rom. 10.20).
[22] See, for example, Ellen Bradshaw Aitken, 'Tradition in the Mouth of the Hero: Jesus as an Interpreter of Scripture', in *Performing the Gospel: Orality, Memory, and Mark: Essays Dedicated to Werner Kelber* (ed. Richard A. Horsley, Jonathan A. Draper and John Miles Foley; Minneapolis: Fortress Press, 2006), 102–3; cf. Philip F. Esler, 'Collective Memory and Hebrews 11: Outlining a New Investigative Framework', in *Memory, Tradition, and Text: Uses of the Past in Early Christianity* (ed. Alan Kirk and Tom Thatcher; Semeia Studies, 52; Atlanta: SBL, 2005), 164–6.
[23] Michael Labahn, 'Scripture *Talks* Because Jesus *Talks*: The Narrative Rhetoric of Persuading and Creativity in John's Use of Scripture', in *The Fourth Gospel and First-Century Media Culture* (ed. Anthony Le Donne and Tom Thatcher; LNTS 426' London; New York: T&T Clark Continuum, 2011), 133–54.

Secondly, the interdependence of textuality and orality in the first-century world is also manifested in and through Jewish and early Christian *scriptural interpretation*, not least in the ways in which written scriptural texts were designed to be publicly and *interpretatively performed and received*. Martin Jaffee, discussing how authoritative Scriptures were appropriated in late Second Temple Judaism, coins the term 'text-interpretive tradition' to denote the fluid, permeable and oral 'body of interpretive understandings that [arose] from multiple performances of a text (written or oral)',[24] some of which were eventually written down and themselves subjected to oral interpretation. Both the individual person reciting the text and the gathered audience would be actively engaged in discussing and expounding Israel's Scriptures. Given that the resource pool of text-interpretative material would exist and be nurtured in the cultural memories of those present, it would form 'an all-but-invisible environment of intertextual associations and ready-to-hand interpretive tropes',[25] belonging to what Werner Kelber has described as the 'biosphere' in which extra-textual traditions reside.[26]

Jaffee proposes that significant glimpses into one specific example of Jewish Palestinian oral–performative literary activity are afforded by the textual artefacts of members of the Qumran community,[27] especially the following description from the *Community Rule* of their collective engagement with scriptural texts:

> And in the place in which the Ten assemble there should not be missing a man to interpret the law (דורש בתורה) day and night, always, one relieving another. And the Many shall be on watch together for a third of each night of the year in order to read the book (לקרוא בספר), explain the regulation (לדרוש משפט), and bless together. (1QS 6.6-8; trans. Martínez and Tigchelaar 1:83)

This description evinces the central role played by the public recitation of authoritative written texts (which probably included the Torah, the Prophets and the Psalms) within the community, while the references to 'interpreting/explaining' (דרש) point to the orally mediated transmission of text-interpretative traditions related to those texts. Indeed, George Brooke has recently proposed that the explicit reference to 'reading' (קרא) in 1QS 6.8 implies more than the act of reciting the text aloud,[28] but rather – based on a study of the use of קרא in other sectarian texts[29] – involved 'active engagement with the text as it was performed'.[30] This interpretative scenario, proposes Brooke, may also account, at least in part, for the striking textual

---

[24] Jaffee, *Torah in the Mouth*, 8; cf. Hezser, *Jewish Literacy*, 452.
[25] Jaffee, *Torah in the Mouth*, 28.
[26] Werner H. Kelber, 'Jesus and Tradition: Words in Time, Words in Space', in *Orality and Textuality in Early Christian Literature*, 159: 'Tradition in this encompassing sense is a circumambient contextuality or biosphere in which speaker and hearers live. It includes texts and experiences transmitted through or derived from texts.'
[27] Jaffee, *Torah in the Mouth*, 31–8.
[28] George J. Brooke, 'Reading, Searching and Blessing: A Functional Approach to Scriptural Interpretation in the יחד', in *The Temple in Text and Tradition: A Festschrift in Honour of Robert Hayward* (ed. R. Timothy McLay; LSTS 83; London: Bloomsbury, 2015), 142–7.
[29] 'Reading, Searching and Blessing', 143–5 (see 1QS 7.1; 8.14-15; 1QSa 1.4; CD 5.2; 1QpHab 7.3).
[30] Ibid., 145.

pluriformity among Torah scrolls in the Qumran library, in that some of the variant forms of authoritative scriptural texts could have resulted from creative readings by scribes who participated in the study sessions mentioned in 1QS 6.6-8.[31] That the two closely related activities of reading/reciting and interpretatively studying Scripture, as presented in the *Community Rule*, was a more widespread phenomenon in late Second Temple Judaism is indicated by other pieces of evidence, including the first-century Theodotus Inscription: 'Theodotus ... built the synagogue for the reading (ἀν[αγ]νωσ[ι]ν νομου) of Torah and for teaching ([δ]ιδαχην ἐντολων) the commandments.'[32]

Scriptural 'reading' as a process involving dynamic interpretative participation, as evidenced in ancient Judaism, can also shed light on some of the ways in which the early Christians engaged in the 'searching of the scriptures' (cf. Jn 5.39). The media-sensitive model or template outlined by Jaffee (and Brooke) opens up a number of possibilities as far as OT/NT studies are concerned, although it has so far only been applied to a small number of NT texts. In a number of analyses of the description of Jesus standing up to read from a scroll of Isaiah (Lk. 4.16-20),[33] Rafael Rodríguez has attempted to reconstruct the text-interpretative traditions underpinning this Lukan passage. He notes that Jesus is presented as physically handling a written scroll of Isaiah (4.17) and yet the passage in question, which is not overtly described as being read (aloud) by Jesus, is actually a composite quotation containing an interpolated line from Isa. 58.6 between Isa. 61.1 and 61.2. Hence, when Jesus proclaims to the Galilean synagogue audience that 'this scripture' (ἡ γραφὴ αὕτη) has been fulfilled in their midst (Lk. 4.21), the curious earlier description of 'reading' (ἀναγνῶναι) along with its contents raises the question as to whether the singular 'scripture' here refers to one or both passages from Isaiah or, as argued by Rodríguez,[34] presents Jesus as *performing and actualizing* the wider 'contextualizing tradition' of God's judgement and restoration of/for Israel, especially as that tradition is embodied in the Isaianic texts. Furthermore, the subsequent appeal to Elijah and Elisha as representative witnesses of how God acts on behalf of those in need and also vindicates against his enemies (Lk. 4.25-7) clarifies *how* Jesus's proclamation in Nazareth fulfils the (broader) Israelite tradition of divine promise of restoration and judgement (cf. Lk. 7.22).[35] Text-interpretative traditions are rooted in, but not confined to, the written corpus of Israel's Scriptures that are said to find their fulfilment in Jesus.

---

[31] Ibid., 146-7, 154. See also idem., 'The Qumran Scrolls and the Demise of the Distinction between Higher and Lower Criticism', in *Reading the Dead Sea Scrolls: Essays in Method* (SBLEJL, 39; Atlanta: SBL, 2013), 12.

[32] See Mladen Popović, 'Reading, Writing, and Memorizing Together: Reading Culture in Ancient Judaism and the Dead Sea Scrolls in a Mediterranean Context', *DSD* 24 (2017): 455 (with references to additional relevant examples).

[33] See in particular *Structuring Early Christian Memory*, 158-63; idem., 'Textual Orientations: Jesus, Written Texts, and the Social Construction of Identity in the Gospel of Luke', in *T&T Clark Handbook to Social Identity in the New Testament* (ed. Brian Tucker and Coleman A. Baker; London: Bloomsbury, 2014), 191-210, especially 200-5.

[34] Rodríguez, 'Textual Orientations', 202-3.

[35] Rodríguez, *Structuring Early Christian Memory*, 162-3; 'Textual Orientations', 203-4.

2 The dynamics of oral performances and listening audiences

Much of the discussion so far in this chapter has centred on certain aspects of the oral–textual continuum attested in 'oral-derived texts',[36] a term that is frequently used for written material designed for oral communication and also for written transcripts of oral performances. Given the immense difficulties of reconstructing the original features of actual performances from the ancient past, as well as the fact that only the written remains of Jewish and early Christian oral-derived texts have survived,[37] the primary task must be to focus on the *written* artefacts themselves and, as far as possible, on their likely function – including their various modes of scriptural referencing – within the dynamics of an oral–performative setting.[38] Since these texts were commonly delivered orally and received aurally, one must enquire how this particular media environment shaped the ways in which they were composed and typically experienced by audiences in the first century CE. In other words, if oral-derived (written) texts functioned as 'sound maps intended to be heard in a rhetorical culture' to emphasize 'the persuasive power of the spoken word',[39] what kind of communicative techniques and strategies can be identified within the NT documents which were devised to enhance their appeals to the Jewish Scriptures?

One of the primary techniques associated with oral-derived texts as *vehicles of communication* is what John Miles Foley has termed 'metonymic referencing', that is, a technique whereby a particular saying or expression stands as shorthand for a much broader tradition with which an audience is already familiar (or where familiarity is assumed by the author and/or performer).[40] Since meaning is generated when the formulaic expression in question metonymically evokes extra-textual associations drawn from a shared cultural inheritance, the 'broader tradition' actively identified by Jewish or early Christian audiences would have included their authoritative Scriptures in addition to associated text-interpretative traditions. Extensive use of Foley's concept of metonymic referencing has been made, in this regard, by Richard Horsley (and in a co-authored volume on Q with Jonathan Draper) to argue that Mark and Q were oral-derived texts originally performed before illiterate audiences in Galilean villages.[41] Through the use of key motifs drawn from Israelite tradition, such as 'the wilderness' to

---

[36] The term 'oral-derived texts' was coined by John Miles Foley; see his *Immanent Art: From Structure to Meaning in Traditional Oral Epic* (Bloomington: Indiana University Press, 1991).

[37] Cf. Eric Eve, *Behind the Gospels: Understanding the Oral Tradition* (London: SPCK, 2013), 124; cf. Holly E. Hearon, 'The Implications of Orality for Studies of the Biblical Text', in *Performing the Gospel*, 4.

[38] For a media-critical *contextual* approach to oral-derived (New Testament) texts, see Rafael Rodríguez, *Oral Tradition and the New Testament: A Guide for the Perplexed* (London: Bloomsbury, 2014), 71–85, 87–118.

[39] Hearon, 'The Implications of Orality', 3–4.

[40] Foley, *Immanent Art*, 5–7. Cf. idem., *The Singer of Tales*, 54: 'the grand, untextualizable network of traditional associations'. See also Katherine M. Hayes, 'Metonymy', in *The Dictionary of the Bible and Ancient Media*, 225–6.

[41] On Mark, see especially Richard A. Horsley, *Hearing the Whole Story: The Politics of Plot in Mark's Gospel* (Louisville: Westminster John Knox Press, 2001); idem., 'A Prophet Like Moses and Elijah: Popular Memory and Cultural Patterns in Mark', in *Performing the Gospel*, 166–90. On Q, see Richard A. Horsley and Jonathan A. Draper, *Whoever Hears You Hears Me: Prophets, Performance, and Tradition in Q* (Harrisburg: Trinity Press International, 1999).

evoke memories of desert wanderings and expectations of future renewal (e.g. Q 3.7-9),[42] together with Moses-like and Elijah-like healings and feedings of crowds, an entire traditional script, it is claimed, is metonymically evoked to present Jesus as the prophetic leader of a new renewal movement.[43]

'Metonymy' bears resemblance, in certain respects, to the concept of 'metaleptic intertextuality', as primarily associated in OT/NT studies with the work of Richard Hays.[44] Both theoretical concepts envisage broad(er) scriptural frames than what are overtly 'cited' in the alluding text, though the interpretative process associated with metonymy takes one out of immediate textual contexts in order to tap into larger traditional networks. The major difference, of course, is that metonymic referencing works specifically with a media-critical model that does not assume the interpreter's ability to consult, quote and interpret other *written* texts but rather draws on culturally inherited memories which do not require visual access to texts. What binds together the concepts of metalepsis and metonymy is that both rely on the hermeneutical premise of scriptural competence on the part of readers and/or hearers. John Miles Foley states plainly that the oral-derived phenomenon of metonymic referencing assumes that the listening audience 'has a deep knowledge of how to "read" the text before them, [and] how to construe the traditional signals',[45] whereas the social and cultural context assigned by Horsley and Draper to the composition and reception of Mark and Q – that is, a rural Galilean setting – similarly presupposes that the immediate audiences of their oral performances would be deeply familiar with the wider traditional register or 'biosphere' in which metonymic evocations were expected to operate successfully.

The notion of orally transmitted texts having been constructed to reflect the scriptural competence of their listening audience(s) raises a number of critical issues. More scripturally literate hearers may well have been adequately equipped to appreciate oral-derived techniques such as metonymic scriptural evocations and text-interpretative traditions, but, as recent audience-centred approaches to OT/NT studies have justifiably noted, this cannot be assumed for all NT texts and their anticipated audiences. In several cases, as Christopher Stanley has proposed with reference to the letters of Paul,[46] there would have been a wide spectrum of familiarity with Israel's Scriptures, ranging from high levels of scriptural literacy (oral and/or visual) to more limited knowledge of 'core stories'.[47]

A related issue of particular relevance to media-sensitive investigations is that hearers inevitably encounter texts differently from readers. In a study of the cognitive

---

[42] Horsley and Draper, *Whoever Hears You Hears Me*, 252–3.
[43] For recent assessments of Horsley's (and Draper's) work on Mark and Q, see Eve, *Behind the Gospels*, 115–23; Rodríguez, *Oral Tradition and the New Testament*, 50–1.
[44] Richard B. Hays, *Echoes of Scripture in the Letters of Paul* (New Haven: Yale University Press, 1989).
[45] Foley, *Immanent Art*, 44.
[46] Christopher D. Stanley, *Arguing with Scripture: The Rhetoric of Quotations in the Letters of Paul* (London: T&T Clark International, 2004). Cf. also James F. McGrath, 'Orality and Intertextuality', in *Exploring Intertextuality: Diverse Strategies for New Testament Interpretation of Texts* (ed. B. J. Oropeza and Steve Moyise; Eugene: Cascade Books, 2016), 176–86, and especially 182, for an audience-orientated approach to the use of Isa. 45.23 in Philippians 2. See further Edward H. Gerber, *The Scriptural Tale in the Fourth Gospel with Particular Reference to the Prologue and a Syncretic (Oral and Written) Poetics* (BIS, 147; Leiden: Brill, 2017), 37–8.
[47] Cf. Hezser, *Jewish Literacy*, 502.

processes involved in the recognition and deciphering of scriptural references ('intertextual devices'),[48] Cynthia Edenburg notes the different capacities associated with short-term memory, 'a clearinghouse in which information is quickly received and processed', and long-term memory as a more permanent form of storage intended for future use.[49] A written text functions as a mnemonic device enabling readers to consult a passage repeatedly and to activate the memory of another, usually accessible, written document in the search for intertextual comparisons and associations.[50] Nevertheless, because of the immediacy of an oral–performative setting,[51] hearers of a text can only recall what is retained in memory 'while searching through long term memory in order to retrieve the recollection of the other text evoked by the association'.[52] And although the recognition of more allusive references may be facilitated through an overt marker textually signposting its 'otherness', Edenburg highlights the cognitively complex, and sometimes impossible, nature of the task of identifying and comparatively evaluating such references in an oral–aural environment.

The kind of performative milieu outlined by Edenburg focuses on the cognitive processes required for the identification of allusive scriptural elements *during a live performance*, with only limited focus given to other channels of communication that would enable hearers to tap into possible scriptural connotations in orally mediated texts.[53] Admittedly, only scant information is available about the ways in which audience members would be able to retrieve or deepen their scriptural knowledge, in the same way that we no longer have access to the original contexts in which oral performances were conducted. Nevertheless, several different scenarios can be envisaged, such as multiple recitations of a text within a communal framework, explanatory prompts provided by the lector, along with combined 'reading' and 'studying' activities during or after individual gatherings.[54]

The detection and interpretation of more veiled scriptural references could also, in some cases, have been activated through communicative techniques already built *within* an oral-derived text, such as the disclosure of possible scriptural connotations through repetition, close-knit configuration and/or the gradual textual–rhetorical unfolding of the traditional register. Related to this is the likelihood that, in a performative context, interactive participation by audience members was expected

---

[48] Cynthia Edenburg, 'Intertextuality, Literary Competence and the Question of Readership: Some Preliminary Observations', *JSOT* 35 (2010): 131–48. Her insights have more recently been applied to New Testament interpretation by Kelly R. Iverson, 'An Enemy of the Gospel? Anti-Paulinisms and Intertextuality in the Gospel of Matthew', in *Unity and Diversity in the Gospels and Paul: Essays in Honor of Frank J. Matera* (ed. Christopher W. Skinner and Kelly R. Iverson; Atlanta: SBL, 2012), 26–31.

[49] Edenburg, 'Intertextuality', 135–6.

[50] Cf. McGrath, 'Orality and Intertextuality', 178.

[51] Cf. Joachim Schaper, 'Hebrew Culture at the "Interface Between Written and the Oral"', in *Contextualizing Israel's Sacred Writings: Ancient Literacy, Orality, and Literary Production* (ed. Brian B. Schmidt; Ancient Israel and its Literature, 22; Atlanta: SBL, 2015), 329: '[speech] generates the illusion of immediate comprehension of and contact with the object signified.'

[52] Edenburg, 'Intertextuality', 137.

[53] Edenburg does refer to the recognition aid provided by 'density of motif recurrence' in performed material ('Intertextuality', 139), although she concludes that extensive use of (often opaque) allusions must have originated in scribal circles and assumes a 'highly literate reading audience'.

[54] See discussion above (Section 1) on 1QS 6.6-8.

and indeed encouraged as texts were orally delivered and aurally received.[55] That is to say, more indirect channels of scriptural communication like metonymic evocations were deliberately aimed at encouraging audiences to seek deeper levels of meaning by filling gaps and making links, and this involved them drawing from their culturally inherited (or acquired) memory pool.[56]

Such strategies could, undeniably, have been intended for readers as well as hearers,[57] but evidence from the ancient sources, including audience-orientated instructions in Graeco-Roman rhetoric on the intended persuasive force of elusiveness, strongly situates this communicative strategy within an oral–aural arena. According to ancient theorists, authors should deliberately withhold certain information to encourage their audiences to fill the gaps and draw conclusions for themselves.[58] In his treatise *On Style* (*Libro Elocutione*) Demetrius cites Theophrastus (frag. 696, third century BCE), noting that the 'essentials of persuasiveness' are that one 'should not elaborate on everything in punctilious detail' but rather omit some points so that an audience can work out the meaning. In this way, listeners are enlisted as 'witnesses' offering 'testimonies' to information otherwise withheld (*Eloc.* 222). Quintilian also underlines the rhetorical value of hinting at arguments instead of stating everything explicitly; audiences will be 'led to seek out the secret which they would not believe if they heard it openly stated, and to believe in that which they have found out for themselves' (*Inst.* 9.2.71). Among the cluster of rhetorical figures identified as encouraging listening audiences to search for deeper levels of meaning are intentionally ambiguous arguments (*emphasis*); open-ended comparisons (such as metaphors, riddles and parables); and, most importantly for this analysis, subtle allusions which, with varying degrees of volume, were used to help people make connections with existing traditional scripts and registers that were already inscribed in textual form.[59]

One NT text that particularly lends itself to an exploration of how it communicates its engagement with the Jewish Scriptures through the (rhetorical) strategy of elusiveness is the Gospel of John, not least because its allusive scriptural references frequently occur in discourses that progressively disclose the Johannine presentation of Jesus's identity, either through appeal to familiar figures from Israel's ancient past or by means of Jesus's self-identification with the aid of well-known metaphors. For

---

[55] On the rhetorical significance of hearing/listening, see Harrison, *The Art of Listening*, 37–46.
[56] Cf. Hayes, 'Metonymy', 226.
[57] Interestingly, Dale Allison, *Studies in Matthew: Interpretation Past and Present* (Grand Rapids: Baker, 2005), 76, draws similar conclusions about the impact of allusions on readers: 'Allusions, which give us more to do and so heighten our attention, invite informed imaginations to make their own contributions. Meaning is infolded not to obscure but to improve communication. The implicit allows the pleasure of discovery, and readers who are invited to fill gaps appreciate authors who respect them enough not to shout.'
[58] From a New Testament perspective, the rhetorical function of elusiveness and indeterminacy to promote audience participation has been examined by Kathy Reiko Maxwell, *Hearing Between the Lines: The Audience as Fellow-Workers in Luke-Acts and Its Literary Milieu* (LNTS, 425; London: T&T Clark, 2010), 27–76. See also Michael R. Whitenton, *Hearing Kyriotic Sonship: A Cognitive and Rhetorical Approach to the Characterization of Mark's Jesus* (BIS, 148; Leiden: Brill, 2017), who investigates the contribution of rhetorical techniques to what he calls 'inference generation' in the characterization of the Markan Jesus.
[59] Maxwell, *Hearing Between the Lines*, 74–6; Whitenton, *Hearing Kyriotic Sonship*, 77–82.

example, and as I have argued elsewhere,[60] the depiction of Jesus as 'shepherd' in John 10 metonymically evokes an intricate configuration of Jewish traditional–scriptural resources; by coupling the discourse's core metaphorical images with wide-ranging scriptural evocations, both are markedly reconfigured and progressively transformed as Jesus's speech develops. The indeterminate and composite[61] character of scriptural referencing in John 10 is therefore part and parcel of the discourse's rhetorical aims: as persuasive speech, it is designed to draw its audiences into a distinctively Johannine understanding of Jesus as 'shepherd'. Similarly, when Jesus calls upon his Jewish interlocutors to follow the example of their ancestor by doing 'the works of Abraham' (τὰ ἔργα τοῦ Ἀβραάμ, Jn 8.39), this metonymically evocative phrase acts as a verbal signal for a wide range of deeds and attributes belonging to the traditional register (scriptural and text interpretive) about Abraham in Second Temple Judaism: his opposition to idolatry, his status as a model of righteousness and faithfulness, and his hospitality and receptiveness to God's word. However, as the discourse develops, it becomes evident that, from a Johannine perspective, the initially open-ended appeal to 'the works of Abraham' is ultimately narrowed to denote the one paramount 'work' that should be reproduced by the children of Abraham, and that is their acceptance of Jesus's true identity and mission (Jn 8.56).[62]

Once again, therefore, for audience members familiar with, even steeped in, the Jewish Scriptures, their distinctive themes and motifs would have been actively recalled through the process of deciphering allusive and metonymically evocative references. But if the audience's profile was marked by cultural diversity, as seems to have been the case in John's gospel and also for several other NT texts (as I have already noted above), the decipherment of an allusion for some hearers may have happened differently or not at all, at least as part of their initial reception of the text. For determining how the Jewish Scriptures could be understood to inform the message of a text, much would depend on its actual shaping and also on how communal engagement with that text could facilitate its aural reception.

3 The workings of memory

Several remarks have already been made in this study about the role of memory within the first-century media environment. Memorization was certainly highly revered in antiquity,[63] though memory, for the purpose of composition and delivery, was a variable and dynamic phenomenon and certainly not tantamount to word-for-word repetition from earlier texts (whether those texts were directly accessible or not). This

---

[60] Catrin H. Williams, 'Persuasion through Allusion: Evocations of Shepherd(s) and their Rhetorical Impact in John 10', in *Come and Read: Interpretive Approaches to the Gospel of John* (ed. Alicia Myers and Lindsey Trozzo; Lanham: Lexington Books/Fortress Academic, forthcoming).

[61] On composite scriptural references, see further section 3.

[62] See further Catrin H. Williams, 'First-Century Media Culture and Abraham as a Figure of Memory in John 8:31-59', in *The Fourth Gospel and First-Century Media Culture*, 212–21.

[63] For the role of memorization within Greek and Roman education, see, for example, Leonard Greenspoon, 'By the Letter? Word for Word? Scriptural Citation in Paul', in *Paul and Scripture: Extending the Conversation* (ed. Christopher D. Stanley; Atlanta: SBL, 2012), 10–13.

is an important consideration for OT/NT studies given that deviations from possible sources (such as the MT or LXX) in scriptural quotations have often been regarded as examples of 'memory lapses' on the part of NT authors as they cited 'fixed' texts. The processes of memory/memorization as understood in ancient media studies shed a very different light on the likely citation practices of NT authors and, more generally, give additional support to the now widely acknowledged phenomenon of textual pluriformity, as attested especially among the Dead Sea Scrolls,[64] during the last Second Temple period.

The impact of memory on the transmission of scriptural texts and their manuscript traditions has been extensively explored by David Carr, leading him to formulate a helpful model of how scribes modified texts when using or citing them from memory.[65] Whereas the *visual* copying of written texts could lead the eye to confuse letters and to overlook certain lines/phrases, and aural variants could arise when orally delivered words were misheard, 'memory variants' amount to what Carr defines as non-significant modifications to texts, such as the exchange of synonymous words, changes in word order and the rearrangement of lines.[66] Categorizing variants in this manner can undoubtedly assist OT/NT scholars in the task of analysing scriptural quotations in NT texts, particularly when seeking to distinguish between media-critical variants and exegetical variants. Both kinds of modifications – 'textual' and redactional – can of course occur within the same scriptural quotation and the differences between them should not be blurred. In a recent article, for example, it has been proposed that the use of the verbal form συντριβήσεται in Jn 19.36 ('Not one of his bones shall be broken') should be classified as a (non-significant) memory variant of Exod. 12.10 LXX (ὀστοῦν οὐ συντρίψετε ἀπ' αὐτοῦ),[67] but without giving appropriate consideration to the possibility that the inclusion of συντριβήσεται, which is identical to the wording in Ps. 33.21 LXX, produces a composite citation in which the divine passive of the psalm text highlights God's protection of the righteous, a key motif in John's presentation of Jesus's death.[68]

It should not be ruled out, moreover, that exegetically motivated conflations and combinations of scriptural elements within individual quotations in the NT (as is probably the case in Jn 19.36) were themselves shaped by a media environment in which memory and oral–textual interaction played a decisive role. The evocation – in combined or conflated quotations – of multiple scriptural texts on the basis of their thematic and/or lexical correspondence was not necessarily the result of

---

[64] On memory as an important factor in the emergence of variant readings in the Scrolls, see George J. Brooke, 'Memory, Cultural Memory, and Rewriting Scripture', in *Reading the Dead Sea Scrolls*, 51–65, especially 55.

[65] David M. Carr, *Writing on the Tablet of the Heart: Origins of Scripture and Literature* (Oxford; New York: Oxford University Press, 2005), 5–6; idem., *The Formation of the Hebrew Bible: A New Reconstruction* (Oxford; New York: Oxford University Press, 2011), 14–36.

[66] For these three categories, see David Carr's more recent article: 'Orality, Textuality, *and* Memory: The State of Biblical Studies', in *Contextualizing Israel's Sacred Writings*, 165–7.

[67] Andrew Montanaro, 'The Use of Memory in the Old Testament Quotations in John's Gospel', *NovT* 59 (2017): 152–3.

[68] Cf. Maarten J. J. Menken, *Old Testament Quotations in the Fourth Gospel: Studies in Textual Form* (CBET, 15; Kampen: Kok Pharos, 1996), 151–2. Intriguingly, Montanaro regards most of the variations from known textual sources in John's scriptural quotations as 'memory variants', but makes no reference to Menken's highly influential study on this subject.

authors' direct and visual engagement with texts in written form (given the practical difficulties of searching for 'distant' passages in literary scrolls) but the product of mnemonic processes. Various mechanisms were available to writers and orators to enable them to memorize and retrieve collections of thematically related passages drawn from disparate textual sources. Such mechanisms included the selection of various extracts to form an anthology of excerpted texts,[69] a practice for which there is strong evidence in the Dead Sea Scrolls.[70] That the gathering together of distinct passages could be driven by *mnemonic operations* is supported by a wide range of Graeco-Roman references to the cataloguing of textual excerpts in the form of complex memory maps to support oral–rhetorical compositions and performances (cf. Aristotle, *On Memory* 451^{b}18-452^{b}6; Cicero, *De Or.* 2.355).[71] Spatial images were systematically constructed so that material containing analogous themes or motifs, but from different texts/passages, was mnemonically deposited and internally visualized. Memorial images could be configured and reconfigured to create new sets of lexical/thematic associations – an interpretative dynamic that is yet to be explored in OT/NT studies when it comes to analysing how composite scriptural quotations and allusions are likely to have been formulated.[72]

What is, nevertheless, now beginning to be subjected to detailed critical scrutiny in OT/NT studies is the rich insights that social and cultural memory theories can bring to the table for investigating the use and reception of the Jewish Scriptures in the NT writings.[73] Building on the work of Maurice Halbwachs,[74] social memory studies consider in particular the ways in which communities and individuals interpret the past in the light of their present social realities. Halbwachs himself defined 'collective memory' as a variable and selective phenomenon relating closely to the identity of a group; that is to say, it does not entail the passive retrieval of stored or memorized data, but rather the construction of a shared past which is continuous with the present and, at the same time, serves to unite the group. Contemporary social memory theorists readily acknowledge the significance of Halbwachs's focus on the ways in which a group's representation of the past is shaped by present concerns and experiences (often labelled as the 'presentist' approach). However, many theorists also emphasize that memory should not be categorized as 'an entirely malleable construction in the present' or, alternatively, as 'the authentic residue of the past'. Rather, it entails a 'fluid

---

[69] See, for example, David Konstan, 'Excerpting as a Reading Practice', in *Thinking Through Excerpts: Studies on Stobaeus* (ed. Gretchen Reydams-Schils; Turnhout: Brepols, 2011), 9–22.

[70] On the Qumran evidence, see, for example, Lutz Doering, 'Excerpted Texts in Second Temple Judaism: A Survey of the Evidence', in *Selecta colligere, II: Beiträge zur Technik des Sammelns und Kompilierens griechischer Texte von der Antike bis zur Humanismus* (ed. Rosa M. Piccione and Matthias Perkams; Hellenica, 18; Allesandria: Edizioni dell'Orso, 2005), 1–38, especially 20–36.

[71] For a discussion of these and other relevant Greek and Roman sources, see Tom Thatcher, 'John's Memory Theatre: A Study of Composition in Performance', in *The Fourth Gospel and First-Century Media Culture*, 76–84. Cf. also Greenspoon, 'By the Letter?', 18–19, 22–3.

[72] Although see Christopher Rowland, 'Imagining the Apocalypse', *NTS* 51 (2005): 323–5, for insightful comments on how ancient and medieval perceptions of memory contributed to the process of linking together scriptural images from related texts.

[73] A number of the relevant studies are noted below.

[74] *Les Cadres sociaux de la mémoire* (Paris: Alcan, 1925); idem., *La Topographie légendaire des évangiles en terre sainte: Étude de mémoire collective* (Paris: Presses Universitaires de France, 1941); idem., *La Mémoire collective* (Paris: Éditions Albin Michel, 1950/80).

negotiation between the desires of the present and the legacies of the past'.[75] Memory can provide a conceptual framework that both mirrors the present and stands in continuity with the past. It is, in other words, a case of complex interplay and perpetual dialogue, 'at times attributing greater force to the remembered past and at times to the remembering present'.[76]

The use of social memory as an analytical category is still at a relatively early stage as far as OT/NT studies are concerned, but there is much interpretative potential in the notion that, for NT authors, the authoritative Scriptures of Judaism functioned as 'sites of remembrance',[77] as figures of memory. Indeed, as Tom Thatcher has unequivocally noted, scriptural references in NT texts are not to be categorized only as quotations, allusions or echoes but as 'instances of early Christian collective memory'.[78] This points to the complementarity rather than incongruity of media-critical and intertextual approaches to OT/NT studies, although it also serves as a reminder that it is not always the (written) scriptural texts but the 'memories ... on which they are based that are "cited" for the audience's consideration'.[79] Thus, mnemonic scriptural evocations are not inevitably tied to identifiable verses or discrete passages; collective memories linked to Scriptures can be drawn from wider commemorative frameworks and are often filtered through known (textual and extra-textual), related Jewish traditions.

More specifically, social memory theorists are interested in how cultural artefacts (such as authoritative texts) use memories of the past to reflect the structures and values of the groups that produced them. In relation, therefore, to how the 'remembering present' shapes the memory of Israel's (scriptural) past, but also how existing memories of a shared past constrain new representations of it, various strategies and processes can be identified in NT texts that demonstrate this interconnectedness between group memory and identity formation/maintenance.

The mnemonic strategy of schematization, in particular, involves the structuring of memories to create a 'master commemorative narrative' that establishes and guides a group's self-understanding.[80] Since 'one of the most remarkable features of human memory is [its] ability to mentally transform essentially unstructured series of events into seemingly coherent *historical narratives*',[81] schematization emerges when

---

[75] Jeffrey K. Olick, 'Products, Processes, and Practices: A Non-Reificatory Approach to Collective Memory', *BTB* 36 (2006): 13. Cf. Barbara A. Misztal, *Theories of Social Remembering* (Philadelphia: Open University Press, 2003), 67–73.

[76] Werner H. Kelber, 'The Works of Memory: Christian Origins as Mnemohistory – A Response', in *Memory, Tradition, and Text*, 234.

[77] Stephen C. Barton, 'Memory and Remembrance in Paul', in *Memory in the Bible and Antiquity* (ed. Loren T. Stuckenbruck et al.; WUNT, 212; Tübingen: Mohr Siebeck, 2007), 326.

[78] Tom Thatcher, 'Cain and Abel in Early Christian Memory: A Case Study in "The Use of the Old Testament in the New"', *CBQ* 72 (2010): 737. He offers a helpful outline of how social memory theories bring a new interpretative lens to understanding how the New Testament authors used the scriptures for their own rhetorical purposes (749–51).

[79] Thatcher, 'Cain and Abel in Early Christian Memory', 750. See also Esler, 'Collective Memory and Hebrews 11', 158–61, 167–8.

[80] See Yael Zerubavel, *Recovered Roots: Collective Memory and the Making of Israeli National Tradition* (Chicago: University of Chicago Press, 1995), 6. See further Anthony Le Donne, *The Historiographical Jesus: Memory, Typology, and the Son of David* (Waco: Baylor University Press, 2009), 52–9; Gerber, *The Scriptural Tale in the Fourth Gospel*, 44–6.

[81] Eviatar Zerubavel, *Time Maps: Collective Memory and the Social Shape of the Past* (Chicago: University of Chicago Press, 2003), 13.

harmonized elements are tied together within a newly constructed framework. The nature of the commemorative narrative emerging from the Jewish Scriptures can vary from one NT text to another, but its construction often entails the reconfiguration of earlier memories so that it can promote and legitimize a collective sense of identity. This applies to the selective reconstruction of remembered 'figures of faith' in Hebrews 11,[82] or to the Johannine reconfiguration of significant patriarchs and prophets – drawing on both scriptural and text-interpretive memories – so that they function as paradigmatic witnesses to Jesus as the definitive revelation of God.[83] Differences between such mnemonic entities are minimized in the process to draw out analogous features to the exclusion of all others. Multiple figures (and events) can be mnemonically clustered together on the basis of their shared/constructed features, although it is often one landmark figure, such as Abraham, who is elevated above all others and placed on a commemorative pedestal as an exemplary model of faith.[84] The prototypical value of scriptural figures can also fulfil a host of different rhetorical-mnemonic purposes, as in diverse early Christian appeals to Cain and Abel in the face of persecution and opposition (Mt. 23.35//Lk. 11.51; Heb. 11.4; 12.24) and to affirm a community's doctrinal convictions at the same time as vilifying the beliefs of others (Jude 11; 1 Jn 3.12).[85] In all such cases, current experiences and normative expectations shape how individual or collective figures from Israel's more distant past are to be remembered.

Nevertheless, for the purpose of analysing mnemonically driven scriptural evocations in NT texts, much of the relevant scholarly work to date has been underpinned by a social memory approach known as commemorative 'keying': this strategy, primarily associated with the work of the sociologist Barry Schwartz, involves the pairing, even conflating, of current figures and events with archetypal images or symbolically meaningful patterns from the past.[86] Keying allows the past to act as a 'frame' for the present, offering coherent models for interpreting and influencing current experiences. Also, if present situations inevitably affect what is seen, and looked for, in the past, the memory of an already salient past functions as an *orienting symbol* for the present, moulding and framing collective values and goals. Commenting on the mirror- as well as lamp-like quality of memory, Schwartz thus notes that 'the past is matched to the present as a model *of* society and a model *for* society'.[87] The remembered past is a model of society because it must be framed in terms that resonate with current circumstances;

---

[82] See Esler, 'Collective Memory and Hebrews 11', 159, 162–3.
[83] Catrin H. Williams, 'Patriarchs and Prophets Remembered: Framing Israel's Past in the Gospel of John', in *Abiding Words: The Use of Scripture in the Gospel of John* (ed. Alicia D. Myers and Bruce G. Schuchard; SBL Resources for Biblical Study; Atlanta: SBL Publications, 2015), 187–212.
[84] Cf. Philip F. Esler, 'Paul's Contestation of Israel's (Ethnic) Memory of Abraham in Galatians 3', *BTB* 36 (2006): 23–34; Jeremy Punt, 'Identity, Memory, and Scriptural Warrant: Arguing Paul's Case', in *Paul and Scripture*, 41–9; Robert L. Brawley, 'Nodes of Objective Socialization and Subjective Reflection in Identity: Galatian Identity in an Imperial Context', in *T&T Clark Handbook to Social Identity in the New Testament*, 138–42.
[85] See especially Thatcher, 'Cain and Abel in Early Christian Memory', 740–9.
[86] Barry Schwartz, *Abraham Lincoln and the Forge of National Memory* (Chicago: University of Chicago Press, 2000), 18–20.
[87] Ibid., 18.

the past is a model for society in that it provides a programmatic template for beliefs and values in the present.

As a number of NT scholars now recognize, the strategy of 'keying' and 'framing' presents an exceptionally valuable theoretical lens for interpreting how the Jewish Scriptures and related extra-textual traditions may 'work' within individual NT texts. In particular, it encourages scholars within the field of OT/NT studies to explore new ways of analysing how NT authors articulate the significance of the past for the present. Keying does not essentially work with a hermeneutical model of foreshadowing or fulfilment; rather, it interprets present realities in analogical terms by *enacting* elements tied to landmark figures and events. The association between two events or eras can be established in such a way that the temporal difference between them is often collapsed to strengthen the connection between them.[88] In the case of the Johannine prologue, for example, the Sinai theophany is evoked in the references to the 'glory' (cf. Exod. 33.18, 22) and 'grace and truth' (Exod. 34.6) manifested in the incarnate Word (1.14-16), but there is no explicit mention of the actual revelation of God's glory in Israel's past, no indication that the Sinai revelation foreshadows or is a type of that which has come through the λόγος made flesh and no hint that Jesus fulfils what was originally promised to Moses. The Sinai event becomes the archetypal–theophanic model for articulating the significance of the revelation of the incarnate Word, but, through mnemonic keying, the two 'events' are assimilated in such a way that the focus is on the fullness of the grace and truth now embodied in Jesus, not on whether these divine qualities were already manifested in the distant past. Similarly, the 'murmuring' of 'the Jews' following the miraculous feeding of the crowds (Jn 6.41, 43) provides yet another example of keying through a process of enactment, since it recalls the behaviour of their Jewish ancestors in the wilderness (Exod. 16.2).[89]

Mnemonic keying also encourages NT interpreters to examine how images drawn from the remembered past have the capacity, particularly in situations of crisis, to explain and 'make sense of things through what we already know'.[90] The impact of the traumatic nature of Jesus's death, when viewed from a social memory perspective, provides a cogent explanation as to why so many scriptural evocations are concentrated in early Christian reflections on the rejection and crucifixion of Jesus, particularly in the passion narratives of the four canonical Gospels.[91] Faced with a 'memory crisis' threatening to dismantle their cohesion as a group, the response of Jesus's followers was to key the events surrounding his violent death to motifs drawn from inherited scriptural traditions, particularly those associated with the suffering of the righteous. Once again, as with other mnemonic strategies, the NT texts provide

---

[88] Thatcher, 'Cain and Abel in Early Christian Memory', 750–1.
[89] Williams, 'Patriarchs and Prophets Remembered', 194–5.
[90] Jeffrey E. Brickle, 'The Memory of the Beloved Disciple: A Poetics of Johannine Memory', in *Memory and Identity in Ancient Judaism and Early Christianity: A Conversation with Barry Schwartz* (ed. Tom Thatcher; Semeia Studies, 78; Atlanta: SBL, 2014), 192.
[91] Chris Keith and Tom Thatcher, 'The Scar of the Cross: The Violence Ratio and the Earliest Christian Memories of Jesus', in *Jesus, the Voice, and the Text*, 197–214; Rafael Rodríguez, '"According to the Scriptures": Suffering and the Psalms in the Speeches of Acts', in *Memory and Identity in Ancient Judaism and Early Christianity*, 241–62. Cf. also Alan Kirk, 'The Memory of Violence and the Death of Jesus in Q', in *Memory, Tradition, and Text*, 191–206, especially 194.

ample evidence of the ways in which commemorative frameworks, keyed to the Jewish Scriptures, enabled members of the early Christian communities to tie their beliefs and experiences to a coherently constructed and meaningful past.

Conclusions

It has been argued in this chapter that recent developments in ancient media studies have much to contribute to the study of the 'what', 'why' and 'how' of the use and reception of the Jewish Scriptures in the NT. The four overarching, and tightly interlinked, topics of orality, textuality, performance and memory bring important new interpretative dimensions to light, not least the extent to which media-critical perspectives present a fuller and arguably more accurate picture of the first-century cultural and social contexts in which early Christians actively engaged with Israel's Scriptures and also of the complex and multifaceted ways in which they did so. Media-sensitive approaches of the kind outlined in this study are not necessarily incompatible with predominantly text-orientated methods, nor do they strive to replace literary-based models, but they do open up the field of OT/NT studies to a whole host of different questions and to promising new methods of enquiry.

Section B

The role of OT context in OT/NT studies

The meaning and place of Old Testament context in OT/NT methodology

Arthur Keefer

Introduction

Studies and methodologies on how the New Testament (NT) uses the Old Testament (OT) often begin with identifying an OT citation or allusion and result in classifying how a NT text employs an OT reference. For example, Hab. 2.24 is first identified as a quotation within Rom. 1.17, meaning that the author of the NT text quoted a certain OT passage. It is later asked how Rom. 1.17 employs the OT passage, often in terms of interpretive uses of the OT, whether promise and fulfilment, eschatological continuity or *sensus plenior*. Between these steps of identification and classification appears an additional concern: what was the meaning of the OT reference in its original 'context'?[1] The term 'context' is used by interpreters in a variety of ways without necessary distinctions, such as a section of text, a theme or a historical event so that appealing to the OT 'context' often facilitates disagreements as to how the NT uses the OT. This semantic problem acquires particular significance within debates about whether a NT author 'respects the context' of an OT quotation, a conclusion that depends largely upon what is meant by 'context' itself, which is the more fundamental assumption lying behind OT/NT studies. In what follows, it will become clear that scholars mean many things by 'OT context'; they assume, for instance, that it refers to a section of text or a theme or to some referent in the mind of the original author, and it will be argued that this variation in meaning bears significance for debates in the NT use of the OT. Wishing only to reveal the assumptions and their interpretative significance, I do not intend to contest certain understandings of 'context' or the interpretations of particular OT texts.

The critique offered here is complemented by a more positive contribution, namely, my hope to delineate a variety of definitions of context as a way forward in methodology. While the semantic problem of what is meant by 'context' within particular case studies certainly requires clarification, I also draw attention to how 'OT

---

[1] For a representative outline of the field, see the dedicated *JSNT* issue but especially, David Allen, 'Introduction: The Study of the Use of the Old Testament in the New', *JSNT* 38 (2015): 3–16.

context' is treated as a step in various explicit methodologies, concluding with a list of meanings for the phrase intended to facilitate a more precise method of analysing the OT and its use in the NT. To demonstrate this, I begin with a comparison of explicit OT/NT methodologies and then present a series of case studies (Rom. 1.17/Hab. 2.24; Mt. 2.15/Hos. 11.1; Lk. 20.37/Exod. 3.6), which expose the many meanings of 'context' and their role within OT/NT interpretation.

1 Explicit methodologies

As one of the earliest interpreters to propose an explicit methodology for examining the NT's use of the OT, Anthony Hanson marks a turning point in the field and unfolds three steps for determining NT interpretation of Scripture.[2] First, 'establish as accurately as possible what text and what form of that text the writer had in mind'. The second includes looking at the OT citation 'in its context in Scripture', which means 'studying the actual historical circumstances in which the passage was written'. Finally, we must consider how the passage was understood in contemporary Judaism. This threefold method accounts for identifying the text and its form, the original 'context' of the OT passage, and its interpretation in Judaism. By 'context', Hanson means not only historical circumstance but also, it seems, the text's meaning and 'significance' in Scripture, three steps that appear in later, explicit methods but with additional steps and further detail.

Craig Evans and Klyne Snodgrass both present a sevenfold process for determining how the NT uses the OT, while Gregory Beale offers nine steps.[3] These scholars order their steps differently, and not all of the steps correspond precisely with the steps of other methodologies. However, the stages from each of these methods organize into four broader categories: identifying the citation or allusion and its textual version, accounting for the OT context, tracing the quotation's history of interpretation and exploring its use by the NT authors. Table 5.1 attempts to present the methodological steps of Evans, Snodgrass and Beale within these four broader categories. The number next to each step corresponds to its order in the respective author's method.

Each of the scholars in Table 5.1 accounts for the context of OT texts that appear in the NT. Evans addresses it in his third step, stated in full, 'Is the OT citation part of a wider tradition or theology in the OT? If it is, the citation may be alluding to a context much wider than the specific passage from which it has been taken.'[4] In one sense, it seems that context means a 'tradition' or theology of the OT. In another sense, 'alluding

---

[2] Anthony Hanson, *The New Testament Interpretation of Scripture* (London: SPCK, 1980), 6–7. Throughout the twentieth century, scholars such as C. H. Dodd, Barnabas Lindars and Henry Shires developed methods implicitly, manifesting a concern with OT context and yet a plurality of conceptions for what it means.

[3] Craig Evans, 'The Function of the Old Testament in the New', in *Introducing New Testament Interpretation* (ed. S. McKnight; Grand Rapids: Baker Books, 1989), 163–9; Klyne Snodgrass, 'The Use of the Old Testament in the New', in *Interpreting the New Testament: Essays on Methods and Issues* (ed. D. Black and D. Dockery; Nashville: Broadman & Holman, 2001), 209–29; Gregory Beale, *Handbook on the New Testament Use of the Old Testament: Exegesis and Interpretation* (Grand Rapids: Baker Academic, 2012).

[4] Evans, 'The Function', 171.

Table 5.1 OT/NT methodologies

	Identification/versions	OT context	History of interpretation	NT use
Evans (1989)	1. What OT text(s) is(are) being cited? 2. Which text type is followed?	3. Is the OT citation part of wider tradition/theology in the OT?	4. Jewish/Christian interpretation	5. How does the NT agree or disagree with other interpretations? 6. Compare NT citation with other citations from the same NT author. 7. Contribution of citation to the argument of the NT passage.
Snodgrass (2001)	2. Analyse the form of the cited text.	1. Determine the original intention of the OT passage.	3. How the OT text was used in Judaism 4. Hermeneutical or exegetical assumptions	5. Analyse the way the NT writer uses the OT. 6. Theological significance and relevance 7. Note used/unused OT texts in the NT
Beale (2012)	1. Identify OT reference 5. Compare text versions (Step 6 may also fit into this category)	3. Analyse OT context	4. Survey relevant uses of OT text in late Judaism	2. Analyse the broad NT context 6–9. Analyse author's use of the OT: textual use (6), interpretive (7), theological (8), rhetorical (9).

to a context much wider than the specific passage' suggests that context refers to a literary unit, whether a single passage or larger section.[5]

Having assumed that the OT text has been identified (the first step for both Evans and Beale), Snodgrass's method instead begins with the OT context. As a first step, 'determine the original intention of the Old Testament passage. Close attention must be given to the context and to the theology at work in the Old Testament text.'[6] It is not clear what context means here, except that it is possibly distinct from the author's original intention and the text's theology. While Snodgrass goes on to claim that the biblical author's original intention must guide interpretations in the case of both testaments, further supporting the place of authorial intent in the interpretive process when linking testaments, a final comment reveals the most plausible referent for Snodgrass's conception of context.[7] He considers approaches to interpreting the OT and, unsatisfied with reading every passage christologically or appealing to *sensus plenior*, prefers 'correspondence to history'. As he explains,

> The presupposition is that the way God worked in the past is mirrored in the way he works in the present and future. There is a correspondence between what happened to God's people in the past and what happens now or in the future.[8]

If Snodgrass underscores the attention given 'to the context and to the theology at work in the Old Testament text' and, when discussing the point of correspondence between the OT and NT, champions 'the way God works' and 'what happens to his people', then perhaps the OT context refers to those divine works and human occurrences that shape a given OT text. This priority suggests that rather than theology and authorial intent, 'context' refers to such historical events or phenomena.

Beale enlarges the approach to OT context, suggesting as his third step that 'one should interpret the OT on its own grounds and within its own redemptive-historical context, without allowing the NT text to influence the interpretation, since it represents a later stage of redemptive history'.[9] Beale's process consciously segregates the OT and NT when studying context and includes a number of substeps: (a) overview the broad OT context; (b) overview the immediate OT context, with special attention to the text's place in the paragraph's flow of thought; (c) relate the OT quotation to what comes earlier and later in the canonical Scripture, incorporating the text's relation to earlier and later stages of redemptive history and considering if the text is a quotation of, or an allusion to, an earlier OT text; and (d) consider if an OT theme influences the OT passage.[10] Then, '*tentatively* apply the findings from this step to the NT quotation: Are

---

[5] Evans' ('The Function', 163–5) additional comments confirm these referents and broach other possibilities. He claims that textual and contextual differences between the OT and the NT are explained through 'biblical pluralism', which occurs on four levels: canon, versions, exegesis or meaning, and theology. If any of these plausibly relate to types of OT 'context', then the use of 'versions' and 'theology' confirm the literary and theological contexts noted above, leaving 'meaning' and 'canon' as additional possible types of contexts.
[6] Snodgrass, 'The Use', 222.
[7] Ibid., 223.
[8] Ibid., 215.
[9] Beale, *Handbook*, 44.
[10] Ibid., 44–6.

there similarities in theme, argument, problems between the OT and NT quotation or allusion, and so on?'[11]

Beale's method for determining the OT context includes thorough attention to the grammatical and literary role of the text in its local and broad 'contexts', such as paragraph, chapter and book, and his first two substeps account primarily for such literary and historical contexts. He then considers the OT text in relation to the canon as a whole and the sweep of redemptive history. Finally, the OT theme arises, with attention to similarities in concept, argument or problem between the OT and NT texts and situations. Thus, under the banner of 'context', Beale includes historical, literary, theological (or redemptive), thematic and argumentative (rhetorical?) perspectives on the OT text. Furthermore, he wants to ensure, for the time being, that the study of these OT contexts is divorced from any NT influence.

To summarize these deliberate enumerations of OT/NT interpretive methods, it seems that Hanson offers the first explicit methodology for studying the NT use of the OT. Incorporating Hanson's three broad steps, Evans, Snodgrass and Beale articulate multistep methods, each of which includes the OT context. While the place of this context varies within their procedures, appearing sooner or later in the sequence, it is the meaning . . . differs, more importantly.[12] Evans refers to the literary and theological contexts. Snodgrass suggests not theology or authorial intent but historical events, and Beale captures the most comprehensive set of OT contexts, which, I will suggest, deserves fuller and more systematic attention in studies of the NT use of the OT.[13] In order to further demonstrate the semantic problem of 'context', as well as its consequences, and contribute to OT/NT methodology, we need to examine several worked-out cases of the NT using the OT.

2 Case studies

The significance of OT context not only appears in theoretical discussions of OT/NT methodology but also arises within studies of particular biblical passages. These

---

[11] Ibid., 46.
[12] The treatment of OT context could change depending on conclusions about the identification of the NT author's source. If scholars disagree about the source (e.g. MT vs. LXX), then this creates different 'OT contexts' altogether. For instance, if assessing the LXX instead of the MT, one would need to account for a possibly expanded or alternative literary context, also implicating different historical situations, authors/audiences and so on.
[13] Two other scholars deserve mention with respect to OT/NT methodology. Richard Hays (*Echoes of Scripture in the Letters of Paul* [New Haven: Yale University Press, 1989], 30) does articulate a method but without thoroughly addressing OT context, and in his fourth step for determining allusions – thematic coherence – draws upon the images and ideas of the OT text. Within his understanding of typology, Hays (156–7, 161) suggests that context refers to historical context, events in a narrative sequence, God's acts, and overarching themes, seeming to leave the meaning of OT context allusive and unspecified, or at least multifarious. Thomas Brodie ('Conclusion: Problems of Method – Suggested Guidelines', in *The Intertextuality of the Epistles: Explorations of Theory and Practice* [ed. R. Brodie, D. MacDonald and S. Porter; Sheffield: Sheffield Phoenix Press, 2006], 285, 293–4) offers guidelines for OT/NT study and presents eight categories for tracing similarities between the OT and NT texts: genre, theme, style, plot, motifs, structure, order and wording. In my judgement, these vie as 'contexts' but are not identified as such.

studies often prompt a debate over whether and how the NT 'respects' or 'misuses' the OT context, a turn of phrase that itself requires clarification.[14] But as mentioned above, the methodological problem of 'respect for context' depends just as much on what scholars mean by 'context'. The use of Hab. 2.4 in Rom. 1.17 provides a good starting point for my concerns and will lead to two additional cases (Mt. 2.15/Hos. 11.1; Lk. 20.37/Exod. 3.6) that provide compelling evidence of alternative treatments in the use of 'context'. These three case studies will expose the variety of conceptions for what OT 'context' refers to, and they will reveal the consequences of this variety for navigating debates about how the NT uses the OT, leading finally to a discussion of implications in which a list of possible meanings for 'context' is supplied and reintegrated into formal discussions of methodology.

2.1 Romans 1.17 and Habakkuk 2.4

The first example of varied conceptions of OT 'context' arises from interpretations of Hab. 2.4 and Rom. 1.17, wherein four scholars reveal at least four different meanings for 'context'. 'For in it the righteousness of God is revealed through faith for faith; as it is written, "The one who is righteous will live by faith"' (Rom. 1.17; NRSV). Rikk Watts has suggested that the explicit quotation of Hab. 2.4 triggers a number of parallels between Romans and Habakkuk, such as Paul's distress and Habakkuk's lament, the groups targeted by both authors, echoes of language, and calls for praise and perseverance.[15] Referring to each of these as a part of the OT 'context', in one sense, Watts aligns the 'context' of Hab. 2.4 with the entire book of Habakkuk. In another sense, he draws parallels between Habakkuk and Romans that reflect linguistic, authorial and rhetorical contexts.

For this same example, Hays has noted different historical 'problems' or situations in the OT and NT texts but does not allow this distinction to mute the commonalities.[16] Habakkuk, he claims, serves as a locus classicus for the theme of theodicy, upon which Paul draws. So while the historical context of Hab. 2.4 and Rom. 1.17 might not align, Hays finds resonance between the thematic contexts of these passages. Similarly, Watson holds that Paul does not wish his readers to see their situation in light of Habakkuk's situation but that he rather creates a tension between Hab. 2.4, Gen. 15.6 and Lev. 18.5 explicit, where Habakkuk represents the positive side of 'the total scriptural testimony to Paul's gospel'.[17] If Paul was therefore not attending to the 'literal sense' of the OT texts, what might 'context' mean in Watson's case? Moyise asks of such an interpretation, 'does this constitute respect for the context of Hab 2:4? It does

---

[14] My examination of context as such advances the work of Moyise ('Does Paul Respect the Context of His Quotations', in *Paul and Scripture: Extending the Conversation* [ed. C. Stanley; ECL 9; Atlanta: SBL, 2012], 97–114) by expanding the selection of NT passages to include non-Pauline texts and by examining the concept of 'context' as such instead of 'respect for context'.

[15] Rikk Watts, '"For I am Not Ashamed of the Gospel": Romans 1:16-17 and Habakkuk 2:4', in *Romans and the People of God* (ed. S. Soderlund and N. Wright; Grand Rapids: Eerdmans, 1999), 3–25.

[16] Hays, *Echoes*, 40–1.

[17] Francis Watson, *Paul and the Hermeneutics of Faith* (London; New York: T&T Clark International, 2004), 48.

if we take "context" to be the role or function of the words in Scripture as a whole.'[18] In short, context refers to the whole of the OT within which Hab. 2.4 is understood.

Lastly, Michael Shepherd finds consistency between Romans and Hab. 2.4 by placing the OT reference within the context of the Twelve, where he concludes that 'Habakkuk is about justification by faith in the eschatological and messianic work of God'.[19] In Moyise's assessment, 'the issue of whether Paul respects the context of his quotations is not a question for Shepherd. He operates with the assumption that the two meanings are identical ... and so has nothing to contribute to our discussion.'[20] While Shepherd may not be concerned with Paul's respect for context, his study certainly contributes to my question about the meaning of context, offering a fourth understanding of the concept: the literary and theological contexts of a wider corpus of literature (in this case, the Twelve) of which a text is part.

Moyise is concerned with the 'respect' question for these studies: 'Does Paul respect the context of Hab. 2:4?'[21] He concludes that 'Watts, Hays, Watson, and Shepherd all think so, but for very different reasons', and while these reasons do include different interpretations of what 'respect for context' means, as Moyise points out, they more fundamentally stem from different meanings of OT 'context'. For Watts, context refers to the whole of Habakkuk and that from a variety of angles, possibly linguistic, rhetorical or otherwise. Hays understands the OT context as thematic (i.e. theodicy). Watson's context refers to the entire OT canon, while Shepherd has the twelve Minor Prophets in view. Some of these conceptions differ in scope, such as Watt's book-wide context versus Watson's canon-wide, both of which deal with a literary-textual context of some sort. Some conceptions also differ in quality. Hence Hays's context, viewed within the literary book of Habakkuk, refers to the prophet's view of a theological concept, which is not a different scope of context but rather a fundamentally different kind of context altogether.

2.2 Matthew 2.15 and Hosea 11.1

Matthew 2.15 is a passage notorious for using an OT text 'out of context', so much so that S. L. Edgar included it among 'the most outstanding instances of contextual inaccuracy'.[22] Matthew 2.15, quoting Hos. 11.1, states, 'This was to fulfill what had been spoken by the Lord through the prophet, "Out of Egypt I have called my son"' (NRSV). According to Edgar, the original meaning is clear for Hosea: 'the "son" is Israel whom God delivered from Egypt.'[23] For Matthew, it is 'a prediction of the return of the infant Jesus from Egypt after the death of Herod'. And in Edgar's judgement, 'there is no real justification for such interpretation'. In the first place, what does 'context' mean in view of the comment about Matthew's contextual inaccuracy? Edgar's remarks indicate that the 'contextual inaccuracy' occurs on a linguistic level, given that in Hosea, the 'son'

---

[18] Moyise, 'Does Paul Respect', 111.
[19] Michael Shepherd, *The Twelve Prophets in the New Testament* (Studies in Biblical Literature 140; New York; Oxford: Peter Lang, 2011), 51.
[20] Moyise, 'Does Paul Respect', 112.
[21] Ibid., 112.
[22] S. L. Edgar, 'Respect for Context in Quotations from the Old Testament', *NTS* 9 (1962): 57.
[23] Ibid.

refers to Israel and in Matthew the 'son' refers to Jesus. In the second place, the mention of God delivering Israel (Hosea) as opposed to the return of infant Jesus after Herod's death (Matthew) suggests that Edgar contrasts different historical situations and thus finds 'inaccuracy' on the level of historical context.

Craig Evans has also said much about Matthew's view of context, noting the change in linguistic context while also clarifying additional differences. He writes, 'Hosea, as the context makes quite clear, is looking back to the exodus, not to a future deliverance. Indeed, the Hosean context is judgmental, not salvific.'[24] The first use of 'context' within which Hosea's comment is understood refers to a literary context, and the second use clearly refers to a redemptive–historical or theological context (i.e. how God acts in history or the nature of his character and relationship to his people), namely the judgement that Hosea addresses. Confirming these understandings of 'context', Evans goes on to say that 'Matthew has not exegeted Hosea 11:1 in a strict linguistic, contextual and historical sense. His is an exegesis of "resignificantion", that is, finding a new element or dimension in the older tradition.'[25] Although Matthew does not adhere to the literary and redemptive–historical contexts of Hosea, according to Evans, Matthew does show some amount of consistency with the OT as a whole by appealing to LXX Num. 24.8a, regarding David as a figure representative of all Israel who then assumes messianic status. This connection allows Matthew to move from Hosea's reference to 'Israel' to God's son as Jesus, showing that the NT author drew upon the wider, canonical OT 'context' in terms of individual passages and themes. For Edgar and Evans, Mt. 2.15 disregards at least the linguistic and redemptive–historical contexts of Hosea. Yet for Evans, Matthew shows consistency with the OT on an inner-biblical level by appealing to other OT passages and on a thematic level by connecting Israel to David to the Messiah.

Where Edgar accuses Mt. 2.15 of 'contextual inaccuracy' and Evans echoes such concerns but also notes an interpretive move of 'resignification' or 're-interpretation', Walter Kaiser has concluded the opposite: 'There is no distortion or abuse of the context of Hosea by Matthew; nor has he added his own interpretation to the text.'[26] Kaiser unfolds the flow of thought in Hosea, a threefold accusation of judgement from the prophet upon Israel with intervening messages of future hope (Hos. 6.1-3; 11.1-11; 14.1-9). According to him, Hosea 11 interrupts the indictment of Israel's lack of covenantal love with claims of God's love for his people, so that in contrast to Evans's 'context' of judgement, the 'context' of salvation is understood.

With an eye towards salvation rather than judgement, Kaiser then aligns the 'contexts' of Hosea and Matthew. He argues that the emphasis in Matthew falls right where it did 'in the context of Hosea: the preserving love of God for his seed, Israel. ... Both Israel and the infant Jesus were the objects of God's love and deliverance in the face of an oppressor.'[27] Furthermore, such salvation occurred early in the life of both Israel and Jesus: Hosea emphasizes God's love as he preserves 'his son, Israel – especially during an early stage in her life. Similarly, Matthew stressed the evidence of

---

[24] Evans, 'The Function', 174.
[25] Ibid., 176.
[26] Walter Kaiser, *The Uses of the Old Testament in the New* (Chicago: Moody Press, 1985), 53.
[27] Ibid., 51-2.

God's love in the preservation of his son once again during the early years of Messiah's life on earth.'[28] Two types of context appear in these remarks: the context of God's salvific action and the context of historical timing (i.e. early in life). Kaiser also points to a third context: 'the NT writer quoted a single verse not as a prooftext, but as a pointer to his source's larger context', suggesting a literary context, the whole book of Hosea.[29] Therefore, in his interpretation of Mt. 2.15's use of Hos. 11.1, Kaiser appeals to the redemptive context (salvation), the historical context (timing of salvation) and the literary context (the book of Hosea).

Edgar, Evans and Kaiser demonstrate the significance of different understandings of OT 'context' for interpretive debates surrounding a NT passage.[30] By limiting the context to the referents of a term – the 'son' as Israel versus the 'son' as infant Jesus – Edgar finds 'contextual inaccuracy' in Mt. 2.15. Evans validates the change in referents by appealing to an understanding of an Israel-David-Messiah representation, which might be called a thematic context. More clearly, however, Evans pulls from the inner-biblical context, using evidence from Numbers to support Matthew's 'contextual' use of the OT. In the end, he counters such a consistent use with discord between the redemptive contexts of Matthew and Hosea, as one features salvation and the other features judgement. Against these interpretations, and yet from the very same redemptive 'context', Kaiser argues positively for Matthew's 'contextual' use of Hosea, finding concord in their treatments of salvation and between their historical and literary contexts.

A swathe of contexts appear in the case of Hos. 11.1 and Mt. 2.15, and on the one hand, the debate over these passages stems from such varied understandings of OT context, such as literary versus redemptive versus historical. On the other hand, in the event that interpreters do appeal to the same 'context', it does not necessitate agreement. Both Evans and Kaiser point to the whole book of Hosea as a context, yet where Evans identifies Hosea's emphasis on judgement, Kaiser identifies a message of salvation. One justifies contextual inconsistency; the other warrants contextual consistency. Thus different interpretations of an agreed-upon OT 'context' may produce alternative arguments about how the NT author uses the OT.[31]

---

[28] Ibid., 52.
[29] Ibid.
[30] Many of these contexts are interdependent. For instance, discerning one context (an OT theme) may arise through studying another context (the book of Hosea). This does not, however, neutralize the significance of their differences and the importance of distinguishing them.
[31] This example challenges Moyise's hypothesis ('Does Paul Respect', 99), where those who advocate that the NT author 'respects' the OT context do so by pointing to a 'wider context', even widening the scope across the entire OT. Those who deny such 'respect' often appeal to (im)possibilities of meaning in the mind of the original author. One group maintains primarily a literary context, while the other points to a historically cognitive context. While often, in the case of Paul, scholars may broaden the OT context to support NT 'respect' for the OT, in the case of Matthew, such widening may support the NT author's respect or disrespect for the OT reference (e.g. Evans and Kaiser broadening the OT context to, say, the entire book of Hosea). I only speculate about why this occurs: perhaps the biblical/historical evidence itself suggests a case for one view or the other and, in this case, would require further discussion. However, prior assumptions about the coherence of OT and NT contexts may motivate interpretations of the evidence, an explanation at which Moyise seems to hint.

2.3 Luke 20.37 and Exodus 3.6

Our final example is the use of Exod. 3.6 in Lk. 20.37, which Peter Enns argues 'is not an example of grammatical-historical exegesis'.[32] Luke 20.37 reads, 'the fact that the dead are raised Moses himself showed, in the story about the bush, where he speaks of the Lord as the God of Abraham, the God of Isaac, and the God of Jacob' (NRSV). Enns justifies his denial of grammatical-historical exegesis by considering the 'context' of Exod. 3.6. According to him, 'when we look at the context of Exodus 3:6, it is hard to see how the Old Testament passage could have been intended to be used as a proof-text for the resurrection'.[33] It seems 'the context of Exodus 3:6' refers, in one sense, to the literary context or the wider narrative of the book of Exodus in which we interpret Exod. 3.6, which leaves no space for finding resurrection as a point of reference. In another sense, Enns implies that context refers to the meaning of Exod. 3.6 for the original audience, since 'no one reading Exodus and coming across 3:6 would think that resurrection was suddenly the topic of conversation'.[34] According to Enns, on these levels of literary context and original meaning, Lk. 20.37 does not cohere with Exod. 3.6.

In counterpoint, David Pao and Eckhard Schnabel argue that Luke does employ Exod. 3.6 in agreement with its original context.[35] In the first place, 'Jesus' interpretation agrees in a fundamental sense with the original meaning of Exod. 3:6: since God's promise to the patriarchs is not a singular but a typical reality'.[36] In other words, the action of God in the Pentateuch aligns with the action of God in Jesus's day, a point that draws on redemptive-historical and theological contexts. In the second place,

> although Exod. 3:6 says nothing about resurrection, Jesus' use of this text as proof for the reality of the resurrection fully and completely grasps its meaning as 'transfer' from the past and present into the future ... that if God has confirmed his covenant relationship with the dead patriarchs, he will therefore resurrect not only the patriarchs but all the dead who have the same covenant relationship with him.[37]

The key point for my concerns here is the remark that Jesus completely 'grasps its meaning', that is, the original, intended meaning of Exod. 3.6, indicating that Pao and Schnabel affirm 'context' as the original meaning of the OT text.

In contrast to Enns, it seems Pao and Schnabel would claim that Lk. 20.37 is an example of 'grammatical historical exegesis', whereby the NT use upholds the redemptive-historical, theological and original-interpretive contexts of the OT.

---

[32] Peter Enns, *Inspiration and Incarnation: Evangelicals and the Problem of the Old Testament* (Grand Rapids: Baker Academic, 2005), 132.
[33] Ibid., 114.
[34] Ibid.
[35] David Pao and Eckhard Schnabel, 'Luke', in *Commentary on the New Testament Use of the Old Testament* (ed. G. Beale and D. Carson; Grand Rapids: Baker Academic, 2007), 251–414.
[36] Ibid., 370.
[37] Ibid.

Interestingly, Enns, Pao and Schnabel actually agree on the original point of the Exodus passage. Enns writes, 'God is simply announcing himself to Moses as the God of his ancestors, the God of Abraham, Isaac, and Jacob.'[38] Pao and Schnabel call Exod. 3.6 'Yahweh's self-identification to Israel' and conclude that 'the words of this text assert the fidelity of Israel's covenant God, who committed himself to Abraham and the other patriarchs'.[39] Thus, in both arguments, Exod. 3.6 communicates God's ancestral identity, showing that these scholars agree in their interpretation of the contexts of theology and original meaning. Yet for Enns, such contexts eliminate the connection between the NT and the OT, while for Pao and Schnabel these very same contexts establish a very valid connection between the NT and the OT. The difference seems to turn on what concepts were, and were not, present in the minds of the OT audience, as for Enns, they needed to have resurrection in mind, and for Pao and Schnabel, such a concept need not have been a necessary thought for the OT audience and could be validly added later by Luke. I will explore this particular issue no further but only note again the varied meanings of 'OT context' to contend that, even when scholars agree on such meanings and primary interpretations, they may draw contrasting conclusions about the OT/NT relationship, based on subtle distinctions in textual reception and, possibly, interpretive or theological presuppositions. For it is possible that the debate about the conscious awareness of concepts for the original audience or author, in this case resurrection, may centre on questions of divine authorship of the text and how this influences coherence in the OT and NT.

3 Implications

I have drawn from three examples of the NT's use of the OT in order to tease out the many understandings of what 'context' refers to, particularly among those who disagree over whether or not the NT 'respects' the OT 'context'. In the first case – Hab. 2.4 in Rom. 1.17 – I argued that discord between interpretations of the OT in the NT arises due to different understandings of the meaning of 'context', which may refer to a dozen verses, a group of texts, the entire OT canon, a theological concept or a single theme. The other two examples – Mt. 2.15's use of Hos. 11.1 and Lk. 20.37's use of Exod. 3.6 – also show a variety of meanings attributed to 'context'. In these cases, though, the root of disagreement is not simply alternative conceptions of what OT 'context' means but rather different interpretations of the same sort of context. For example, in the case of Lk. 20.37, disagreement results from different requirements for the OT audience's conceptual stock. In addition to this, Mt. 2.15 reveals how the definition of context can be expanded from the verses surrounding the OT passage to the OT book as whole or to a redemptive-historical theme and then used to argue for either respect or disrespect of the OT. Since my aim is not to evaluate the arguments for how a particular NT passage uses the OT, the remaining task is to compile the many definitions of context and then reassess explicit methodologies for OT/NT interpretation. The preceding case studies

---

[38] Enns, *Inspiration*, 114.
[39] Pao and Schnabel, 'Luke', 370.

produce a catalogue of OT 'contexts', organized by starting with more literary aspects, moving on to thematic and then historical aspects:[40]

(a) the language of the original (linguistic/grammatical);
(b) the surrounding verses of the quotations;
(c) similar texts elsewhere in the OT;
(d) major section(s) of the OT (esp. a single book);
(e) OT theme(s);
(f) God's redemptive-historical action (salvation history/theology);
(g) the historical situation of the original authors;
(h) the meaning within the mind of the original authors.

Again, I do not have particular objections to these definitions of context and only wish to suggest that the plurality of meanings for context and the unsystematic method with which they have been addressed carry implications for OT/NT methodology. These findings will particularly aid those interested in explicit methodologies for examining the NT's use of the OT. As one of the first explicators of such methods, Hanson's initial proposal – to look at the OT citation 'in its context in Scripture', especially the historical situation – while necessary, does not offer enough detail for the host of OT 'contexts' discovered here.[41] The forward strides of Evans, Snodgrass and Beale offer more with which to work. Evans uses OT 'context' to refer to OT theology and literary units – (f) and (b) in my list – and while it is unclear what all Snodgrass includes within 'context', he at least means historical events or situations and possibly OT theology and authorial intent, which capture (f), (g) and (h) of my list. Beale's method includes historical, literary, theological or redemptive, and thematic perspectives on the OT text, that is, respectively, (g), (a)–(d), (f), (e), leaving out only (h) – the meaning within the mind of the original authors. Therefore the plurality and significance of contexts in actual studies of how the NT uses the OT, which I have investigated here, indicate that Beale's method supplies the most adequate set of steps for scholars.[42]

The question arises as to how interpreters should prioritize the proposed eightfold catalogue. I wish to neither advocate for one of these context types at the expense of another nor enumerate them in order to ensure that at least one category allows us to cohere the OT and NT.[43] However, the debates presented in this study, though limited, highlight the role of certain categories. Arguments that oppose coherence between the OT and NT appeal to (g) – the historical situation of the original authors – and sometimes (a) – the language of the original (linguistic/grammatical) – while arguments for coherence often call upon numbers (c) through (f): similar texts

---

[40] These categories supplement Moyise's list of 'respect for context' ('Does Paul Respect', 112–13) notions in three ways: OT themes, redemptive-historical action and the meaning within the mind of the original author.
[41] Hanson, *The New Testament*, 6.
[42] Beale's method not only accounts for the meanings of context listed above but actually suggests an additional category that has possibly been overlooked in studies on the NT use of the OT: rhetorical.
[43] Attention should be given to exploring the normative understandings of 'context' in antiquity. This may start by identifying the primary concerns in interpretive debates over biblical texts. For example, what is the meaning and place of 'context' within the interpretive debates between Jesus and the Pharisees according to Matthew (e.g., 5.43-8)?

elsewhere in the OT; major section(s) of the OT (esp. a single book); OT theme(s); God's redemptive-historical action (salvation history/theology). Interpreters of both stances, however, draw from numbers (d) through (f) to support their points. These categories – (d) major sections of the OT; (e) OT themes; and (f) God's redemptive-historical action – while used to support both coherence and incoherence for OT/NT, then depend upon interpretation, either supporting or countermanding coherence between the OT and NT passages. Therefore clarity about what is meant by 'context' to a great extent helps to resolve some disputes over the NT's use of the OT, and yet such delineation does not reconcile all disagreement. For each notion of context requires interpretation, even if only in the selection of evidence, and thereby gives rise to variant understandings of the OT passage. In terms of priority within the (a)–(h) list, particularly in view of the tendentious nature of those meanings for context just identified, I would suggest that numbers (d) through (g) deserve priority, as they seem to play a decisive role in determining coherence and incoherence.[44]

Conclusion

Since the early and mid-twentieth century, within studies of how the NT uses the OT, the meaning of 'OT context' has been largely assumed, often unspecified, and used in a plurality of senses. The term continues to be employed with a variety of meanings, and because its distinctions are unstated, it often facilitates disagreements as to how the NT uses the OT, especially in the debate over whether or not the NT 'respects' the OT text. I have pointed out these semantic distinctions and offered a list of definitions for OT context, not intending to restrict how 'context' should be understood but rather aiming to identify assumptions and provide a resource for further studies in methodology and OT/NT research. For as Paul Foster[45] has recently stated, 'a more controlled methodology needs to be employed' in this area. The contributions of the present study, while suggesting at least the third step in Beale's method as most adequate for this process, should facilitate a more controlled approach to analysing OT references.

---

[44] This may at the same time suggest (a), (b), (c) and even (h) as more objective criteria and thus lend them priority. See, for example, Paul Foster, 'Echoes without Resonance: Critiquing Certain Aspects of Recent Scholarly Trends in the Study of the Jewish Scriptures in the New Testament', *JSNT* 38 (2015): 96–111. His discussion, however, prioritizes these categories for questions of the identification and existence of textual links rather than relations of context.

[45] Foster, 'Echoes without Resonance', 109.

6

Selective versus contextual allusions: Reconsidering technical terms of intertextuality

Beate Kowalski

Introduction

How can allusions be defined? This is an important question in intertextuality. Is it an allusion if an author uses the same word or topic as another text source? How objective would such an assumed allusion be? How sure are we in detecting allusions in NT texts? How crucial is the original context of an allusion? Are there further parallels between the pre-text and the receiving text? How much does an author change the meaning of an allusion by using it in a new literary and historical context? Intertextual study requires answers to these questions in defining what an allusion is and in developing clear methodological rules; in the past, different scholars have approached these questions in different ways.

From time to time, it is necessary to take stock of research on this topic. The number of exegetical publications has exploded in response to the multidimensional nature of textual interpretation, and this necessitates a broad variety of methods and approaches. The interdisciplinary focus and working method of exegesis incorporates technical terms and theories from related disciplines, and historical, literary, and philological approaches are applied to sacred texts. So, biblical research on intertextuality is becoming complex and produces inconsistent results. Especially for students, this can be very confusing, so that they do not know what results to accept or which method to apply. The entire discussion about quotations and allusions in a text concerns the right balance between parallelomania – (apparent) similarities without historical and literary context – and context sensitive awareness.[1]

Before presenting a short review of research on intertextual studies which focus on Revelation of John, it is necessary first to give account of my understanding of what 'context' means. In my opinion, atomistic allusions do not exist at all; even small allusions refer to a context. Language is always more than a collection of words. Even if a characteristic single word or phrase is used from a pre-text, it evokes the entire literary and historical context – this can be the specific text segment in which the phrase

---

[1] Cf. S. Sandmel, 'Parallelomania', *JBS* 81 (1962): 1–13.

is used or the macrotext, the entire biblical writing. This function can be observed with insider language (the special way of communication within a closed social group) as well, such as in the lamentation psalm (Ps. 22.1) in the Passion Narrative of the Synoptics. Even though only the hopeless cry of abandonment is quoted (cf. Mk 15.34), the entire psalm is a witness of deep trust and hope in addition to this expression of despair. While v. 1 is quoted directly, trust and hope are evoked in order to anticipate Jesus's salvation. Or to use another example, the song of Moses (τὴν ᾠδὴν Μωϋσέως), which is mentioned but not quoted in Rev. 15.3, alludes to the theological message of liberation in the book of Exodus. John alludes to it by just mentioning the heading and provides his readers with the theological message that liberation is again possible. The NT authors count on 'biblical' insider knowledge of their readers; NT writings make evident that their authors lived in a religious world with a very vivid biblical tradition.

Even though the literary context and the genre of a text is emphasized, its historical context cannot be ignored. If a text is understood as a response to a situation (i.e. part of a communication process), the initial situation to which the text refers cannot be disregarded; there will be a basic human experience relating the two texts. Regardless of the cultural, social and historical differences, interconnectedness on the level of human experiences must be possible according to Gadamer's hermeneutic: 'Understanding is reached in the fusion of the differing horizons of text and reader (*Horizontverschmelzung*). This is possible only to the extent that there is a "belonging" (*Zugehörigkeit*), that is, a fundamental affinity between the interpreter and his or her object.'[2]

In what follows, a review of recent publications on intertextuality will be presented. It is followed by case studies and reflections on the implications for the discussion about selective versus contextual allusions.

1 Review of recent publications on intertextuality

1.1 Short review of the beginnings of intertextual biblical research

The laying of the foundation stone on intertextual research in biblical studies is marked by G. K. Beale, J. Paulien, S. E. Porter, S. Moyise and S. Bøe who developed the methodology, reflected on it self-critically and clarified the technical terms.[3]

---

[2] H-G. Gadamer, *Truth and Method* (trans. J. Weinsheimer and D. G. Marshall; 2nd edn; New York: Bloomsbury, 1989).

[3] Just to mention a few major publications on Revelation of John of these scholars: G. K. Beale, *The Use of Daniel in Jewish Apocalyptic Literature and in the Revelation of St. John* (Lanham; New York; London: University Press of America, 1984); S. Bøe, *Gog and Magog. Ezekiel 38–39 as Pre-text for Revelation 19,17-21 and 20,7-10* (WUNT 2/135; Tübingen: Mohr Siebeck, 2001); J. Paulien, *Decoding Revelation's Trumpets: Literary Allusions and the Interpretation of Revelation 8:7-12* (Andrews University Seminary Doctoral Dissertation Series 11; Berrien Springs: Andrews University Press, 1988); S. E. Porter, 'The Use of the Old Testament in the New Testament: A Brief Comment on Method and Terminology', in *Early Christian Interpretation of the Scriptures of Israel: Investigations and Proposals* (ed. C. A. Evans and J. A. Sanders; JSNTSup 148; SSEJC 5; Sheffield: JSOT Press, 1997), 79–96, 80; cf. also C. A. Evans, '"It is not as through the Word of God had Failed": An Introduction to Paul and the Scriptures of Israel', in *Paul and the Scriptures of Israel* (ed. C. A. Evans and J. A. Sanders; JSNTSup 83 SSEJC 1; Sheffield: JSOT Press, 1992), 13–17; Steve Moyise, *The Old Testament in the Book of Revelation* (JSNTSup 115; Sheffield: JSOT Press, 1995).

Moreover, they conducted important studies on the reception of the OT in the NT in particular text corpora. It is a quite small research community in English-speaking countries which is primarily concerned with the intertextuality of Scripture; however, despite conflicting opinions and results, constructive discussions between the above-mentioned scholars have been possible and have encouraged further studies.

In what follows, I want to recall the landmarks of these beginnings, after which I discuss open questions and desiderata that have led to the next stage of intertextual studies. The purpose of this review is to observe their fundamental results and note their shortcomings which point to the way forward.

Among other things, G. K. Beale has published a study of Daniel in Jewish literature in which he distinguishes between

> 'clear allusion': which features 'word order which is almost in the same form as the O.T. text and usually has the same general meaning, although this latter element may be absent'.
>
> 'probable allusion (with more varied wording)': '[a] wording which is not as close to that of the O.T. text but still having links with it, and [b] the presence of an idea uniquely traceable to that text sometimes only [b] may be present'.
>
> and 'possible allusion or echo': 'parallel in wording or thought, but of a more general nature than in the other categories'.[4]

As far as I have studied his publications, including his commentary on Revelation, he is aware of contextual allusions and avoids an atomistic view.[5] Nevertheless, he does not always look at the wider context (in terms of the text segment to which the allusion belongs to) of the pre-texts he identifies.[6]

J. Paulien evaluates ten different commentaries on the OT background of a text segment;[7] he defines the term 'allusion' and criticizes the missing catalogue of criteria: 'In addition, there is some evidence that many commentators operated more by intuition than on the basis of consistent criteria.'[8] In discussing exegetical and literary studies and approaches, he comes up with the solution of distinguishing between unconscious ('echoes') and conscious allusions.[9] He argues that linguistic, thematic

---

[4] Beale, *Use of Daniel*, 43, n. 62.
[5] G. K. Beale, *The Book of Revelation: A Commentary on the Greek Text* (NIGTC; Grand Rapids: Eerdmans, 1999). G. K. Beale, *John's Use of the Old Testament in the Revelation* (JSNTSup 166; Sheffield: Sheffield Academic Press, 1988), 67–75, considers contextual and non-contextual use of the OT. He distinguishes between literary/thematic and historical context.
[6] See for example Beale, *Revelation*, 1136f where he proposes Isa. 40.10 as pre-text of Rev. 22.12. It also can be observed in his excursus on the Jewish background of silence (448–54). I would expect a close examination of the text segment to which the allusion belongs to. It is almost impossible to discuss this in a biblical commentary.
[7] Paulien, *Decoding Revelation's Trumpets*.
[8] J. Paulien, 'Elusive Allusions: The Problematic Use of the Old Testament in Revelation', *BiR* 33 (1988): 37–53 (48).
[9] Paulien, 'Allusions', 39f. It can be doubted if a distinction between conscious and unconscious usage can be demonstrated on a linguistic level.

and structural[10] similarities are helpful indications for the use of a direct allusion.[11] In addition, he distinguishes between the following levels of allusions:

> 'certain allusions': '"Certain allusions" exist when the evidence for dependence is so overwhelming that *the interpreter* is certain that John was pointing to the antecedent text.'[12]
>
> 'probable allusions': 'A "probable allusion"' occurs when the evidence for a direct allusion is considerable but falls short of certainty.'[13]
>
> 'possible allusions': '"Possible allusions" are *more problematic*. With a possible allusion there is enough evidence to indicate that John **may** have been making a direct allusion to the OT, but not enough to be reasonable certain.'[14]
>
> 'nonallusions': 'The category of "nonallusions" is relevant only when evaluating lists of suggested allusions. After examination, the *interpreter* concludes that there is no evidence that the author intended a parallel between two texts.'[15]

Paulien criticizes a methodology that can tend towards subjectivity, as it operates with the intuition of the modern commentator. Therefore, he tries to develop linguistic criteria which even distinguish between different certainties of allusions. It is debatable whether one can refer to conscious or unconscious allusions, and I would prefer to think about a deliberate usage. Nevertheless, Paulien underlines the necessity of looking at the context of a certain allusion.

S. E. Porter has collected the variety of technical terms which are in use to describe the reception of the OT in the NT: 'citation, direct quotation, formal quotation, indirect quotation, allusive quotation, formal quotation, indirect quotation, allusive quotation, allusion (whether conscious or unconscious), paraphrase, exegesis (such as inner-biblical exegesis), midrash, typology, reminiscence, echo (whether conscious or unconscious), intertextuality, influence (either direct or indirect), and even tradition, among other terms'.[16] This problem of the large number of terms is not solved yet, as Garrick Allen said in 2017: 'The cacophony of competing terms and definitions currently in use in Biblical Studies increases the chances for misunderstanding and imprecision.'[17] While the freedom of research and researchers is essential, the diversity of technical terms and methodologies is the crux of the matter. I am pretty sure that the problem will not be solved in the future as exegetes are not necessarily known for reaching agreements.

S. Moyise published a study on the use of the OT in the Revelation of John in which he reflects on methodological and hermeneutical questions. In terms of context, he states that

---

[10] Paulien, 'Allusion', 43 with footnote 49 referring to M. D. Goulder, 'The Apocalypse as an Annual Cycle of Prophecies', NTS 27 (1981): 342–67 (343–50).
[11] Paulien, 'Allusion', 41, presupposes a written *Vorlage*: 'We do not know the content of his library or his reading habits' (44).
[12] Paulien, 'Allusion', 46.
[13] Ibid.
[14] Ibid., 47. Bold text original.
[15] Ibid., 46. Italics added.
[16] Porter, 'The Use of the Old Testament', 79–96, 80; cf. also Evans, 'Word of God', 13–17, 13f.
[17] G. Allen, *The Book of Revelation and Early Jewish Textual Culture* (Cambridge: Cambridge University Press, 2017), 7.

every allusion is removed from the original context and placed in a new literary frame. He raises the important question: 'How does the Old Testament context interact with the New Testament context?'[18] He concludes that the NT develops a new understanding of OT pre-texts. He describes the correspondence between the OT allusion and the new context: the OT reflects on the NT context and the NT context changes OT allusions.[19]

S. Bøe has worked on the reception of Ezekiel 38–9 and critically reflected on the method of the use of Scripture in Revelation.[20] He uses the term 'correspondence' in order to describe topics, structures and the arrangement of texts and events. In his additional analyses, he differentiates between *allusions, citation/quotation/isolated echo* and *no real correspondence*.

If we evaluate these publications in terms of selective versus contextual allusions, we can observe that they avoid an atomistic analysis in favour of a precise definition of allusions. Certainly, some technical terms open the door for a more subjective perception of texts, but nevertheless an allusion is defined as the accordance of more than one single word and scholars try to detect allusions on the level of a sentence or long phrase. However, some technical terms indicate a greater awareness of parallels between literary contexts, like paraphrase, exegesis (such as inner-biblical exegesis), midrash, typology, reminiscence, echo, intertextuality,[21] influence (either direct or indirect) and tradition.

1.2 Recent publications on intertextual biblical research on Revelation of John

Before presenting recent publications on intertextual research on Revelation of John, the NT writing with the highest number of OT allusions, it should be noted that it is an ongoing discussion, particularly among English-speaking scholars. Only very few publications are recorded in German language, and these are not well integrated into English research.

B. Kowalski applies the intertextual methodology of L. Gregory Bloomquist which he developed as a socio-rhetorical analysis to identify apocalyptic.[22] Four aspects have to be observed:

(a) *Reference* (with what texts and textual traditions are these phrases in dialogue?);
(b) *Recitation* (exact, modified or different words);

---

[18] Moyise, *Old Testament*, 19.
[19] Ibid., 116.
[20] Bøe, *Gog and Magog*.
[21] Since 1967 the term 'intertextuality' is discussed in literary studies and entered exegetical research. S. Gillmayer-Bucher, 'Intertextualität. Zwischen Literaturtheorie und Methodik', *PzB* 8 (1999): 5–20 (9) has called attention to forty-eight different possible uses of the term. A text is regarded as multidimensional space in which various writings overlap.
[22] B. Kowalski, '"Let My People Go, That They May Serve Me" (Exod. 10:3). Exodus Motifs in the Revelation of John', *Henoch* 38 (2016): 32–53; L. G. Bloomquist, 'Methodological Criteria for Apocalyptic Rhetoric: A Suggestion for the Expand Use of Sociorhetorical Analysis', in *Vision and Persuasion: Rhetorical Dimensions of Apocalyptic Discourse* (ed. G. Carey and L. G. Bloomquist; St. Louis: Chalice Press 1990), 181–203.

(c) *Recontextualization* (placing of attributes, narration or speech in a new context without announcing its previous attribution);
(d) *Reconfiguration* (modification of a word, phrase, topic or theme).

Consequently, she explores the verbatim allusions to Exod. 3.14 in the various verses in Revelation. Next she observes the closer context of the Exodus verse in order to ask how it influenced the thoughts of John the prophet.

M. Jauhiainen, the Finnish scholar, follows the methodology of Ziva Ben-Porat which is based on literary allusions, so-named devices for 'simultaneous activations of two texts'.[23] In particular, the actualization of the OT pre-text is emphasized. He analyses the function of allusions and avoids an atomistic intertextual method. Jauhiainen applies his method to the use of Zechariah in Revelation[24] and distinguishes three types of allusions: literary allusions, simple allusions and echoes. Unfortunately, he does not sort them in terms of probability, nor does he develop clear criteria for allusions, because he does not recognize the problem of parallelomania (for him the function of an allusion is crucial). He examines interaction of a text in the new text. The prophet Zechariah is used to express the restitution by God, his coming and the building of the eschatological temple.

Garrick Allen wrote his dissertation on the use of the OT in Revelation.[25] He 'demonstrates that John read, interpreted, and reused scripture in a manner commensurate with the norms of scriptural reuse operative in Second Temple Judaism'. He 'highlights the close relationship between Revelation and the literature of the Second Temple period in terms of their author's shared exegetical repertoires'.[26] It is a special feature of his study that he analyses 'the reuse of scripture ... in the context of its textual culture. Placing Revelation within its proper textual context provides a base from which to test its reuse of scripture against works that are native to the broader compositional ethos in which it was constructed'. In that sense, the author understands context in both historical and textual terms.

In terms of methodology, Allen distinguishes between reference, quotation, explicit and implicit allusion. Furthermore, he pays attention to textual pluriformity, textual fluidity and variant editions; he also is aware of the anachronism of the applied terms as they had not been in the minds of ancient authors. Thus, he uses them in a phenomenological, not in a constitutive sense. In relation to our question, he argues for contextual allusions in a very broad sense, one which includes textual variants in manuscripts and the Jewish-Christian literature. He is also aware of the pluriformity and fluidity of texts in antiquity. This view implies a fundamental questioning of intertextual terms which assume a final stage of an almost fixed text.

M. Sommer wrote his doctoral dissertation on the reception of the Exodus 7–10, the Exodus plagues in Revelation. Before presenting his own methodology, he evaluates studies that are dealing with the production and reception of the OT. They are aware

---

[23] Z. Ben-Porat, 'Intertextuality and Cosmopolitanism in Cyberspace', *Primerjalna književnost* 32 (2009): 137-58 (146). See also Z. Ben-Porat, 'The Poetics of Literary Allusion', *PTL* 1 (1976): 105-28.
[24] M. Jauhiainen, *The Use of Zechariah in Revelation* (WUNT 2/199; Tübingen: Mohr, 2005).
[25] Allen, *Revelation*.
[26] Ibid., 5.

that the literary relationship between Revelation and its pre-texts exceed merely punctual contacts. Thus he points to the influence of OT pre-texts on the structure of Revelation.[27] He criticizes studies with a mono-perspective, namely those which argue for the influence of a single OT writing on the structure of Revelation. The frequent use of composite allusions and quotations supports his view.[28] Another argument that demonstrates his idea of a multi-perspective approach is the technique of multiple usages of pre-texts in Revelation which even can form the structure of Revelation (Kowalski).[29] The major question is whether John was aware of the context of the OT texts he used.

Sommer's dissertation responds to three desiderata of research: (1) With regard to the content, Sommer argues against any kind of harmonization of the plague narratives and Revelation. He disproves the recapitulation theory which regards the plagues as final judgement; he also rejects the interpretation of the plagues as a warning. According to Sommer, NT scholars do not always read the Exodus in an appropriate way; they interpret the plagues as a warning. (2) With regard to the reception history, scholars also apply interpretations as mentioned above and rejected by Sommer (recapitulation theory, plagues as warning). The major criticism of Sommer is that scholars compare Revelation with totally irrelevant or later Jewish interpretations of the book of Exodus. (3) Sommer himself regards the prophetic writings as a connective link between Exodus 7–11 and Revelation. According to him, John has read the Egyptian plagues against the background of the idea of the coming day of the Lord. Therefore, he titles his book 'The Day of the Plagues' – a combination of the two motifs. In terms of methodology, Sommer applies a multi-perspective approach which is necessary as the usage of the plague motif is characterized by blending motifs and traditions in Revelation. John has connected the Egyptian plagues with intratextual back references with the two text passages dealing with the day of the Lord (Rev. 6.12-17; 16.14). At the same time, he can show that the motif of the day of the Lord has the potential for associations which enable a link to the Egyptian plagues.[30]

One of the advantages of this study is that Sommer starts with a source-critical analysis of Exodus 7–10 and not with the text of Revelation. He reads the NT writings in continuation of the OT, instead of reading the NT writings through the lens of the OT. Secondly, he studies the two scenes dealing with the day of the Lord (Rev. 6.12-17) including their pre-texts at the beginning. They precede the three visions of the seven trumpets and bowls and are part of the seven seals. In another major chapter, the intratextual relationships between the Egyptian plagues and the day-of-Lord motif are precisely studied. Further aspects are the connection between the Egyptian plagues, the creation theology, the day-of-Lord motif and the identity of the Christian communities. Sommer also explores the judgement over Babylon, the day of the Lord in connection with the second Exodus (Jeremiah 50–1) and the Egyptian plagues.

---

[27] Michael Sommer, *Der Tag der Plagen. Studien zur Verbindung der Rezeption von Ex 7-11 in den Posaunen- und Schalenvisionen der Johannesoffenbarung und der Tag des Herrn-Tradition* (WUNT 2 387; Tübingen: Mohr, 2015), 5.

[28] Ibid., 6–9.

[29] Cf. B. Kowalski, *Die Rezeption des Propheten Ezechiel in der Offenbarung des Johannes* (SBS 31; Stuttgart: Verlag Katholisches Bibelwerk, 1996).

[30] Sommer, *Tag*, 27–9.

Thus, he is aware of the reception of a motif in the OT itself. He analyses not only the intertextual relationship between Exodus 7–10 and Revelation but also the connection between the motif of the grasshoppers, the day of the Lord, the war and the plagues.[31]

Sommer summarizes his research as follows: the day-of-the-Lord motif offered the background for the reception of the plagues. This connection was prepared by the late prophetic writings (Joel 3; Isaiah 34, 50; Ezekiel 38) which already open the possibility for such associations. Readers at the end of the first century CE were able to connect the two motifs with each other, as John already did in the plagues of the seven bowls and seven trumpets. In effect, Sommer detects a literary dependency in Revelation upon the plague narratives and a connection to Rev. 6.12-17. John's usage of Exodus 7–11 can be described as universalization which includes a connection between plagues and the day of the Lord. The plagues have another function in the bowl visions. In regard to the interpretation of Rev. 18.4 as second Exodus, Sommer recognizes a connection to Jeremiah 50–1 and the day of the Lord as well.

In terms of methodology, Sommer has a very broad understanding of context. His multi-perspective reading is on the right track as he is aware of composite allusions, source-critical problems, inner-biblical rewriting processes and influences on multiple levels of a text. He argues for a synchronic connection between the images and motifs of the plague narratives and the day-of-the-Lord motif which had already been provided by the prophets.[32] A weakness of his study is that it is not aware of further allusions to other OT writings – but that is a very complex issue.

Stefan Alkier, Thomas Hieke and Tobias Nicklas edited a collection of essays on poetics and intertextuality of the Revelation of John.[33] In its third part, nine essays on intertextuality and intermediality are presented. They discuss the literary and theological function of the OT in Revelation (Thomas Hieke), the rewriting of prophets (Adela Yarbro Collins), transtextual adventures of sin (Edmondo F. Lupieri), the motif of Sodom and the final judgement (Michael Sommer), the son of man in Revelation (Luca Arcari), Revelation as prophetic remembrance of Jesus's words (Daniele Tripaldi), the intertextual nexus of Revelation and Graeco-Roman literature (Jan Willem van Henten),[34] the reception history of Rev. 6.1-2 (Ian Boxall) and the heavenly liturgy and its interaction with orthodox liturgy (Sotirios Despotis). The volume does not intend a systematic reflection on methodological issues. It focuses on the last book of the NT and its theological implications of intertexual relationships.

The long-term project of the École Biblique et Archéologique Française de Jérusalem (EABF) in Jerusalem 'The Bible in its Traditions' is conducted in the three languages: English, French and Spanish. 'Our goal is to create a comprehensive research, study, and reading tool for the Bible, emphasizing the variety of traditions in the biblical text,

---

[31] Ibid., 217–31.
[32] Ibid., 259–63.
[33] S. Alkier, Thomas Hieke and T. Nicklas, *Poetik und Intertextualität der Johannesapokalypse* (WUNT 346; Tübingen: Mohr Siebeck, 2015).
[34] 'For the Corpus Hellenisticum approach the focus is on individual passages, mostly just a few words and usually short Greco-Roman parallel passages. The outcome is often an atomistic view of Revelation's text as well as its parallel passages. For a careful interpretation of the parallels it is often important to take the larger context of these passages into consideration and to explore their own socio-cultural contexts' (421).

and the depth and breadth of its interpretations throughout centuries, persuasions, and disciplines.'[35]

They present the variety of the original biblical versions (Hebrew, Greek, Latin, Syriac and Aramaic) and their reception in history up to the current time (information on how the text came to be and what it meant then, but also how the text has been used ever since, in the Jewish tradition, in the theology and liturgy of the Church, and how it has shaped world culture). The context of an allusion or quotation is understood as 'notes dealing with archaeology, history, geography, realia or texts of the ancient world and cultures, relevant to the production of a Biblical text'.[36] The term context is broadly defined; it is not limited to the literary context.

The use of the OT in the NT is also part of reception history.[37] The relationship between biblical texts comprises two lines: (1) A structural, synchronical and theological line as the texts of the biblical canon are based on its interaction ('elle postule que l'ensemble du canon constitue une structure dans laquelle toutes les parties sont en interaction').[38] (2) A historical and intentional line searches for the possibility that an author or redactor/composer of a text has quoted or alluded to a certain text passage ('elle s'interroge sur la possibilité que l'auteur/le rédacteur/le compilateur du texte en question ait, consciemment, pu faire telle citation, ou allusion, etc. à tel ou tel passage des Écritures'). The basic theory which is applied is the perspective of dialogue which can include the use of an expression, a narrative motif, an idea, a history or praxis, or a complete narrative scheme/literary genre. The traditional hermeneutics of intra-biblical typology and fulfilment of Scripture are employed.

The term fulfilment is refined in terms of legislation, fulfilment, certain/probable/possible allusion, enigmatic citation and quotation of a commandment. Also typology is further developed: 'Either type or antitype may be a person, thing, or event, but often the type is messianic and frequently related to the idea of salvation (http://www.theopedia.com/Biblical_typology).' Also scenarios, rituals and laws can be used for typology. Typological narratives include the following elements: language (form, refrain and phrase), motifs, scenario (theophany), time frame, situation (Jesus's situation resembles the psalmist of Ps. 22), episodes, sequences, characters and attributes. Typological semantics include symbols, themes, fulfilment of Scripture, messiahship, glory, speaker and wisdom.

The project also focuses on the connection between OT texts, in terms of rewriting processes and the references to text corpora (ἐκ τοῦ νόμου καὶ τῶν προφητῶν: 2 Macc. 15.9; τῶν δώδεκα προφητῶν: Sir. 49.10). In terms of selective versus contextual allusions, a critical evaluation of the intertextual method reveals a high sensitivity for the context and the avoidance of an atomistic view on texts. The entire method is text orientated; it is not author centred, nor does it apply a reader-response criticism.

The downside of this method is its narrow hermeneutics which reduces the relationship between the two parts of the Bible to analogy and fulfilment. It is not

---

[35] Information about this project is translated from an unpublished handout for researchers who collaborate with the project. See also: http://blog.bibletraditions.org/about-the-research-project/.
[36] http://blog.bibletraditions.org/about-the-research-project/.
[37] Ibid.
[38] Ibid.

always practicable to describe the use of the OT in terms of fulfilment, as the OT does not only consist of prophecies and the NT has prophetic texts and writings itself (Revelation). Furthermore, prophecies are usually not fulfilled in the distant future but in the near present. Finally, not all OT prophecies are fulfilled in the NT.[39]

2 Application examples/case studies

In terms of methodology, can we speak about an allusion if two texts with different historical and literary contexts have only one single word in common? What further conditions have to be fulfilled in order to avoid atomistic intertextual analysis? In the following text, examples of different quality will be presented, to determine what implications they have for the method of intertextuality.

2.1 Ruth and the prodigal son

While preparing a paper on the so-called parable of the prodigal son, I came across a small note about a surprising connection with the book of Ruth. Karl-Heinrich Ostmeyer mentions it in his interpretation of the famous parable in the extensive manual edited by Ruben Zimmermann.[40] He argues for a contrast between the two narratives, a kind of 'inverted'[41] or antithetical usage. The only word both narratives have in common is the verb κολλάω, which occurs in Ruth 2.8 LXX and in Lk. 15.15. It means 'to join closely together, to join oneself to, to join, to cling to, to associate with, to become a follower of someone'.[42]

In Ruth, κολλάω is used by the actor Boaz, who advises Ruth to keep close to his maidens. In Luke, it is used to describe the younger son's behaviour towards a Gentile citizen of the foreign country who sent him to his fields to feed the pigs (v. 15). This negative attachment is contrasted by Ruth, who joins her mother-in-law and her God (Ruth 1.14: דָּבַק/ἀκολουθέω;[43] cf. 1.16 – the Hebrew verb is surprisingly rendered with what will become, for the Gospels, a technical term for discipleship and the only time that it is rendered with ἀκολουθέω) and follows the advice of Boaz to keep close to his maidens (2.8: דָּבַק/κολλάω). While Ruth receives abundantly and has enough to eat, the younger son receives nothing and goes hungry (Lk. 15.16). The difference between the two of them results from their motives: while Ruth leaves everything to serve and follows her mother-in-law to God's promised land, the younger son selfishly demands

---

[39] Ibid.
[40] Karl-Heinrich Ostmeyer, 'Dabeisein ist alles (Der verlorene Sohn)–Lk15,11-32', in *Kompendium der Gleichnisse Jesu* (ed. R. Zimmermann; Gütersloh: Gütersloher Verlagshaus 2007), 618–33.
[41] Beale, *Revelation*, 94–6.
[42] William Arndt, F. W. Danker, W. Bauer and F. W. Gringrich, eds, *A Greek-English Lexicon of the New Testament and other Early Christian Literature* (3rd edn; Chicago: University of Chicago Press, 2014).
[43] דָּבַק is translated with ἀκολουθέω and not with κολλάω.

his heritage and follows his own path going to the Gentiles. As Ruth is fully integrated into the Jewish people, the younger son suffers social isolation.[44]

Ruth	Prodigal Son
Ruth as stranger in Israel	Younger Son as stranger in Gentile country
Named	Anonymous
Woman	Man
Poor widow	Rich son
Gentile → Israel	Jew → Gentile land
Famine → bread	Bread → famine
Conversion at the beginning of the journey	Conversion at the end of the journey
2.8 κολλάω Positive attachment of Ruth to Boaz's maidens, following his advice	15.15 κολλάω Negative attachment of the younger son to a Gentile citizen, following his own advice
Free response to a vocation	Dependence on a human being
1.14: ἀκολουθέω˙ Ruth following her mother-in-law and her God	15.13 ἀποδημέω Younger son leaving his father
2.9, 14-18; 3.15 Receiving abundantly	15.15 Receiving nothing
Full integration	Social isolation
Representing Abraham//Israel	Representing a converted sinner
Hero (like Abraham)	Antihero
Reversed life journeys **Common biblical motifs**	

At first glance, the arguments for an antithetical contrast between the Ruth narrative and the parable of the prodigal son seem to be convincing. But the only characteristic word they have in common is the verb κολλάω, which is used quite frequently in the OT,[45] so that it is justified to question this potential allusion. Therefore, we will look at the textual contexts including the Hebrew text version, perhaps leading to a refining of the methodology at the end.

What does this mean in terms of the parable of the prodigal son and a probable allusion? The twofold translation of דבק with κολλάω and ἀκολουθέω characterizes the Ruth narrative as a conversion narrative of a Gentile woman who comes to believe in the God of Israel. Although the precise allusion is only based on this single word, the

---

[44] Cf. Ostmeyer, 'Der verlorene Sohn', 627. He mentions further allusions to OT texts like the narrative about Jacob and Esau or Genesis 37–50.
[45] Deut. 6.13; 10.20; 28.60; 29.19; Ruth 2.8; 2 Sam. 20.2; 3 Kgdms 11.2; 4 Kgdms 1.18; 3.3; 5.27; 18.6; 1 Esd. 4.20; Tob. 6.19; 1 Macc. 3.2; 6.21; Ps. 21.16; 24.21; 43.26; 62.9; 100.4; 101.6; 118.25, 31; 136.6; Job. 29.10; 38.38; 41.8.15; Sir. 2.3; 19.2; Jer. 13.11; Bar. 1.20; 3.4; Lam. 2.2; 4.4. Occurrences in the NT: Mt. 19.5; Lk. 10.11; 15.15; Acts 5.13; 8.29; 9.26; 10.28; 17.34; Rom. 12.9; 1 Cor. 6.16f; Rev. 18.5.

plot of both narratives includes similarities. Therefore we could assume an allusion to a narrative pattern.

2.2 Ruth and the vocation narratives in Gospel tradition

After reading the parable of the prodigal son (Lk. 15.11-32) through the lens of the Ruth short story, I would like to ask if another perspective is possible: a re-reading of Ruth through the lens of NT vocation narratives that focus on discipleship. We are aware that such a reading implies an anachronistic interpretation, but it might support the argumentation presented in the previous section. Almost all Jewish and Christian commentaries interpret Ruth 1.16 as an expression of faith but not as a response to a call by God. Although scholars notice the connection between Ruth 2.11 and Gen. 12.1, they do not apply this connection to Abraham's vocation to Ruth's solemn promise to her mother-in-law.

Ruth. 1.14: Ρουθ δὲ ἠκολούθησεν (דָּבְקָה) αὐτῇ;

The LXX book of Ruth describes Ruth's decision for her mother-in-law as a response to a call with ἀκολουθέω. Her oath of fidelity, her solemn vow, underlines the vocation: She is following Naomi to her people and her God. This formula illustrates that her decision is not an expression of dependence but rather a free choice and response to God calling her through the need of her mother-in-law. Just as Abraham, she is leaving her family and her country (Ruth 2.11//Gen. 12.1), unconditionally and with deep faith. The Greek rendering ἀκολουθέω of the Hebrew דָּבַק in Ruth 1.14 is rendered with what will become, for the Gospels, a technical term for discipleship; דָּבַק is normally translated with κολλάω.[46] It is the only verse in the entire OT in which דָּבַק is rendered with ἀκολουθέω.[47] The context of v. 14 supports the assumption that the author describes the call of Ruth by the God of Israel to which she responds by following. She professes her faith in the God of Israel in a solemn promise in v. 16 (ὁ λαός σου λαός μου καὶ ὁ θεός σου θεός μου) which underlines that Ruth follows not only her mother-in-law but also the call of the God of Israel to the Promised Land. It is an implicit allusion to Gen. 12.1 which is directly alluded to in Ruth 2.11, where Boaz reveals his knowledge about her decision. The important part of the verse refers back to Abraham's call in Gen. 12.1.

In summary, it can be said that the book of Ruth is a female rewriting (= rewriting of the Abraham story with a female hero); instead of the male hero Abraham, the author

---

[46] Occurrences in the NT (in particular in the Lukan tradition): Mt. 19.5; Lk. 10.11; 15.15; Acts 5.13; 8.29; 9.26; 10.28; 17.34; Rom. 12.9; 1 Cor. 6.16f; Rev. 18.5.

[47] Gen. 2.24 (προσκολλάω); 19.19 (καταλαμβάνω); 31.23 (καταλαμβάνω); 34.3 (προσέχω); Num. 36.7 (προσκολλάω) 9 (προσκολλάω); Deut. 4.4 (πρόσκειμαι); 10.20 (κολλάω); 11.22 (προσκολλάω); 13.5 (προστίθημι) 18 (προσκολλάω); 28.21 (προσκολλάω) 60 (κολλάω); 30.20 (ἔχω); Jos. 22.5 (πρόσκειμαι); 23.8 (προσκολλάω).12 (προστίθημι); Judg. 18.22 (καταλαμβάνω); 20.42 ([κατα-]φθάνω) 45 (προσκολλάω); Ruth 1.14 (ἀκολουθέω); 2.8 (κολλάω) 21 (κολλάω) 23 (κολλάω); 1 Kgdms 14.22 (συνάπτω); 31.2 (συνάπτω); 2 Kgdms 1.6 (συνάπτω); 20.2 (κολλάω); 23.10 (προσκολλάω); 3 Kgdms 11.2 (κολλάω); 4 Kgdms 3.3 (κολλάω); 5.27 (κολλάω); 18.6 (κολλάω); 1 Chr. 10.2 (καταδιώκω); 2 Chr. 3.12 (ἅπτω); Job. 19.20 (σήπω); 29.10 (κολλάω); 31.7 (ἅπτω); 38.38 (κολλάω); 41.9 (προσκολλάω) 15 (κολλάω); Ps. 22.16 (κολλάω); 44.26 (κολλάω); 63.9 (κολλάω); 101.3 (κολλάω); 102.6 (κολλάω); 119.25 (κολλάω) 31 (κολλάω); 137.6 (κολλάω) 13.11 (κολλάω); 42.16 (καταλαμβάνω); Lam. 4.4 (κολλάω); Ezek. 3.26 (συνδέω); 29.4 (προσκολλάω).

is portraying Ruth with the same characteristics of the Abraham story, including God's call, the famine, the promises of land and descendants. The canonical positioning of the book of Ruth between the time of the Judges and the time of the Kings makes it a bridge narrative; moreover, the history of Israel can continue because of Ruth's decision to accept and follow God's call.

> 2.11: καὶ ἀπεκρίθη Βοος
> καὶ εἶπεν αὐτῇ
> ἀπαγγελίᾳ ἀπηγγέλη μοι
> ὅσα πεποίηκας μετὰ τῆς πενθερᾶς σου μετὰ τὸ ἀποθανεῖν τὸν ἄνδρα σου
> καὶ πῶς κατέλιπες τὸν πατέρα σου
> καὶ τὴν μητέρα σου
> καὶ τὴν γῆν γενέσεώς σου
> καὶ ἐπορεύθης πρὸς λαὸν
> ὃν οὐκ ᾔδεις ἐχθὲς καὶ τρίτης
> Gen 12.1: καὶ εἶπεν κύριος τῷ Αβραμ
> ἔξελθε ἐκ τῆς γῆς σου
> καὶ ἐκ τῆς συγγενείας σου
> καὶ ἐκ τοῦ οἴκου τοῦ πατρός σου
> εἰς τὴν γῆν ἣν
> ἄν σοι δείξω

What do the two examples mean in terms of methodology? Although the allusion consists only of one single word, we cannot speak about a selective usage. The verb κολλάω is connected with a narrative pattern which is reused in an inverted manner. Allusions to an entire narrative, to a specific literary genre or narrative pattern, are the ideal case of contextual allusions.

2.3 Exodus and Revelation of John

Now I would like to come to a field of study which needs further exploration: The reception of the book of Exodus in Revelation of John. A short review of research to date will present the desiderata.

At first glance the book of Exodus and the widespread Exodus motifs, typology and theology seem to be of secondary importance. On closer inspection, this impression is proven to be wrong, since many motifs belong to the pivotal theological idea of liberation, as will be demonstrated below. Little enough attention has been paid to this tradition in Revelation. Two doctoral dissertations have been written since the early 1980s. Unfortunately, one is published in Danish, the other remains unpublished. It was J. S. Casey who presented first, in 1981, his thorough study on the Exodus Typology in the Book of Revelation,[48] eleven years later followed by G. S. Adamsen on the 'Exodusmotiver i Johannes' Åbenbaring'.[49] In 2008, an

---

[48] Cf. J. S. Casey, 'Exodus Typology in the Book of Revelation' (PhD diss., Southern Baptist Theological Seminary 1981; Ann Arbor: Microfilm, 1984).
[49] G. S. Adamsen, 'Exodusmotiver i Johannes' Åbenbaring' (M. Theol. Diss., Århus, 1992).

interesting article on the Exodus background of Revelation 15–16 was published by L. Gallusz, a Hungarian scholar. It is an extract of his PhD on the throne motif in the Revelation of John.[50] The approaches and results of these three studies are presented in what follows.

Casey obviously has a theological approach. He basically addresses John's understanding of OT Exodus theology. The Exodus is not only an epoch of Israel's past but also of John's present: Jesus Christ is the fulfillment of God's promise of liberation. Therefore he explores the image of God in Revelation as the redeemer of the people, as judge of the oppressed and guarantor of his eternal inheritance. Hence, he concentrates on christological and soteriological key verses in 1.5f, the plagues in Rev. 8.6–11.19; 15.5–16.21, and the description of the inheritance in 7.1-17; 14.1-5; 15.1-5; 20.1-6; 21.1-8; 21.22–22.5.[51] Due to his theological interest, Casey's selection of texts does not cover thoroughly all crucial text passages with Exodus motifs in Revelation of John. He shows no interest in covering all possible allusions and/or quotations on the basis of the common lists in text-critical editions of the Greek New Testament (UBS[5], NA[28]). The results of his dissertation are therefore restricted to his theological question. Casey characterizes John's method of alluding to the Exodus as a typological usage.[52]

Adamsen, who published his PhD in Danish, has a solid philological and methodological interest. He not only presents the history of research,[53] but also reflects on hermeneutical problems. The dissertation reveals his awareness of recent intertextual discussions of the technical terms 'allusion' and 'quotation' following J. Paulien's suggestions. Consequently, he examines all verses and text passages in Revelation which allude to the Exodus (1.5b-6; 2.12-17; 5.9f; 7.9-17; 8–9; 11.15-19; 10; 11.1-14; 12-13; 14.1-5; 15.2-4; 15.5–16.21; 17.1–21.8; 21.9–22.5). In concluding his research, he follows Casey's position that John's usage of Exodus can be described well with the term 'typology' and that the Exodus motif influenced Revelation structurally and theologically. Finally, he states that Exodus plays a major role for John.

Casey and Adamsen generally agree with their findings, but neither treat nor respond to all probable questions. An exhaustive examination of all probable allusions and/or direct quotations based on the text-critical editions (UBS[5], NA[28]) still is a lacuna within Revelation scholarship. Hence, one might mention other motifs which influenced John, such as his characteristic description of God with the *Dreizeitenformel* (a formula which expresses the eternity of God), the key verse 18.4 and the many hymns which interrupt the dramatic visionaries. In the following, first an overview of all possible allusions and quotations of Exod. 3.14 will be given on the basis of NA[28]. Then the

---

[50] L. Gallusz, *The Throne Motif in the Book of Revelation* (LNTS 487; London: Bloomsbury, 2013); L. Gallusz, 'The Exodus Motif in Revelation 15-16: Its Background and Nature', *AUSS* 46 (2008): 21–43;

[51] The three passages 7.1-17; 14.1-5; 15.1-5 have a common scene in heaven, the three others (20.1-6; 21.1-8; 21.22–22.5) describe the inheritance more completely. Cf. J. S. Casey, 'Das Exodusthema im Buch der Offenbarung vor dem Hintergrund des Neuen Testaments', *Concilium* (D) 23 (1987): 22–8; Casey, 'Exodus', 171–214.

[52] He also uses the category of typology to describe the Exodus theology in the OT and its reception in the Jewish and NT writings.

[53] He underlines the importance of the studies of L. Goppelt regarding the OT typology and E. Schüssler Fiorenza's focus on the ecclesiological aspect (Exodus 19 in Revelation).

Exodus background of the God question in Revelation of John will be explored. It can be explicated that there is a connection between God, the hymns, the plagues and the exhortation to separate from Babylon (18.4) which is deep-rooted in the book of Exodus (3.10-14; 10.3).

Old Context of Exod. 3.14 and Reception of the Motifs in Revelation		
	Context of Exod. 3.14 ...	... in Revelation
Exod. 3.4	Appearance of God (ὁράω)	Heavenly throne (4–5), Mount Zion (21–2); seeing (ὁράω) God's face (22.4)
Exod. 3.13,15	Revelation of God	Revelation of God (1.1, 8; 4–5, etc.)
Exod. 3.7	Affliction (κραυγή)	End of affliction (κραυγή 21.4)
Exod. 3.8	God coming down (καταβαίνω)	Jerusalem coming down (καταβαίνω) (3.12; 21.2, 10)
Exod. 3.9	Oppression (θλιμμός)	Tribulation (θλιμμός) (1.9; 2.9, 10, 22; 7.14)
Exod. 3.12	Liberation to worshipping God	Exhortation to separate from Babylon idolatry (18.4), hymnic-liturgical frame (4.8; 11.17; 16.5)
Exod. 3.6, 14	God's self-revelation (divine speech)	God's self-revelation (divine speech) (1.8; 21.6)
Exod. 3.12, 20	Wonder (θαυμάσιος) (sign [σημεῖον] and plagues [πληγή])	Eschatological signs (12.1, 3; 13.13, 14; 15.1; 16.14; 19.20); plagues (seals, trumpets, bowls) (11.17; 16.5)

New Context of Exod. 3.14 in Revelation Usages		
	Context	Usage
Rev. 1.4	Epistolary greeting – threefold clause –	Theological–contextual usage as part of a Trinitarian formula
Rev. 1.8	Theological formula – threefold clause –	Combined (prophetic writings) and theological usage to emphasize God's sovereignty
Rev. 4.8	Hymnic context – threefold clause (changed order) –	Combined (Isa. 6.3 and further prophetic writings) and theological usage to emphasize God's sovereign over history
Rev. 11.17	Hymnic context – Binomial clause –	Theological–contextual usage to emphasize God's judgement and sovereign over history
Rev. 16.5	Hymnic context – Binomial clause –	Theological–contextual usage to emphasize God's judgement
Rev. 17.8	Judgement scene	Inverted, antithetical–polemical usage to emphasize God's judgement (negation)

New Context of Exod. 3.14 in Revelation: Changing Speakers and Contexts					
Reference	Speaker		Context		
Rev. 1.4	John describing God		combination with the titles κύριος ὁ θεός and ὁ παντοκράτωρ	ἅγιος	hymnic context and response to a plague	Judgement
Rev. 1.8						
Rev. 4.8		4 living beings				
Rev. 11.17		24 elders				
Rev. 16.5		angel of the waters		δίκαιος ὅσιος		
Rev. 17.8		1 bowl angel				
	describing **or rather** addressing		God's sovereignty over			
	God's name		history **or rather** judgement			
	shift of speaking		**shift of meaning**			

The advantage of this methodology is that it pays tribute to the original contexts and studies the new context likewise.

3 Implications

It is almost impossible to develop an overarching concept of intertextuality which can be used for all biblical writings. It is an illusion to believe that all intertextual connections follow the same technique. The discussion about selective versus contextual allusions is a crucial issue which could be demonstrated above. Scholars have achieved a certain consensus in regard to which the following aspects can be observed:

- It can be stated that elective allusions are not used by the NT writers at all. Scholars have to take this result into account when they discuss definitions of technical terms and develop intertextual methods. The contexts are almost always important as NT authors did not have an atomistic understanding of texts. They did not use sacred texts like a dictionary but rather like a memory stick containing a complexity of theological messages. It would be very useful to benefit from memory theories which are already applied to the Synoptics in order to explain the connection between memory, narrative and Christology. Orality and written forms keep and transport memories. A re-reading of NT writings through the lens of a memory theory might be the way of the future. As all memory techniques are aware of context, they can help avoid an atomistic view of intertextual relationships. A multi-perspective approach to intertextual relationships between texts is absolutely appropriate. Mono-causal explanations of textual relationships, however, are not suitable at all.

- The technical term 'context' includes an awareness that attention to variations of a text in different manuscripts is necessary (see, for example, Garrick Allen's research who pays close attention to text criticism). Of course, NT authors did not have a text-critical edition of the OT writings. Maybe they only used an oral tradition or a mix of different manuscripts. But scholars need to be aware of the complex history of NT manuscripts. Therefore, it is important to look at text-critical variations, in particular of the LXX, in order to reconstruct the tradition history.
- Awareness of an inner-biblical rewriting process is also necessary. A certain motif which is used by NT authors can have been used previously by various OT traditions. For example, the Exodus motif was reused and retold in the exile period. The prophetic writings developed various ideas further and announced a second Exodus.
- The phenomenon of composite allusions in NT writings which can be found quite frequently demonstrate that NT authors had been aware of the wider biblical context or tradition. Composite allusions might indicate that NT authors had been aware of an inner-biblical rewriting process. In combining several pre-texts they place the allusions in new context with a new function which has to be analysed.
- Allusions even can have a structural influence on a NT writing as it is discussed by G. K. Beale (Daniel) and B. Kowalski (Ezekiel) in regard to the Revelation of John. Only a comprehensive study of all allusions to a certain OT book in a particular NT writing provides us with a full picture. Thus, it is necessary to compare two complete writings with each other.
- Some exceptions in terms of contextual allusions have to be mentioned: The allusion to narrative patterns might not include an exact accordance of a single word or phrase but the frequently told memory of an important theological message or experience. A second issue is of *hapax legomena*, words that are used only once. While allusions to a single word of a pre-text should be regarded critically, *hapax legomena* are an exception.
- Finally, a critical view on the lists of selective allusions in text-critical editions of the NT indicates that a revision would be needed. These lists are by no means complete and correct. They also convey the false impression that NT authors used the OT in a selective manner.

Old Testament context: Insights from Philo

Kenneth Schenck

Introduction

To what extent and in what ways did Philo engage the contexts of the Scriptures that he interpreted and appropriated? On the one hand, Philo gives his reader clear statements about his hermeneutic as it related to the distinction between literal and allegorical interpretation (e.g. *Mig.* 89). Beyond these, he has left us with ample examples of his engagement with Scripture, allowing us to induce patterns in his use of context. What we will find is that Philo paid a great deal of attention to various details of the immediate literary context of passages in the Jewish Scriptures. However, his keen eye in this regard more often than not served non-contextual goals. That is to say, his eye for details in the context more typically served to find figural meanings rather than contextual ones.

Before examining Philo's hermeneutic, we should first identify what texts he considered to be Scripture as well as which textual tradition served as the object of his interpretation. First, most agree that Philo functioned out of the *Greek* text of the Pentateuch rather than the Hebrew.[1] Philo does not seem to have known Hebrew, although he probably had access to sources that gave etymological information on various Hebrew words.[2] Accordingly, when we ask the extent to which Philo engaged the context of the Scriptures, we are largely asking the extent to which he engaged the literary context of *Greek* texts, not the original Hebrew. Philo simply was not equipped to engage the original meaning of the Jewish Scriptures from a linguistic perspective. Furthermore, the exact nature of the Greek text that Philo used is debated. For one, there are variations among the manuscripts of Philo themselves. Overall, however, it would seem that Philo generally used the Septuagintal text and that those variations closer to the Hebrew reflect later editing of his quotes to coincide with the later

---

[1] Cf. Gregory E. Sterling, 'The Interpreter of Moses: Philo of Alexandria and the Biblical Text', in *A Companion to Biblical Interpretation in Early Judaism* (ed. Matthias Henze; Grand Rapids: Eerdmans, 2012), 427. The most notable exception to this conclusion is Harry A. Wolfson, *Philo: Foundations of Religious Philosophy in Judaism, Christianity, and Islam* (Cambridge: Harvard University, 1947).

[2] For example, Lester L. Grabbe, *Etymology in Early Jewish Interpretation: The Hebrew Names in Philo* (BJS 115; Atlanta: Scholars, 1988).

renderings of Aquila and others.³ Certainly, Philo considered the translation of the Septuagint at Alexandria to be an inspired event.⁴

Second, Philo's 'canon' – if it is not anachronistic to speak of one – consisted more of the Pentateuch rather than the larger Jewish canon as we know it today. In an important comment, Philo says, 'I myself was initiated into the great mysteries by Moses, the God-beloved. Nevertheless, when I saw Jeremiah the prophet and knew that he was not only an initiate, but also a worthy revealer of the sacred, I did not hesitate to become his disciple' (*Cher.* 49).⁵ The impression we get is that while Philo ascribed the highest sense of inspiration to the writings of Moses, the Pentateuch, he also believed that a text like that of Jeremiah could be inspired as well.⁶ The two related to each other similar to the way that 'lower' mysteries were subordinate to 'higher' mysteries. Gregory Sterling's catalogue of Philo's engagement with the Jewish Scriptures indicates that Philo quoted or alluded to the Pentateuch over forty times more frequently than the other books that would end up constituting the Hebrew canon.⁷ While Philo thus considered many of these other books sacred, they clearly were not as significant to him as the Pentateuch.

1 Philo's hermeneutic

The classic text in relation to Philo's hermeneutic is found in *Migration* 89.

> There are some who, because they consider the literal laws to be symbols of things that pertain to the intellect, are extremely attentive to the latter but flippantly make light of the former. I for one would blame those who treat the literal meaning so lightly. For it is necessary to take care with both: both a more accurate investigation of the unseen meanings and to be beyond reproach in the way you preserve the visible aspects of the text.

In this statement, Philo shows himself to take seriously both the literal meaning of the biblical texts as he understood them and the hidden, deeper meanings he thought they also had. This attention to both the literal and the figural was unusual in Philo's day. There were certainly those who took the Jewish laws literally, whom Philonists

---

³ For example, Peter Katz, *Philo's Bible: The Aberrant Text of Bible Quotations in Some Philonic Writings and Its Place in the Textual History of the Greek Bible* (Cambridge: Cambridge University, 1950), 83 and Sterling, 'Interpreter of Moses', 427–31.
⁴ Cf. *Mos.* 2.37-40. Philo did not consider the translators of the Septuagint mere translators but 'hierophants and prophets'.
⁵ All translations of Philo are mine unless otherwise noted.
⁶ For a recent exploration of the intersection between Philo and Jeremiah, see Gregory E. Sterling, 'Jeremiah as Mystagogue: Jeremiah in Philo of Alexandria', in *Jeremiah's Scriptures: Production, Reception, Interaction, and Transformation* (ed. Hindy Najman and Konrad Schmid; Brill: Leiden, 2016), 417–30, as well as the responses by René Block, 'Philo and Jeremiah: A Mysterious Passage in *De Cherubim*. A Response to Gregory E. Sterling', 431–42, and by Franz Tóth, 'Jeremiah as Hierophant: Jeremiah in Philo of Alexandria. A Response to Gregory E. Sterling', 443–69.
⁷ Sterling, 'The Interpreter of Moses', 425.

sometimes call the 'literalists'.[8] There were certainly those who only took the Jewish laws allegorically (e.g. *Contemp.* 28–9), sometimes deemed the 'allegorists'. What was unusual was for Philo to take both literal *and* allegorical interpretations seriously.

Philo's attention to the literal especially came into play with regard to the traditional practices of Judaism. He also saw symbolic and allegorical significance to these practices, but the literal practice of the law remained important to him as well, unlike other Jewish allegorists in his context. For example, while Philo saw symbolic significance in the Jewish Sabbath, he believed that, in literal practice, Jews should also not 'light a fire or till the ground or carry a load or call a meeting or sit in judgment or seek deposits or recover debts' (*Mig.* 91). Similarly, while the symbolic significance of circumcision was primary for Philo, he strongly affirmed its literal practice as well (*Mig.* 92).[9] Philo valued the literal Jerusalem Temple, even though its greater significance was allegorical (cf. *Spec.* 1.67).

In *Creation* 1–2, Philo also indicates that Moses did not invent 'myth' in the Pentateuch.[10] Adam Kamesar hereby concludes that Philo did not see these books overall as mimetic or fictional but rather as didactic literature.[11] We can assume that Philo believed that individuals like Abraham, Isaac, Jacob, Joseph and Moses were real people who had once lived and walked the earth. We should also note that Philonists generally consider the treatise *On the Creation* as the first in a series of books within Philo's corpus known as the *Exposition of the Law*.[12] This collection is the least allegorical of Philo's three exegetical series and possibly aimed at a broader readership. It thus makes sense that Philo's interpretation would stay on more a literal level in this series.

By contrast, Philo's two other series, the *Allegorical Commentary* and *Questions and Answers on Genesis and Exodus*, utilized allegorical interpretation significantly more in their engagement with the Pentateuch. *Questions and Answers* gives not only literal but also deeper allegorical understandings of Genesis and Exodus. Then his series known as the *Allegorical Commentary* gives his most extensive allegorical understandings of the Pentateuch.[13] The relationship between the literal and the allegorical meanings of a passage to Philo was like the relationship between the body and the soul. In a passage with vocabulary similar to Col. 2.17 and Heb. 10.1, Philo encourages interpreters to move beyond the literal interpretation of the Tower of Babel story and 'go on to the figurative benefit. They should consider that the letters of the oracles are like the shadows of bodies, while the values revealed are the truly underlying realities' (*Conf.* 190).

---

[8] An early treatment of those in Philo's context who read the Scriptures literally was Montgomery J. Shroyer, 'Alexandrian Jewish Literalists', *JBL* 55 (1936): 261–84. Interestingly, some in Philo's world dismissed the Jewish Scriptures *because* they took them literally (e.g. *Conf.* 2–3).

[9] Interestingly, Philo did not seem to find much practical value in the food laws, even though he probably kept them in a general way. See Kenneth Schenck, *A Brief Guide to Philo* (Louisville: Westminster John Knox, 2005), 35–6.

[10] Cf. also *Mos.* 2.46-7 and *Praem.* 1–2.

[11] Adam Kamesar, 'Biblical Interpretation in Philo', in *The Cambridge Companion to Philo* (ed. Adam Kamesar; Cambridge: Cambridge University, 2009), 65–91, esp. 75–7.

[12] Of the surviving writings of Philo, the following are usually included within this series: *Creation, Abraham, Joseph, Decalogue, Special Laws, Virtues,* and *Rewards.*

[13] The surviving treatises in this series include *Allegorical Interpretation, Cherubim, Sacrifices, Worse, Posterity, Giants, Unchangeable, Agriculture, Planting, Drunkenness, Sobriety, Confusion, Migration, Heir, Preliminary Studies, Flight, Names, God,* and *Dreams.*

While Philo often considered both literal and allegorical interpretations of the same passages to be valid, in some instances, he did move to the figurative or allegorical because he considered a literal interpretation to be problematic (*defectus literalis*). The statement in Gen. 6.6 that God changed his mind was one such occasion. Philo considered the notion that the unchangeable God might change his mind to be one of the worst impieties possible (e.g. *Deus* 22). Accordingly, he does not take this statement straightforwardly but interprets it in terms of the foreknowledge of God and the fact that all of time is a present existence to God (*Deus* 29, 32). Similarly, Philo rejects the possibility that someone might actually hide from God, so rejects out of hand the apparent literal sense of Gen. 3.8 (*Leg.* 3.4). No one could possibly hide him or herself from God.

When Philo did shift into allegorical interpretation, he usually did so in predictable ways. One of the most common allegories to which Philo turned was the so-called 'allegory of the soul.'[14] In this allegory, figures such as those in the Adam and Eve story come to be symbols of the faculties of the soul. Adam becomes a symbol of mind and Eve a symbol of sense perception. The serpent then represents pleasure. This sort of anthropological allegory carried with it moral implications for the way individuals should conduct themselves in the world.

Other allegorical interpretations are also common in Philo. One that he shared with his environment was the tendency to see cosmological and numerological symbolism in the Pentateuch. Like other Jewish thinkers, Philo could see the temple as a microcosm of the universe (e.g. *Spec.* 1.66). The six days of creation find in the number six a perfect number that is equal both to the sum and the product of its factors (*Opif.* 13). It suggests the orderliness of creation, the productivity of creation, and the combination of both male and female. We repeatedly find Philo drawing allegorical significance from the numbers in the Pentateuch.

Two further allegories worth mentioning are (1) those relating to God, the Logos and the Powers of God, and (2) those relating to Abraham, Isaac and Jacob as types of humans. The Logos, of course, featured large in Philo's allegorical agenda. On any number of exegetical occasions, he allegorically identified elements in the biblical text with the Word of God, including Bezalel who fashioned the tabernacle (*Leg.* 3.96), the sword of the angels that guarded the Garden of Eden (*Cher.* 35), Aaron (*Her.* 201), and the high priest in general (e.g. *Mig.* 102; *Fug.* 108), to name only a few examples.[15] The Powers of God related to the two names for God in Genesis – *theos* and *kyrios*. Philo related these to the creative/beneficent and the royal/punitive aspects of God respectively. Here we see Philo's astute eye for detail in the biblical text, although he uses it in the service of allegory.[16] With regard to Abraham, Isaac and Jacob, they served Philo as allegorical representatives of three types of virtuous human (e.g. *Abr.* 52). Jacob is a person who becomes virtuous by practice. Abraham represents the person

---

[14] For a helpful analysis of Philo's sense of this allegory, see Thomas H. Tobin, *The Creation of Man: Philo and the History of Interpretation* (CBQMS 14; Washington DC: Catholic Biblical Association, 1983).
[15] For a classic text in Philo on the various names of the Logos, see *Conf.* 146.
[16] His anticipation of later source hypothesis in this regard is striking.

who becomes virtuous by way of instruction. Isaac meanwhile, is the person who is virtuous by nature, needing neither instruction nor practice to become virtuous.

What we find in Philo's hermeneutic, then, is not an inattentiveness to the details of immediate literary context but an approach that often used those details intentionally in the service of a different hermeneutical agenda than that of modern exegesis. Although Philo is not always aware when he is interpreting out of context, he may have been more aware than many a pre-critical interpreter who *thinks* he or she is reading in context. For Philo, the shift to figural and allegorical interpretation was often a conscious one. Further, he was not unlike some of his contemporaries who practised theological interpretation in his reinterpretations of texts whose literal meanings he found to be problematic. Potential meanings for the text that conflict with Christian orthodoxy are rejected in deference to interpretations that are more amenable to Christian faith.

2 The meanings of words

In the remainder of the chapter, we look in more detail at Philo's engagement with specific elements of context. His approach to the meanings of words is an appropriate place to begin. To what extent did Philo interpret words in context? What we find is that Philo had a penchant for finding deeper meanings to words in their etymologies, as well as a tendency to incorporate specific words of the text into his allegories in a 'this is that' fashion. From the standpoint of modern exegesis, both of these practices are non-contextual in nature.

The etymological fallacy is well known, even if all too common in mid-twentieth-century biblical scholarship. The history of a word's meaning in the past, including its etymology, does not determine the contemporary meaning of a word in general, let alone its meaning in a specific context. For this reason, even if Philo's etymologies were correct, his interpretations based on them would likely be extensively non-contextual.[17] However, his understandings of etymologies – probably themselves derived from other sources – are often wildly inaccurate in themselves.[18] Take his sense that the name Abraham meant, 'chosen father of sound' (*Abr.* 82). Having defined his name in this way, Philo then connects sound to the spoken logos and father to the ruling mind. None of these understandings are accurate in relation to the original, contextual meaning of any text associated with Abraham.

Of more interest to students of the New Testament is Philo's interpretation of Melchizedek, king of Salem. Similar to Heb. 7.1-2, Philo understands the name to mean 'righteous king' and the connection to Salem to mean that he is a king of peace (*Leg.* 3.79). The text of Gen. 14.18-20 makes no use of either of these etymologies. Nothing in the context of Genesis suggests that the Hebrew meaning of the word *Salem* played any role in the meaning of these verses. Similarly, no attention is drawn to the

---

[17] The Hebrew language arguably did play upon etymology in a way that other languages do not. This dynamic suggests that the *culture* of the Hebrew-speaking world may have assigned contemporary meaning with some interaction with etymology.
[18] See n. 2 above.

name Melchizedek in the text, although we can imagine that the name could have had significance to the first audiences of Genesis. Almost predictably, Philo goes on to see the Melchizedek of the text as symbolic of the Logos.

Certainly within Philo's allegories, individual words/elements in the biblical narratives took on symbolic meanings unrelated to the contexts of those texts. As an example, Philo interprets the robe of the high priest allegorically in a way that is meant to be a likeness of the universe (*Spec.* 1.82-97). So the dark colour and roundness of the garment symbolizes the air, since air is black and stretches from below the moon to just above the lowest recesses of the earth (1.85). The breastplate symbolizes heaven with its shoulder emeralds of great value, both circular to represent the hemispheres above and below the earth (1.86). Twelve stones on the breast represent the zodiac (1.87). These meanings for the various words in the text have no obvious relationship to the context of the Exodus 28 text.

Various Philonists have also noted Philo's use in his interpretations of expressions like *tout' estin* ('that is') and *ison* ('equal to').[19] For example, in *Cherubim* 17, Philo is interpreting the comment in Num. 5.18 that a wife under scrutiny for possible adultery is to have her hair uncovered (LXX). What does it mean for her hair to be uncovered? Philo says, 'It has been appointed to the priest and prophet, Reason, to cause the soul "to stand before God" with uncovered head (that is, with the soul's primary doctrine naked and its intentions stripped).' Philo uses the expression *tout' estin* to equate the uncovering of the woman's head in Numbers with the nakedness of our souls before God (cf. Heb. 4.12-13).

This whole section is a case study in Philonic exegesis. It begins with the question of what it means to say that the cherubim were set 'over against' Paradise (*Cher.* 11; Gen. 3.24). The question of this expression's meaning leads Philo to a discussion of three meanings to the phrase: a hostile sense, a sense of judgement and a sense of intimacy. Philo here is performing a word study on the expression 'over against', with an allegorical twist. He finds an example of the first usage in the verse that says Cain dwelt in Nod 'over against' Eden. Allegorically, Nod represents the inner turmoil that is opposed to Eden, which is true delight (12).

Philo goes on to give multiple interpretations of what the cherubim represent in the Genesis passage. His interpretation clearly assumes that multiple interpretations can be valid. The highest interpretation is a mystical one, one that came 'from my own soul', which he says is often God-possessed and receives oracles about things it does not know.[20] Turning to a familiar theme, he suggests that the two cherubim represent the two powers of God. One represents God's goodness (*theos*), the other his authority (*kyrios*). Meanwhile, the sword represents the Logos (*Cher.* 27–8).

Philo's interpretation of words is thus a particular hermeneutical mixture of contextual and non-contextual elements. On the one hand, he is highly attentive to

---

[19] For example, Maximilianus Adler, *Studien zu Philon von Alexandreia* (Breslau: Marcus, 1929), 23; Peder Borgen, *Philo of Alexandria: An Exegete for His Time* (SNT 86; Leiden: Brill, 1997), 154; 'Philo – An Interpreter of the Laws of Moses', in *Reading Philo: A Handbook of Philo of Alexandria* (ed. Torey Seland; Grand Rapids: Eerdmans, 2014), 91.

[20] It is tempting to compare Philo at this point to charismatic interpreters of the biblical text today, although his mysticism was far more rational in orientation. For a discussion of Philo as a mystic, see David Winston, 'Philo's Mysticism', *SPhA* 8 (1996): 74–82.

minute details in the Greek text. On the other, his hermeneutic uses these details primarily to serve non-literal purposes in interpretation. He shows the ability to perform word studies, much as we teach in the modern inductive Bible study classroom. However, these studies in Philo usually turn quickly to allegory and typologies. Throughout the process, his work draws on etymological and overload fallacies to reach his desired interpretive ends.

3 Attention to grammar

Grammar as we think of it today is not the grammar of Philo's day. In his day, 'grammar' was the first subject of study in the general education of the highly privileged, the course of study called the *enkyklios paideia* (e.g. *Cong.* 11).[21] However, grammar referred at that time to the overall study of Greek poets and historians (*Cong.* 15). By contrast, when we speak of grammar today, we refer to the observation of items such as case and number in nouns, tense and mood in verbs, or the syntax of clauses. Nevertheless, although he did not call it grammar, Philo did make observations about grammatical aspects of the biblical texts he interpreted. These are observations of context, and Philo was astute at making them. Further, Philo asked questions about his grammatical observations, as all good exegetes do. As we have come to expect, Philo does not diverge from modern interpretive method in his attention to detail but rather in the hermeneutic he uses to move from observation to interpretation.

For example, Philo observes correctly that the commandments of the Decalogue are addressed in the singular rather than the plural: 'You [singular] shall not kill' (*Dec.* 36). As all good exegetes should, he then asks why the singular is used instead of the plural and proceeds to give three reasons as answers (*Dec.* 37–43). Two of his answers almost certainly introduce extraneous meaning into the text, namely, his claim that the singular implies that every individual is equal in worth to the whole nation and his sense that God values each individual no matter how humble. However, his third explanation focuses on the importance of every individual keeping the command, as opposed to a corporate command to which an individual might take exception. This answer may actually come close to the real answer to the question.

On another occasion, he uses the presence and absence of the article on the word *theos* to solve a theological conundrum posed by the Greek text of Gen. 31.13 (*Somn.* 1.227-30). The Septuagint at this point does not render Bethel as a place name in Greek but rather translates 'at Bethel' rather woodenly as 'in the place of God' (*en topō theou*). The ambiguity of this phrase leads Philo to ask whether the text pictures *two* Gods. Since there is only one God, Philo notes that the first mention of God in Gen. 31.13 has the article: 'I am *the* God.' However, the rendering of Bethel as 'place of God' does not have the article. Philo uses this grammatical observation to argue

---

[21] For an excellent overview of Graeco-Roman education in Philo's day, see Erkki Koskenniemi, 'Philo and Classical Education', in *Reading Philo*, 102-28.

that the second mention of God refers to the Logos rather than to the one who is truly God.

In this case, the translation in front of Philo catalysed an interpretation that was rather foreign to the original meaning of the passage. Similarly, his hermeneutic led him to see the Logos in a passage completely devoid of such a concept. Nevertheless, in both the examples above, Philo paid keen attention to the grammatical aspects of the passage in question. We might say that Philo had extensive skills of observation on the level of detail. His primary mode of exegesis – question and answer – led him to ask important exegetical questions. From an original meaning standpoint, his failing was that he did not use context to answer those questions.

4 Immediate literary context

In both Philo's *Allegorical Commentary* and his *Questions and Answers on Genesis and Exodus*, he proceeds verse by verse through the biblical text. While modern commentaries often approach the biblical text in a similar way, the effect in Philo is to atomize the text and remove it from its train of thought, not entirely unlike those who use proof texts or quote memory verses out of context today. Philo's method is often midrashic, especially in the *Allegorical Commentary*. He begins with the focal Scripture, which, by way of catchwords and other techniques, leads him to other passages that he uses to shed light on the initial passage.[22] This use of Scripture to interpret Scripture is usually non-contextual, for it does not take into account the individual historical and literary contexts of each passage.

Nevertheless, Philo does not always ignore the train of thought in a passage. In *Creation* 77, Philo rightly asks why humanity is created last in the series of creations in Genesis 1. A modern exegete might answer that Genesis 1 presents humanity as the climax of the creation, a being that is unique in the sense that humans are made in the image of God as ruler of all (cf. Gen. 1.27-8). Philo incorporates these aspects of the text into thoughts that, as we might expect, extend well beyond the text. He assumes, for example, that the other creations are part of a 'feast' prepared for humanity (*Opif.* 78). God gets everything prepared before he brings in the guest of honour. Philo also recognized the dynamic of rulership in Genesis 1, probably key to the original sense of the image of God in 1.27. As humanity comes last, the other creatures are amazed and give humanity homage (83). Philo thus observed correctly the general climax of the train of thought in Genesis 1 with the creation of humanity, yet moved beyond it with his characteristic interests and themes as well.

It is perhaps worth noting that *Creation* is part of Philo's series the *Exposition of the Law*, the least allegorical of his three commentary series. It is thus the least atomistic of his series exegetically. Philo's two-volume *Life of Moses* may have introduced this series, and its first volume largely follows the plot of Exodus in its presentation of Moses as king. As we would expect of an ancient *bios*, Philo does interject morals he sees in the

---

[22] The catchword method is called *gezerah shewa* and can be seen at work in a New Testament passage like Heb. 4.1-11.

story of Moses and draws both positive and negative examples from it.[23] Further, he does not have the modern goal of identifying what the 'evaluative point of view' of Exodus *itself* might be on its own terms.[24] As a pre-critical interpreter, he largely uses the text as a mirror of the values he already has.

As an example, Philo's exposition of the story of Moses at the burning bush largely follows the train of thought and sequence of events in Exodus 3-4 (*Mos.* 1.63-84). Moses is shepherding when he notices a bush that is aflame but not burning up. An angel appears to him, and God portends Israel's exodus. God reveals his name and gives Moses signs to convince the Israelites to believe. Philo thus correctly observes the train of thought of the story. Philo correctly observes other details of the text, such as the way the Exodus text has God's direct speech (3.4) and yet speaks of the angel of the LORD appearing in the bush (3.2). At the same time, Philo sees a more profound symbolism in this story than we find in Exodus itself. He takes this scene as a description of Israel's situation in Egypt at that time. Metaphorically speaking, Israel is the bush and the fire is Egypt, bent on consuming Israel (*Mos.* 1.67). The fire of Egypt will not consume Israel, but Israel will prick its enemies.

If we were to use the model of Paul Ricoeur, Philo was incredibly adept at observing the 'world within the text.'[25] However, he was not paradigmatically equipped or orientated to answer interpretive questions to any great degree based on the 'world behind the text.' Rather, he answered interpretive questions primarily on the basis of his own definitions and assumptions in the 'world in front of the text.' When he read these assumptions into what he took as the literal meaning of the text, he did so without realizing it. At other times, he intentionally allegorized the text in keeping with his hermeneutical paradigms. Nevertheless, even in such cases, he believed that these meanings were truly in the text.

5 Broader literary context

Philo viewed the Pentateuch as a single literary piece. We thus would not expect him to factor into his interpretation the potential impact of multiple sources redacted together into a unified whole. Like non-contextual interpreters today, Philo did not account for the repetition of similar stories with source theories. However, unlike many readers today, his penchant for allegory provided other ways to read such doublets.

---

[23] Jewish writings that retell biblical stories are sometimes categorized as 'rewritten Bible'. Cf. Borgen, *Philo*, 63–79, following the lead of Philip S. Alexander, 'Retelling the Old Testament', in *It Is Written: Scripture Citing Scripture: Essays in Honour of Barnabas Lindars* (ed. D. A. Carson and H. G. M. Williamson; Cambridge: Cambridge University, 1988), 99–121, esp. 116.

[24] Narrative criticism asks what the implied, evaluative perspective of the text is towards various events in the story. For example, Acts 2.43-7 does not merely *describe* what community life was like in the early Church. It aims to *endorse* this form of community life as an ideal and may even idealize the life of the early Church. For a recent discussion of point of view in biblical narratives, see Gary Yamasaki, *Perspective Criticism: Point of View and Evaluative Guidance in Biblical Narrative* (Eugene: Cascade, 2012). See also the older and more general introduction to narrative criticism by Mark A. Powell, *What Is Narrative Criticism* (Minneapolis: Fortress, 1991).

[25] For the three worlds of the text, see Paul Ricoeur, *Interpretation Theory: Discourse and the Surplus of Meaning* (Fort Worth: Texas Christian University, 1976), 87–8, 92–5.

For example, Philo does not even make mention of the fact that Abraham and Sarah seem to be making the same mistake again with Abimelech in Genesis 20 that they made with Pharaoh in Genesis 12. Rather, both Pharaoh and Abimelech allegorically represent the licentious person (*Abr.* 103; *QG* 4.61). Similarly, the double creation stories of Genesis 1 and 2 provide an opportunity for Philo to see an allegory of the soul. The human created in Gen. 1.27 is the ideal human, while the man created in Genesis 2 is the shadowy person of flesh (e.g. *Opif.* 134–5).[26]

Within Philo's assumptions, however, he does see patterns in the overall shape of these texts, patterns that do fit with the canonical shape of the Pentateuch. In his series the *Exposition of the Law*, he analyses the structure of the Pentateuch and divides it into three parts: (1) the creation, (2) the history and (3) the legislation (*Praem.* 1). This outline does indeed correspond roughly to (1) Genesis 1–2, (2) Genesis 3– Exodus 19 and (3) Exodus 20–Deuteronomy 34. Philo also sees other patterns that may or may not have been intended by the redactors of the Pentateuch. For example, Philo saw the Decalogue of Exodus 20 as a general statement that was played out in the specific legislation of the remaining books (e.g. *Praem.* 2; *Spec.* 1.1). Further, he saw the lives of Abraham, Isaac and Jacob as the exemplars or embodiment of the legislation that followed, so that the concrete laws of the Pentateuch were copies of their lives (*Abr.* 3).

Beyond these macro-patterns that Philo saw in the Pentateuch, we have already mentioned the midrashic technique Philo often used in his *Allegorical Commentary*, interpreting a primary text by way of secondary texts. Philo usually made these connections by way of a catchword or some other more or less superficial commonality between the two texts. For example, *Heir* 22–62 give Philo's interpretation of Gen.15.2 LXX; 'Master, what will you give me, for I continue childless, and the son of Masek born in my house is this Eleazar of Damascus.' Philo interprets the verse almost word by word, in the process reaching out to fifteen other texts (in the order of his referencing: Isa. 1.4; Exod. 4.12; Gen. 18.27; 33.5; 31.28; 31.14-15; Exod. 18.7; Deut. 21.15-17; Gen. 29.31; 3.20; Lev. 17.11; Gen. 2.7; 1.27; Exod. 18.4; and Gen. 22.12). Isaiah 1.4 relates to knowledge of when to speak to God. Exodus 4.12 relates to God giving Moses knowledge of when to speak. Genesis 18.27 addresses Abraham's general humility when speaking to the Lord. From a modern exegetical perspective, only the last of these is a potentially relevant text when it comes to literary context that legitimately might bear on the interpretation of the original passage.

We reach the same conclusion again. Philo was incredibly observant, and he was able to see overarching patterns to a literary text. However, he was much more interested in deeper allegorical meanings he found in the text. He did not draw on broader literary context as evidence to build an interpretation but as corroboration of an existing one. For him, all the Scriptures taught the same acontextual, universal truths. For the modern exegete, by contrast, the meaning of each passage relates to an individual, contextual moment in history.

---

[26] Again, see Tobin, *Creation of Man* for a thorough analysis of Philo's allegory of the soul.

6 Historical context

We can divide the historical contexts of biblical texts into three general categories: (1) general historical referents, (2) situational factors behind each writing and (3) social–cultural dimensions to the text. Of these, Philo was largely unaware of the last two. On the one hand, he had the advantage of living in a world that was closer to the Ancient Near East than the modern world – especially the so-called Western world. On the other hand, the Graeco-Roman world was quite different in itself from the Ancient Near East. Additionally, Philo was not hermeneutically wired to think of the biblical texts in terms of situational factors. For him, they were collections of divine teaching with universal, timeless import. His interpretations are thus largely ahistorical in the same way that pre-critical interpreters today tend to read the Bible as one book written by God directly for all time – meaning directly to them.

Occasionally, Philo does engage sociocultural background. In the passage from *Heir* discussed in the previous section, one of the texts to which he links Gen. 15.2 is Deut. 21.15-17, which legislates the way in which one distributes inheritance among sons from multiple wives. Although a modern exegete would note that Philo is using a text purported to be several centuries later than the time of Abraham, it is an example of Philo bringing sociocultural, historical information (albeit from a biblical text) to bear on the interpretation of Gen. 15.2. Philo's discussion of adultery in *Decalogue* 121–31 also brings sociocultural assumptions from his world that probably approach some of the original connotations of the prohibition in terms of honour–shame and social upheaval. Philo notes that adultery brings three households into ruin (*Dec.* 126). The husband of the woman involved is stripped of his hopes for legitimate offspring. The woman and adulterer are disgraced, and their families will be the object of outrage. Philo correctly notes that the interconnections between people and families can result in the event touching the whole *polis* (127). These dynamics arguably applied to the Ancient Near Eastern context of Israel just as they did in the time of Philo.

Aside from Philo's historical and apologetic treatises, which addressed actual figures and groups from his own day,[27] Philo's engagement with the historical referents of the Pentateuch was more literary in nature than historical. Again, in the passage from *Heir* interpreting Gen. 15.2, Philo is not interested in the figures of 'Masek' or Eliezer as historical persons.[28] He is not interested in Damascus as a historical place. He takes *Masek* to mean 'from a kiss', leading to a sequence of allegorically enriching but exegetically irrelevant thoughts. Damascus means, 'the blood of a sackcloth robe,' while Eliezer means, 'God is my helper.' As is typical of pre-critical interpreters, the Scriptural texts become a world of ideas into which the interpreter inserts him or herself, not a witness to meanings located at a particular place and time in history.

---

[27] Four of his writings are generally placed in this category: *Flaccus, Embassy, Hypothetica,* and *Contemplative Life*.

[28] The expression 'son of Masek' itself is a Septuagintal mistranslation or overly literal translation of the Hebrew idiom, *ben mesek*, which probably meant something like, 'son of possession' – that is, 'heir'.

Conclusion

By now it should be abundantly clear that, while Philo paid close attention to literary clues in the context of the biblical writings, he largely was not a contextual interpreter as we would understand one today. The canons of contextual interpretation today aim to induce the historical meaning of the texts, drawing on both literary and historical evidence. For literary evidence, we observe grammatical and syntactical features of the text. We observe how one thought flows into the next, looking for connecting words and implicit relationships between sentences. We locate the meaning of an individual passage within an overall work, taking into account the possibility of sources and redaction. For historical evidence, we examine how words in the original language were being used at the time of writing. We try to identify the historical referents of the text, the specific occasion that gave rise to it and the relevant sociocultural background.

This process of contextual exegesis was largely foreign to Philo. For Philo, the text gave the inspired reader access to the world of God's ideas. The meaning of Scripture was not a function of the world in which it was written, but Scripture was a world in itself into which the interpreter entered.[29] The modern exegete reads the Bible as part of the world and part of the truth. Philo read the world and truth from within the text of Scripture. So while Philo paid keen attention to contextual elements of the text, they did not primarily serve as determiners of meaning. Rather, they served as symbolic embodiments of higher, timeless, non-contextual truths.

---

[29] Although the work of Hans Frei addressed interpreters of the eighteenth and nineteenth centuries, it remains helpful for understanding premodern hermeneutical paradigms. Cf. *The Eclipse of Biblical Narrative: A Study in Eighteenth and Nineteenth Century Hermeneutics* (New Haven: Yale University, 1980).

8

Old Testament context: Insights from the Dead Sea Scrolls

Benjamin Wold

The extent to which citations of Old Testament (OT) passages in Qumran discoveries are informed and shaped by their context(s) is a sub-question related to the larger issue of the interpretation of Scripture. Like other Second Temple period literature, the Hebrew Scriptures were the source and framework for shaping and composing theological ideas. Reflected in the interpretation of the OT texts are attempts to address a wide variety of issues; they seek to solve linguistic problems, deal with perceived gaps, harmonize and integrate laws, and wrestle with material that came to be at odds with ethical or moral positions in another generation. Ancient Jewish exegetes also searched for meanings from, and answers to, OT passages that did not always seem to ask the same questions at a later time.[1] The aim here is to contextualize questions about 'Old Testament context' within the particularities of the Qumran discoveries and the variety of ways that Scripture was used.

The publication history of the Dead Sea Scrolls – namely the release of Cave 1 materials in the 1950s and Cave 4 materials in the 1990s – has resulted in misperceptions of these discoveries and their significance. It is worthwhile to remind ourselves that this is not a monolithic corpus of compositions, and it is more accurate to refer to the Scrolls as a 'repository' rather than a 'library'. Scroll discoveries in the eleven caves around Khirbet Qumran contained the remains of about 930 manuscripts, which survive in more than 15,000 fragments. The vast majority of manuscripts were found in Cave 4 (ca. 10,000 frags. preserving 574 mss.). In total among the 11 Caves, 760 of these manuscripts were composed in Hebrew, 140 in Aramaic and 30 in Greek. Out of these, 222 are 'biblical', and it is now common knowledge that every book in the OT is preserved in at least fragmentary form except for Esther and Nehemiah. Around 140 of the manuscripts preserve the remnants of previously known Jewish religious documents such as apocryphal and 'pseudepigraphical' works. Nearly 600 manuscripts preserve 300 previously unknown documents. Since the 1990s, three divisions are typically used to think about these Scrolls. They are (1) biblical texts (i.e. OT), (2) Yaḥad

---

[1] Moshe J. Bernstein, 'Interpretation of Scriptures', in *Encyclopedia of the Dead Sea Scrolls* (ed. Lawrence H. Schiffman and James C. VanderKam; New York: Oxford University Press, 2000), 376–83.

texts (i.e. 'sectarian') or (3) early Jewish texts (i.e. non-sectarian).[2] Therefore, in asking questions about how context informs biblical citations, this is treated below in two separate sections: section 1 addresses Yaḥad texts and section 2 previously unknown non-Yaḥad texts.[3]

Within Qumran discoveries, there is no unified way that OT compositions were interpreted or a single understanding of the message they were to communicate. It is far beyond the scope of this study to treat the interpretation of Scripture in all of its varieties, but rather the point of departure here is specific questions related to explicit, or nearly explicit, uses of the OT.[4] The seminal article on OT citations in the Qumran Scrolls, as it relates to our question of context, is that of Joseph Fitzmyer.[5] However, in his study of explicit citations, Fitzmyer leaves out of consideration, for the most part, *pesharim* and instead focuses mainly on other Yaḥad compositions (esp. CD, 1QS and 1QM).[6] In this regard, the non-explicit use of the OT – whether by allusion, echo or rewriting – is much more dominant than direct quotations.[7] There is a fundamental difference between explicit and implicit uses of the OT that effects the direction of the line of questioning here. Explicit ones use and present OT passages as divine authority. Implicit ones use biblical materials to form the texture of their compositions and, in so doing, recreate, by identifying with biblical authors, a biblical atmosphere (e.g. the Hodayot).[8] Therefore, when asking how and if OT contexts carry over when Scripture is cited in their new contexts, the dominance of non-explicit usages already indicate a lack of interest into original context(s). Moreover, the widespread practice of rewriting Scripture as found among the Scrolls, and throughout early Jewish literature, was a particularly dominant exegetical activity which is an expansion upon and reinvention of a biblical text.[9]

---

[2] Devorah Dimant, 'The Library of Qumran: Its Content and Character', in *The Dead Sea Scrolls Fifty Years after their Discovery* (ed. L. H. Schiffman, E. Tov and J. C. VanderKam; Jerusalem: IES, 2000), 170–6. The misperception that continues to this day is that there are only two divisions: biblical and sectarian.

[3] Another possible approach, which is a different line of questing than taken here, is to explore intertextuality within the biblical texts themselves.

[4] For example, comprehensive studies like Michael Fishbane, 'Use, Authority and Interpretation of Mikra at Qumran', in *Mikra: Text, Translation, Reading, and Interpretation of the Hebrew Bible in Ancient Judaism and Early Christianity* (ed. M. J. Mulder; CRINT 2/1; Assen: Van Gorcum, 1988), 339–77.

[5] Joseph Fitzmyer, 'The Use of Explicit Old Testament Quotations in Qumran Literature and in the New Testament', *NTS* (1960–1): 297–333; re-published in idem., *Essays on the Semitic Background of the New Testament* (SBS 5; Atlanta: Scholars Press, 1974), 3–58.

[6] Fitzmyer, 'The Use of Explicit', 5–6 explains that since *pesher* does not occur in the NT it is not relevant to his comparative study. The breakdown of explicit citations is 30 in CD, 5 in 1QM, 4 in 4QFlorilegium and 3 in 1QS. Therefore, Fitzmyer's study is predominately a study of the use of scripture in CD. Pace Fitzmyer, cf. Acts 2.14ff. where Joel 3.1-5 is used in a pesher-like style.

[7] Devorah Dimant, 'Use and Interpretation of Mikra in the Apocrypha and Pseudepigrapha', in *Mikra: Text, Translation, Reading and Interpretation of the Hebrew Bible in Ancient Judaism and Early Christianity*. CRINT (II 1; ed. M. J. Mulder and H. Sysling; Philadelphia: Fortress Press, 1988), 379–419 (410); Cf. Casey D. Elledge, 'Exegetical Styles at Qumran: A Cumulative Index and Commentary', *RevQ* 21 (2003–4): 165–208.

[8] Dimant, 'Use and Interpretation', 419.

[9] George W. E. Nickelsburg, 'The Bible Rewritten and Expanded', in *Jewish Writings of the Second Temple Period* (ed. M. E. Stone; Assen: Van Gorcum, 1984), 89–156; Philip S. Alexander, 'Retelling the Bible', in *It is Written: Scripture Citing Scripture* (ed. D. A. Carson and H. G. M. Williamson; Cambridge: Cambridge University Press, 1988), 99–121 sees rewritten Bible as a distinct genre;

Fitzmyer identifies forty-two passages in the Damascus Document, Community Rule, War Scroll and 4QFlorilegium that contain explicit citations and use introductory formulae. Fitzmyer's study cannot be considered comprehensive and is focused exclusively on Yaḥad compositions. To date, there is no comprehensive study that systematically identifies or adjudicates biblical *citations* in Qumran discoveries. Armin Lange and Matthias Weigold exhaustively identify 'biblical quotations and allusions'; however, they do not distinguish between these two and the vast majority of those listed are allusions.[10] No attempt is made here to offer an exhaustive list of citations but rather to provide examples and analysis of explicit citations to demonstrate how OT context(s) were regarded.

One genre from Qumran deserves special mention because it cites the OT in a unique way. *Pesharim* were popular at Qumran and, at least in the case of the continuous style (i.e. systematically to a single book), are not known elsewhere. In regard to continuous *pesher*, commentaries on at least nine OT books were found; these are Isaiah (4Q161–65; 3Q4; 4Q515?), Hosea (4Q166–67), Micah (1Q14; 4Q168), Nahum (4Q169), Habakkuk (4QpHab), Zephaniah (1Q15; 4Q170), Psalms (1Q16; 4Q171; 4Q173; 4Q173a), Song of Songs? (4Q240), and Malachi (4Q253a). Among the most important thematic *pesharim* (i.e. in an anthology style) are 4QFlorilegium (4Q174), 4QTestimonia (4Q175), and 11QMelchizedek.

It is possible to make inferences about which OT texts were the most popular among the Qumran Scrolls. If the frequency of manuscripts discovered communicates popularity, then it is worth noting that the top twelve most frequent, in order of most to least, are Psalms (39 mss.), Deuteronomy (33 mss.), Genesis (24 mss.), Isaiah (22 mss.), Exodus (18 mss.), Leviticus (17 mss.), Numbers (11 mss.), the Minor Prophets (10 mss.), Daniel (8 mss.), Ezekiel (6 mss.), Jeremiah (6 mss.) and Job (6 mss.). In relationship to the number of manuscripts discovered, an important question here is the frequency of citations to a specific biblical book within the Qumran discoveries. An exhaustive list of all citations found in the Scrolls, that is, without being lumped together with allusions, is not available. However, James VanderKam and Peter Flint offer a reliable list of just

---

Michael Segal, 'Between Bible and Rewritten Bible', in *Biblical Interpretation at Qumran* (ed. M. Henze; Cambridge: Eerdmans, 2005), 10–28 rewriting is a way of appropriating the authority of the biblical text; Hindy Najman, *Seconding Sinai: The Development of Mosaic Discourse in Second Temple Judaism* (JSJSup 77; Leiden: Brill, 2003) frames her questions around authorial inscription and the authority a text claims for itself.

[10] Armin Lange and Matthias Weigold, *Biblical Quotations and Allusions in Second Temple Jewish Literature* (Göttingen; Oakville: VandenHoeck & Ruprecht, 2011), 259–344 and at 345–78 list uncertain quotations and allusions and at 379–84 Scrolls that do not contain any certain quotations or allusions to the Hebrew Bible. James C. VanderKam and Peter Flint, *The Meaning of the Dead Sea Scrolls: Their Significance for Understanding the Bible, Judaism, Jesus, and Christianity* (San Francisco, CA: HarperSanFrancisco, 2002), 427–33 list 'definite or reasonably so' quotations and allusions, however by 'allusion' they actually mean that sometimes it is not a quotation but rather a paraphrase. Lange and Weigold, *Biblical Quotations and Allusions in Second Temple Jewish Literature*, 17 imply criticism of VanderKam and Flint as not being comprehensive when they claim to be; however, as a narrower list of explicit or nearly explicit uses of the Bible it is far more useful than an exhaustive list that is composed of mostly allusions and echoes. Johann Maier, *Die Qumran-Essener: Die Texte vom Toten Meer, vol. 3: Einführung, Zeitrechnung, Register und Bibliographie*, UTB.W 1916 (München: Reinhardt, 1996), 161–82 has an index that includes allusions and quotations that is neither exhaustive nor does it distinguish between the two.

citations and make no claims that it is comprehensive.[11] Following Vanderkam and Flint, the frequency of manuscripts and explicit uses of the OT have some correlations. The most frequently cited OT books according them are Isaiah (109x), Psalms (75x), Deuteronomy (45x), Genesis (27x), Leviticus (27x), Numbers (24x) and Exodus (18x). The number of manuscripts of specific OT documents at Qumran parallels, to a great extent, the frequency of these intertextual occurrences in the NT; that is, the five books of Moses, Psalms and Isaiah are the most frequently cited in the NT too.

1 Yaḥad literature

Two sets of criteria may be used to adjudicate which texts belong to the Yaḥad and which do not. Because Fitzmyer treats 'sectarian' texts alone, these criteria also enable us to reflect on underlying assumptions of these texts that influence the use of the OT. Indeed, when we turn to Fitzmyer's classifications, while the first three may be applicable to non-Yaḥad texts, instances of the fourth (i.e. *eschatological*) may be scarce or seldom present. The following characteristics exclude a composition from being a product of the Yaḥad: (1) a free use of the tetragrammaton; (2) disinterest to at least attempt to reconcile calendrical issues with the 364-day solar calendar (i.e. 354-day lunar calendar); (3) any text written in Aramaic or Greek since the Yaḥad only wrote in Hebrew; and (4) any document produced before ca. 150 BCE when the Yaḥad community first developed. If a composition reflects any of the following characteristics then they may, but not necessarily, be ascribed to the Yaḥad: (1) use of sobriquets ('nicknames'); (2) a critical distance from the Jerusalem Temple and its priesthood; (3) a clear understanding that the Jerusalem priests abandoned the Torah and that revelation and interpretation of Torah is given to the Teacher of Righteousness; and (4) a cosmic and ethical dualism, in which anyone who is not part of the Yaḥad has been predestined to perish in eschatological judgement.

A particularly valuable contribution that Fitzmyer makes in his study is the suggestion of four classifications into which his forty-two examples are categorized. A summary of these classes is offered here along with one example related to each:

1. *Literal or Historical*: the OT is cited in the same sense that it was intended by the original writers. In this category, every instance Fitzmyer gives is from the Damascus Document (CD VII 8-9; IX 2, 5, 7-8; X 16-17; XVI 6-7).[12] For instance, when CD X 16-17 cites Deut. 5.12 ('observe the Sabbath day and keep it holy'), the Deuteronomic Decalogue is cited in the same sense as originally intended: keeping the Sabbath.[13]

---

[11] James C. VanderKam and Peter Flint, *The Meaning of the Dead Sea Scrolls*, 427–33. They list 'definite or reasonably so' quotations and allusions; however by 'allusion' they actually mean that sometimes it is not a quotation but rather a paraphrase. Prophetic works are also frequently cited in their list because they are the subject of *pesharim*.

[12] 'CD' refers to the mss. discovered in the Cairo Geniza while '4QD' to the mss. from Qumran. These represent two distinct recensions, and here I follow Fitzmyer referring to CD because considerably more text is extant in CD. Any divergences between recensions are noted.

[13] Fitzmyer, 'The Use of Explicit', 19–20.

2. *Modernization*: the OT text refers to an event in its own contemporary scene, which is vague enough to be applied to an event in the history of the Yaḥad. Therefore, the general sense of the OT text is preserved but is applied to a new subject. An example of this use is found in CD IV 12-18 which cites Is. 24.17 ('panic, pit and net against you, earth-dweller!'); the vision of Isaiah is of catastrophe on the day of judgement and is applied in CD to the present wicked era of the author's own time, when Belial is set loose against Israel.
3. *Accommodation*: the OT text is lifted from its original context and modified or deliberately changed in order to adapt it to a new situation or purpose. Here we encounter a category under which non-verbatim citations may be found. As such, a great many passages could be described as accommodating OT texts. For instance, in the Community Rule (1QS V 17-18) there is a gloss of Is. 2.22 ('Shun the man whose breath is in his nostrils, for how much is he worth [כיא במה נחשב הואה]?'). The Hebrew term נחשב in Isaiah straightforwardly expresses: 'for what account are they' (i.e. mortal humanity). The meaning in the Community Rule is applied to being 'reckoned' into the community.
4. *Eschatological*: the OT text is seen to express a promise (or threat) about something that is to be accomplished in the eschaton. An instance of this use is found in CD XX 15-17 where Hos. 3.4 is cited ('there shall be no king, no prince, no judge, no-one who reproaches in justice'). CD takes the days described by Hosea to be comparable to the situation of a later time, a period spanning from the death of the Teacher of Righteousness until the destruction of the men of war who returned with the Man of Lies.

In general, the relevance of the historical setting means very little in these examples taken from Yaḥad texts. We may observe that OT passages were applied to the history of the group. There is a desire to inform their own recent history, the significance of an individual or a theological idea; in this way, they draw analogies between their community and Israel's history.[14] While there are clear stylistic and genre differences between CD, 1QS and 1QM (the latter two are categorized as 'rules'), *pesharim* follow these same basic tendencies.

Whether continuous or thematic *pesher*, Scripture has two levels of meaning: (1) the ordinary and (2) a level concealed and understood only to the elect and those possessing divine knowledge or understanding of mysteries. Our best instances of the continuous style come from Pesher Habakkuk; for example, 1QpHab IX 3-5 reads: '"Since you pillaged many peoples all the rest of the nations will pillage you" [Hab. 2.8], its interpretation [*pishro*] concerns the last priests of Jerusalem who will accumulate riches and loot from plundering the nations.' Within Fitzmyer's categories, this is an example of *modernization* and not *accommodation* because, in Habakkuk, the last generation is addressed and in 1QpHab this vision finds fulfilment in an end-time period during which the Teacher of Righteousness and his community live.[15] Therefore, this is the sense of the OT text, but it is applied to a new context.

---

[14] Ibid., 53.
[15] Fitzmyer only lists two occurrences of OT citations in 1QpHab (VII 1-5; VII 7-8), which are not counted among his '42' explicit quotations; therefore, one assumes that these two passages are indicative of how this *pesher* uses OT and is applicable to other occurrences.

A number of compositions found at Qumran have been labelled or described as 'Midrash'. While there are similarities between Midrash and Pesher there are significant distinctions as well. *Pesharim* quote an entire passage of Scripture and follow it with an interpretation that has a tenuous relationship to the biblical passage. Rabbinic texts often cite single words and phrases and directly present their interpretation, oftentimes citing specific rabbis. Unlike Midrash, *pesharim* are always anonymous. Rabbinic texts are collections of statements, some of whose original contexts are unknown and some of whose original contexts were probably in non-midrashic settings; comments in the *pesharim* make sense only as commentaries on the biblical text. Presuppositions behind the *pesharim* and *midrashim* are different; the single purpose of the author(s) of the *pesharim* was to demonstrate that the biblical prophecies were coming into being in their community, while the rabbis had a variety of purposes for creating their *midrashim* and midrashic collections.

Some of the best examples of scriptural anthology found at Qumran (cf. 11QMelchizedek) are 4Q174 (4QFlorilegium; Latin for 'gathering of flowers') and 4Q175 (4QTestimonia, a title usually referring to a list of proof texts in classical works). Within Fitzmyer's scheme, both 4QFlorilegium and 4QTestimonia fall into two categories: *accommodation* and *eschatological*. Based upon palaeographic analysis, 4Q174 dates to the late first century BCE. References to the community's experiences align themselves with a date similar to Pesher Habakuk and a conflict with a Hasmonean high priest. That this document is to be located among the so-called 'sectarian' compositions is clear from the reference to the council of the Yaḥad in 4Q174 i 17. The community is also referred to with the sectarian terminology 'sons of light' in 4Q174 i 8. 4QTestimonia is also widely regarded as deriving from the Yaḥad. Because 4Q174 contains the phrase 'the last days', John Allegro initially referred to it as the 'Eschatological Midrash', which is not an accepted title today.

A major concern of 4QFlorilegium is the captivity of Israel, which is attributed in this composition to the ultimate adversarial character: Belial and the sons of Belial. A time is anticipated when the situation of ongoing captivity will be set straight and the elect of the elect, a remnant community that is the faithful of Israel, will be restored and the wicked will be judged. When considering the future, the author is particularly interested in a select number of passages that are interpreted in connection with the eschaton. These passages are 2 Sam. 7 (related to Exod. 15.17-18 because of a common interest in Israel as something that will be 'planted'); Ps. 2 (related to 2 Samuel 7 because of interest in a 'son'); and Deut. 33. Part of Israel's restoration in 4QFlorilegium is rebuilding the second temple and raising up anointed ones. The anointed ones in the fragment are found in 4Q174 i 19 which cites Ps. 2.1-2 ('[why ar]e the nations [in turmoil] and hatch the peoples [idle plots? The kings of the earth t]ake up [their posts and the rul]ers conspire together against the Lord and [his anointed one]') referring to the community.

4QFlorilegium envisages a future temple which is expressed with a Hebrew phrase that has been interpreted in more than one way: '*Miqdash Adam*' (i 6) in reference to Exod. 15.17-18 ('[the temple of] the Lord your hands will est[a]blish, the Lord will reign forever and ever').[16] On the one hand, this may be translated in relation to the

---

[16] See J. George Brooke, *Exegesis at Qumran: 4QFlorilegium in Its Jewish Context* (JSOTS 29; Sheffield: Sheffield University Press, 1985).

proper name of the first man Adam; on the other hand, one may understand 'humanity' (Hebrew אדם) more generally. Thus, several translations offered are 'sanctuary of Adam', 'human sanctuary' or a 'sanctuary *among* humanity'.

While an anthology collects excerpts, 4QFlorilegium goes beyond simply gathering passages. The concern of the author, which is the lens through which the OT passages are interpreted, is his community and how they have suffered and await a time of restoration and vindication. Therefore, the selected passages communicate about the present situation and more recent history of the community.

Four biblical passages frame 4QTestimonia, and the author has conveniently placed these in four separate paragraphs. Central to interpreting 4QTestimonia is to assess how these four passages relate to one another. The first citation is found in the OT (Masoretic Text) in Deut. 5.28-9 and 18.18-19, but 4QTestimonia is actually following Exod. 20.21 in the Samaritan Pentateuch. The author is citing a tradition from the Samaritan Pentateuch that merges these two passages from Deuteronomy. After this first paragraph, the next two passages, cited in paragraphs three and four, are straightforwardly from Num. 24.15-17 and Deut. 33.8-11.

The fourth and last passage in 4QTestimonia clearly reflects Josh. 6.26 ('Then Joshua charged them at that time, saying, "Cursed be the man before the Lord who rises up and builds the city of Jericho; he shall lay its foundation with his firstborn, and with his youngest he shall set up its gates."'), but should likely not be referred to as a 'citation', but rather an interpretation of Josh. 6.26 that was circulating in the period. This interpretation of Josh. 6.26 is also found in the Apocryphon of Joshua (4Q379 22 ii 7-14), a manuscript that may be dated considerably earlier than 4QTestimonia, and when 4QTestimonia uses Josh. 6.26, the adaptations and changes are the same as those found in the Apocryphon of Joshua. To explain this interpretive tradition by concrete example, 4QTestimonia and the Apocryphon of Joshua begin their citation of Josh. 6.26 and then stop near the middle in order to add a statement about the accursed one being a 'man of Belial'. Another addition is found at the conclusion of the citation where comments occur that are found only in these two Qumran Scrolls. Such observations indicate a common way of thinking about Josh. 6.26 and many have suggested that 4QTestimonia is actually quoting the Apocyrphon of Joshua as a source.[17]

That the author conceives of himself and his community as living in an end-time period and enduring persecution as a righteous community is suggested by the particular use of these four biblical citations. The first three paragraphs of 4QTestimonia take up passages to portray three messianic figures. Exod. 20.21 (=Deut. 5.28-9, 18.18-9) refers to the raising up of a prophet like Moses. Num. 24.15-17 is concerned with the expectation of royal and priestly messiahs collectively. Deuteronomy 33.8-11 is about a future high priest like Aaron. The man of Belial is convincingly taken as a reference to a corrupt Hasmonean ruler. The expectation of messianic figures underscores the interpretation of this manuscript as a work concerned with the fulfilment and expectation of the community in the eschaton.[18]

---

[17] Hanan Eshel, 'The Historical Background of the *Pesher* Interpreting Joshua's Curse on the Rebuilder of Jericho', *RevQ* 15 (1992): 409–20.

[18] Noteworthy is that this is a forward-looking fulfilment whereas NT texts are backward looking (i.e. using OT to demonstrate what occurred in Christ).

2 Previously unknown Non-Yaḥad literature

In addressing previously unknown non-Yaḥad literature, the aim is to avoid a treatment of the use of the OT in works such as Ben Sira, Jubilees or the Enochic tradition. How each of these examples of previously known compositions uses Scripture is exhaustively treated elsewhere and does not necessarily fall within Qumran studies per se. It is striking that in Fitzmyer's original study the majority of examples of scriptural citation are from CD and are otherwise relatively sparse. As we turn to quotations of the OT in this section, there are in fact a small number of explicit citations, especially ones that are introduced with a formula. Instead, the majority of instances fall into the category of *accommodation* by making slight alterations to the OT text. Another tendency is to take two or more passages and merge them together into a pastiche (e.g. Is. 61.1 and Ps. 146.5-8 in 4Q521 ii 8-13), which is also a characteristic of thematic *pesharim*. One particular use of the OT that is found at Qumran merits at least mention, namely that there are also a number of phylactery and *mezuzot* from Cave 4 (4Q128-55) which mostly cite Deuteronomy 5–6, 11 and Exodus 13, 20. Similar to section 1, Fitzmyer's categories are used and examples are given; however, *modernization* and *eschatological* are less helpful because they describe a use of the OT specific to the Yaḥad.

Literal or Historical. 4QTohorot^a (4Q274) is concerned with ritual purity and may or may not be a product of the Yaḥad. Joseph Baumgarten comments that 'the Qumran texts reflect the variety of means of lustration which were employed in the Second Temple era, when the maintenance of purity was a widely shared concern among Jewish pietists'.[19] Moreover, 4QTohorot is concerned to instruct about purity as it relates to women ('she shall …') which distances it from the Yaḥad. 4Q274 1 i 3-4 cite Lev. 13.45-6: 'Anyone of the unclean [wh]o [touches] him shall bathe in water and wash his clothes and afterwards he may eat; for this is as said, "Unclean, unclean!", shall he call out all the days [טמא טמא יקרא כול ימי].' Whereas in Leviticus 13 this is applied to a leper, in 4QTohorot^a it appears to be extended to other impure people: by analogy to the *zab* ('gonorrheic').[20] Therefore, this Qumran composition uses Leviticus in its original sense and only follows a wider application to the statement: 'unclean, unclean'.

Modernization. An indeterminate text that is difficult to assess is 4Q463 1 2-3 (Narrative D) which cites Lev. 26.44. An introductory formula is used when introducing Lev. 26.44 in 4Q463 1 2-3: '[sa]ying, even while they are in the lands of the[i]r enemies [I do not spurn them and do not reject them].' This may be an example of *modernization*; in Lev. 26.44 the word 'land' is singular and refers to Egypt, whereas 4QNarrative D has plural 'lands' which is applied to a different time of exile. One indication that this may be a Yaḥad text is an expression of opening ears to, presumably, hidden things and deeper matters.

Accommodation. There are a number of examples of OT texts being accommodated. Here three examples are given. Firstly, an instance of a nearly explicit use of Scripture from the wisdom composition called 4QInstruction (4Q415-18, 4Q423, 1Q26).

---

[19] DJD 35:92.
[20] DJD 35:101–2.

4QInstruction is replete with allusions to Genesis 2–3. One passage where Genesis plays a significant role is in 4Q416 2 iii-iv. Most reconstructions of 4Q416 2 iii 21-4Q416 2 iv 1 assume a verbatim citation of Gen. 2.24 ('walk together with the helpmeet of thy flesh [*According to the statute of God that a man should leave*] his father and mother And should cl[eave to his wife, so that they … should become one flesh]'), which would be the only explicit citation of a biblical passage in the document.[21] Alternatively, Elisha Qimron offers a theoretical reconstruction of Gen. 2.24 at the end of iii 21 and iv 1 that is a paraphrase.[22] In the biblical tradition, Gen. 2.24 may be interpreted as a man leaving his *Patria potestas* (i.e. his father's house) and joining his wife's *potestas*.[23] Lines 2–7 are concerned to instruct, *contra* Gen. 2.24, that when a daughter is given in marriage she moves from her own household to her husband's, and that he is the one who then has rightful authority over her (4Q416 2 iv 2-7). Therefore, reconstructing line 1 as a direct citation of Gen. 2.24 seems unlikely; instead, it is likely being accommodated by deliberately modifying it to fit with his view of women in their roles as wives and daughters.

Clear from the broader context of 4QInstruction is that justification for the authority of a husband over his wife is not straightforwardly derived from Gen. 3.16 but rather is asserted by reflecting on the two becoming one flesh (iii 21; iv 4; iv 5) and perhaps also the creation of woman from the side of man (i.e. iii 20 'understand [her] origins'; iv 13 'wife of your bosom'; ii 21 'vessel of your bosom').[24] 4QInstruction has a positive view of marriage, and when the author teaches on this topic, he reflects on Gen. 2.18-24 but avoids an explicit use of v. 24 because he wants to emphasize that a woman leaves her parents and joins with her husband.

A second example of *accommodation* is found in the Plea for Deliverance (11QPs^a XIX 15-16) which is structured on Ps. 51 and at lines 15–16 alludes to Ps. 119.133 ('let not iniquity rule over me'), replacing און ('iniquity') with שטן ('satan') and רוח טמאה ('unclean spirit'): 'let not a satan rule over me, or an unclean spirit, let not pain nor an evil inclination rule over my bones'. By these substitutions, the Plea for Deliverance begins to transform the origin of evil and the reason for human sin from being straightforwardly a part of anthropology to deriving from reified agents.

A third example of *accommodation* is found in 4QPseudo-Ezekiel (4Q385-6, 4Q385^c, 4Q388, 4Q391) and also falls into the category of *eschatological*. The oldest copy of 4QPseudo-Ezekiel is 4Q391, which dates to the mid-second century BCE.[25] There is no reason to believe that this composition originates from the Qumran community. 4QEzekiel (4Q385 2) retells the vision of the valley of dry bones found in Ezekiel 37. While this is an example of rewritten Bible, it draws our attention here because there are also nearly verbatim phrases of the OT. The best example is in 4Q385 2 5 (cf. Ezek. 37.4) where we read: '[and He said], "Son of man, prophesy over the bones and speak."'

---

[21] DJD 34:123–5.
[22] Elisha Qimron, מגילות מדבר יהודה. החיבורים העבריים / *The Dead Sea Scrolls: The Hebrew Writings, Volume Two* (Jerusalem: Yad Ben-Zvi Press, 2013), 156–7.
[23] Cf. Jub. 3:6b–7 which also supplements Gen. 2:23b-24.
[24] 4Q303 (Meditation on Creation A) the creation of woman from the side of Adam is mentioned (l. 9).
[25] 4Q391 is a papyrus that survives in seventy-eight fragments and was published several years before the other five manuscripts, DJD 19:391.

This fragment is replete with other small phrases found in Ezekiel 37 (e.g. 'four winds' of heaven in ln. 7 and Ezek. 37.9).

The vision of Ezekiel 37 is often seen, and with good reason, as concerned with national redemption.[26] What is particularly striking about 4QPseudo-Ezekiel is that it reworks a prophetic rather than narrative text, which is then given an apocalyptic context.[27] In this way, 4QPseudo-Ezekiel is an example of *accommodation* and *eschatological*. The new apocalyptic version of rewritten Ezekiel is historicized and related to a contemporary context; this is similar to the *pesharim*, though without the formal literary characteristics of the *pesharim*. 4QPseudo-Ezekiel's adaptation of the Vision of Dry Bones transforms the image of national restoration to that of individual redemption. 4Q385 2 depicts God directing Ezekiel to prophesy three times over the bones: (1) that the bones be joined together (ln. 5); (2) that they be covered with veins and skin (ln. 6); and (3) that the four winds of heaven blow on them (ln. 7). This retelling of the Vision of Dry Bones, in keeping with other examples of rewritten Bible, simplifies the Ezekiel account by abbreviations and clarifies it with additions. This column of 4QPseudo-Ezekiel has been widely viewed as depicting personal resurrection.[28] Dimant summarizes four modifications to the vision that make it 'refer explicitly to an actual resurrection'. These are (1) the event belongs in the eschatological era; (2) the vision applies only to the righteous of Israel; (3) it is a reward for the righteous; and (4) the benediction given after revival makes the resurrection concrete.[29] The author produces a type of commentary on the original prophecy and thus decodes it. That this vision is about personal reward becomes even more apparent when in line 2 the vision is established as a response to the personal righteousness of those who love God.

4QPseudo-Ezekiel's Vision of Dry Bones is now more concretely a resurrection of individuals and recompense for the righteous in the eschaton.[30] That these fragments are concerned with an eschatological era is found in the twice-repeated question: 'when will these things happen?' (lns. 3, 9). Dimant draws attention to the (reconstructed) thrice-repeated 'and it was so' (lns. 6, 7, 8) formula, which is convincingly taken as an allusion to Genesis 1 and the response to each day of creation. 4QPseudo-Ezekiel's association of resurrection with creation is likely the earliest witness to this tradition.

---

[26] The view that Ezekiel's vision is about national restoration and not personal end-time resurrection has been found esp. in 37.11-12; cf. Andrew Chester, 'Resurrection and Transformation', in *Auferstehung – Resurrection* (ed. H. Lichtenberger and F. Avemarie; WUNT 135; Tübingen: Mohr Siebeck, 1999), 47–77 (53).

[27] See Mladen Popović, 'Prophet, Books and Texts: Pseudo-Ezekiel and the Authoritativeness of Ezekiel Traditions in Early Judaism', in *Authoritative Scriptures in Ancient Judaism* (ed. M. Popović; SJSJ 141; Leiden: Brill, 2010), 227–51 (229–30) argues that '*Pseudo-Ezekiel* was also responsible for, or contributed to, the formation of the final form of biblical Ezekiel in the Masoretic text'.

[28] For example, Menahem Kister and Elisha Qimron, 'Observations on 4QSecond Ezekiel', *RevQ* 15 (1992): 595–602.

[29] DJD 30.33. Another eschatological characteristic of *4QPseudo-Ezekiel* is the speeding up of time to hasten the redemption of Israel (4Q385 4).

[30] DJD 30.29; Kister and Qimron, 'Observations', comment: 'It may therefore be surmised that lines 5-8 represent an implicit answer: the author indicates, in the words that he ascribes to God, that the vision of the Dry Bones (Ez. 37,4-10) was His way of demonstrating to the Children of Israel that the righteous would be rewarded by being resurrected.'

Conclusions

When asking questions about how OT quotations reflect concern for their original context(s) in the Qumran discoveries, it has been necessary here to organize a response in relationship to the categories of Yaḥad texts and previously unknown non-Yaḥad texts. Moreover, this study has focused mainly on explicit citations of the OT because other styles of interpretation, such as literary allusion and rewritten Bible, have a significantly different relationship to context. This follows Joseph Fitzmyer who asked similar questions in the early 1960s and likewise limited his analysis to quotations. Whereas Fitzmyer only analyses Yaḥad texts, his categories for considering how context was regarded remain valuable. Here, his categories are taken up and applied to compositions that were not available to him (viz. Cave 4 mss.).

Several observations may be made in conclusion. First, both in Yaḥad or non-Yaḥad texts, scriptural citation is not the most popular way to use the OT. Among Yaḥad compositions the majority of occurrences are from the Damascus Document. In non-Yaḥad works there are few examples of OT texts cited verbatim and even fewer that are introduced with a formula (e.g. 'as it is written'). Second, by setting Yaḥad and non-Yaḥad texts alongside one another, we may observe that the expectation of 'fulfilment' is much less pronounced in the non-Yaḥad scrolls. Specific to Yaḥad literature is a re-application of OT passages to the history of the group and individuals who are identified with it. Finally, among the non-Yaḥad texts there is a tendency to accommodate texts, they are lifted from their context, amended at times and adapted to convey or support theological (and halakhic) viewpoints. In general terms, the use of OT in its many varieties, not only citations, as represented in Qumran discoveries reflects little interest in original contexts. When OT context is regarded, it is found predominately in a small handful of explicit quotations, particularly those called here literal/historical and modernization.

Section C

The role of criteria for OT/NT studies

9

The use of criteria: The state of the question

David Allen

Discussions and debates concerning the use of the Old Testament in the New (OT/NT) are a long-standing and well-recognized discourse within biblical studies. Many of the *methodological* issues pertaining to such discourse remain less well recognized, however, particularly in respect of recognizing and 'justifying' an alleged or mooted relationship between a NT text and its OT precedent or source.[1] While 'parallelomania' has rightly been viewed as a dangerous potential pitfall for biblical scholarship,[2] scholars have tended to be more successful at diagnosing the symptoms and effects of that condition than in offering preventative treatment that remedies the malaise and gives confidence for *secure* identification of parallels, allusions and intertextual associations.[3] While one recognizes the significant work and influence of Michael Fishbane, and his promulgation of theories of inner-biblical exegesis,[4] the very fact that his work is so well regarded arguably derives from the relative lack of a substantive, methodological discourse or corpus on the process of identifying such links.

Indeed, a cursory review of salient, landmark OT/NT texts – Dodd, Lindars, Hanson and Juel, for example[5] – reveals that the *criteria* for identifying and categorizing the multivalent relationships between the texts have tended to invite

---

[1] For example, G. K. Beale, *The Right Doctrine from the Wrong Texts?: Essays on the Use of the Old Testament in the New* (Grand Rapids: Baker, 1994), while bringing together a number of essays pertaining to key hermeneutical or philosophical matters, does not engage significantly with *how* one proves or evidences the mooted relationship. Energy tends to be devoted to the significance of an allusion or echo, rather than to demonstrating its existence. There are some exceptions to the general rule, particularly in the study of specific texts or studies – cf. Kelli S. O'Brien, *The Use of Scripture in the Markan Passion Narrative* (LNTS 384; London: T&T Clark, 2010). However, wider analyses of such matters are relatively rare (a factor this volume seeks to address).

[2] Samuel Sandmel, 'Parallelomania', *JBL* 81 (1962): 1–13.

[3] Albeit written at the end of twentieth century, Michael B. Thompson, *Clothed with Christ: The Example and Teaching of Jesus in Romans 12.1-15.13* (JSNTSup 59; Sheffield: JSOT Press, 1991), 30, notes: 'Little has been written about how to identify allusions in biblical literature.'

[4] Cf. Michael A. Fishbane, *Biblical Interpretation in Ancient Israel* (Oxford: Oxford University Press, 1988). One notes further the essential indebtedness of Hays's *Echoes* to the prior principles and approach of Fishbane.

[5] C. H. Dodd, *According to the Scriptures: The Sub-Structure of New Testament Theology* (London: Nisbet, 1952); Barnabas Lindars, *New Testament Apologetic* (London: SCM, 1961); Anthony Tyrrell Hanson, *The Living Utterances of God: The New Testament Exegesis of the Old* (London: Darton, Longman & Todd, 1983); Donald Juel, *Messianic Exegesis: Christological Interpretation of the Old Testament in Early Christianity* (Philadelphia: Fortress, 1988).

fairly limited discourse and discussion. Goppelt's influential *typos* discourse does not dig deeply into methodological questions,[6] and even the recent OT/NT-specific Carson/Beale commentary does not really embrace such matters, focusing instead on the interpretative implications of the proposed link.[7] The exegetical techniques so deployed by the NT authors are, of course, highly significant areas for discussion, and the comparison with other Second Temple strategies is likewise engaging and insightful, but it is these matters that tend to dominate the ensuing OT/NT discussion rather than those engaging with the existence of the mooted allusion. This is perhaps because the identity of the quotation was deemed to be secure and/or the existence of the allusion was deemed sufficiently 'probable' not to warrant an extended discussion of appropriate criteria or any methodological consideration of what makes the allusion probable (or otherwise).[8] Instead, it is the *use* of the (mooted) text, and the associated hermeneutical and exegetical questions, that become primary rather than any initial process for declaring the relationship in the first place.[9] There are some exceptions to this rule (Christopher Stanley's work on citational technique, for example),[10] but generally speaking, relatively little has been said on such matters.

The publication of Richard Hays's *Echoes of Scripture in the Letters of Paul*,[11] however, has been a benchmark contributor in framing issues surrounding OT/NT discourse, and particularly in terms of how one 'recognizes' an OT allusion or echo, and one might describe it as effectively changing the proverbial rules of the OT/NT enterprise.[12] Hays's work effectively placed an intertextual 'marker in the sand', thereby expanding the way in which intertextuality was seen to be operative within the Pauline corpus, and any work on Paul's use of the Jewish Scriptures has subsequently had, in some way, to engage with its claims.[13] Paul Foster's recent critical

---

[6] Leonhard Goppelt, *Typos: The Typological Interpretation of the Old Testament in the New* (trans. Madvig; Grand Rapids: Eerdmans, 1982).

[7] G. K. Beale and D. A. Carson, *Commentary on the New Testament Use of the Old Testament* (Grand Rapids: Baker Academic, 2007).

[8] This is implicit in Beale and Carson, *Commentary*.

[9] Cf. also the comprehensive review of OT/NT methodological issues in Dennis L. Stamps, 'The Use of the Old Testament in the New Testament as a Rhetorical Device: A Methodological Proposal', in *Hearing the Old Testament in the New Testament* (ed. Stanley E. Porter; MNTS; Grand Rapids: Eerdmans, 2006), 10–23. Stamps rightly draws attention to the lack of consensus as to how to describe citations (as a quotation, echo, allusion and the like), but makes no connections to 'criteria' in this regard.

[10] Christopher D. Stanley, *Paul and the Language of Scripture: Citation Technique in the Pauline Epistles and Contemporary Literature* (SNTSMS 69; Cambridge: Cambridge University Press, 1992).

[11] Richard Hays, *Echoes of Scripture in the Letters of Paul* (New Haven: Yale University Press, 1989).

[12] Alec J. Lucas, 'Assessing Stanley E Porter's Objections to Richard B Hays's Notion of Metalepsis', *CBQ* 76 (2014): 93–111, rightly terms it 'a watershed moment in the history of Pauline scholarship'. Stephen Fowl, 'The Use of Scripture in Philippians', in *Paul and Scripture: Extending the Conversation* (ed. Christopher D. Stanley; ECL 9; Atlanta: Society of Biblical Literature, 2012), 163 similarly notes that it 'is one of those books that changes the shape of conversations'. Cf. Christopher D. Stanley, 'Paul's "Use" of Scripture: Why the Audience Matters', in *As It Is Written: Studying Paul's Use of Scripture* (ed. Stanley E. Porter and Christopher D. Stanley; Society of Biblical Literature Symposium Series 50; Leiden: Brill, 2008), 128: 'The influence of Hays' "metaleptic" approach to analysing Paul's engagement with the Jewish Scriptures is hard to overstate.'

[13] Cf. Francis Watson, *Paul and the Hermeneutics of Faith* (London: T&T Clark, 2004), xii: Hays's 1989 volume was 'the first indication that insights drawn from contemporary hermeneutics and literary theory could fruitfully be applied to Pauline interpretation in general, and to Paul's reading of Scripture in general'.

review of OT/NT discourse (one essentially sceptical of Hays' approach), nonetheless, noted that, with the publication of *Echoes*, 'a new phase in research dealing with the use of Jewish scriptures in the New Testament commenced'.[14] While there is more to Hays's work than just methodological questions (its suggestion of Paul's espousal of an ecclesiological hermeneutic, for example), and while its focus was primarily on Pauline texts,[15] the methodological focus of *Echoes* (and its development and clarification in subsequent essays)[16] demonstrably changed the framework in which OT/NT discourse has outworked. Relative methodological silence in terms of criteria for identifying allusions to, and echoes of, the Jewish Scriptures was transformed into a much louder (or 'echoey') consideration of such matters.

1 Hays's approach

Key to Hays's approach was its engagement in matters of intertextuality, and it is probably fair to say that, more than any other scholar, he has brought the concept/techniques into the vocabulary and world view of NT studies, particularly the theory of metalepsis. Hays alludes to the work of Julia Kristeva, normally seen as the one who coined the intertextuality term, but his approach lacks the ideological dimension to Kristeva's project; instead he borrows far more from the work of the literary critic John Hollander,[17] and his is an essentially minimalist approach to intertextuality. Indeed, Hays's lens is essentially intra-biblical and limited in that way; it borrows more from the approach of Michael Fishbane in terms of inner-biblical exegesis or the idea of ongoing scriptural reinterpretation. For Hays, Paul's 'discursive space' is Israel's Scripture.[18]

---

[14] Paul Foster, 'Echoes without Resonance: Critiquing Certain Aspects of Recent Scholarly Trends in the Study of the Jewish Scriptures in the New Testament', *JSNT* 38 (2015): 98. Cf. G. K. Beale, *Handbook on the New Testament Use of the Old Testament: Exegesis and Interpretation* (Grand Rapids: Baker Academic, 2012), 34: 'Hays's approach is one of the best ways to discern and discuss the nature and validity of allusions (though he like the term "echoes"), despite the fact, as we have seen, that some scholars have been critical of his methodology.'

[15] It is notable that Hays's proverbial follow up to *Echoes* (Richard B. Hays, *Echoes of Scripture in the Gospels* [Waco: Baylor University Press, 2016]) effectively assumes his prior discourse and does not revisit the criteria. Indeed, the 2016 volume is notable for its *lack* of explicit engagement with the previous methodological questions that had permeated his prior discourse. See likewise Richard B. Hays, *Reading Backwards: Figural Christology and the Fourfold Gospel Witness* (London: SPCK, 2015). See also John Goldingay, *Reading Jesus's Bible: How the New Testament Helps Us Understand the Old Testament* (Grand Rapids: Eerdmans, 2017), and his recent work on OT/NT allusion-confirming criteria.

[16] Richard B. Hays, 'Who Has Believed Our Message: Paul's Reading of Isaiah', in *New Testament Writers and the Old Testament: An Introduction* (ed. John Court; London: SPCK, 2002); the essay is re-presented in Richard B. Hays, *The Conversion of the Imagination: Paul as Interpreter of Israel's Scripture* (Grand Rapids: Eerdmans, 2005). See also Richard B. Hays, 'Echoes of Scripture in the Letters of Paul: Abstract', in *Paul and the Scriptures of Israel* (ed. Craig A. Evans and James A. Sanders; JSNTSup 83; Sheffield: JSOT Press, 1993) and his responses to critiques of his work.

[17] John Hollander, *The Figure of Echo: A Mode of Allusion in Milton and After* (Berkeley: University of California Press, 1981).

[18] Kenneth D. Litwak, 'Echoes of Scripture? A Critical Survey on Paul's Use of the Old Testament', *CurBS* 6 (1998): 262–3.

One of the most significant aspects of Hays's thesis was its attention to the titular 'echoes' of the Jewish Scriptures that could be found within the Pauline corpus,[19] and particularly the proposal that one might identify or confirm the existence of such echoes by the use of a set of criteria.[20] Hays's proverbial seven criteria are now reasonably well known within biblical scholarship and have been subsequently used by many of his successors. They offer a 'useful and succinct procedure'[21] for echo identification, and any review of methodological criteria must necessarily begin with them.[22]

1. *Availability*: Was the original source available to the author and the readers? This may just be a temporal categorization, but it also draws on the potential for the author to be familiar with the source text (and thus related to where else they may be seen to be using it).

2. *Volume*: This tends to be one of the more critiqued of Hays's criteria, and the one that has (in his view, at least) been often misunderstood. Conceding that the 1989 work did not make the criterion sufficiently explicit, Hays subsequently expands on its definition – it is 'how insistently the echo impresses itself upon the reader'.[23] In so doing, Hays sets out three particular aspects to the criterion:[24]

   - The *amount of verbatim repetition* of the requisite words or phrases (it is an essentially lexical or linguistic similarity). The higher the number of common words, the louder the volume.
   - The *distinctiveness of the phrase* – essentially its prominence or significance within the contemporary context. As such, one might encounter a potential tension between this and the previous aspect – an otherwise quiet echo becomes loud (though Hays does not really acknowledge this).
   - *Rhetorical role of the text* – the 'rhetorical stress placed upon the phrase(s) in question' (55). This is hard to assess or quantify (something Hays concedes), and that is perhaps why the volume criteria tends to focus just on the first two elements.

3. *Recurrence*: How frequently does Paul use, refer or cite this text? Hays subsequently calls this 'multiple attestation',[25] and also categorizes it as 'clustering', namely that where potential allusions to a particular source are closely located, they become more probable in that regard.

---

[19] Our discussion is not so much about how the recognized echo functions, or the exegetical technique Paul employed, for example, but more the methodology Hays advocated for recognizing its presence in the first instance.

[20] Hays does not restrict the location of where the echo can take place: it can occur in the mind of the author, in the original readers, in the text itself, in the modern reader, or in the community of engagement with it, 'creative tension' of them all.

[21] O'Brien, *Use*, 29. Shiu-Lun Shum, *Paul's Use of Isaiah in Romans: A Comparative Study of Paul's Letter to the Romans and the Sibylline and Qumran Sectarian Texts* (WUNT 2/156; Tübingen: Mohr Siebeck, 2002), 6 suggests that Hays's criteria have become a 'set of rules' for the 'game' that is detecting biblical allusions and echoes.

[22] Hays, *Echoes*, 29–32.

[23] Hays, 'Who Has Believed', 54.

[24] Ibid., 53–62.

[25] Ibid., 56.

4. *Thematic coherence*: Does it fit? This feels like a more slippery or subjective assessment and one based more on interpretative judgement than textual witness. As such, this (and the subsequent criteria) has tended to receive a more critical assessment from other scholars, some of whom argue that this subjective dimension effectively disqualifies from being a legitimate criterion.[26]
5. *Historical plausibility*: This pertains to the historical reality of the mooted allusion. Does it equate or resemble other Jewish exegetical approaches? Or is it anachronistic? The difficulty perhaps with this criterion is the degree to which it precludes innovation on Paul's part; Francis Watson, for example, has shown the essential novelty of the Pauline reading strategy and Paul's fundamental difference from contemporary readers in this regard.[27]
6. *History of interpretation*: Have others identified this point of connection? What have they made of it?
7. *Satisfaction*: This is more than thematic coherence; it is a more 'macro' assessment that attends to the overall effect of the mooted allusion. While he concedes its potential subjective dimension, this criterion becomes the most significant one for Hays, or so he declares: 'It is the most important test: it is in fact another way of asking whether the proposed reading offers a good account of the experience of a contemporary community of competent readers.'[28]

2 Analysis of criteria

It is probably worth stating that, from the outset, Hays himself offers some caveats or qualifications in terms of the use of his criteria. They possess no particular pecking order or hierarchy,[29] and they should therefore be used corporately, rather than independently, of each other. It is also fair to say that the (wider) arguments of *Echoes* are only partially dependent upon the criteria and the particular echoes that they supposedly evidence. Ross Wagner notes, for example, that 'while attention has naturally focused on the figure of echo in Hays' work and on his criteria for discerning echoes, the extent to which his study relies on indisputable instances of citation and allusion often goes unnoticed. Hays allows his ear to be tuned by his disciplined attention to Paul's *explicit* appropriations of Scripture.'[30] Echoes and criteria are thus only one piece within the larger jigsaw of Paul's scriptural engagement.

More significantly perhaps, Hays himself warns against applying the criteria in mechanical or slavish fashion, and with any restrictive or limiting sense – that is, 'texts

---

[26] See below and the critique of Hays from, for example, Stanley E. Porter, *Sacred Tradition in the New Testament: Tracing Old Testament Themes in the Gospels and Epistles* (Grand Rapids: Baker Academic, 2016).
[27] Watson, *Paul*.
[28] Hays, *Echoes*, 31–2.
[29] Cf. Hays, 'Who Has Believed', 53: 'no one of these criteria is decisive: they must be employed in conjunction with one another.' Yet, as noted above, he still applies a particular significance to the satisfaction criterion.
[30] J. Ross Wagner, *Heralds of the Good News: Isaiah and Paul 'in Concert' in the Letter to the Romans* (NovTSup 101; Leiden: Brill, 2002), 10n37, emphasis added.

can generate readings that transcend both the conscious intention of the author and all the hermeneutical strictures that we promulgate'.[31] The potentiality of echoes, the capacity within them one might say, exceeds the capacity of the criteria to evidence or demonstrate their existence. Hence from the outset, the most significant advocate of a criteria-driven approach, its primary proponent one might suggest, seems slightly hesitant as to its potential efficacy, and Hays himself latterly qualifies the criteria as merely 'serviceable'[32] or 'modestly useful rules of thumb'.[33] It is interesting, then, that Hays does not overtly apply the criteria in his subsequent analysis within *Echoes*, at least not in any quasi-scientific proof mode. As such, the term 'criteria' may be something of a misnomer, for it suggests a formality or objective quality that the categories cannot, nor ever were intended to, bear. Michael Thompson, in a similar quest focused on finding allusions to Jesus tradition in Paul, likewise cautions against over-expectation or precision, proposing that the value of criteria 'lies in assisting the judgement of relative probability'.[34]

3 Other criteria proposals

Hays's work has generated a variety of responses. Some, as we shall see, have been less persuaded by his proposals. Others – many, one might say – have embraced the Hays approach,[35] and the restatement of the Hays criteria has been a feature of many monographs on OT/NT related matters, notably in volumes beyond Pauline discourse (though perhaps with less explicit examination of the criteria – they are commonly presented as 'given').[36] In effect then, since the publication of *Echoes*, the principle of applying criteria to ratify or justify an echo or allusion has become effectively associated with the Haysian seven.[37] Indeed, if one were applying Haysian criteria to Hays's own

---

[31] Hays, *Echoes*, 32.
[32] Ibid., 32.
[33] Hays, 'Who Has Believed', 53.
[34] Thompson, *Clothed with Christ*, 36.
[35] Sylvia C. Keesmaat, 'Exodus and the Intertextual Transformation of Tradition in Romans 8.14-30', *JSNT* 16 (1994): 29–56; Christopher A. Beetham, *Echoes of Scripture in the Letter of Paul to the Colossians* (BIS 96, Leiden: Brill, 2008); Wagner, *Heralds of the Good News*; Brian J. Abasciano, *Paul's Use of the Old Testament in Romans 9:10-18: An Intertextual and Theological Exegesis* (LNTS 317; London: T&T Clark, 2011); Roy E. Ciampa, *The Presence and Function of Scripture in Galatians 1 and 2* (WUNT 2/102; Tübingen: Mohr Siebeck, 1998); Benjamin L. Gladd, *Revealing the Mysterion: The Use of Mystery in Daniel and Second Temple Judaism with Its Bearing on First Corinthians* (BZNW 160; Berlin: Walter de Gruyter, 2008).
[36] Inter alia David M. Allen, *Deuteronomy and Exhortation in Hebrews: An Exercise in Narrative Re-Presentation* (WUNT 2/238; Tübingen: Mohr Siebeck, 2008); Kelly D. Liebengood, *The Eschatology of 1 Peter: Considering the Influence of Zechariah 9-14* (SNTSMS 157; Cambridge: Cambridge University Press, 2013); Külli Tõniste, *The Ending of the Canon: A Canonical and Intertextual Reading of Revelation 21-22* (LNTS 526; London: Bloomsbury T&T Clark); Kenneth D. Litwak, *Echoes of Scripture in Luke-Acts: Telling the History of God's People Intertextually* (JSNTSup 282; London: T&T Clark, 2005) though with some appreciative moderation.
[37] Cf. Abasciano, *Paul's Use*, 22: 'Hays has provided what has become an almost standard list of criteria "for testing claims about the presence and meaning of scriptural echoes in Paul."' See also Beale, *Handbook*, 32–5, who, even with some critique and amendment, still classifies them as the established framework for validating echoes and allusions.

work, the volume criterion would be both loud and seemingly confirmatory of his proposals; such has been the general embrace of his criteria thesis.[38]

But, of course, Hays is not the only protagonist in the methodological debate; while he may have been among the first to formally propose a framework for evidencing allusions and echoes, his voice is not the only one in the criteria choir. Exploring how one might account for echoes or allusions to the OT in the Gospel texts, for example, Mark Alan Powell proposes three indicative criteria: the *availability* of the alluded text, the latter's *degree of repetition* and the *thematic coherence between the two texts*.[39] The first of these parallels Hays's initial one, and the second is effectively a combination of his recurrence and volume criteria;[40] the third perhaps combines aspects of the thematic coherence and satisfaction criteria.

Robert Brawley essentially embraces Hays's approach but prefers the language of 'intertextual reverberations' to 'echoes' and reduces his predecessor's seven criteria to just two: volume and availability.[41] The other five criteria thus assume some form of confirmatory or supportive role, rather than a determinative one. Brawley also critiques Hays for defining 'volume' merely as shared phrasing – there is actually a wider discourse of genre and form that can contribute to that category. Kenneth Litwak follows Brawley's lead (interestingly so, bearing in mind their common Lucan focus), likewise embracing availability and volume, and observing that the remaining five criteria in many ways overlap and/or restate what is embraced under the other two. Külli Tõniste concurs that availability and volume are the primary criteria for assessing the existence of the echo but finds a variant role for the other five; they act more as tests for the echo's presence, and without them being satisfied, the mooted echo 'can be excluded as 'noise'.[42]

Sometimes Hays's criteria have been adopted and subtly nuanced. Kelli O'Brien, for example, essentially embraces Hays's core premise but reduces the list to five criteria: availability, reoccurrence or clustering (effectively combining volume and reoccurrence), clarity (lexical similarity – so a form of volume too), thematic coherence and distinctiveness (the degree of influence). Such terms feel on the same level as Hays's, but are calibrated a little differently. Likewise, Sylvia Keesmaat also endorses Hays's criteria or at least restates them with some expansion. In particular, as with others, she advocates sharpening the volume criterion (a critique Hays subsequently addresses). Keesmaat's approach is also notable for the way in which she uses the criteria to *test* her overall conclusions; as such, her methodology is less about using the criteria to

---

[38] Beetham, *Echoes of Scripture* notes, for example, that the title of his work is effectively an 'echo' of Hays's prior discourse. Stanley, 'Paul's "Use" of Scripture', 126n1 likewise recognizes this foundational and central role: 'Virtually all scholars who have worked in this area in recent years have relied on the criteria set forth by Richard B. Hays' (i.e. in the 1989 volume).

[39] Mark Allan Powell, *Chasing the Eastern Star: Adventures in Biblical Reader-Response Criticism* (Louisville: Westminster John Knox, 2001), 101–2.

[40] Jeannine K. Brown, 'Metalepsis', in *Exploring Intertextuality: Diverse Strategies for New Testament Interpretation of Texts* (ed. B. J. Oropeza and Steve Moyise; Eugene: Cascade, 2016), 33.

[41] Robert L. Brawley, *Text to Text Pours Forth Speech: Voices of Scripture in Luke-Acts* (ISBL; Bloomington: Indiana University Press, 1995).

[42] Tõniste, *Ending*, 25–6. See also Steve Smith, *The Fate of the Jerusalem Temple in Luke-Acts: An Intertextual Approach to Jesus' Laments over Jerusalem and Stephen's Speech* (LNTS 553; London: Bloomsbury T&T Clark, 2017), 33–4 who suggests attending to the usage of the text (e.g. within liturgical contexts) as a factor in assessing the recognition of the allusion.

identify or focus on one textual link but rather to see if they make actual overall sense of the *thematic* argument. Do they work corporately? To put it another way, and in a sense which one suspects Hays would endorse, the Haysian seven become more akin to 'tests' rather than 'criteria'.

Holly Carey increases the list of criteria to eight, clearly influenced by Hays's work, but equally differentiated from it. She lists the following: shared circumstances, shared vocabulary, recurrence, interruption, illumination, availability, historical likelihood and historical parallels.[43] Alternatively, Shiu-Lun Shum generally adopts Hays's seven but expresses hesitation about availability; interestingly, though, it is the availability to *Paul* (as much as to the audience) that Shum questions, and he conjectures that Paul may not necessarily have been aware of the full gamut of Scripture.[44] At the same time, Shum accredits particular significance to the thematic coherence criterion, and where Hays discourages such prioritizing, Shum notably seems to prioritize. Likewise, while resolutely embracing the Haysian seven, Brian Abasciano draws particular attention to volume and thematic coherence,[45] finding them decisive in discerning the presence of an echo.

One might also consider other ways in which the criteria have been enhanced or developed, or their usage reshaped in a particular form. Here one might suggest Jeannine Brown's work on metalepsis,[46] and particularly the way in which 'story' functions as the primary link between texts. Brown attends to the role of 'storied' associations between the different texts – that is, they may lack formal verbal associations, but there is a strong connection in terms of character or plot. Because the nature of the association is different, so the nature of the criteria varies. Brown employs Powell's three criteria, but to these she adds a further three borrowed from Hays: historical plausibility, history of interpretation and satisfaction. As such, she ends up implicitly advocating the existence of the Haysian seven, but with a wider spectrum or lens of discourse for their employment.[47] She avers: 'Intertextuality moves beyond allusion and quotation to include "a common nexus of images and themes informing a whole passage."'[48] Her approach, for this author at least, is notable for widening the scope of Haysian intertextuality, but at the same time, one suggests that it puts further burden on the legitimacy question; that is, Brown does not really resolve the question as to the efficacy of criteria but merely restates or reframes it from an alternative position. By appealing to wider, broader and more storied connections, the legitimacy question becomes only more prominent.

---

[43] Holly J. Carey, *Jesus' Cry from the Cross: Towards a First-Century Understanding of the Intertextual Relationship between Psalm 22 and the Narrative of Mark's Gospel* (LNTS 398; London: T&T Clark, 2009), 43–4.
[44] Shum, *Paul's Use of Isaiah*, 7.
[45] Abasciano, *Paul's Use*, 24.
[46] Brown, 'Metalepsis'.
[47] Brown's way of reading is akin to that picked up in Hays, *Echoes-Gospels*. Here Hays terms it figural reading – less overtly intertextual – but the storied or narrative connections seem to be implicit within his approach.
[48] Brown, 'Metalepsis', 40, referencing Litwak, *Echoes of Scripture in Luke-Acts*, 52–3.

4 Further responses to criteria

The scope of the engagement with Hays's work is extensive and picks up on matters related to, but also beyond, the criteria question. Matthew Bates, for example, while generally appreciative of Hays's contributions, is nonetheless critical of the (restricted) contours in which it works, concluding that Hays's methodology and scope is too narrow. While there is attention in Hays to discerning how the source text has impacted textually, Bates avers that his method makes little reference to the wider world view it inhabits and needs to take account of the coeval and subsequent texts in terms of how intertextual relationships work. In effect, Bates contends that Hays was wrong to concentrate solely on the LXX – it does not embrace the work of text reception and makes the context too narrow.[49] He makes the same criticism of the Beale/Carson volume; for Bates, it too makes no use of coeval (non-NT) Christian texts, so any aspiration to genuine intertextual engagement remains consequently limited.

At the same time, however, in terms of the criteria, there has been relatively little embrace with the nitty-gritty principles of Hays's methodology – or at least relatively so when compared to the level of embrace of his proposal and associated criteria.[50] As noted above, debates have been about the number and definitions of the criteria, rather than the existence or very concept of the criteria per se. Indeed, many responses to Hays's intertexual play have just preferred *not* to engage with the criteria question.[51] Some significant critique of Hays's approach, however, may be found in the work of Christopher Stanley, specifically Stanley's focus on the rhetorical effect of Paul's use of Scripture, and its reception by the various audiences.[52] Adopting an essential reader-response perspective to Paul's scriptural engagement, Stanley has contended that more attention must be given to the capacity of the readers to understand or engage with the mooted allusions; such audiences would have been unlikely to make such connections, and this cautions against the intertextual expansion post-Hays. It is fair to say that Stanley's approach is directed less to the criteria, though it has ramifications for them; if, for example, the audience are 'ignorant', what of the availability criteria?

But perhaps the most significant Haysian conversation partner – or critic, one might surmise – is Stanley Porter,[53] and it would be not unfair to describe the 'discourse' between Porter and Hays as a primary locus for criteria discussion. Porter's critiques have been formulated in a number of locations and publications but are set forth most recently in an overarching OT/NT volume addressing the NT's use

---

[49] Matthew Bates, 'Beyond Hays's *Echoes of Scripture*', in *Paul and Scripture*, 263–91.
[50] See Stanley, 'Paul's "Use" of Scripture', 128–9.
[51] For example, a dedicated multi-author review of the Hays 1989 volume does not significantly engage with questions of criteria, offering only brief comment on them – see Craig A. Evans and James A. Sanders, eds, *Paul and the Scriptures of Israel* (JSNTSup 83; Sheffield: JSOT Press, 1993).
[52] See Christopher D. Stanley, *Arguing with Scripture: The Rhetoric of Quotations in the Letters of Paul* (London: T&T Clark, 2004); Stanley, 'Paul's "Use" of Scripture'. For an assessment of Stanley's thesis, see Brian J. Abasciano, 'Diamonds in the Rough: A Reply to Christopher Stanley Concerning the Reader Competency of Paul's Original Audiences', *NovT* 49 (2007): 153–83.
[53] See Lucas, 'Assessing', 93–111; also Beale, *Handbook*.

of what Porter terms 'sacred tradition'.⁵⁴ A core element of Porter's critique pertains to the methodological assumptions present within OT/NT discourse, especially that practitioners might be more attentive to the precision with which terms like 'quotation', 'allusion' and 'echo' are deployed; in Porter's assessment, 'the boundaries between quotation, allusion and echo are significantly (and increasingly) blurred' and this undermines methodological precision and accurate identification for the specified relationship. A cursory examination of the way in which particularly allusion and echo do get used (and whether the criteria function as evidence for either allusion or echo or both) suggests that there is some validity to Porter's objection and that tighter terminological nomenclature is required.⁵⁵

More significantly for our concerns, beyond this terminological disputation, Porter is also critical of the criteria premise that he finds present in Hays's work. In particular, Porter dissents from the availability criterion, contending that it is 'inadequate' in this regard. As Hays – at least in Porter's construal – advocates for a reader-response reception of the echo, responsibility for its perception lies with the audience; Porter contends that if it were so, then the echo effectively disappears if the audience is not aware of it, and thus the availability criterion is not fit for purpose.⁵⁶ Similarly, the volume criterion is queried for defining one metaphor (echo) with another (volume), and recurrence merely counts the number of such echoes rather than serving as a genuine text for the existence of the echo. Moreover, criteria four to seven relate, Porter contends, to the 'interpretation' of the echo rather than to testifying to its existence; that satisfaction, one such instance, is also Hays's most significant criterion Porter finds 'perplexing', as it is 'not in fact a criterion for discovering echoes, only for interpreting them'. Porter essentially concludes that Hays effectively only has three criteria for evidencing echoes – and even these are problematic.

A more middling voice may be that of Greg Beale. Beale acknowledges the significance of the seven criteria, recognizing that 'Hays' approach is one of the best ways to discern and discuss the nature and validity of allusions'.⁵⁷ However, he too expresses some reservation as to their efficacy; thematic coherence and satisfaction overlap (and could potentially be one criterion), as do availability and historical plausibility, and thus Beale conjectures that five rather than seven criteria might be a more appropriate summation.

---

⁵⁴ Porter, *Sacred Tradition*. See also Stanley E. Porter, 'The Use of the Old Testament in the New Testament: A Brief Comment on Method and Terminology', in *Early Christian Interpretation of the Scriptures of Israel: Investigations and Proposals* (ed. Craig A. Evans and James A. Sanders; JSNTSup 148; Sheffield: Sheffield Academic Press, 1997); Stanley E. Porter, 'Allusions and Echoes', in *As It Is Written*. Andreas J. Kostenberger, 'Hearing the Old Testament in the New Testament: A Response', in *Hearing the Old Testament in the New Testament*, offers an appreciative assessment of Porter's critique.

⁵⁵ Cf. B. J. Oropeza and Steve Moyise, *Exploring Intertextuality: Diverse Strategies for New Testament Interpretation of Texts* (Eugene: Cascade, 2016), xvii: 'The fact that each of these terms resists such precise definition is one of the reasons why many have turned to intertextuality, a word that suggests complexity.'

⁵⁶ Cf. Porter, 'Use', 83: 'Apart from audience perception, what means are available to recognize an author's echo?'

⁵⁷ Beale, *Handbook*, 34.

5 Intertextuality

The parent to the children of criteria is of course the very 'intertextual' project in which Hays seeks to work and which has become a broad or umbrella designation for the type of arena OT/NT discourse inhabits. Scholars deploy terms of echo and allusion differently, sometimes with care and sometimes without, and this generates a diversity of criteria for recognizing the existence of the term.[58] The same may be said of the term 'intertextuality'. Intertextual engagement manifests itself in a plethora of directions[59] and continues to expand its remit in both Hebrew Bible and NT studies; debates also ensue as to the appropriateness of the title, with many advocates reminding us that intertextuality is simply wider than *texts*.[60] It is perhaps more akin to a matrix of 'cultural codes'[61] and certainly transcends just the solely intra-scriptural lens Hays adopts.[62]

In a recent essay on such terminology, Russell Meek assesses the definitions of 'intertextuality', 'inner-biblical exegesis' (IBE) and 'inner-biblical allusion' (IBA). Meek draws significant terminological difference between the first two terms. Intertextuality, for example, pertains to the world view of the text; that is, the words bring their own world view or usage which impacts upon reading, and intertextuality properly includes the oral tradition that sits behind it. Unlike the more diachronic inner-biblical exegesis, which maps the temporal evolution of the text, intertextuality is synchronic, multivalent even, mapping 'a network of traces' accordingly. Significantly for our concerns, Meek conjectures therefore that 'the intertextual method is unconcerned with developing criteria for determining intertextual relationships between texts'.[63] Indeed, if Meek is right, one might tentatively suggest that the very notion of criteria is counterproductive or contrary to the intertextual enterprise, inimical to it perhaps, or rather that it is only appropriate to the more narrow IBE discourse in which the diachronic textual associations are the considered subject and where the scholar must demonstrate/prove the point of connection and authorial intent. As such, this makes the case for arguing and demonstrating criteria more pressing, as that is the essential burden of IBE, but also cautions against calling the OT search for allusions and echoes 'intertextuality'.

6 Where are we now?

One might therefore suggest some summary conclusions on the state of the question and the particular role or function of criteria for assessing the validity of allusions and echoes.

---

[58] See Porter, *Sacred Tradition*.
[59] Oropeza and Moyise, *Exploring Intertextuality*; see also Richard B. Hays et al., *Reading the Bible Intertextually* (Waco: Baylor University Press, 2009).
[60] Keesmaat, 'Exodus and the Intertextual Transformation of Tradition'.
[61] Daniel Boyarin, *Intertextuality and the Reading of Midrash* (Bloomington: Indiana University Press, 1990), 12–13.
[62] Hays is, of course, aware of his limited range of vision, even if others have critiqued his narrow focus.
[63] Russell Meek, 'Intertextuality, Inner-Biblical Exegesis, and Inner-Biblical Allusion: The Ethics of a Methodology', *Bib* 95 (2014): 284.

1. Hays's criteria still remain the primary set or corpus against which to evaluate mooted OT/NT associations, or at least they appear to have withstood the various challenges set before them. Porter's scepticism notwithstanding, the lack of any wide consensus *contra* Hays is notable, and even those scholars whose appropriation of Hays's seven is more selective effectively still endorse his essential premise.[64] Thirty years on from *Echoes*, there is no 'new kid on the block', and it is a testimony to the ongoing influence and legacy of Hays's volume that it remains the primary and necessary conversation partner when one seeks to utilize a criteria-driven methodology.

2. Thus in many ways, the 'completeness' of the Haysian seven remains in place. There have been proposed reworkings or amendments to them, but the basic core/shape remains consistent. But at the same time, one wonders if the discipline is approaching some form of impasse or stalemate in this regard.[65] For the post-Hays discussion around criteria has actually not moved the discourse on substantially. Debates remain as to how much (if any) lexical similarity is required to prove the link, how much audience competency is required (and whether that is even relevant), and the degree to which proposed criteria are even allowed to be 'criteria' likewise remains contested. And it is not evident that criteria are being significantly used, for example, to 'disprove' the existence of a mooted allusion; at best, they seem to serve merely a confirmatory or vindicatory role.[66] To put the matter another way, Hays's criteria potentially 'serve to open the field, not narrow it',[67] and, without such constraint, the consequences of such openness can easily generate overly creative exegesis, and Pauline interpretation shaped according to the whim of the interpreter. As Beker notes in response to Hays's 1989 volume, 'how can "echoes" serve as constraints, when they are muffled, subliminal or "latent"?'[68]

3. Hence, in the light of this discussion, one wonders whether criteria (Haysian or otherwise) are capable of being the measures or benchmarks that scholars wish them to be and thus whether they are proverbially 'fit for purpose' in this regard. Hays himself speaks of the criteria as essentially 'aesthetic judgements', a view echoed (no pun intended) by many of his advocates, and even their most confident proponents recognize that they yield a more subjective than objective assessment.[69] Determining

---

[64] Litwak, *Echoes of Scripture in Luke-Acts* seems exemplary in this regard; he may only adopt two of the seven criteria, but he still places him essentially in the Haysian camp, as the title of his volume seemingly testifies.

[65] Assessments of Thompson's Paul-Jesus criteria (Thompson, *Clothed with Christ*) are perhaps illustrative in this regard. James D. G. Dunn, 'Jesus Tradition in Paul', in *Studying the Historical Jesus: Evaluation of the State of Current Research* (ed. Bruce Chilton and Craig A. Evans; Leiden: Brill, 1994), 160 notes how Thompson's eleven criteria may bring scientific rigour to Paul-Jesus discourse, whereas Porter, *Sacred Tradition*, 15 ends up dismissing them as 'virtually unworkable'.

[66] One thinks of just war theory in similar fashion; it is invariably used to 'justify' military action already practised, rather than as a process undergone to stop or cease a decision for war.

[67] Matthew Scott, *The Hermeneutics of Christological Psalmody in Paul: An Intertextual Enquiry* (SNTSMS 158; New York: Cambridge University Press, 2014), 3. Scott's consideration offers a more hesitant – if still appreciative – assessment of the Hays legacy and cautions against inappropriate assumptions regarding Paul's use of metalepsis.

[68] J. Christiaan Beker, 'Echoes and Intertextuality: On the Role of Scripture in Paul's Theology', in *Paul and the Scriptures of Israel*, 64.

[69] After carefully outlining a series of eleven criteria for discerning Jesus citation/allusion in Paul, Thompson, *Clothed with Christ*, 36 still concedes: 'Their value lies in assisting the judgment of relative probability.'

echoes and allusions is as much an art as it is a science (and probably more so),[70] and this seemingly precludes the exactness or rigour for which some criteria advocates seek. As such, are criteria – however defined – round pegs in a square hole? Is 'guidelines', for example, a more methodologically sound language to use in OT/NT allusion discourse and one which offers a qualitative rather than quantitative assessment?

One might identify parallels or similarities perhaps in other related discourses where discussions relating to criteria have taken place. One thinks, for example, of the debates within Historical Jesus (HJ) studies pertaining to the criteria used to evidence the authenticity (or otherwise) of Jesus sayings. If, as elsewhere in this volume, the 'what might we learn' question has been posed, what might OT/NT discourse learn from HJ studies? As with OT/NT discourse, a variety of criteria have been suggested as characterizing the authenticity of Jesus tradition (inter alia dissimilarity, coherence or multiple attestation), and these have perhaps assumed a similar 'status' to the Haysian seven (and probably an even more influential one in HJ studies). However, recent work has tended to query the authenticity-criteria approach, and it would seem – to the outsider looking in, at least – that the days of such criteria are numbered and found to be no longer helpful.[71] The HJ quest is not over – at least the majority of scholars seem to still aver that – and likewise, the quest for discerning connections between OT and NT is not over; by contrast, one surmises that it is flourishing. However, the search for authentic or genuine OT allusions *based on criteria* may be over, or require similar rethinking to that HJ study has occasioned. And it may be the case that the *incapacity* of criteria to satisfactorily 'demonstrate' an OT/NT allusion serves both to illustrate that incapacity and also, therefore, to open up alternative methodologies or approaches.

4. It may be that we need to offer a different lens to the allusion discourse, one no longer predicated in terms of criteria or 'criteria' utilized or understood in a different way. One example might be found in Tom Thatcher's use of social memory theory as a quasi-criterion for making sense of a mooted OT–NT association. Rather than finding the link in terms of textual orientation, Thatcher suggests that the intertextual relationship draws on shared memory: 'the sacred texts of Israel informed, and were often foundational to, these memories, yet it is the memories themselves, not the texts on which they are based, that are "cited" for the audience's consideration.'[72] This may be dangerous ground for a scholarly sub-discipline traditionally honed on textual association and may raise even more pressing questions as to how one can confidently authenticate perceived associations (textual links at least offer some form of evidencing these, even if the nature of that is contested); but it nonetheless offers a different, potentially fruitful framework for the way in which the New Testament uses the Old.

---

[70] As Hays, *Echoes*, 29 himself declares: 'exegesis is a modest, imaginative craft, not an exact science.'
[71] See in this regard: Chris Keith and Anthony Le Donne, *Jesus, Criteria, and the Demise of Authenticity* (London: T&T Clark, 2012). While the contributors are not univocal in their assessment of criteria, there is a core thesis advocating the relegation of criteria of authenticity.
[72] Tom Thatcher, 'Cain and Abel in Early Christian Memory: A Case Study in "The Use of the Old Testament in the New"', *CBQ* 72 (2010): 750.

10

The use of criteria: A proposal from relevance theory

Steve Smith

Introduction

For almost thirty years, Richard Hays's *Echoes of Scripture in the Letters of Paul* has had a significant effect on OT/NT study, with many writers influenced by Hays's criteria for the identification of OT echoes: *availability, volume, recurrence, thematic coherence, historical plausibility, history of interpretation and satisfaction*.[1] While they have had a significant effect on OT/NT scholarship with many scholars referring to them, these criteria are not uniformly applied by scholars: some use them unchanged,[2] others make them the basis of their approach but adapt them by emphasizing some criteria more than others,[3] still others add other criteria to them.[4] However, many scholars do not use them, and even Hays does not make explicit use of them as standard criteria for identifying echoes in his recent volume.[5] In addition to this, there are some significant limitations with their use as criteria, not

---

[1] Richard B. Hays, *Echoes of Scripture in the Letters of Paul* (New Haven; London: Yale University Press, 1989), 29–32; Richard B. Hays, *The Conversion of the Imagination: Paul as Interpreter of Israel's Scripture* (Grand Rapids: Eerdmans, 2005), 34–45.

[2] For example, Roy E. Ciampa, *The Presence and Function of Scripture in Galatians 1 and 2* (WUNT 2/102, Tübingen: Mohr Siebeck, 1998), 24–5; Brian J. Abasciano, *Paul's Use of the Old Testament in Romans 9:1-9: An Intertextual and Theological Exegesis* (JSNTSup 301; London: T&T Clark, 2005), 22–4.

[3] For example, Jeannine K. Brown, 'Genesis in Matthew's Gospel', in *Genesis in the New Testament* (ed. Maarten J. J. Menken and Steve Moyise; LNTS 466; London: Bloomsbury T&T Clark, 2012); Kenneth D. Litwak, *Echoes of Scripture in Luke-Acts: Telling the History of God's People Intertextually* (JSNTSup 282; London: T&T Clark International, 2005). Volume, availability and thematic coherence are typically favoured; however, Wagner emphasizes satisfaction, thinking this as what Hays frequently bases his decisions on: J. Ross Wagner, *Heralds of the Good News: Isaiah and Paul 'in Concert' in the Letter to the Romans* (NovTSup, 101; Leiden: Brill, 2002), 11–13.

[4] Michael B. Thompson, *Clothed with Christ: The Example and Teaching of Jesus in Romans 12.1-15.13* (Sheffield: Sheffield Academic Press, 1991), 30–6; Brian S. Rosner, *Paul, Scripture and Ethics: A Study of 1 Corinthians 5-7* (Leiden: Brill, 1994), 17–20.

[5] Richard B. Hays, *Echoes of Scripture in the Gospels* (Waco: Baylor University Press, 2016).

least their appearance of objectivity while being essentially *subjective* assessments.[6] So fundamentally, Dave Allen is correct to question their role in his chapter in this volume.

In a 2015 article, Paul Foster focuses on what he regards as 'some of the worrying excesses of the method';[7] part of his critique concerns how well it is able to reject 'spurious cases of perceived echoes'.[8] While Foster overstates the problem, in part through a too narrow definition of what constitutes an echo, there surely is a need in scholarship for some way of assessing potential intertexts for those who are attempting to recover something resembling the original meaning of the text. Because the identification of intertexts can be intuitive and hard to quantify, it is vital to understand how a reader approaches the text in order to determine how their decisions over potential echoes are made. In this chapter, I propose that relevance theory (RT) can offer a way of doing just that, not in order to give alternative criteria but by providing a framework for understanding how readers approach texts.

The first section outlines RT and proposes four variables of reader intertext detection from a relevance framework that can serve as guides for the contemporary interpreter in the process of identifying intertextual echoes. The second section discusses wider contributions that RT can make to OT/NT studies, focused around the detection of OT echoes, before it finally suggests how this relevance framework can be used in place of criteria in identifying allusions in NT texts.

1 Relevance theory

Relevance theory offers a comprehensive theory of human communication based on inference.[9] In particular, it regards communication as not simply a matter of encoding and decoding thoughts but as dependent on inference in a process directed by *relevance*.[10]

A hearer combines what they hear in the utterance – both its explicit content and what it implies – with what they already know, and where it modifies their context or *cognitive environment* to produce new *contextual effects*, it is said to be relevant.[11] The hearer orders their thinking in processing the utterance around this search for

---

[6] Availability and historical plausibility can be measured to an extent, but the others cannot. See Steve Moyise, 'Intertextuality and the Study of the Old Testament in the New', in *The Old Testament in the New: Essays in Honour of J. L. North* (JSNTSup 189; Sheffield: Sheffield Academic Press, 2000), 18–19.
[7] Paul Foster, 'Echoes without Resonance: Critiquing Certain Aspects of Recent Scholarly Trends in the Study of the Jewish Scriptures in the New Testament', *JSNT* 38 (2015): 100.
[8] Ibid., 104.
[9] The classic work is Dan Sperber and Deirdre Wilson, *Relevance: Communication and Cognition* (2nd edn; Oxford: Blackwell, 1995). Also helpful are the essays in Deirdre Wilson and Dan Sperber, eds, *Meaning and Relevance* (Cambridge: Cambridge University Press, 2012) and the summary in Deirdre Wilson and Dan Sperber, 'Relevance Theory', in *Handbook of Pragmatics* (ed. Laurence Horn and Gregory Ward; Oxford: Blackwell, 2003).
[10] Sperber and Wilson, *Relevance*, 3–5.
[11] Ibid., 48, 58, 108–9.

relevance because the speaker has assumed the utterance is relevant to the hearer[12] and has sought to make it optimally relevant to the hearer. The degree of relevance of an utterance is determined by a combination of maximizing contextual effects and minimizing the mental effort the hearer needs to expend.[13] The hearer of an utterance therefore follows this process: presuming the utterance to be relevant, the hearer searches through their cognitive environment – the range of contexts available to them – to see where the utterance is relevant to them;[14] these contexts will include the wider context of the utterance and so-called *encyclopaedic information* (data associated with a concept which may include cultural beliefs, personal opinion and experiences). The hearer does not need to be thinking about these contexts at the time but rather merely to be able to access them (such contexts are said to be *manifest* to them). Critically, for the utterance to be successful, the speaker and the hearer need to have the same assumptions manifest to them, and the speaker must realize that the hearer has access to these assumptions. It is important to note that some of these contexts will be more immediately accessible,[15] and in order to minimize their interpretive effort, the hearer will begin their search for relevance with these more immediate contexts (the speaker is aware that the hearer will do this, designing the utterance such that the appropriate context is most manifest). Because the hearer seeks *optimal relevance*, not maximal relevance, they will stop searching once they have found relevance and will not search in other contexts for further relevance because this demands too much effort.[16]

This process is well described for spoken communication, though some argue it is less applicable to texts because they are more stylistic and less dialogical.[17] However, texts are communication just like speech, and texts do not signal that they need to be treated any differently to utterances,[18] so RT has been applied with benefit to textual communication as well as spoken communication.[19]

---

[12] Ibid., 260–79.
[13] 'Extent condition 1: An assumption is relevant to an individual to the extent that the positive cognitive effects achieved when it is optimally processed are large. Extent condition 2: An assumption is relevant to an individual to the extent that the effort required to achieve these positive cognitive effects is small.' Ibid., 265–6. For a fuller discussion see also pp. 118–71.
[14] Ibid., 38–46, 138.
[15] Some information is only attainable through an indirect route involving the activation of other encyclopaedic information first, ibid., 137.
[16] Deirdre Wilson, 'Relevance and Understanding', in *Language and Understanding* (ed. Gillian Brown; Oxford: Oxford University Press, 1994), 44–50.
[17] As noted by Keith Green, 'Relevance Theory and the Literary Text: Some Problems and Perspectives', *JLS* 22 (1993): 210.
[18] Tzvetan Todorov, *Genres in Discourse* (trans. Catherine Porter; Cambridge: Cambridge University Press, 1990), 1–12.
[19] See David Trotter, 'Analysing Literary Prose: The Relevance of Relevance Theory', *Lingua* 87 (1992) and especially the recent Terence Cave and Deirdre Wilson, eds, *Reading Beyond the Code: Literature and Relevance Theory* (Oxford: Oxford University Press, 2018). In biblical studies there are many examples, see Steve Smith, *The Fate of the Jerusalem Temple in Luke-Acts: An Intertextual Approach to Jesus' Laments over Jerusalem and Stephen's Speech* (LNTS 553; London: Bloomsbury T&T Clark, 2017), 28, n. 107.

When dealing with intertextuality,[20] RT treats the allusion as a form of *echoic language*.[21] In alluding to another text, a text will have shared words or content with it: a hearer noting this link will follow the usual relevance process and search for implications that the two texts have in common, stopping when expectations of relevance are achieved.[22] Being a text, the reader can expect some more effort to be expended in interpretation than one would spend in interpreting a spoken utterance, so the intertext can be relatively difficult to interpret; however, there must not be a simpler way to achieve relevance than the intertext, otherwise the reader will find relevance there, and not in the intertext.[23] This means that if relevance is attained with less effort through a motif, story or theme, then a reader will not proceed to process the verse itself; it also means that when relevance is attained in the most obvious intertext to the reader, then they will not continue processing other possible allusions.

There is more to interpreting allusions than this, and some of the processes of adding implicatures can be understood more fully by examining how RT handles metaphors.[24] Briefly, in requiring more interpretive effort from a reader, difficult intertexts promise an increase in cognitive effects through implicatures (if explicatures arise from the logical form of the utterance, then implicatures are other contextual effects that are implied from it).[25] These implicatures fall on a spectrum: some are strong and a writer can reasonably assume that a reader will derive these implicatures from the intertext; others are weaker, and when a reader forms weaker implicatures they need to take more interpretive responsibility for them (a writer may have intended that the reader derive some weaker implicatures but not the specific ones that the reader derived).[26] Therefore, the stronger implicatures are necessary for optimal relevance and some of the weaker ones will be too; however, a reader can also go beyond the author's communicative intention in searching too hard for meaning.[27]

This theory can therefore be applied to the process of identification of allusions.

---

[20] Several have written about RT and OT allusion in the NT, including Stephen W. Pattemore, *The People of God in the Apocalypse: Discourse, Structure and Exegesis* (SNTSMS 128; Cambridge: Cambridge University Press, 2004); Peter S. Perry, 'Relevance Theory and Intertextuality', in *Exploring Intertextuality: Diverse Strategies for New Testament Interpretation of Texts* (ed. B. J. Oropeza and Steve Moyise; Eugene: Cascade Books, 2016); Smith, *Fate*; Nelson R. Morales, *Poor and Rich in James: A Relevance Theory Approach to James's Use of the Old Testament* (BBRSup 20; University Park: Eisenbrauns, 2018).

[21] Humans can create mental *representations* about a concept. Quotations are a form of *metarepresentation*, 'a representation of a representation', the 'ability to form *thoughts* about attributed thoughts'. See Deirdre Wilson, 'Metarepresentation in Linguistic Communication', in *Meaning and Relevance*, quotes p. 230, italics original.

[22] Ibid., 244.

[23] For the significance of effort in textual interpretation, see Terence Cave and Deirdre Wilson, 'Introduction', in *Reading Beyond the Code*, 12–13.

[24] Smith, *Fate*, 30–3.

[25] Sperber and Wilson, *Relevance*, 182, 93–202.

[26] This is seen very clearly in poetry and the use of metaphor there: ibid., 199–200.

[27] For a good discussion of this see Anne Furlong, 'Relevance Theory and Literary Interpretation' (PhD, University College London, 1996), 189–204.

2 The application of relevance theory

According to RT, a reader of the NT text seeks relevance for what they read in a range of contexts beginning with the context that is most closely available to them (the most manifest context); often that interpretive context will be the loose association of thoughts that have been forming in the reader's mind as the discourse of the text develops. Where an intertextual relationship successfully occurs between the NT and OT, the reader is led to the OT text as the interpretive context for finding relevance. For such a link to be made, three steps typically need to happen in the mind of the reader: (i) the reader will notice a signal in the text that another text is being referred to; (ii) the prior text is identified; and (iii) sufficient cognitive effects are developed to satisfy relevance.[28] Of course these steps can occur simultaneously in the mind of the reader, but they can also occur sequentially in a short space of time, and it is important to bear all of them in mind when noting how likely it is for a reader to identify an intertext. There are several variables which are important in determining if this process will be successful, and the evaluation of these variables is important for those attempting to determine how likely a potential intertext is. In this way, they can serve as guides to interpretation.

First, the presence of a *textual signal*. Signals in the text indicate to the reader that a reference to the OT is being made.[29] If such a signal is present in the verse, then the reader will search through a catalogue of available OT contexts to access one in which expectations of relevance are fulfilled. If an intertext is important for meaning, then RT indicates that a writer should signal it as part of their guarantee of optimal relevance: in other words, the writer uses the signal to ensure that the most manifest context for the reader is the one in which the writer needs them to find relevance.[30]

Signals can be introductory formulae, such as the γέγραπται and εἴρηται before the quotations from Scripture in the temptation narratives in Lk. 4.4, 8, 10, 12, or the ἀναπτύξας τὸ βιβλίον εὗρεν τὸν τόπον οὗ ἦν γεγραμμένον which precedes the quotation of Isa. 61.1-2 in Lk. 4.18-19. Such signals before quotations are obvious, but other more subtle signals may be present, such as a statement which directs the reader to a specific OT text (see below); a change in style of writing (Rom. 3.10-18); the use of a grammatical signal such as ὅτι (Lk. 2.30, referring to Isa. 52.10, especially in the context of the frequent allusions in the infancy songs); or a distinct motif followed by a textual fragment (Lk. 1.13 echoes Gen. 17.19 and is signalled by the similar situation of a childless couple).[31] Where a signal is strong, then the echo does not need to be as recognisable because the signal encourages the reader to explore the available interpretive contexts until relevance is found; the increased effort is compensated by an expectation of more cognitive effects. The characteristics of an allusion which make

---

[28] The first two stages are similar to the first two stages in Ziva Ben-Porat, 'The Poetics of Literary Allusion', *PTL: A Journal for Descriptive Poetics and Theory of Literature* 1 (1976): 105–28.

[29] In RT terms, this signal points to the ostension of the writer, signalling to the reader that relevance is to be found in a certain context: Deirdre Wilson, 'Relevance Theory and Literary Interpretation', in *Reading Beyond the Code*, 198.

[30] Ibid., 187–90.

[31] See Benjamin D. Sommer, *A Prophet Reads Scripture: Allusion in Isaiah 40-66* (Stanford: Stanford University Press, 1998) for such ideas of signalling.

it more distinctive (as discussed below) are still important, but the presence of an independent signal means that the text does not have to be so clear that it requires no effort to process. Signalled but difficult texts can be a deliberate strategy: for example, Lk. 24.44-7 uses a clear signal to point to the OT (πάντα τὰ γεγραμμένα ἐν τῷ νόμῳ Μωϋσέως καὶ τοῖς προφήταις καὶ ψαλμοῖς περί ἐμοῦ), but the texts it points to are unclear. As a result, the reader expends increased interpretive effort and is forced to make assumptions about what the verses may be in order to derive weak implicatures; these are then confirmed or denied when turning to the apostolic exegesis in the Acts speeches, which give the content of such scriptural exegesis. On other occasions, the signal points the reader to a specific OT verse or story: Jesus's sermon in Luke 4 contains specific details of the stories from Elijah and Elisha which point to particular narratives (Lk. 4.25-7); Lk. 17.32 uses μνημονεύετε τῆς γυναικὸς Λώτ to point to a story in the Genesis narrative (Gen. 19.26); and the reference to καθὼς ἐγένετο ἐν ταῖς ἡμέραις Νῶε in Lk.17.26 is used to signal the specific reference for the comments in the following verse.

Where there is no extrinsic signal, allusions function differently. The signal for such intertexts is intrinsic to the intertext itself; in other words, the reader only spots the intertext because they recognize it. So these intertexts are only likely to be identified if they are clearly recognizable, and if they come from a text that is the most manifest context available to the reader, because processing will stop when relevance is found in the most immediate context – anything else requires too much processing effort. So even among readers with an excellent knowledge of the LXX, there will be occasions when a reader would not make a connection with an OT text because another context is closer. It is intertexts like this that frequently cause scholarly debate.

Secondly, it is important to assess the *echoic strength* of the intertext. There is some overlap with Hays's concept of volume here: Hays refers to the degree of verbatim repetition of the prior text, the distinctiveness or prominence of the words used (i.e. they are clearly associated with the prior text) and the degree of rhetorical stress the echo receives,[32] though the latter has more to do with signalling than *echoic strength*. Verbal parallels are undoubtedly very important,[33] but the place of shared vocabulary can be overemphasized.[34] Shared words can direct a reader to a text when a textual signal has alerted the reader to the presence of an intertext, but where there is no extrinsic signal, matters are different. No matter how many words texts have in common, an intertext is not going to be noted by a reader unless it is distinctive and pointing to a text that is immediately manifest for the reader (see *accessibility* below). But there is more to echoic strength than verbal parallel, and shared themes are vitally important because these bring certain encyclopaedic information to the mind of a reader, ensuring that certain OT contexts where they are dealt with are the most manifest environment for finding relevance. So shared themes are capable of forming textual links when there is no extrinsic signal, and once this link is created, then verbal similarity may have some

---

[32] Hays, *Conversion*, 34–7.
[33] For example, Jeffrey Leonard demonstrated the significance of shared language beyond other markers of intertexts in OT inner-biblical allusions, Jeffery M. Leonard, 'Identifying Inner-Biblical Allusions: Psalm 78 as a Test Case', *JBL* 127 (2008): 241–65.
[34] Ziony Zevit, 'Echoes of Texts Past', in *Subtle Citation, Allusion, and Translation in the Hebrew Bible* (ed. Ziony Zevit; Sheffield: Equinox Publishing Ltd., 2017), 12.

role in directing the reader to a particular text. However, it is significant that shared themes do not always point to a text: a reference to a motif will often lead to a motif as the intertext; mention of an event (or story) will often lead to that event (or story) being the intertext. For example, Lk. 13.34 makes reference to gathering under wings; with no extrinsic signal, the intertextual link is dependent on echoic strength.

Luke 13.34 ποσάκις ἠθέλησα ἐπισυνάξαι τὰ τέκνα σου ὃν τρόπον ὄρνις τὴν ἑαυτῆς νοσσιὰν ὑπὸ τὰς πτέρυγας ... (How often have I desired to gather your children together as a hen gathers her brood under her wings ...)

While commentators typically note a list of potential intertexts, settling for one of them on the basis of lexical similarity,[35] I have demonstrated elsewhere that Lk. 13.34 does not have particular similarity with any text but to the motif of YHWH's care of his people, the motif shared by all these texts and several later Jewish texts.[36] The distinctive thematic coherence of this verse to the OT motif is sufficient to ensure that the OT theme is the most manifest context for interpretation. A reader would find expectations of relevance satisfied here and not spend more effort identifying a particular text.

To give a couple of further examples, verbal parallel can be sufficient when the text is distinctive and well known, and there is some signalling, for example the echo of Ps. 36.6 (LXX) in Lk. 23.46, where the last words of Jesus perhaps indicate an echo is possible. However, verbal similarity on its own may not be enough for many readers. In the interpolation of Isa. 58.6 in the middle of Isa. 61.1-2 in Lk. 4.18-19, readers may not notice the interpolation immediately (unless the co-location of these texts in 4Q521 suggests they were commonly used together); but as they examine the highly signalled quotation to Isa. 61.1-2 in detail, the interpolation will become apparent.[37]

Thirdly, the *accessibility* of the OT text. For RT, availability (whether readers and writers had access to the LXX) is not the principal issue,[38] *accessibility* is more important. Because NT texts are interpreted in their most manifest interpretive context, the critical issue is whether a proposed intertext is the most manifest context for a reader or whether there is a more immediate context where expectations of relevance may be satisfied. For example, there may be occasions where relevance would be found in other contexts associated with the use of a text, such as its liturgical use (like a Hallel Psalm in the context of Jewish feasts),[39] or its place in a Christian *testimonia*.[40] Similarly, an OT story, motif, event or theological idea (e.g. the so-called Isaianic New Exodus) could be closer at hand for the reader than a specific text, and they would stop processing after achieving relevance there. These contexts are still OT based, but the encyclopaedic data associated with them is slightly different to the data associated with a particular text. In these cases, it is unlikely that the writer intended a specific verse

---

[35] For example, Hays, *Gospels*, 260–1.
[36] Smith, *Fate*, 39–42.
[37] For details of the text and possible co-location, see David W. Pao and Eckhard J. Schnabel, 'Luke', in *Commentary on the New Testament Use of the Old Testament* (ed. G. K. Beale and D. A. Carson; Grand Rapids: Baker Academic, 2007), 288–9.
[38] This is the significant issue for Christopher D. Stanley, *Arguing with Scripture: The Rhetoric of Quotations in the Letters of Paul* (New York; London: T&T Clark International, 2004), 38–61.
[39] Smith, *Fate*, 51.
[40] See Martin C. Albl, *And Scripture Cannot Be Broken: The Form and Function of the Early Christian Testimonia Collections* (NovTSup 96; Leiden; Boston: Brill, 1999).

to be the sole intertext because the principles of relevance require the writer to signal the context clearly for the reader (as they did for Lot's wife above). Accessibility is far more important where there is no signal because a reader may not access anything related to the OT at all if the text is relatively unavailable and relevance can be found in a closer unrelated context, no matter how strong the apparent *echoic strength* of the OT context.

As part of accessibility, it is important to think about what makes a text accessible. This may be that it is well known, but it can be through repetition: if there is some *local repetition* of an OT text within a NT passage, this serves to make associated OT texts, stories and motifs manifest for the reader when they come across another possible intertext. So the dense references to the OT prophets in Lk. 19.41-4 ensure readers have these contexts available as they continue deeper into the text.[41]

Fourth, the role of *interpretive benefit* cannot be understated. Ultimately, a reader is only going to accept an intertext if its context satisfies expectations for optimum relevance, because the acquisition of relevance serves to indicate to the reader that the intertext is one that the writer intended.[42] If sufficient relevance it is not found in an intertext, then the reader will explore other contexts; so without interpretive benefit a text cannot be an intertext.[43] In many ways this is similar to Hays's criteria of satisfaction, but there are two ways that it is different. (i) For Hays, this is one of several criteria; following RT it becomes clear that without it there is no intertext. (ii) Because principles of relevance apply to scholarly readings of texts just as they do to ancient readers, one must differentiate whose satisfaction is involved. Scholars are likely to favour an intertext being present based on whether it brings interpretive benefit to them, not benefit to the primary readers. Similarly, the way that the discussion of an intertext is set up in any scholarly work ensures that certain interpretive contexts are made most manifest to the modern reader; in this way the proposed intertext is likely to offer sufficient cognitive effects to satisfy the expectations for relevance of the reader of the scholarly work. In other words, because the intertext fits well with the scholar's argument, it proves satisfying to agree that it is an intertext. The important question to ask is whether the *original* reader would have found the text brought interpretive benefit, and that requires the kind of orientation into their cognitive environment that has been discussed above.

Of course, there is some overlap with ideas contained in Hays's criteria in these elements: *textual signals* incorporate ideas of *recurrence*, among other things; *echoic strength* includes considerations of what Hays terms *volume* and *thematic coherence*; *accessibility* incorporates and expands on Hays's *availability*; and *interpretive benefit* adds some specificity to *satisfaction*. In addition, while *historical plausibility* and *history of interpretation* are not explicitly included as independent items, the sort of things they assess form part of the careful historical work that needs to be done to demonstrate what contexts would be accessible to the ancient reader. In covering some of the same ground, the guides recognize the significance of the factors that Hays identified, but they are not the same as his criteria, and they seek to address some of

---

[41] Smith, *Fate*, 59–67.
[42] Wilson, 'Literary Interpretation', 187–90.
[43] Pattemore, *People*, 40; Morales, *Poor and Rich*, 65.

the weaknesses contained within the very idea of criteria. This will be addressed below, but before doing this it is important to note some wider contributions of how these guides apply to intertextuality.

3 Wider contributions

There are four wider aspects of the identification of echoes in OT/NT study that RT can also make a contribution towards, and it is important to note these before defining how the guides above can be used in practice.

3.1 Types of allusion

The discussion above helps to demonstrate that there are several different types of echo that are possible in a NT text.

Essential references are required for the communication of the message of the text. The author requires these textual references to be noted and they should be clearly identifiable because the author will ensure their accessibility.

Enriching references are those that some readers will notice, thereby adding implicatures, but which other readers will miss without causing detriment to the central message of the text. An author wants readers to note these echoes because it increases understanding, but the contextual effects are additional to the essential ones.

Compositional references are those that were in the mind of the author as the NT text was written and have a formative effect on the theology of the NT text, but which do not represent a part of the communicative intent of the writer on any level. Discovering these echoes helps to reconstruct the theology of the author, and if a reader notes them they will probably enrich a reader's understanding of the text – because they are in tune with the themes of the text – but they are not part of the communicative intention of the text, and the reader takes responsibility for their interpretation.

Unintentional references are references to texts that the author knew but was not consciously aware of while writing the NT text. Such texts will have had an effect on the writing of the text on a subconscious level but are not part of the communicative intent. NT authors have an excellent knowledge of Scripture, and OT texts will likely be part of the apparatus of their thinking and inevitably affect what they write subconsciously – but they are not part of the communicative intent of the text.[44] A reader takes responsibility for their interpretation, and their contribution can be less in line with the overall message of the text than *compositional references*.

---

[44] As Lucas notes, 'for one so steeped in the language of Scripture as Paul, he was bound to express himself in ways that subconsciously echoed scriptural texts on a regular basis without any metaleptic intentions': Alec J. Lucas, 'Assessing Stanley E Porter's Objections to Richard B Hays's Notion of Metalepsis', *CBQ* 76 (2014): 95.

Post-authorial references are those that are discovered by modern readers to literature that the author did not know. These are not part of the communicative intent of the author.

This is a more helpful way of subdividing OT references than the more usual quotation, allusion, echo and so on because it concerns their function and not their structure. The differences between these types is not always sharply defined in practice because they form a spectrum of allusion types, but it is important to attempt (as far as possible) to differentiate between an echo that is part of the writer's communicative intent (and ostensively placed in the text) and an echo that is there because it was formative in the writer's mind whether consciously or unconsciously.[45] Too often OT/NT studies blur these distinctions and pursue the re-creation of the thoughts of the NT writer rather than the 'meaning' of the textual communication. There is considerable theological merit in re-creating the author's mind, but to assume that these then form intertexts that a reader would note confuses the issue.

3.2 Re-reading the text

This list of types of allusion makes it clear that there are likely to be more intertexts involved in a NT text than are immediately obvious, and a reader who makes a close study of the text will often find echoes below the surface reading. One may question whether the additional cognitive effects from these further echoes are part of the intended communication of the text, because where readers expend extra effort in the identification of additional relevance, they go beyond the expectation of the writer. However, with biblical texts this may not be true. NT documents were written expecting some form of re-reading rather than with the expectation of being read once only.[46] Epistles are likely to have been written anticipating group readings with the explanation of the text by a teacher in the church; as such, Paul expected that the potential echoes in his text would be discovered by his readership. Although the case for the audience of the Gospels is a heated debate,[47] it is surely likely that their authors did not anticipate a single reading.

This means that the category of *enriching intertexts* is probably broader than one might expect, and some of the intertexts on the border between *enriching* and *compositional intertexts* actually belong in the enriching category. The key arbiter has to be the provision of relevance by the text: if an intertext gives sufficient contextual effects (for sufficiently limited effort) then it is likely to be intended by the author, as long as a more immediate intertext does not satisfy relevance expectations.

---

[45] See Wilson, 'Literary Interpretation', 198.
[46] If ideals in the wider culture are anything to go by, see William A. Johnson, *Readers and Reading Culture in the High Roman Empire: A Study of Elite Communities* (Classical Culture and Society; New York: Oxford University Press, 2010).
[47] See the discussions in Richard Bauckham, ed., *The Gospels for All Christians: Rethinking the Gospel Audiences* (Grand Rapids: Eerdmans, 1998).

3.3 Original and contemporary readers

In reading the text today, the principles of relevance govern our reading, but we are not the primary readers of the text.[48] If we are attempting to recover the original communication of the text then we cannot be driven by the contextual assumptions that are most available to us – it is those of the primary readers that matter. Similarly, the relevance that modern readers derive from texts may differ from the relevance primary readers would attain – consequently the relevance achieved by primary readers may feel somehow incorrect to modern readers who are expecting something different. This reemphasizes the importance of careful evaluation of the cognitive environment of the primary readership.

3.4 Author- and reader-centred reading

The relevance theoretic approach is neither reader centred nor author centred, and as such it avoids the pitfalls of other methods that are closely associated with one or the other. Relevance theory does not require a reader to recover authorial intention, instead it regards the text as a communicative event where the writer provides everything that the reader requires to arrive a certain meaning with minimal effort; however, the fulfilment of this intention of the writer is the responsibility of the reader. Readers, therefore, are free to explore the text but use the principles of relevance to impose interpretive limits on themselves, searching for relevance in what is likely to be the intention behind an utterance.[49]

Bearing these wider issues in mind, it is possible to indicate how RT can contribute to evaluating echoes.

4 Using a relevance theory approach

The goal of the application of the guides here is to provide more precision and flexibility to the process of detecting echoes in OT/NT studies. There are four things that need to be borne in mind while applying them to OT/NT research.

First, as the four guides for interpretation are applied to texts they need to be used in the context of an overall framework of the theory of human communication. It is difficult to decide the overall weighting of the different Hays's criteria, and a significant reason for this is that they do not have an overall frame of reference, nor do readers follow them in reading a text. However, because the guides to interpretation are evaluated together as part of overall theory of communication, this allows consideration of how important individual elements are on a case-by-case basis. For example, a text needs considerable *echoic strength* (often thematic) and availability if there is no clear extrinsic *textual signal*; and no matter how well signalled an intertext, it is unlikely to form part of the communicative intent of the writer unless it gives contextual effects

---

[48] Morales, *Poor and Rich*, 25.
[49] See the discussion in Adrian Pilkington, *Poetic Effects: A Relevance Theory Perspective* (PBNS 75; Amsterdam: John Benjamins Publishing Company, 2000), 66.

not available in a more immediate context. As such, the RT communicative framework is essential.

Secondly, it is important to recognize that the process is essentially subjective. The guides above are not criteria for identifying allusions, instead they offer a more careful focus on the various stages that a reader goes through in reading a text, thereby permitting the interpreter to think about the various subjective (and often unconscious) choices that readers face; they force the interpreter to slow down and think about steps that are often quickly passed over in reading. The decision is still subjective, but based on more detailed information.

Third, interpreters need to be aware of the kind of reader they are evaluating because the model permits the interpreter to shift weighting depending on the reader that is being evaluated: these readers may be the primary reader of the text in the original context or a modern reader; they may be a first-time reader of the text or may be re-reading in a group setting where more interpretive effort would be expended. This is one of the great strengths of the approach: it realizes that different readers come to the text, and the text will not necessarily yield the same depth of meaning to each reader. Relevance theory therefore deals with how *real readers* read, not how an imagined idealized reader could approach the text.

Fourth, the model should be used dynamically, taking account of the essentially dynamic nature of the reading process. As readers progress through a text, they make judgements that are provisional and which develop as the text continues;[50] Relevance theory describes readers utilizing *ad hoc concepts*, temporary clusters of thoughts about a certain subject which may be developed as the text progresses.[51] A relevance approach to the text bears this dynamic in mind as prior contexts are more manifest to the reader and developed as the text revisits them.

On one level using RT is not anything new, because if relevance describes human communication then all interpreters are subconsciously using the principles of relevance in making their textual decisions anyway. What is more, RT is not strictly a method for interpretation; it is a linguistic theory of communication. However, it does give a framework for interpretation, and focusing on the four guides permits the interpreter to focus in on key steps in the interpretive pathway foregrounding the mental processes that are important to real-life readers. As such, it offers a valuable contribution to the definition of echoes in the NT.

Conclusion

This chapter has offered a set of guides which can help in deciding whether a proposed echo is present in the NT and what sort of echo it is. Based on a universal theory of human communication, it permits the interpreter to focus in on aspects of the reading process that are normally taken for granted. It is not an alternative set of criteria for finding allusions, and such concepts are questionable, but in answer to Paul Foster's

---

[50] Terence Cave, 'Towards a Passing Theory of Understanding', in *Reading Beyond the Code*, 168–70.
[51] Pilkington, *Effects*, 96–108.

criticism it does permit the scholar to identify whether an allusion was likely to be part of the author's communicative intent (the kind of allusion with which Foster is most concerned). This approach is adaptable, and it is capable of giving evidence that an allusion is essential for communication or that it exists for enriching purposes in further study. In addition, because of its focus on the availability of contexts, it is also capable of differentiating intertexts which are appealing to modern readers from those noted by the original readers because it can focus on the relevance that each group derives from the text, and this should help modern interpreters develop more precision in textual decisions.

Section D

Responses

11

Rethinking context in the relationship of Israel's Scriptures to the NT: Character, agency and the possibility of genuine change

Rikk Watts

Introduction

The first part of this chapter will survey and offer some commentary on key aspects of the current conflicted state of our field. The second half is where the new work begins. It seeks to offer a way forward by employing R. G. Collingwood's notion of 'historical imagination' to re-imagine how the NT writers related to Israel's Scriptures. It will argue that two interrelated assumptions appear foundational for them. First, Israel's Scriptures as the unbroken and unfailing word of the Lord God were normative and sufficient in revealing his character and thus articulating his relationship with his creation and especially his people. If so, it makes better sense, methodologically, to begin, not with NT authors' use of the OT but with Israel's Scriptures' normative influence on the NT. Second, given those Scriptures' emphasis on Yahweh's unique character and his unparalleled interest in humans, the grammar of Israel's 'theology' is primarily neither conceptual nor even literary but personal. Since persons are known through their agency,[1] that is words (including speech acts) and deeds over time, the fundamental orientation of Scripture is necessarily historical and narrative.

One would expect, therefore, that 'context' is likewise primarily personal, focused on God's response to a particular situation. The hermeneutical question when discussing the rationale behind a particular NT appeal to Israel's Scriptures would be: What does this text reveal about a faithful God's particular actions in the past that helps us understand the significance of his actions in the present? This chapter proposes that, when viewed from this perspective, the NT authors see what Yahweh has done in Christ to be both entirely consistent with his past and promised future interventions, and more profoundly revealing of his constant and unfailing character.

---

[1] John Macmurray, *The Self as Agent* (Gifford Lectures 1953; London: Faber & Faber, 1957).

1 Current debate

David Allen's useful survey of current discussion in the study of the NT use of the OT highlights four key areas of continuing discord.[2] They concern: context, interpretative technique, textual form and 'macro versus micro' approaches. Regarding context, the question focuses on the extent, if any, to which the cited text's original setting and meaning in Israel's Scriptures bears on its function in a given NT document. Proposals range across the spectrum from the OT context being broadly determinative (to use Allen's language), through a dialogical approach where there is a 'legitimate' two-way interchange (though what constitutes 'legitimate' is unstated), to the NT setting being the only significant consideration. Concerning the latter, it is sometimes asserted that in reflecting contemporary Jewish exegetical practice, the NT usage often goes far beyond the original contextual meaning.[3] This naturally raises the question: what exactly is contemporary Jewish exegetical practice(s)? The contested notions of *sensus plenior* and typology (one could perhaps add figural readings) also emerge here.

Directly related to the above, the second question, concerning interpretative technique, arises from the fact that the authors of the NT were either (mostly) first-century Jews or, for example, in Luke's case, heavily invested in a Jewish *Weltanschauung*, while at the same time influenced to some degree by the Hellenism of the world in which they found themselves.[4] Now, depending on their particular histories, social settings and identities, individuals might be happy to assume a broadly Hellenistic fashion in one area, yet remain conservatively Jewish in another, while integrating elements from both in still others. But at the same time, human individuality being scripted in the grammar of our relationships, we need to take account of the fact that the writers of the NT belonged to a self-consciously distinct and disliked community. Originally and distinctively self-titled 'the Way', they faced early harassment (Acts 9.2; 19.9, 23; 24.14, 22; cf. Mk 1.2-3's 'way of the Lord'). Not much later, in a mixed community of Jews and Gentiles, outsiders soon identified them, perhaps with some hostility, as Christian. This was probably because they no longer conformed to a characteristically Jewish or Gentile way of life and because of their apparent partisan zeal for Christ (Acts 11.26; 26.28).[5] Relatively small, and facing opposition on several fronts, the

---

[2] David Allen, 'Introduction: The Study of the Use of the Old Testament in the New', *JSNT* 38 (2015): 3–16. See also, Susan E. Docherty, 'New Testament Scriptural Interpretation in Its Early Jewish Context', *NovT* 57 (2015): 1–19.

[3] Allen, 'Introduction', 8, citing Peter Enns, *Inspiration and Incarnation: Evangelicals and the Problem of the Old Testament* (Grand Rapids: Baker Academic, 2005).

[4] This is not to rerun the older debate classically addressed by Martin Hengel, *Judaism and Hellenism* (trans. John Bowden; 2nd edn; Philadelphia: Fortress Press, 1981). It reflects instead the kinds of social dynamics raised by E. A. Judge and David M. Scholer, *Social Distinctives of the Christians in the First Century: Pivotal Essays* (Peabody: Hendrickson Publishers, 2008), and deeper 'philosophical' differences over, for example, education, again, Judge, 'Higher Education in the Pauline Churches', in *Learning and Teaching Theology: Some Ways Ahead* (ed. Les Ball and James Harrison; Eugene: Wipf and Stock, 2015), 23–31, or 'worldview', my 'Christianity and the Ancient World', *Crux* 53 (2017): 2–26; cf. Larry Hurtado, *Destroyer of the Gods: Early Christian Distinctiveness in the Roman World* (Waco: Baylor University, 2016).

[5] For example, Harold B. Mattingly, 'The Origin of the Name "Christiani"', *JTS* 9 (1956): 26–37. Edwin A. Judge, 'St Paul and Classical Society', *JAC* 15 (1972): 16–36; David Horrell, 'The Label *Christianos*: 1 Peter 4:16 and the Formation of Christian Identity', *JBL* 126 (2007): 361–81.

earliest Christians were thus marked by their singular devotion to the person of Jesus as Lord (cf. 1 Cor. 8.6) in whom they believed the ends of the ages (Kingdom of God) had begun and whose supremely authoritative teaching was mediated through his still-living designated and therefore authorized apostles. Sociologically speaking, and given their profoundly Jewish roots, one would expect to find in this earliest period a relatively cohesive hermeneutics, more akin to the homogeneity of Qumran than the varied opinion which characterizes the (later?) rabbis.

In addition, it might not be unexpected that a movement both as radical (e.g. a crucified Messiah, a high Christology [1 Cor. 8.6] and Law-free Gentile inclusion) and yet as conservative (e.g. grounded in Israel's Scriptures; see Jesus's rebuke of Pharisaic innovation in e.g. Mk 7.1-13 and 10.2-9) as 'the Way' might also, like its founder, both innovate and conserve in its handling of Israel's Scriptures. As most would agree, descriptions are not prescriptions. The mere fact that an interpretive option was available did not require a NT writer to take it; a new reading was always a possibility and, given the above, not unlikely. One apparently new development was Paul's extended conflations of scriptural texts (e.g. Rom. 3.10-18; or 2 Cor. 6.16-18). The single closest contemporary example is CD 8.14-15 (combining Deut. 9.5; 7.8).[6] Since it is improbable that Jesus copied Paul, the practice likely originated with him (e.g. Isa. 56.7 and Jer. 7.11 in Mk 11.17; Dan. 7.13 and Ps. 110.1 in Mk 14.62).

It might be appropriate here to comment here on wide-ranging scholarly appeals to the various hermeneutics of intertestamental literatures. It is difficult to know how much familiarity populations in rural centres like Capernaum or smaller urban centres such as Colossae would have had with these writings. On the one hand, to the extent that the Targums reflect first-century Palestinian Synagogue interpretations, one might argue for greater local familiarity (in the Gospel narratives) with the views and methods contained therein. On the other, that Qumran's Teacher of Righteousness actively forbade any communication of his ideas with outsiders (CD 5.15-17) might suggest caution in assuming those texts as background. The presence of an educated Apollos suggests some knowledge of Alexandrian (Philonic?) views in major centres like Ephesus and Corinth, but what about, for example, *1 Enoch* or the *Psalms of Solomon*? How many such texts were even designed for 'public' consumption, let alone enjoyed sufficiently wide circulation to be considered a realistic influence on the NT writings? That the NT writers themselves specifically appeal very infrequently to these writings – vanishingly small compared to the citations of, and allusions to, Israel's Scriptures – might give us pause as to what familiarity with them they either assumed, themselves had or if indeed they even cared about them. It seems clear that such writings – and presumably the interpretative opinions expressed therein – had for them nowhere near the authority of Scripture. Moreover, since the Jesus of the Gospels appears uncompromisingly hostile to the speculative traditions of men that according to him went beyond what was written (e.g. again Mk 7.1-13 and 10.2-9; and as his

---

[6] 4Q174[Flor] and 4Q175[Test] merely string texts together; see James M. Scott, 'The Use of Scripture in 2 Corinthians 6.16c-18 and Paul's Restoration Theology', *JSNT* 56 (1994): 77. Later rabbinic materials do cite related texts, for example, Exod. 23.20 and Mal. 3.1 in *Exod. Rab.* 32.9, but not in the same composite form we find in the Gospels.

own citation patterns bear out), why would we assume his earliest followers were any different (cf. Paul in 1 Cor. 4.6)?

This should not be taken to imply that the Gospels' Jesus nor the NT authors themselves were unaware of or uninfluenced by how Scripture had previously been interpreted, elements of which alternative readings can still be found in the various intertestamental literatures. But as Samuel Sandmel famously articulated some time ago, the problem lies in discerning whether similarity necessitates genealogical dependency or even familiarity.[7] Presumably, it is not unlikely that intelligent readers indwelling the same larger tradition and reflecting on the same limited corpus could come, independently, to a very similar understanding. My point is simply to note that the NT writers present themselves as engaging primarily with Scripture, not necessarily with others' interpretations of it. And when they adopt readings that are different to other interpreters, any resulting conflict is usually with the person(s) who holds the differing view, not their interpretative traditions per se, which are rarely if ever cited.

Now, if only in order to communicate to outsiders, something they were apparently keen to do, we should expect some common hermeneutical ground (e.g. a shared expectation of how to read biographies, historiography and letters). But more than that, their willingness to engage in public lecture and debate suggests that they also expected their hearers to find their arguments persuasive. Indeed, while we have accounts of Jesus and his apostles (including Paul) being attacked on various counts, the charge of abuse of Scripture is not among them (cf. Acts 17.11). At the same time, since it appears that Jesus and his apostles were convinced that in Jesus, they alone, of all of Israel's various 'religious'[8] groupings, had inherited and were already experiencing God's eschatological promises, one would expect a unique hermeneutical certainty in their handling of Scripture. Why follow others when the proof of one's own pudding was there for the eating?[9] Then there is the simple historical likelihood that the earliest Christian communities would be more inclined to expend their limited resources on the books (which were likely not as expensive as sometimes suggested[10]) that apparently matter most to them: Scripture, the apostles' letters and the gospels. It might be that the absence of such might explain the relative absence of specific scriptural citations in several letters (e.g. Colossians, Philippians), although this does not, of course, necessarily mean the absence of Scripture in the mind of the author (e.g. perhaps Isa. 29.13 in Col. 2.22; Ps. 110.1 in 3.1; Gen. 1.26-7 in 3.10; and Isa. 45.23

---

[7] Samuel Sandmel, 'Parallelomania', SBL 81 (1962): 1–13.
[8] 'Religious' because it is not clear that anyone in the ancient world thought there were practising 'religion'; Edwin Judge, 'The Social Identity of the First Christians: A Question of Method in Religious History', in *Social*, 130–1; also Brent Nongbri, *Before Religion: A History of a Modern Concept* (New Haven: Yale University Press, 2013); *pace*; for example, Hurtado, *Destroyer*, 38–44.
[9] The persistent canard that sets 'faith' against 'reason' ignores the fact that according to Israel's own Scriptures their knowledge of God was based, not on imagination or speculative philosophy, but (historical) experience, often in the face of Israel's resistant un-faith; see Yael Avrahami, *The Senses of Scripture: Sensory Perception in the Hebrew Bible* (New York: T&T Clark International, 2012); and Ian W. Scott, *Implicit Epistemology in the Letters of Paul: Story, Experience and the Spirit* (WUNT 205; Tübingen: Mohr Siebeck, 2006).
[10] Based on the figures in Martial, i.117.17 and xiii.3.2, and assuming thirty-two letters per line (P46) a copy of LXX Isaiah might cost from thirty to as low as eight denarii depending on the quality and one's bargaining power; not cheap but hardly beyond the reach of the average patron.

in Phil. 2.10; Deut. 32.5 and Dan. 12.3 in 2.15). All this to say greater care might need to be taken in how NT scholars use various intertestamental and rabbinic literatures.

In Allen's third area of discussion, proposals for the origins of the NT textual form range from variation originating in the author's creativity to the use of a currently unknown but at that time legitimate text form. Currently, the LXX as the 'bible' of the early Greek-speaking Church is rightly making a comeback. But unless there was a complete break with earlier tradition, it is worth remembering that Paul's training was in Jerusalem and, before that, his Lord and the Twelve were Palestinian. The NT writers might pragmatically cite the Greek texts available to them and their churches, but that should not rule out a prior foundational familiarity with the Scriptures in Hebrew. The fourth and final question concerns the macro and micro distinction which turns primarily on the role or not of Israel's larger narrative – for example, exodus and new exodus patterns – in informing the hermeneutics of NT authors and the extent to which it substantiates putative 'echoes'. The following discussion will suggest some ways forward on this point as well.

2 Two steps back and …

All this said, my purpose in this chapter is not simply to rework old ground, but instead to ask how people of good 'scholarly' will and facility can come to such widely differing conclusions. While it might be that our data is so pluriform and indeterminate that no other result is possible, the fact that this diversity often arises in response to the same NT text suggests that at least part of the problem lies elsewhere. Since every question presupposes something of the answer, a hopefully non-controversial possibility is that this diversity of outcomes results in part from our different initial assumptions. It might be that these differences are unresolvable, in which case we will continue to talk past one another. On the other hand, perhaps in reconsidering where we start, we can move forward.

During my early training as an engineer, I sometimes encountered situations where a particularly intractable problem had given rise to two mutually exclusive, but individually not entirely satisfactory, theoretical solutions. Over long debate, they began to take on a life of their own, eventually becoming the unconscious lenses through which everyone subsequently examined the problem. The lines of the theoretical debate and our ways of conceptualizing the problem had become not only determinative for all future discussion but effectively more 'real' than the data itself. The tricks played by the human mind (mine included!) had come into play. For example, when confronted with a situation that we cannot immediately explain and the human mind being very good at discerning patterns in random data, we quickly fashion a hypothesis that renders the data coherent and comprehensible. But the problem is that we are equally poor at assessing the likelihood of the hypothesis and, once committed, find it very difficult to see the evidence in any other light.[11]

---

[11] Michael Lewis, *The Undoing Project: A Friendship that Changed Our Minds* (1st edn; New York: W.W. Norton & Company, 2017), 205–8.

One way of trying to escape the impasse was, intellectually, to take two steps back, one step sideways and then to come at the problem from a new angle. The two steps back were essential. At only one step, the subject was still within reach and in a sense subject to my manipulation. Two steps created an emotional distance, a stepping back from the prior commitment, that allowed the subject space to 'breathe' as it were. The step sideways opened up a different vantage point and line of approach. It might be that something similar could help us here.

3 Collingwood's re-enactment

The 'new angle' I would like to propose begins with R. G. Collingwood's idea of historical imagination or re-enactment.[12] This turns on his characteristic distinction between the outside and inside of history. The former deals with external 'objective' observables and the latter with the 'subjective' personal element, that is, with what we might 'know' of the participants and their aims. Using the example of the chess game,[13] one can learn a great deal about chess simply by careful attention to the 'outside', that is, the externals. One can observe the board and its shape and pattern, the initial placement of the various pieces, their characteristic movements, and, over time, even possible strategies in given situations, perhaps even discerning the differences between beginning, middle and end games. But one could never tell the difference between a Friday-night friendly at the local pub and a contest between Boris Spassky and Bobby Fischer at the height of the Cold War. This 'inside' view builds on the humanity we hold in common with the players and, consequently and especially, a shared understanding of human action as intentional 'agents' which, ultimately, is what makes 'history' interesting.[14]

Two brief asides are necessary. First, not unexpectedly, this attempt to rethink 'the very same thoughts' as historical figures has been, for a number of historians, the most problematic and even bizarre aspect of Collingwood's approach to history (e.g. at one point, he seems to imply the metaphysic that thoughts are eternal).[15] Criticized by some as an example of the idealist fallacy,[16] William H. Dray, although acknowledging some

---

[12] R. G. Collingwood, *The Idea of History* (ed. T. M. Knox; Oxford: Clarendon Press, 1967), 213–16; Peter Johnson, *R. G. Collingwood: An Introduction,* Bristol introductions (Bristol, England; Dulles: Thoemmes, 1998), 79–90. For a more detailed analysis, R. G. Collingwood, *The Principles of History: and Other Writings in Philosophy of History* (ed. William H. Dray and W. J. van der Dussen; New York: Oxford University Press, 1999).

[13] Borrowed from my student, Mark Cheeseman, based on a similar example in W. J. van der Dussen, *History as a Science: The Philosophy of R. G. Collingwood* (Dordrecht: Springer, 2012), 153.

[14] On shared stable and predictable meaning systems which enable meaningful social action, M. Weber, *The Theory of Social and Economic Organization* (trans. A. M. Henderson and Talcott Parsons; Glencoe: Free Press, 1947), 112–13.

[15] Cf. Elazar Weinryb, 'Re-Enactment in Retrospect', *The Monist* 72 (1989): 568–80; but defended by Margut Hurup Nielsen, 'Re-Enactment and Reconstruction in Collingwood's Philosophy of History', *History and Theory* 20 (1981): 1–31. Collingwood's treatment is more nuanced than sometimes represented, see his *Principles,* 220–2.

[16] David Hackett Fischer, *Historians' Fallacies: Towards a Logic of Historical Thought* (New York: Harper Torchbooks, 1970). However, Collingwood's emphasis on such subjective elements as training and experience suggest to me that he is already closer to Polanyi and Lonergan.

of Collingwood's own ambiguous statements, has nevertheless argued that in essence this is what we all do, all of the time, when seeking to understand why others do what they do.[17] And for Bernard Lonergan, if we take instead a critical-realist approach,[18] we can retain the substance of what Collingwood taught regarding historical imagination and evidence.[19] We, as knowingly and self-aware subjective observers[20] in attempting to take proper account of another's culture and historical timeframe, can seek to interpret their words and actions as indicators of their intention, and that on the assumption of a shared notion of rational behaviour. In one sense, this is what some recent NT studies have tried to do.[21] The problem for us, however, is that the past being past we no longer have direct access to the actions of the NT authors; all we have are the artefacts those actions left (in this chapter, particularly the writings of the NT).[22]

Second, it is important to distinguish between data and evidence ('the facts of the case') and how they function in respect of historical explanation. Obviously, not all data is evidence. The historian needs to make some initial judgements, based on training and experience, as to what data might or might not be relevant. But in the final analysis, it is only in the light of the progression towards the coherence and comprehensiveness of the final explanation, and of the role that any given datum plays in that explanation, that one can come to know what is or is not evidence ('the facts of the case'), whether a source is to believed or not and whether the historian's explanation is likely to be correct.[23] This, as Collingwood argued, is precisely the autonomous historian's prerogative as a knowing and trained subject exercising authority over the relevant sources.[24] This chapter will likewise progress by bringing together some additional data – in particular the central place of Yahweh's character and his commitment to human transformation – with a view to offering a more comprehensive explanation of how the Scriptures shaped the NT documents.

In the light of the above, this chapter is an attempt to make a beginning at 'thinking the NT authors' thoughts after them' and, particularly, in regards to two questions. First, what can we know of how they might have thought of Scripture and hence how this might shape their engagement with it? Second, how might Israel's unique conception of 'deity' – if that is not already a false conceptualization[25] – and creation have shaped the fundamental character of that engagement? In particular, and to put things starkly, were they operating, for example, with a rationalist abstract Stoic mindset in a world where

---

[17] William H. Dray, *History as Re-Enactment: R. G. Collingwood's Idea of History* (Oxford [England]; New York: Clarendon Press; Oxford University Press, 1995).
[18] Not simply to be identified with that of N. T. Wright, *The New Testament and the People of God* (Minneapolis: Fortress Press, 1992).
[19] Bernard Lonergan, *Method in Theology* (New York: Herder and Herder, 1972), 206.
[20] See also, for example, H. A. Veeser, ed., *The New Historicism* (London: Routledge, 1989).
[21] In Jesus studies, for example, initially and specifically Ben F. Meyer, *The Aims of Jesus* (London: SCM Press, 1979).
[22] Leon J. Goldstein, 'Dray on Re-Enactment and Constructionism: Review of William H. Dray, *History as Re-Enactment*', *History and Theory* 37 (1998): 409–21; especially 416–18.
[23] Cf. Collingwood, *Idea*, 245–55.
[24] This correlates to the critical element in Lonergan's critical realism.
[25] The idea of a general class 'deity' seems necessarily excluded by Israel's fundamental assertion that there is only one creator, Yahweh, and his creation.

everything was already determined by the Logos,[26] or in the realm of subjective and interpersonal history where genuine change and transformation were real possibilities and hence personal agency and character of primary concern? If it is the latter, as I think more likely, what might this combination of agency and character contribute to our understanding of the NT authors' fundamental hermeneutical stance?

4 Hearing the Scriptures

To the first question then: what can we say as to the significance and centrality of Scripture for the NT authors? Clearly, the Scriptures are far and away their most pervasive and influential literary source. Granted the difficulties in verse counting, not least when it comes to allusions (I leave aside the even more problematic 'echo'), and recognizing the variation in scriptural presence (e.g. from the impressive density of Scripture in Romans 9–11 to the above-noted relative absence in Colossians), according to one estimate, the NT writings appeal some 2,500 times to some 1,800 scriptural texts.[27] By way of contrast, the mere handful of references to intertestamental Jewish literature and Graeco-Roman authors serves to emphasize this extensive dependence. Even more remarkable is the complete absence of Hellenistic greats such as Plato or Aristotle. And it is not as if the NT writers could have been unaware. While matters of distinct Jewishness were marked by Law (and for Christians, the gospel of Jesus Christ and hence, as we saw above, their unique sobriquet), there is little evidence to suggest that this applied in educational circles.[28] Even if not the recipient of a full rhetorical or philosophical education, Paul grew up in Tarsus where, according to Strabo, 'the zeal for philosophy and other kinds of education surpasses that in Athens and Alexandria and any other place renowned for schools and occupation in philosophy' (*Geog.* 14.5.13). Half of his teacher Gamaliel's one thousand students were familiar with Greek wisdom (*b. Sota* 49b; Acts 22.3).

The reason for the Scriptures' unparalleled ubiquity is not hard to find. They are unapologetically described as the oracles of God (τά λόγια τοῦ θεοῦ; Rom. 3.2; cf. Acts 7.38; Heb. 5.12). According to John's Jesus, they can neither 'be broken' (Jn 10.35) nor 'fail', as Paul is also at pains exhaustively to demonstrate in his discussion of Israel's continued priority in God's plan (Rom. 9.6). Speaking of Paul, he employs the conclusively authoritative 'it is written' over thirty times in Romans, 1 and 2 Corinthians and Galatians. Its nominal cognate and equally authoritative γραφή occurs some twelve times. When making the argument in Galatians for the temporary place of Torah observance in defining God's people,[29] Paul does so on the basis of a thoroughgoing appeal to that same authoritative Scripture, indeed Torah itself. Of course, none

---

[26] For example, Chrysippus: 'There will never be any new thing other than that which has been before; but everything is repeated down to the minutest detail' (Fr. 625); see below.
[27] Roughly based on UBS 4 figures.
[28] Judge, 'St Paul and Classical Society', in *Social*, 87–8.
[29] Namely. since the Law was promulgated after the foundational Abrahamic covenant (3.17a) and primarily to keep Israel until the promise came (3.19b, 23-24), God is also free to rescind it once that purpose was served; after all, one cannot change covenants retrospectively (3.15, 17b), the Law came because of sin (3.19a), and it could never 'make alive' (3.21).

of this impugns the Law's status as holy, just, good and spiritual (cf. Rom. 7.12, 14), and hence there is no contradiction in, for example, Deuteronomy still playing a major role in his thinking.[30] Similarly, while in the four Gospels 'it is written' appears just slightly less frequently (27) though with equally conclusive authority, similarly, at critical points in their argument, γραφή is found nearly twice as often (23).[31] Even if the presence of this precise language varies across the rest of the NT documents, the same high view appears to obtain unquestioned throughout.

This bears developing. Just as the NT authors have their contexts so too do we; and perhaps part of our difficulty is our own educational experience and terminology. From very early on, we have to choose between the OT and the NT. Consequently, in spite of the overwhelming popularity of Isaiah both in first-century Judaism and the NT,[32] it is the rare *Neutestamentlicher* indeed who could, on the spot, give a one-hour coherent explanation of the basic shape and themes of that all-important prophetic book. Only slightly less problematic is the label 'Old Testament'.[33] The unhelpful implications hardly need articulating, but it ought to give us serious pause that not one NT author, nor the Jesus they present to us, ever uses such a designation. If we allow that the NT authors speak of them as the Scriptures, and that Jesus was about the reconstitution of Israel, into whom, according to Paul, Gentiles are grafted, then Israel's Scriptures might be a more accurate designation and hence is the terminology preferred herein.

It is, then, Israel's Scriptures that both undergird and drive the NT's 'high Christology'. For example (and forgive the long list), Jesus's binding of Satan, forgiveness of sins (as his interlocutors' protest affirms), setting the authority of his words over and above Scripture (contentious but I think clear in Mt. 5.21-48; Mk 7.14), authority over the sea, feeding his people in the desert, transformation into the Transfiguration's shining splendour long before the cloud appears, reworking the Passover by making himself the centre of its celebration, death, resurrection and his followers' subsequent experience of the Spirit, together only take on their full revelatory significance in the light of Israel's Scripture.[34] Given the historical and contextual priority of the Scriptures, it makes better sense methodologically to begin, not with the NT use of the OT, but with Israel's Scriptures' normative shaping of the NT. Francis Watson's (and

---

[30] For example, David Lincicum, *Paul and the Early Jewish Encounter with Deuteronomy* (WUNT 2/284; Tübingen: Mohr Siebeck, 2010).

[31] Craig A. Evans, 'Why did the New Testament Writers Appeal to the Old Testament?' *JSNT* 38 (2015): 36–48.

[32] Based on the literary evidence of Qumran, the NT and reconstructions of triennial Synagogue readings, Charles Perrot, 'The Reading of the Bible in the Ancient Synagogue', in *Mikra: Text, Translation, Reading, and Interpretation of the Hebrew Bible in Ancient Judaism and Early Christianity* (ed. M. J. Mulder and Harry Sysling; Assen: Van Gorcum; Philadelphia: Fortress, 1988), 137–59.

[33] It is true that Heb. 8.13 claims that Jeremiah's promise of a 'new' covenant was fulfilled in Jesus (cf. Lk. 22.20). But to extend an argument for the obsolescence of the ('old') Levitical priesthood such that Israel's Scriptures en toto can also be deemed 'old' ignores their clearly continuing authority as assumed throughout the NT.

[34] See further Rikki E. Watts, *Isaiah's New Exodus and Mark* (Tübingen: Mohr Siebeck, 1997), 137–82; followed by Richard B. Hays, *Echoes of Scripture in the Gospels* (Waco: Baylor University Press, 2016), 21.

before him C. H. Dodd's) fundamental stance is correct.[35] In my own words, Paul, the Christ-devoted Jew, owns and appeals to the unquestioned authority of Christ and the Gospel precisely because of what authoritative Scripture continues to declare about Yahweh, his character, actions and promises.

Consequently, the NT authors can freely and repeatedly use the same 'word of God' for both the Scriptures and the Gospel (e.g. Mk 7.13; Lk. 5.1; Jn 10.35; Acts 4.31; Rom. 9.6; 1 Cor. 14.36; 1 Thess. 2.13; etc.). The latter is for them no aberrant innovation but instead fulfilment (Matthew's Jesus is well aware that this might not immediately appear so – Mt. 5.17), and hence of no less authority. It is, from their perspective, of one cloth with those Scriptures. One recalls here Professor Morna Hooker's response to Chris Stanley, whose 'Paul', although regularly employing Scripture simply to buttress his personal authority, nevertheless had 'a deep respect' for it:

> Paul ... needed to quote Scripture because he was convinced that the God of Abraham, Isaac, and Jacob, who had revealed himself to Moses and the prophets, was the God and Father of our Lord Jesus Christ, through whom Gentiles, as well as Jews, had been made members of his holy people. In order to persuade others of this outrageous gospel, he had to demonstrate its truth from Scripture, not because he had 'a deep respect' for it, but because the Torah was the embodiment of the Jewish faith.[36]

While Hooker is surely correct, re-enactment suggests we can go further. These texts are not merely the embodiment of Israel's faith. For the NT authors, they are the living and present word of the one and only true God.

Given that we deal with documentary artefacts, the fundamentally personal dimension of scriptural communication needs constantly to be borne in mind. The only reason Israel's faith ultimately matters is because its Scriptures are the oracles of the one true creator and *living* God (cf. e.g. Mk 12.27; Rom. 9.26; 2 Cor. 6.16; 1 Thess. 1.9; Heb. 9.14; 10.31). They centre on, and originate in, the prior actions of a faithful and unchanging Yahweh. They are the living word of a personal God, who was intensely interested in his creation and especially humanity, whom the NT authors had apparently experienced in profoundly life-changing ways, and to whom they were deeply committed. And if Paul's letters, in one sense, were seen to mediate his presence through the Spirit to their recipients (cf. 1 Cor. 5.3-5), how much more Israel's Scriptures the presence of Israel's God (cf. the prophets' 'utterance Yahweh' which Spirit-inspired speech implies Yahweh's presence in his agents, through whom he himself was speaking directly to his people)?[37]

---

[35] Francis Watson, *Hermeneutics of Faith* (London: T&T Clarke, 2004). See his response to his critics in 'Paul the Reader: An Authorial Apologia', *JSNT* 28 (2006): 363–73. C. H. Dodd, *According to the Scriptures: The Sub-Structure of New Testament Theology* (London: Nisbet, 1952).

[36] M. D. Hooker, 'Review of Christopher D. Stanley, Arguing with Scripture: The Rhetoric of Quotations in the Letters of Paul', *JTS* 57 (2006): 270.

[37] Analogous perhaps to the sense of near and active presence implied by the *Tg. Isaiah*'s 'Memra'; see B. D. Chilton (ed.), *The Isaiah Targum: Introduction, Translation, Apparatus and Notes* (ArB 11; Edinburgh: T&T Clark, 1987), xv–xvi. See also Markus Bockmuehl's remarks on the 'text's own agency' in his response to Hays, in Richard B. Hays, *Reading Backwards: Figural Christology and the Fourfold Gospel Witness* (Waco: Baylor University, 2014), x–xi.

This is hardly the mindset of academic literary theory or of academic biblical studies in general. Both still seem to operate, in part, on a pre-Lonerganian and pre-Polanyian assumption of the epistemological sanctity of disinterested objectivity. Let me explain. As Bernard Lonergan and Michael Polanyi demonstrated,[38] and I suspect most would agree, 'disinterested objectivity' is not only impossible but fails to achieve its stated aims precisely because this is not how we actually come to know. However, I want to suggest, *mutatis mutandis*, a similar subjective commitment is essential if we are to know how the NT authors used Scripture, that is, by thinking their thoughts after them. In other words, 'disinterested objectivity' is hardly the stance of the NT authors.[39]

The Scriptures were, for the NT authors, not a literary artefact, even less the communication of abstract 'theological' concepts, accessible only to the enlightened few.[40] They were not primarily of religious,[41] literary, historical or even 'theological' interest, as more recent NT scholarship tends to regard them. Indeed, to construe the NT authors' use of Scripture in such terms is seriously to misinterpret the NT authors. Thus, while Paul Foster's critique of the way some authors have used (abused?) Richard Hays concept of echoes[42] is to my mind valid – too much is regularly built on too little – his criticism that this is due to Hays's repeated situating of Paul's discourse solely within the symbolic field of Israel Scripture seems misdirected; as implied by his admission 'while … at one level true' (98). Foster's thinking primarily in terms of literary borrowing seems not to take with sufficient seriousness what Scripture being *Scripture* means to the NT authors. This is not to say that these Scriptures are not in one sense literature. It is to remind us that they were neither written nor received merely, or even primarily, 'as literature'. The NT authors' hermeneutic reflects a 'red-blooded' conviction that the living God himself continued to speak with creational immediacy through Scripture. That we so often discuss the NT authors' engagement with the Scriptures in merely literary and often detached terms says, I suspect, far more about us and our situation than it does about them and theirs. To borrow a phrase, perhaps it is our pale faces that we see at the bottom of the hermeneutical well.

For them, Scripture is the living, present and active word of the one and only creator God, with whom, through Christ and the indwelling Spirit, they were reconciled as children to their father, and to whom they had bold access to make their requests known. I fully realize that this language sounds foreign, perhaps even distasteful, in an

---

[38] Respectively, *Insight: A Study in Human Understanding* (New York: Philosophical Library, 1957); and *Personal Knowledge: Toward A Post-Critical Philosophy* (Chicago: University of Chicago Press, 1962).

[39] Both the Stoics and the Christians believed that one could not understand them from the outside. One could only come to know either on the basis of a total commitment to their respective ways of life; see C. Kavin Rowe, *One True Life: The Stoics and Early Christians as Rival Traditions* (New Haven; London: Yale University Press, 2016).

[40] In contrast, for example, to the view of Plato where '[God is] incorporeal, one, immeasurable, … whose nature is difficult to find and if found cannot be expressed among the many', Plato, *Timaeus* 28e; Apuleius, *On the Teaching of Plato* 1.5.

[41] See n. 8.

[42] 'Echoes without Resonance: Critiquing Certain Aspects of Recent Scholarly Trends in the Study of the Jewish Scriptures in the New Testament', *JSNT* 38 (2015): 96–111.

academic work. But the otherwise familial intimacy and easy familiarity of Paul's letters is in large part due to this reality.[43] The Collingwoodian question, then, is whether modern literary theory and putative academic objectivity, instead of clarifying, distorts the intentional or inside element of the NT authors' history – that is, of seeking to think the NT authors' thoughts after them. On this view, in order to do so, we need to begin where they do. This means indwelling their world (*Weltanschauung*[44]) wherein a faithful, personal God continues to speak through his unfailing and 'unbreakably' authoritative Scriptures and now, above all, in his Christ, the Lord Jesus. This is not to say that one has to agree with them. But since understanding should precede critique, we need to begin with the discipline of a reconstructive instead of deconstructive historical imagining.

5 The centrality of character, agency and the possibility of genuine change

It can be argued that the Scriptures' primary concern is the normative revelation of the unique character of this Yahweh, a god unlike any other (Exod. 8.10; 15.11; 33.17–34.9; Dt. 3.24; 1 Sam. 2.2; 1 Chr. 17.20; 2 Chr. 6.14; Pss 35.10; 36.6; 86.8). From this flows Scripture's articulation of the nature and terms of Yahweh's relationship with his creation, and its relationship with him. This is especially so for humans who, made in his image, and particularly Israel, his son (Exod. 4.22; etc.), are expected to embody his life-giving mercy, faithfulness, righteousness, justice and compassion. From the NT perspective, this same Yahweh is now fully revealed in the Lord Jesus (where Lord reflects the high Christology evident in, for example, Mk 1.2-3 and 1 Cor. 8.6).[45]

The significance of this emphasis on Yahweh's character, and the Scriptures' subsequent unparalleled, even offensive, view of the importance of humanity, derives at least in part, from Israel's and Jerusalem's radically different cosmology. The ancient world by and large was troubled by change. For Egypt, the good Pharaoh's reign was one in which essentially nothing happened. By the first century, Hellenism's two main alternatives were Stoicism and the less popular Epicureanism. For the former, according to Chrysippus, the eternal cyclic restoration of the cosmos, governed as it was by the unchanging logos, meant there was no possibility of any new thing but everything was repeated down to the very last detail (Frag. 625). It was the same for the Epicureans, only now it was the unchanging randomness of eternally swerving

---

[43] Bruce W. Winter, 'Revelation versus Rhetoric: Paul and First-Century Corinthian Fad', in *Translating Truth: The Case for Essentially Literal Bible Translation* (ed. Wayne A. Grudem; Wheaton: Crossway, 2005), 135–50.

[44] This is not the place to pursue the question, but I suspect that the history/theology tension which lies at the heart of Samuel V. Adams's critique of N. T. Wright's emphasis on worldviews carries more weight in the context of Hellenistic cosmology and epistemology than it does in Jerusalem where history and knowing God go hand in hand; *The Reality of God and Historical Method: Apocalyptic Theology in Conversation with N. T. Wright* (NET; Downers Grove: IVP Academic, 2015); see n. 4.

[45] Mk 1.2-3, Mal. 3.1 and Isa. 40.3 identify Jesus with the coming of Yahweh; and 1 Cor. 8.6 similarly identifies Jesus as the Lord in the Shema.

atoms. What Jerusalem offered was the possibility of genuine change, the inexpressible gift inherent in a good, but emphatically not perfect, creation.[46] Humans could become genuine agents of change and transformation. Since every 'design' choice reflects the character of the designer, character becomes central in Israel's Scriptures and hence in the NT. And since humans are made in God's image, only in conforming to his character will our actions lead to life and genuine freedom (e.g. classically, Gal. 5.16-26; Mt. 7.12; Mk 12.28-33).

Equally important is how this character is revealed. Characterized by the gift of change, Jerusalem's world was what it actually was, not what human myth imagined (the gods of the ANE or Homer) or what rational speculation (Stoic or Epicurean) reasoned it should be. The same applies to Israel's Yahweh, the 'I am', who is who he is (Exod. 3.13-14; 6.2). The prohibition against making an image (which at the very least implies knowledge of what one is imaging) and the Torah's thorough-going emphasis on seeing and hearing[47] indicates that this revelation is not a matter of either human poetic imagination or reasoned speculation but what can be seen, and touched, and handled (1 Jn 1.1-3).

The implications for our chapter are several. First, one would expect the NT authors to engage with Scripture in ways that reflect Yahweh's faithful character, especially now in keeping with the cross-bearing Christ who laid down his life for others. This for me is the fatal weakness of those proposals that see, for example, Paul using Scripture primarily to enhance his own authority or ideological hegemony.[48] We have no evidence of any NT author having to face accusations along such lines. Moreover, given their own manner of life and their exhortations to others (e.g. 1 Thess. 1.1; 2.7-8; 2 Cor. 1.12-14, 24), such Foucauldian power mongering would require an unparalleled degree of hypocrisy, for which, again, we have no evidence. Second, this rejection of any human speculation concerning Yahweh might be what lies behind Jesus's previously noted withering denunciation of the Pharisees for going beyond or ignoring what was written and thus Paul's similar sanction (again, Mk 7.1-13; 1 Cor. 4.6). Third, it suggests that the NT authors' fundamental hermeneutical assumption in reading Scripture is the faithfulness of Yahweh's unchanging character.

This being so, we are not surprised that Paul's extended argument in Romans 9–11 – namely, that Israel's current rejection of the gospel means neither that God's word has failed nor Israel's loss of primacy, much less rejection by God – is not a tour de force but a dense interweaving of scriptural accounts of Yahweh's past, current and prophesied future dealings with his people.[49] At stake is not Paul's need to construct ad hoc a coherent 'theology', let alone fabricate a case out of whole cloth. Instead, his presupposition being a personal God's faithful character, all he need do is simply lay

---

[46] The logic is obvious. A perfect world cannot change since the moment it does, it would no longer be perfect.
[47] Avrahami, *Senses*.
[48] Cf. for example David Lincicum's 'Review of Christopher D. Stanley, Arguing with Scripture: The Rhetoric of Quotations in the Letters of Paul', *JETS* 49 (2006): 430.
[49] See Watts, 'Israel's Scriptures and the Character of God – an Initial Exploration of Romans 9-11', https://www.academia.edu/13778590/Israels_Scripture_and_the_Character_of_God_an_Exploration.

out the relevant scriptural evidence concerning a God for whom, to use a more modern expression, his word is his bond. The texts themselves demonstrate that the issue is less one of justice than a faithful God's overwhelming predilection to mercy – that his word has not failed. As John Macmurray has argued against Descartes,[50] because persons, including Yahweh, are not just thinkers but agents, then the narrative of their agency, that is, of their words and deeds is how we come to know them as persons.[51] If so, this would explain the fundamentally narratival and personal character of Israel's Scriptures. Beyond the scope of this chapter, this understanding might help bring some resolution to the question noted in Allen's fourth point of debate: the macro–micro distinction and the role or not of Israel's larger narrative. On the view argued here, the content and shape of Israel's Scriptures seems to presuppose that knowing Yahweh is impossible apart from the larger narrative of his engagement with his creation and especially through Israel.

6 'Authorial intention'

This combination of authority and 'personal' origin has ramifications for the question of authorial intention. It has become popular, in some circles, to read Israel's Scripture and/or the NT texts as though the original authors' intention is irrelevant. But this is both a confusion of categories and anachronistic. It is a confusion of categories in that, historically, questions around the accessibility and relevance of authorial intention emerged in the context of assessing the success of poetry as a work of art: did the poet achieve her artistic intention?[52] But 'intention' in this sense is not our concern. Neither Israel's Scriptures nor the NT are 'works of art', nor were they written with art critics in view. It is anachronistic in that the question really came to the fore with the peculiar achievements of the English romantic poets. It should go without saying, but both the Scriptures and the NT documents not only long antedate that movement but are neither English nor romantic.

On the other hand, as Peter Head argues, one of the key reasons for having letter carriers accompany letters was that, having been intimately involved in the letter writing process, they could offer firsthand clarification of what the letter writer intended.[53] In other words, ancient letters were all about authorial intention in the more basic sense of trying to understand what the author was saying through these texts, and, like all of us do in everyday interaction, to discern what they intended.[54] This is not to say that for us discerning the NT authors' intention will be easy. It is to say that to dismiss their intention altogether is not an option if we are serious about thinking the NT authors'

---

[50] Macmurray, *Self*, and *The Clue to History* (London: Faber and Faber, 1981).
[51] On the essentially narrative character of persons for example, Stephen Crites, 'The Narrative Quality of Experience', *JAAR* 39 (1971): 291–311; Kay Young and Jeffrey L. Saver, 'The Neurology of Narrative', *SubStance* 30 (2001): 72–84; Jonathan A. Carter, 'Telling Times: History, Emplotment, and Truth', *History and Theory* 42 (2003): 1–27.
[52] See William K. Wimsatt and Monroe C. Beardsley, 'The Intentional Fallacy', *Sewanee Review* 54 (1946): 468–88.
[53] 'Named Letter-Carriers among the Oxyrhynchus Papyri', *JSNT* 31 (2009): 279–99.
[54] See Dray, *History as Re-Enactment*.

thoughts after them. A former student, Michael Theophilus, has noted that the forty or so instances of the expression 'it is written' in the papyri occur in legal contexts where the intention of what is written lies at the heart of the matter.[55] Since the Torah is nothing if not legal, then one might rightly assume that a concern with what Yahweh intended also lies at the heart of NT citations of the same.[56]

This seems borne out in that, as is widely noted, the hermeneutical and methodological questions arising from how the NT authors engage with legal aspects of Torah are, in general, far fewer and more straightforwardly answered than those concerning how they deal with the prophets.[57] While, on the one hand, it shows that in terms of Torah the NT authors are apparently concerned with context (cf. on the rabbis, below), it also makes the apparently different quality of some of their engagements with the prophets all the more problematic. How does one explain this apparent inconsistency between the NT authors' apparently 'literal' and contextually aware reading of the Law with what appears to be, at times, a very different approach to the prophets and the psalms?

This tension is only heightened if we recall that the prophets too speak the word of God – as indicated by their previously noted 'utterance Yahweh' declarations, often in the legal context of a *rib* or trial, some of which clearly take up the language of Deuteronomy.[58] Ought not their words also be received with a similarly authoritative and equally 'legal' weight, as appears to be the stance of the Pharisees, the Essenes, the NT authors and the Jesus the NT presents to us? If so, would not the matter of the prophets' authorial intent be of equal importance to the NT authors? Consequently, would we not also expect that matters of promise and claimed fulfilment were equally weighty, legally binding and hence also centred on authorial intent? On this view, when the NT authors speak of the Law and Prophets, it is less a literary statement addressing two distinct genres or collections of writings (though it is that), than a matter of attesting a shared and equally binding authority. And that authority is directly grounded in the person of a faithful and consistent Yahweh.

Before we go on to discuss the implications for the NT authors, this might be an appropriate time to comment briefly on some recent proposed 'solutions' to the question of the NT's relationship to Israel's Scriptures that seem to me to be problematic in principle.

---

[55] Personal communication; work forthcoming.
[56] For this reason, Steve Moyise's appeal to the Hellenic tradition of quotation seems misplaced; we are not dealing with maxims whose authority needs bolstering (Aristotle), nor using poetry for relief (Quintillian), nor seeking to imitate Homer's expression (Longinus); 'Scripture in the New Testament: Literary and Theological Perspectives', *Neot* 42 (2008): 305–26.
[57] For example, the well-known crux of Paul's citation of Deut. 25.4 in 1 Cor. 9.9 is more readily explained if we see that God's primary concern is that human action reflects his character; and hence the question of how humans treat their co-working animals. Paul's logic then runs: if God is concerned that humans permit their co-working animals to participate in the harvest, how much more those other humans (cf. Ps 8) who sow, reap and thresh? And if this applies to material benefits, how much more to those who help us reap spiritual benefits?
[58] For example, K. Neilson, *Yahweh as Prosecutor and Judge: An Investigation of the Prophetic Lawsuit (Rib Pattern)* (JSOTSup 9; Sheffield: JSOT Press, 1978).

7 Excursus: Some proposals

Take, for example, *sensus plenior*. First, in terms of explanatory power, as I have argued elsewhere,[59] it is essentially ad hoc. Invoked only when the normal reading practices associated with the Gospels (biography), Acts (historiography) or Paul (letters) do not work, it less explains than it explains away. That is, there appears to be no underlying rationale as to why a faithful and unchanging God speaks this way in some places and not others. Second, nowhere do the prophets themselves suggest they were speaking out of a two-tiered hermeneutic such that, while they meant one thing, God might have meant something quite different. The latter sounds more like the enigmatic Delphic oracle than it does the unique God of Israel who himself speaks plainly to his people (Deut. 30.11-14).

Figural reading, as proposed by Richard B. Hays, is more sophisticated, attending as it does to the dynamics of reading in the context of a broader cultural intertextuality. It is surely correct in its fundamental assumption that, since, for the NT authors, God had acted decisively in Jesus (and God being consistent), there had to be a scriptural precedent. Matthew, in my view, assumes just this in explaining the significance of Jesus's astonishing and universal healings.[60] But figural reading's origin in modern literary theory strikes me as problematic. Modern literary critics might present autonomous English romantic poets as expressing their creativity by engaging subliminally with the earlier work of Milton.[61] But, while not at all denying an inner-biblical reference[62] and bearing in mind the preceding remarks on authorial intention, attributing this mindset to the NT authors seems anachronistic. Further, it seems to me that for them, God is the active agent, not literary correspondences or echoes of a text.[63] And as with *sensus plenior*, this approach strikes me as essentially ad hoc in that it seems unable to explain why the NT authors and the Jesus they describe choose to read some Scriptures figurally but not others.

Recently, Matthew W. Bates offered his 'prosopological' solution whereby, for Paul, the real voice behind Israel's Scriptures is that of Christ, the eternal logos,[64] an approach that seems more appropriate to Hebrews' personification of Scripture ('he says', 1.6, 7, 8; 5.6; 8.8) than Paul's impersonal 'it is written'. Unlike Hays, Bates grounds his 'figural' hermeneutic in ancient Hellenistic practice, though still running the risk of anachronistically reading post-apostolic hermeneutics into Paul. By way of introduction, he cites Paul's use of Isa. 65.1-2 in Rom. 10.20-1. Problematically for

---

[59] Rikk E. Watts, 'How Do You Read? God's Faithful Character as the Primary Lens for the NT Use of the OT', in *Essays in Honor of Greg Beale: From Creation to New Creation – Biblical Theology and Exegesis* (ed. Daniel M. Gurtner and Benjamin L. Gladd; Peabody: Hendrickson, 2013), 199–220.

[60] Rikki E. Watts, 'Messianic Servant or End of Israel's Exilic Curses? Isaiah 53.4 in Matthew 8.17', *JSNT* 38 (2015): 81–95.

[61] Richard B. Hays, *The Conversion of the Imagination: Paul as Interpreter of Israel's Scripture* (Grand Rapids: Eerdmans, 2005), 166.

[62] See my 'Echoes from the Past: Israel's Ancient Traditions and the Role of the Nations in Isa 40-55', *JSOT* 28 (2004): 481–504.

[63] See Hays, *Reading*, xi, where he still speaks primarily in terms of the text, as though for the NT authors the text had its own autonomy apart from the one whose voice it embodies.

[64] Matthew W. Bates, *The Hermeneutics of the Apostolic Proclamation: The Center of Paul's Method of Scriptural Interpretation* (Waco: Baylor University Press, 2012).

Bates, although Paul follows Isaiah in applying 65.2 to Jews, he switches the identity of those addressed in 65.1 to Gentiles. The solution, following the later church fathers, is to look for the voice behind the text, which for Justin Martyr is Christ himself.[65] In one sense, this is of course right. If Jesus is the Lord, and in Isaiah it is the Lord who speaks, then yes, insofar as Christ the Lord is identified with Yahweh, it is he who speaks. But this is not what Justin means, and even so it is not clear how having Jesus as the speaker resolves the problem of a two-tier identification (originally to Jews then later to Gentiles). Furthermore, in appealing to ancient Hellenistic literary 'theory', Bates appears implicitly to assume key elements of Hellenism's upstairs/downstairs ontology with its suspicion of the immediate and changeful world of the senses (and hence history) and prioritizing of the unchanging abstract rationality of the eternal logos. This seems to me to be in stark contrast to Jerusalem's conception of reality.[66] Furthermore, there appears to be an easier solution, and it turns on the Lord's unchanging character and Paul's experience of the same in his preaching the gospel among the nations. As Yahweh had once presented himself to an Israel who did not seek him, he now does so to the Gentiles. The resulting contrast, between the Gentiles' positive response and Israel's continued hostility, is precisely the reality that Romans 9–11 was written to explain.

Ephraim Radner's figural reading, while erudite, strikes me as even more invested in Hellenistic ontology, such that his speculative *theologia* finds its true home, as it did with Aristotle, in the metaphysic of the unchanging where 'reality' is necessarily tenseless.[67] Not only does this mode of discourse seem utterly foreign to the outlook and argument of Scripture and the NT authors (with their assumption of the solid reality of creation and emphasis on the immediacy of experience and testing), but Radner's opening construal of 'exile' as a 'timeless' universal experience blurs and beats level Scripture's emphatic declaration of the particularity of Israel's unique covenant with Yahweh (e.g. Amos 3.2). There is also a certain irony in his offering an explanation of what NT authors were doing that they themselves in their historical particularity would almost certainly have not understood.

The point of this small survey is to suggest that any explanation of the NT authors' engagement with Scripture must be able to do so in terms that take seriously both the assumptions of that scriptural world – Israel's affirmation of the reality and goodness of creation – and the first-century horizons of the NT's essentially Jewish authors.

8 To return …

Now it might be that the NT authors are also ad hoc in their approach to the prophets. But several factors suggest caution. First, it seems very odd that authors who, in one context, can make a clear and convincing case based on a contextually aware and more literal reading of Scripture – and indeed their very own works regularly reflect an

---

[65] Ibid., 2–3.
[66] See my 'Christianity', 5–13; and, for example, Collingwood, *Principles*, 'Reality as History', 171–80.
[67] Ephraim Radner, *Time and the Word: Figural Reading of the Christian Scriptures* (Grand Rapids: Eerdmans, 2016).

awareness of context, consistent argument and literary structure – would then go on to do something entirely different with other Scriptures and in the very same work. This, of course, is where recourse is made to 'contemporary Jewish exegetical techniques'. But as I suggested earlier, there might be more going on here than meets the eye. A number of examples might help make the point.

Although commonly assumed that the rabbis were notoriously acontextual in their readings, David Instone-Brewer's underappreciated 1992 study on pre-70 CE rabbis has shown that our mistake was in not recognizing that, as lawyers, they were looking for legal precedents. When that is taken into account, they were characteristically aware of the original context.[68] It might just be that we are making a similar mistake with regard to the NT authors and the prophets. They were looking, not for strictly legal, but *historical* precedent; remembering that both Torah and Yahweh's prophetic word originate in, and therefore equally reflect, his righteousness, mercy and faithfulness. Hence in the above case of Romans 10's appeal to Isaiah 65, Paul shows that God's kindness in revealing himself to a people who did not seek him, whether Jew or Gentile, is not only not new – nor, sadly, is Israel's continuing rebellion – but entirely consistent with whom he is.

Awareness of context can sometimes be so assumed that less informed readers (such as most NT scholars) might miss it. In his classic *Messianic Exegesis*, Donald Juel discusses the rabbis' difficulty with Exod. 14.15. Here God rebukes Moses for crying out to him for deliverance ('Then the Lord said to Moses, "Why do you cry out to me?"'), which is surely exactly what the righteous are supposed to do in time of trouble, before instructing him: 'Tell the Israelites to go forward!' Among the various rabbinic solutions Juel provides, Simon of Kitron's runs: '"For the sake of the bones of Joseph I will divide the sea for them." For it is said, "And he left his garment in her hand and fled" (Gen. 39.12). And it also says, "The sea saw it and fled" (Ps. 114.3).' For Juel, this is an example of *Gezerah shawah*, an artful but hardly convincing analogy based largely on wording.[69]

But again, there might be more going on, and it is worthwhile looking a bit closer. Simon apparently understands that Moses should have known better, and the reason involves the bones of Joseph. This is no small matter, since being permanently buried in a foreign land was unthinkable. Joseph's bones are mentioned in only three places in Scripture, two of them in Torah – a legal text of some importance for the rabbis. The first instance is Gen. 50.24-5. Righteous Joseph, now full of years, reconciled to his father's household, and with several generations of offspring, is about to die. His last words express great confidence that God will 'surely come to you, and bring you up out of Egypt to the land he swore to Abraham, Isaac, and Jacob' (v. 24). This is exactly the phraseology and concern that Yahweh, faithful to his patriarchal promises, later expresses when, in setting in motion the Exodus, he first appears to Moses (Exod. 3.6, 8-10). And Joseph makes his children swear that when God 'surely comes to you' (v.

---

[68] David Instone-Brewer, *Techniques and Assumptions in Jewish Exegesis before 70 CE* (Texte und Studien zum antiken Judentum 30; Tübingen: Mohr Siebeck, 1992).
[69] Donald Juel, *Messianic Exegesis: Christological Interpretation of the Old Testament in Early Christianity* (Philadelphia: Fortress, 1988), 42–5. Though alert to how much is assumed, like Moses before him, he seems to miss the significance of the accompanying bones of Joseph.

25) – note the repetition (v. 24a) – they must carry his bones up with them. The critical point is that the final sign of God's faithfulness to him and Yahweh's presence among his people is that he will finally rest in the land of promise. The third reference, Josh. 24.32, relates the fulfilment of that 'prophetic' hope: his bones are buried at Shechem. The linking middle term is God's faithfulness to be present, notably expressed in the Exodus and particularly in the iconic event of dividing the sea, which just happens (!) to be the setting of the second reference: Exod. 13.19. In specific fulfilment of Joseph's explicit request, cited again in full, we are told that Moses took his bones with him. Of particular interest for us is that this fact is related just two paragraphs before the text at hand, that is, the Lord's rebuke of Moses.

Now, my point is not to justify Simon's 'exegesis'. It is, however, to note the contextual awareness. Simon's 'bones of Joseph' reference draws on material only several paragraphs prior and hence clearly related to Yahweh's rebuke. This does not seem coincidental. Yes, there is the memorable word linkage of Joseph's righteous act with one of the great psalms recalling Israel's exodus deliverance. It is this celebrated faithfulness that ensures God will respond, causing even the unruly sea to flee if need be. But there is more to it than simple wordplays (or creative figuration). There is also an underlying narrative integrity predicated on God's faithfulness in Israel's historical memory.

Two lessons can here be learned. First, a wordplay that artfully aids memory need not rule out a concern for context; indeed, the choice of words might be determined by context. And if Simon's contextual awareness runs to several paragraphs prior, then perhaps in 'thinking their thoughts after them', we might consider following suit. Second, and not to put too fine a point on it, our hermeneutical problem might lie less with the rabbis than with our ignorance both of what they were trying to do and, more generally, of Scripture itself.

4Q174 (Florilegium) is often cited in discussions of testimony books as an example of a pre-Christian collection of scriptural passages. What is often not noted is the way it organizes those texts (I have italicized relevant texts and key words). The section we have begins with God's promise to David in *2 Sam. 7.10-11a* to appoint a *place* for his people. This *place* is the Lord's *Temple*, whose permanent *presence* among his people was after all the point of the Exodus, citing *Exod. 15.17*. The metonymic logic is that of Moses (Exod. 33.15-16): Yahweh's *presence* is what defines and constitutes Israel; without it there is no *rest*. But since not every Israelite is a true Israelite, the text goes on to list all those who are to be excluded from this rest. It then returns to *2 Sam. 7.11b*'s unfulfilled promise of *peace* from all David's *enemies*. Clearly addressed only to faithful Israel (hence the preceding exclusion), the sectarians 'rightly' apply this to themselves with their *enemies* now being the children of Belial. It then continues on with *2 Sam. 7.11c, 12b, 13b-14a*'s promise of an heir to whom God will be a father and he as son (cf. Ps. 2.7; also Exod. 4.22), whose fallen *tent* God had promised to restore in order to deliver Israel (citing *Amos 9.11*). Here too, the recipients of this deliverance are the righteous who do not walk in the way of the wicked (*Ps. 1.1a*) against whom the prophets warned (*Isa. 8.11*) and who will never be defiled with idols (*Ezek. 37.23*). These are the sons of Zadok (David's true priests), namely, and on the sectarians reasoning obviously so, those who join the *Yahad* (community). And as in the past, so in the present. Citing *Ps. 2.1-2*, which given that it is a Davidic psalm and hence also an eternal promise is naturally read eschatologically: the nations will conspire also against them but, given God's faithfulness, similarly in vain. Since there is only one eschaton, and since Scripture speaks with one voice, this is also the time of great persecution during which the righteous will be refined (*Dan. 12.10*). What is to be noted is that, even though the text cites single verses, their selection is guided by a larger and perfectly reasonable historical–'theological' coherence. Framed in the outset around God's promises to David, it draws on the Torah, the prophets and the psalms from an overarching 'large picture' perspective not usually associated with 'atomistic' exegesis.

These few examples suggest to me that we need to be more careful in assuming that contemporary Jewish exegesis necessarily meant radically acontextual and unconstrained over-readings. Moreover, what this last example suggests is that there might be another alternative to the view that the NT authors read Israel's Scriptures backwards.

Many of the texts cited in 4Q174 already have a future aspect. They describe events that were expected to continue and have not, or were yet to come. This is why, for example, the Davidic psalms are preserved, even though Israel had not had a Davidic king for nearly 600 years. The as-yet-unfilled promise of a true messianic king adds a prophetic edge to them and that directly because of the unquestioned assumption of Yahweh's faithfulness and commitment to his creation and especially his people. On this view, it is not that the sectarians read themselves back into the texts. Instead, the prophetic texts (now including the Davidic psalms) themselves already read forward, creating a potential future into which the sectarians, simply by virtue of being faithful righteous Israel, can now locate themselves in their present. No sleight of hand is necessary. The promise of the future was always on offer. They have simply fulfilled the conditions.

It is because something similar happens with Paul that I query David Lincicum's claim that Paul reads Christian experience back into Deuteronomy.[70] Deuteronomy, by the very fact of its offering blessing and curse, not least in Moses's third discourse (29–30), is already a forward-looking document, opening up Israel's possible futures. The distinction may be fine, but I think it is vital. Jesus is not read back into Deuteronomy but instead comes into the future space that Deuteronomy along with Scripture in general opens up.

Undergirding the rabbis', the sectarians' and Paul's reading of Scripture is the faithful character of the eternal God. It is on this basis that Paul can draw comparisons between Deuteronomy and Christian life. Yes, Deuteronomy dealt with Israel's past but also with its future, and uniting both was Israel's God as the faithful and unchanging active agent. Since there is no question that God had acted in Jesus, righteously effecting both his promise of resurrection and the out-pouring of the Spirit on all flesh, then even if God's people are no longer required to 'observe Torah' it is still the same God at work. Again, it is not so much reading the Church back into Israel's Scriptures as God's

---

[70] Lincicum, *Encounter*.

faithful character reaching out, as it were, into the future to form, as he had promised, a people for himself.

Stepping back, from this larger perspective, 'fulfil' is less a matter of proof-texting than an assertion. What Israel experiences in Jesus is the climactic expression of God's work in that future which the texts themselves 'created'.

Conclusion

In seeking to understand the relationship between the NT authors and Scripture, we have, following Collingwood, endeavoured to think their thoughts after them. This chapter has argued for a more personal, agency-centred hermeneutic whose fundamental assumption is the faithful character of Yahweh who created a world in which the possibility of genuine change and human agency are profound gifts. Hence, the Scriptures are fundamentally future orientated and not only expect but are intended to effect transformation.

This transformation is predicated on God's faithful character and presence; which character humans, as his agents, are expected to imitate through the indwelling presence of his Spirit. Since God is a person, and persons are known through their unique 'histories', Scripture's normative and identity-defining status is predicated on its being the narrative of Yahweh's words and deeds, whether revealed, from a first-century perspective, in foundational Torah, or subsequent prophetic history (thus, the 'Law and the prophets').

Consequently, for the NT authors, Scripture's engagement with them, as the living word of the living God, was first and foremost a deeply personal and relational matter, with primary emphasis on trust and personal transformation. This immediately raises questions about scholarly proposals which imply a fundamentally different character in either Yahweh or the reader (let alone foreign ontologies which devalue the particularities of history or undermine the fundamental reality of a changeful creation).

In this context, given the conviction that Jesus was, however mysteriously, the presence of Yahweh among them, it is axiomatic that the NT authors should expect consistency: as God the father had spoken and acted in the past so now in the Lord Jesus his son. This suggests that the NT authors' primary orientation is not one of reading Jesus back into Scripture, but instead reading Yahweh forward in him. Scripture is necessarily the normative lens through which God's present actions are to be clarified, explained and understood. It might be more accurate, then, to speak less of the NT authors' use of Scripture than of Scripture's normative shaping of them.

Finally, if this approach is correct, then, as suggested at the outset, the question we should be asking is: what does this scriptural text reveal about a faithful God's particular actions in the past that helps us understand the significance of his actions in the present?

12

Concluding reflection

Steve Moyise

I am very pleased to write a concluding reflection for this volume on the occasion of the fortieth anniversary of the 'Annual Seminar for the Study of the OT in the NT', for which I acted as chair from 2000 to 2013.[1] During that period, the seminar was foundational for the series of books edited by Maarten Menken (RIP) and myself on the use of particular OT books (Genesis, Deuteronomy, Psalms and Isaiah) or collections of books (Minor Prophets) in the NT (T&T Clark, 2004–12),[2] and many of the contributors are or have been regular members of the seminar. Indeed, many doctoral students tested out their ideas at the seminar before successfully completing their PhDs and developing academic careers. It has indeed been a fruitful forum for research and discussion in a friendly collegiate atmosphere, and I hope it continues for many years to come.

    I will not comment on every chapter but will draw some reflections on the three main sections that make up the volume. First, what insights can those of us who work in OT/NT draw from Hebrew Bible (HB) studies? I was particularly struck by William Tooman's description of 'Assimilation' and 'Amalgamation' in his account of the reuse of Scripture in the HB. Theories of intertextuality have often been used to bypass questions of authorial intention and chronological priority and focus instead on a broad range of literary effects produced when two or more texts are linked together. For example, clearly the books of Daniel and Ezekiel have an important role in the book of Revelation, but no one who has read Revelation will look at Daniel and Ezekiel in quite the same way. This is obviously true for those like Richard Bauckham, who believe that Revelation is the 'climax of prophecy',[3] but it is also true (albeit in a different way) for those who are simply acquainted with the book. As I have said

---

[1] A Festschrift for the previous chair (Lionel North) was published in 2000: S. Moyise, ed., *The Old Testament in the New Testament* (London: T&T Clark).

[2] Steve Moyise and Maarten J. J. Menken, eds, *The Psalms in the New Testament* (London: T&T Clark, 2004); Maarten J. J. Menken and Steve Moyise, eds, *Isaiah in the New Testament* (London: T&T Clark, 2005); Steve Moyise and Maarten J. J. Menken, eds, *Deuteronomy in the New Testament* (London: T&T Clark, 2007); Maarten J. J. Menken and Steve Moyise, eds, *The Minor Prophets in the New Testament* (London: T&T Clark, 2009); Maarten J. J. Menken and Steve Moyise, eds, *Genesis in the New Testament* (London: T&T Clark, 2012).

[3] Cf. R. Bauckham, *The Climax of Prophecy* (Edinburgh: T&T Clark, 2003).

elsewhere: 'Each new text disturbs the fabric of existing texts as it jostles for a place in the canon of literature.'[4]

Of course, traditionally trained historical critics oppose such 'impositions' and strive to interpret Daniel and Ezekiel on their own terms. But as Tooman illustrates, mutual interpretation is part of the reality of the collection and transmission of the HB. If Revelation alludes to Ezekiel, it is alluding to a book that is already 'mutually evoking and mutually interpreting'[5] and adds further 'voices' to the conversation. Many will still want to preserve chronological priority (when it can be determined), but there is no escaping the dialogical nature of biblical interpretation. Although Richard Hays is famous for his seven criteria for assessing the validity of allusions (as discussed by David Allen in this volume), it was his dialogical approach to Paul's use of Scripture that most influenced my own work: 'Paul's urgent hermeneutical project ... is to bring Scripture and gospel into a mutually interpretive relation, in which the righteousness of God is truly disclosed.'[6]

What is sometimes forgotten is that Hays was not suggesting that this is true of every quotation or allusion. Paul's use of the 'threshing ox' example in 1 Cor. 9.8-10 and the 'psalmist's graceful depiction of the heaven's glory' (from Ps. 19.4) in Rom. 10.18 are appropriations of language that 'lend rhetorical force to his own discourse, with minimal attention to the integrity of the semiotic universe of the precursor'.[7] Not all have been as cautious as Hays, however, leading critics such as Paul Foster to write an article entitled 'Echoes without Resonance: Critiquing Certain Aspects of Recent Scholarly Trends in the Study of the Jewish Scriptures in the New Testament'.[8] In Katherine Dell's article, she is generally appreciative of Craig Bartholomew's attempt to find echoes of Ecclesiastes in the NT but finds some of his suggestions somewhat farfetched.[9]

Was Jewish exegesis 'atomistic'? Susan Docherty draws attention to Michael Fishbane's groundbreaking book (1985), as well as rabbinic studies by Daniel Boyarin (1990) and Alexander Samely (1992, 2002), to argue that there was often a perceived problem in the text that 'made it a suitable "target" for exegesis'.[10] That is not to say that it was 'contextual' in a modern sense (to be discussed below) but there was an attempt to *relate it* to other texts of Scripture.

---

[4] S. Moyise, 'Dialogical Intertextuality', in *Exploring Intertextuality: Diverse Strategies for New Testament Interpretation of Texts* (ed. B. J. Oropeza and Steve Moyise; Eugene: Wipf and Stock, 2016), 3.
[5] Tooman, 28.
[6] R. B. Hays, *Echoes of Scripture in the Letters of Paul* (New Haven: Yale University Press, 1989), 176.
[7] Ibid., 175. What I find interesting is that even here, Hays uses poetic language to describe what he admits is a somewhat mundane use of Scripture. Indeed, he goes on to say that the 'citation of Ps. 19.4 does not prove that Jews have had the opportunity to hear the gospel; rather, it gives Paul a "vocabulary of a second and higher power" with which to assert that they have heard it' (the quoted phrase is from T. M. Green, *The Light in Troy: Imitation and Discovery in Renaissance Poetry* [New Haven: Yale University Press, 1982], 39).
[8] Paul Foster, 'Echoes without Resonance: Critiquing Certain Aspects of Recent Scholarly Trends in the Study of the Jewish Scriptures in the New Testament', *JSNT* 38 (2015): 96–111.
[9] Ecclesiastes is one of the few books where Hays's criterion of 'availability' is relevant, since it is by no means certain that a Greek version was in circulation before the first century CE.
[10] Susan E. Docherty, 'New Testament Scriptural Interpretation in Its Early Jewish Context', *NovT* 57 (2015): 1–19.

Similarly, Tooman cites two studies (Teeter, 2012; Lyons, 2015) where the book of Daniel and Psalm 22 draw widely on Isaiah and not just on a single verse or section. His conclusion is worth quoting:

> The ways that we validate the presence of scriptural reuse, in particular, looking for explicit citations or density of rare and unique words and phrases, tends to focus our attention on very small text segments, individual lines, or verses, or pericopae. Perhaps because of this, there is an understandable tendency to miss wider arguments when they are evoked.[11]

Tooman also suggests that polysemy ('the facility of any sign, word, phrase, sentence or text to bear multiple meanings in a single context') might be more frequent in the HB than previously thought. His example of how Genesis 20 gives *one* way that the gaps of Gen. 12.10-20 might be filled is clearly instructive for many of the fulfilment texts in the NT. The difficulty of the quotation formulae in Mt. 1.22 and Rom. 2.24 is that they seem to suggest that the interpretations offered are, and always have been, the true meaning of these texts. But if the norm was to think of texts like Isa. 7.14 and Isa. 52.5 as polysemic, it might be that Matthew and Paul are showing how the 'semantic potential' or 'latent meaning' of the texts corresponds with the interpretations being offered. Indeed, Craig Blomberg suggests that the semantic range of the verb πληρόω includes the concepts of 'completing' or 'filling full' and hence 'allowed for multiple fulfillments of prophecy of varying kinds'.[12]

Scholars today often talk of 'quotation', 'allusion' and 'echo' as belonging to a spectrum of 'explicitness' when referring to particular texts, but little has been done to date on the oral/aural background that the word 'echo' suggests. Catrin Williams offers a wide-ranging chapter on such topics as memory and performance which illuminates many aspects of OT/NT studies. For example, following the work of the sociologist Barry Schwartz, 'commemorative keying' explores the way that the past is used as a 'frame' for bringing coherence to the present. Bypassing traditional debates about foreshadowing and fulfilment, it 'interprets present realities in analogical terms by *enacting* elements tied to landmark figures and events'.[13]

Next we come to the vexed question of the role of context when interpreting quotations and allusions. Given that Philo is commonly regarded as a non-contextual exegete, Kenneth Schenk provides a number of examples where Philo does attend closely to the text and its surrounding context (e.g. *Opif.* 77; *Mos.* 1.63-84). However, this is different from what we would call 'contextual interpretation' today, for, according

---

[11] Tooman, 34.
[12] C. Blomberg, *Jesus and the Gospels* (2nd edn; Nashville: B&H Academic, 2009), 234. Mitchell Kim, in a response to my treatment of 'respect for context', argued that Paul's use of Hos. 2.23 in Rom. 9.25-6 can be said to 'respect the context' because, even though Paul's meaning is different to the original sense of Hos. 2.23, it is consistent with a 'latent sense' of it. I have no problem with the idea of 'latent sense' (though I prefer to speak of the 'semantic potential' of a text) but disagree with Kim's apologetic use of it, for we have no way of assessing whether Paul's application of Hos. 2.23 to Gentiles is a latent sense of not. See my original article, Kim's challenge and my response in Christopher D. Stanley, ed., *Paul and Scripture: Extending the Conversation* (Atlanta: SBL, 2012).
[13] Williams, 68.

to Schenk, Philo did not *use* this information to guide his exegesis: 'Rather, they served as symbolic embodiments of higher, timeless, non-contextual truths.'[14]

The results are similar in Benjamin Wold's study of the DSS. Using categories derived from Joseph Fitzmyer's famous article,[15] there are a 'small handful of explicit quotations' from among the Literal/Historical and Modernization groupings that show some interest in the original context (4Q274, 4Q463) but they are in the minority: 'In general terms, the use of OT in its many varieties, not only citations, as represented in Qumran discoveries reflects little interest into original contexts.'[16] That is not to say that such exegesis was arbitrary or ad hoc. Other studies have shown that a rationale can often be discovered behind such exegesis,[17] but it is not contextual interpretation in the way that we would understand that term today.

Where does this leave OT/NT studies? Should we assume that the NT authors had little interest in the original context of their quotations and allusions or were they operating with a different set of hermeneutical principles? Arthur Keefer builds on my earlier study of 'respect for context' in two ways. First, he expands on the number of ways that scholars understand the term 'context'. Typically, this has often been the half dozen or so verses either side of the citation but others have expanded this to the chapter, book, major division of Scripture (e.g. Pentateuch) or indeed the whole canon of Scripture. Keefer expands this further to include OT themes, redemptive-historical action and authorial intention. He does not wish to make a judgement on the legitimacy of these wider contexts and in one sense, neither did I. However, I did want to make the point that these wider contexts are not what most people have in mind when discussing 'respect for context' and so can be misleading. In one of Keefer's examples, it seems to me that Walter Kaiser's attempt to show that Mt. 2.15 (Jesus's sojourn in Egypt) *is* the true meaning of Hos. 11.1 when understood in the context of the whole book is quite erroneous.

Keefer's second point challenges my assumption that scholars tend to adopt these wider definitions of context because they wish to argue for respect (or consistency as he calls it), when the surrounding verses would make this difficult to maintain (e.g. Hos. 11.2: 'The more I called them, the more they went from me; they kept sacrificing to the Baals, and offering incense to idols'). His example is that both Craig Evans and Walter Kaiser draw on the whole of Hosea in order to interpret Matthew's use of Hos. 11.1, but their different understandings of the book lead them to different conclusions.[18] The point is well made, though I was not intending to state an absolute principle. I was simply observing that those that look to the wider context of chapter, book or canon of

---

[14] Schenk, 114.
[15] J. Fitzmyer, 'The Use of Explicit Old Testament Quotations in Qumran Literature and in the New Testament', *NTS* 7 (1960-1): 297-333.
[16] Wold, 125.
[17] See George J. Brooke, *Exegesis at Qumran: 4QForilegium in its Jewish Context* (JSOTSup 29; Sheffield: JSOT Press, 1985).
[18] On the other hand, Evans goes on to argue that Matthew also had LXX Num. 24.8a in mind and it is this that allowed him to make the connection between Israel as God's son and Jesus, son of David, as God's son. Thus although Kaiser and Evans both expand the context of Hos. 11.1 to include the whole book, Evans goes further in bringing in related texts, so they are not actually operating with the same understanding of context.

Scripture do not usually conclude that the NT author *still* has little interest in context. It is usually in the service of an argument for 'respect of context' or consistency.

Beate Kowalski presents a review of research on the question of whether NT allusions are what she calls 'selective' or 'contextual'. If I have understood her correctly, she is using the term 'selective' in the sense of 'atomistic' and denies this in the strongest terms. Initially, this appears to be on theoretical grounds, for she claims that an allusion is *always* more than a simple reproduction of words. Words have meaning because they have been used before, and in that sense, all language is intertextual. There is no such thing as 'atomistic' allusions for words can never exist in isolation from other influences.

I am reminded of the words of Meir Sternberg, who, also on theoretical grounds, claimed the exact opposite. He asserted that 'tearing a piece of discourse from its original habitat and reconstructing it within a new network of relations cannot but interfere with its effect'.[19] If the citation is recognized, there is inevitably a process of 'recontextualization', because the text has been severed from its original moorings and forced to serve a different purpose. Thus from this perspective, it could be said that all 'reuses' of OT language are in a sense 'out of context'.

I think most people would recognize the truth in both of these positions but deem them irrelevant for the discussion at hand. If there is no such thing as an 'atomistic' allusion and the only other choice is 'contextual', then of course Revelation's use of the OT is 'contextual'. But then so is Philo, the DSS and every other writing, ancient or modern. On the other hand, if all uses of the OT are, by definition, out of context, then the claim that the quotation of Hos. 11.1 in Mt. 2.15 is out of context has no particular significance. What we are interested in is where on the scale of contextual awareness should these various writings be placed? By common consent, the ancient writers were not as concerned with context as we (academics) are, but then it would be anachronistic to expect them to be. However, we can ask whether the NT authors follow in the footsteps of (say) Philo or the DSS or show greater awareness of context and expect the same of their readers.

Despite the works surveyed by Kowalski, this remains a matter of debate in Revelation studies. For example, the words of Rev. 3.7 ('These are the words of the holy one, the true one, who has the *key of David, who opens and no one will shut, who shuts and no one opens*') are rightly regarded as an allusion to Isa. 22.22 ('I will place on his shoulder the *key* of the house *of David; he shall open, and no one shall shut; he shall shut, and no one shall open*'). But is it a contextual allusion? The original reference is to Eliakim, to whom God made the following promise: 'On that day I will … clothe him with your robe and bind your sash on him. I will commit your authority to his hand, and he shall be a father to the inhabitants of Jerusalem and to the house of Judah' (22.21). However, it will all end in disaster: 'On that day, says the LORD of hosts, the peg that was fastened in a secure place will give way; it will be cut down and fall, and the load that was on it will perish, for the LORD has spoken' (22.25). Does John really

---

[19] Meir Sternberg, 'Proteus in Quotation-Land: Mimesis and the Forms of Reported Discourse', *Poetics Today* 3 (1982): 108.

wish his readers to call to mind this context in order to understand the meaning of the 'open door' laid before the church in Philadelphia (Rev. 3.8)?[20]

More broadly, Michelle Fletcher has written a monograph entitled *Reading Revelation as Pastiche*.[21] She argues that in order to maintain a contextual understanding of John's visions, it is necessary to silence disparate voices. For example, John's inaugural vision (Rev. 1.12-18) has been explained by identifying a core text in either Daniel 7 (Beale) or Daniel 10 (Moyise) and then showing how other texts have been brought in by common wording or theme. However, Fletcher claims that this disguises the most obvious feature of the vision, the fact that texts have been taken from a wide variety of contexts and even combined with non-textual allusions, such as the seven stars (1.16). She argues that this 'pastiche' of allusions is more characteristic of John's use of the OT than what we would call a 'contextual' approach.

The third section of the volume looks at how allusions and echoes may be verified. As David Allen observes, there has been a widespread loss of confidence in the objectivity of applying criteria in NT research, whether in OT/NT studies or Historical Jesus scholarship. In part, this is due to the general postmodern suspicion of scholars claiming 'objectivity', when in fact it is just a disguise for promoting personal agendas.[22] This manifests itself in various ways in OT/NT studies: (1) It distorts the analogue nature of allusions and their effects by forcing them into a digital 0-1 (NO/YES) pattern; (2) If a coincidence of language is given a 1 (YES), it opens the door to importing huge swathes of OT theology into the NT words; (3) By using the criteria of 'thematic coherence' and 'satisfaction' to establish a 1 (YES), it virtually guarantees the conclusion that all NT allusions are contextual.

Fletcher offers an interesting example to test this out. In the complex description of the 'one like a son of man' in Rev. 1.12-18, the figure is said to have a golden sash draped across his breasts (καὶ περιεζωσμένον πρὸς τοῖς μαστοῖς ζώνην χρυσῆν).[23] This is disguised in most modern translations ('chest' – NRSV/NIV/ESV)[24] but would have stood out in Greek as much as it does in English. Indeed, Fletcher claims that the reader of Song 1.2 LXX would also have stumbled over the masculine pronoun (NETS: 'Let *him* kiss me from his mouth's kisses! For your breasts (μαστοί) are good beyond wine'). Here and in Song 1.4, 4.10 (x2) and 7.12(13), the MT has דֹּדֶיךָ ('your love') from the root דוד, but the LXX has assumed it is from דד ('breast'; cf. Ezek. 23.3, 8, 21). Given that this 'single word sits strangely among the other resonances in this image, and also is distinct on the linguistic register,'[25] Fletcher suggests that the allusion should be

---

[20] Gregory K. Beale (*The Book of Revelation* [NIGTC; Grand Rapids: Eerdmans, 1999]) thinks John is making a typological connection between Jesus and Eliakim: 'Whereas Eliakim's control was primarily political, Christ's was to be primarily spiritual, as well as ultimately universal in all aspects' (285).

[21] Michelle Fletcher, *Reading Revelation as Pastiche: Imitating the Past* (LNTS 571, London: Bloomsbury T&T Clark, 2017).

[22] See Walter Brueggemann, *The Bible and Postmodern Imagination* (London: SCM, 1993), 8-9. Watts claims that given Paul's manner of life and his exhortations to others, we can rule out any possibility that he would use Scripture to 'enhance his own authority or ideological hegemony' (169). Ironically, it seems to me that this is precisely what this statement is trying to do, against those like Christopher Stanley who wish to explore Paul's rhetorical use of Scripture.

[23] Drawing on Jesse Rainbow, 'Male μαστοί in Revelation 1.13', *JSNT* 30 (2007): 249–53.

[24] But RSV 'breast' and KJV 'paps'. The Vulgate has *mamillas*.

[25] Fletcher, *Pastiche*, 94.

accepted and that its effect is to add 'the lover' to the pastiche of other images in Rev. 1.12-18.[26]

Fletcher's main argument is an ideological one, namely, that we should allow 'the "quieter" voices of the text to be heard alongside those which are generally given primacy and subsume other voices'.[27] Indeed, we should be willing to give them 'equal importance'. More specific justification comes in the observation that when the reader gets to Revelation 19–22, the 'marginalized lover, which undermines some of the more dominant textual voices at the start, in fact refuses to stay silent as the text culminates in nuptials'.[28] She might also have referred to Rev. 3.20 ('Listen! I am standing at the door, knocking; if you hear my voice and open the door, I will come in to you and eat with you, and you with me'), which is commonly regarded as an allusion to Song 5.2.[29]

However, I think most would agree that the application of Hays's seven criteria would result in the allusion being rejected. Song of Songs barely registers in lists of allusions (only Jn 7.38 and Rev. 3.20 according to NA[28]) and there is no suggestion that the nuptial imagery of Revelation 19–22 is related to the book. So there is no recurrence, very little volume (one word) and little coherence, as Fletcher is at pains to point out. It has not featured in the history of interpretation and historical plausibility usually requires specific verbal or thematic links with other texts. This leaves satisfaction, which is clearly true for her 'pastiche' interpretation but not, I suspect, for the majority of readers. On the grounds of Hays's seven criteria, the single word 'breasts' should not be regarded as an allusion to LXX Song 1.2.

Nevertheless, I am in sympathy with her view that the quieter voices in the text should not be supressed out of some (ideological) desire to obtain coherence. Indeed, developing the echo metaphor, echoes can be quite loud when they occur between two buildings or in a tunnel and the same is true of textual echoes. However, I cannot agree that such allusions have 'equal importance' with more prominent allusions. It seems to me that this falls into the trap of forcing essentially analogue data into a digital 0–1 NO/YES pattern. Why can it not be true that a faint echo in the text is allowed to produce a faint effect on the reader? This seems to be the nub of Foster's criticism of 'echoes without resonance'. Accepting that there might be a faint echo of LXX Song 1.2 in Rev. 1.13 does not imply that the figure of 'the lover' should be given equal weight to the more overt images in Rev. 1.12-18.

When I first came across relevance theory (RT) in Stephen Pattemore's book on Revelation (2004),[30] it seemed to me that Christopher Stanley's hypothetical 'ignorant'

---

[26] Ibid. Another example is the comparison of the figure's face with the brightness of the sun (ὁ ἥλιος φαίνει ἐν τῇ δυνάμει αὐτοῦ). This is a rather obvious metaphor and Christian readers are likely to think of the Transfiguration (Mt. 17.2). However, R. H. Charles (*A Critical and Exegetical Commentary on the Revelation of St. John* [Edinburgh: T&T Clark], I: 30-1) suggested it was an allusion to LXX B Judg. 5.31 (ὡς ἔξοδος ἡλίου ἐν δυνάμει αὐτοῦ) but since there is little contextual similarity (contra Beale, *Revelation*, 212), most commentators ignore it.
[27] Fletcher, *Pastiche*, 96.
[28] Ibid., 97.
[29] Pointed out by Rainbow, 'Male μαστοί', 251–2, and supported by NA[28] (but not UBS5).
[30] Stephen W. Pattemore, *The People of God in the Apocalypse: Discourse, Structure and Exegesis* (SNTSMS; Cambridge: Cambridge University Press, 2004).

reader (also 2004) had become Sperber and Wilson's 'lazy' reader.[31] Readers are said to expend only that amount of energy required to find relevance and then give up. It is perhaps an accurate description of the majority in the early Church, trying desperately to eke out a living and avoid harassment and persecution. For them, it was probably enough to hear Rev. 1.12-18 as a description of the most radiant of all beings, with little interest (or ability) to trace the origins of each and every phrase. But Stanley also posited an 'informed audience', who would know the original context of Paul's quotations and (in some cases) be able to contest his interpretations. Does RT not accept the existence of the 'curious reader', one who always wants to dig deeper, leave no stone unturned and (apparently) derive huge satisfaction from the effort expended?

Where I think RT can make a contribution, as Smith similarly suggests within his chapter, is to push the discussion back to analogue characteristics and speak about probabilities rather than just a YES/NO to validating allusions. Thus I think Fletcher is correct that a reader is more likely to conclude that Rev. 1.12-18 points to a whole variety of images rather than an exegesis of Daniel 7 or 9. In that sense, optimal relevance is achieved by noticing this diversity and the use of 'breasts' rather than the more customary 'loins' could serve this purpose. However, this very point mitigates against seeking relevance in the context of each and every phrase. It is enough to note the diversity of images and gain whatever 'rhetorical impact' it induces. For the more curious reader, I think RT would suggest that they would start with Daniel and perhaps explore the allusions in Zechariah (golden lamp stands) and Isaiah (sharp sword from the mouth) but whether they would ever get to Song of Songs seems unlikely.

Lastly, Rikk Watts wishes to refute the view that the NT authors 'read backwards' (Hays), allowing their Christian experience to reconfigure the meaning in Scripture. Thus commenting on David Lincicum's monograph, he claims that 'Jesus is not read back into Deuteronomy but instead comes into the future space that Deuteronomy along with Scripture in general opens up'.[32] Indeed, he is willing to make the same point about Qumranic exegesis, which does not read the community back into the texts, for the texts themselves create a 'potential future into which the sectarians, simply by virtue of being faithful righteous Israel, can now locate themselves in their present'.[33] I have no problems with this as an explanation for what the various authors thought they were doing but I think it obscures more than it illuminates. It is like asking why rain fell on Monday and snow fell on Tuesday and receiving the answer: gravity. It is true and it is fundamental but not what we were (probably) enquiring about. One might say that Gen. 15.6 opened up a space that both Paul and James felt they could inhabit but why then do we have such different interpretations? I appreciate that the phrase 'read back' could be taken as 'simply read back', as if the text had nothing to contribute, but

---

[31] Christopher D. Stanley, *Arguing with Scripture: The Rhetoric of Quotations in the Letters of Paul* (London: T&T Clark, 2004). Stanley actually refers to them as the 'minimal audience' but he describes them as those with a 'general ignorance of the content of the Jewish Scriptures' (69).
[32] Watts, 176.
[33] Ibid.

this is hardly Hays's view.³⁴ I do not see how you can avoid the conclusion that the very different rhetorical situations of Paul and James has had an *influence* on the way they have read Gen. 15.6.

In conclusion, this is a rich collection of essays that shows that many traditional questions are being rethought, as well new avenues of research opening up. I wish the present chair (Professor Susan Docherty) every success in continuing to provide a forum for such research.

---

[34] 'In short, to gain Paul's kind of reader competence we must learn from him the art of dialectical imitation, bringing Scripture's witness to God's action in the past to bear as a critical principle on the present, and allowing God's present action among us to illumine our understanding of his action in the past' (Hays, *Echoes*, 183).

Bibliography

Abasciano, Brian J. 'Diamonds in the Rough: A Reply to Christopher Stanley Concerning the Reader Competency of Paul's Original Audiences'. *NovT* 49 (2007): 153–83.

Abasciano, Brian J. *Paul's Use of the Old Testament in Romans 9:1-9: An Intertextual and Theological Exegesis*. JSNTSup 301. London: T&T Clark, 2005.

Achtemeier, Paul J. '*Omne Verbum Sonat*: The New Testament and the Oral Environment of Late Western Antiquity'. *JBL* 103 (1990): 3–27.

Ackroyd, P. 'The Vitality of the Word of God in the Old Testament: A Contribution to the Study of the Transmission of Old Testament Material'. *ASTI* 1 (1962): 7–23.

Adams, Samuel V. *The Reality of God and Historical Method: Apocalyptic Theology in Conversation with N. T. Wright*. NET. Downers Grove: IVP Academic, 2015.

Adler, Maximilianus. *Studien zu Philon von Alexandreia*. Breslau: Marcus, 1929.

Aitken, Ellen Bradshaw. 'Tradition in the Mouth of the Hero: Jesus as an Interpreter of Scripture'. In *Performing the Gospel: Orality, Memory, and Mark: Essays Dedicated to Werner Kelber*, edited by Richard A. Horsley, Jonathan A. Draper and John Miles Foley, 97–103. Minneapolis: Fortress Press, 2006.

Albl, Martin C. *And Scripture Cannot Be Broken: The Form and Function of the Early Christian Testimonia Collections*. NovTSup 96. Leiden; Boston: Brill, 1999.

Alexander, Philip. 'The Bible in Qumran and Early Judaism'. In *The Text in Context*, edited by A. D. H. Mayes, 35–62. Oxford: Oxford University Press, 2000.

Alexander, Philip. 'Midrash'. In *A Dictionary of Biblical Interpretation*, edited by C. J. Coggins and T. L. Houlden, 452–9. London: SCM & Trinity, 1990.

Alexander, Philip. 'Retelling the Bible'. In *It Is Written: Scripture Citing Scripture*, edited by D. A. Carson and H. G. M. Williamson, 99–121. Cambridge: Cambridge University Press, 1988.

Alexander, Philip. 'Retelling the Old Testament'. In *It Is Written: Scripture Citing Scripture: Essays in Honour of Barnabas Lindars*, edited by D. A. Carson and H. G. M. Williamson, 99–121. Cambridge: Cambridge University Press, 1988.

Alexander, Philip. 'Why No Textual Criticism in Rabbinic Midrash? Reflections on the Textual Culture of the Rabbis'. In *Jewish Ways of Reading the Bible*, edited by George Brooke, 90–175. JSSSup 11. Oxford: Oxford University Press, 2000.

Alkier, S., Thomas Hieke and T. Nicklas. *Poetik und Intertextualität der Johannesapokalypse*. WUNT 346. Tübingen: Mohr Siebeck, 2015.

Allen, David M. *Deuteronomy and Exhortation in Hebrews: An Exercise in Narrative Re-Presentation*. WUNT 2/238. Tübingen: Mohr Siebeck, 2008.

Allen, David M. 'Introduction: The Study of the Use of the Old Testament in the New'. *JSNT* 38 (2015): 3–16.

Allen, Garrick V. *The Book of Revelation and Early Jewish Textual Culture*. SNTSMS 168. Cambridge: Cambridge University Press, 2017.

Allison, Dale C. 'The Old Testament in the New Testament'. In *The New Cambridge History of the Bible: From the Beginnings to 600*, edited by James Carleton Paget and Joachim Schaper, 479–502. Cambridge: Cambridge University Press, 2013.

Allison, Dale C. *Studies in Matthew: Interpretation Past and Present*. Grand Rapids: Baker, 2005.

Anderson, William H. 'The Curse of Work in Qoheleth: An Exposé of Genesis 3:17-19 in Ecclesiastes'. *EvQ* 70 (1998): 99-113.

Arndt, William, Frederick W. Danker, Walter Bauer and F. W. Gringrich, eds. *A Greek-English Lexicon of the New Testament and Other Early Christian Literature*. 3rd edn. Chicago: University of Chicago Press, 2000.

Avioz, Michael. *Nathan's Oracle (2 Sam 7) and Its Interpreters*. Bern: Peter Lang, 2005.

Avrahami, Yael. *The Senses of Scripture: Sensory Perception in the Hebrew Bible*. New York: T&T Clark International, 2012.

Barbour, Jennie. *The Story of Israel in the Book of Qohelet: Ecclesiastes as Cultural Memory*. Oxford: Oxford University Press, 2012.

Bartholomew, Craig. 'The Intertextuality of Ecclesiastes and the New Testament'. In *Reading Ecclesiastes Intertextually*, edited by Katharine J. Dell and Will Kynes, 226-39. LHBOTS 587. London: Bloomsbury, 2014.

Barton, John. 'Beyond Hays's *Echoes of Scripture*'. In *Paul and Scripture: Extending the Conversation*, edited by Christopher D. Stanley, 263-91. ECL 9. Atlanta: Society of Biblical Literature, 2012.

Barton, John. 'Déjà Lu: Intertextuality, Method or Theory?' In *Reading Job Intertextually*, edited by Katharine J. Dell and Will Kynes, 1-16. LHBOTS 574. London: Bloomsbury, 2013.

Barton, John. 'Intertextuality and the "Final Form" of the Text'. In *Congress Volume: Oslo 1998*, edited by Andre Lemaire and Magne Sæbø, 33-7. Leiden; Boston: Brill, 2000.

Barton, John. *Oracles of God: Perceptions of Ancient Prophecy in Israel after the Exile*. London: Darton, Longman & Todd, 1986.

Barton, Stephen C. 'Memory and Remembrance in Paul'. In *Memory in the Bible and Antiquity*, edited by Loren T. Stuckenbruck, Stephen C. Barton and Benjamin G. Wold, 321-39. WUNT, 212. Tübingen: Mohr Siebeck, 2007.

Bates, Matthew W. *The Hermeneutics of the Apostolic Proclamation: The Center of Paul's Method of Scriptural Interpretation*. Waco: Baylor University Press, 2012.

Bauckham, Richard. *The Climax of Prophecy: Studies on the Book of Revelation*. Edinburgh: T&T Clark, 1993.

Bauckham, Richard. *James: Wisdom of James, Disciple of Jesus the Sage*. NTR. London: Routledge, 1999.

Beale, Gregory K. *The Book of Revelation: A Commentary on the Greek Text*. NIGTC. Grand Rapids: Eerdmans, 1999.

Beale, Gregory K. *Handbook on the New Testament Use of the Old Testament: Exegesis and Interpretation*. Grand Rapids: Baker Academic, 2012.

Beale, Gregory K. *John's Use of the Old Testament in the Revelation*. JSNTSup 166. Sheffield: Sheffield Academic Press, 1988.

Beale, Gregory K. *The Right Doctrine from the Wrong Texts?: Essays on the Use of the Old Testament in the New*. Grand Rapids: Baker, 1994.

Beale, Gregory K. *The Use of Daniel in Jewish Apocalyptic Literature and in the Revelation of St. John*. Lanham; New York; London: University Press of America, 1984.

Beale, Gregory K., and D. A. Carson. *Commentary on the New Testament Use of the Old Testament*. Grand Rapids: Baker Academic, 2007.

Beentjes, Pancratius C. 'Inverted Quotations in the Bible: A Neglected Stylistic Pattern'. *Bib* 63 (1982): 506-23.

Beetham, Christopher A. *Echoes of Scripture in the Letter of Paul to the Colossians*. BIS 96. Leiden: Brill, 2008.

Beker, J. Christiaan. 'Echoes and Intertextuality: On the Role of Scripture in Paul's Theology.' In *Paul and the Scriptures of Israel*, edited by Craig A. Evans and James A. Sanders, 64–9. JSNTSup 83. Sheffield: JSOT Press, 1993.
Ben-Porat, Ziva. 'Intertextuality and Cosmopolitanism in Cyberspace'. *Primerjalna književnost* 35 (2009): 137–58.
Ben-Porat, Ziva. 'The Poetics of Literary Allusion'. *PTL: A Journal for Descriptive Poetics and Theory of Literature* 1 (1976): 105–28.
Bernstein, Moshe. 'The Contribution of the Qumran Discoveries to the History of Early Biblical Interpretation'. In *The Idea of Biblical Interpretation: Essays in Honor of James L. Kugel*, edited by Hindy Najman and Judith Newman, 215–38. SJSJ 83. Leiden; Boston: Brill, 2004.
Bernstein, Moshe. 'Interpretation of Scriptures'. In *Encyclopedia of the Dead Sea Scrolls*, edited by Lawrence Schiffman and James Vanderkam, 376–83. New York: Oxford University Press, 2000.
Bernstein, Moshe. 'Re-Arrangement, Anticipation, and Harmonization as Exegetical Features in the Genesis Apocryphon'. *DSD* 3 (1996): 37–57.
Bernstein, Moshe, and Shlomo Koyfman. 'The Interpretation of Biblical Law in the Dead Sea Scrolls: Forms and Method'. In *Biblical Interpretation at Qumran*, edited by Matthias Henze, 61–87. SDSSRL. Grand Rapids: Eerdmans, 2005.
Bertholet, Katell. 'Les Titres des Livres Bibliques: Le Témoignage De La Bibliothèque De Qumrân'. In *Flores Florentino: Dead Sea Scrolls and Other Early Jewish Studies in Honour of Florentino García Martínez*, edited by A. Hilhorst, É. Puech and E. J. C. Tigchelaar, 127–40. JSJSup 122. Leiden: Brill, 2007.
Bertrand, Daniel A. 'Le Chevreau D'anna: La Signification De L'anecdotique Dans Le Livre De Tobit'. *RHPR* 68 (1988): 269–74.
Blomberg, C. *Jesus and the Gospels*. 2nd edn. Nashville: B&H Academic, 2009.
Bloomquist, L. Gregory. 'Methodological Criteria for Apocalyptic Rhetoric: A Suggestion for the Expand Use of Sociorhetorical Analysis'. In *Vision and Persuasion: Rhetorical Dimensions of Apocalyptic Discourse*, edited by G. Carey and L. G. Bloomquist, 181–203. St. Louis: Chalice Press, 1990.
Blum, Erhard. 'Formgeschichte – A Misleading Category? Some Critical Remarks'. In *The Changing Face of Form Criticism for the Twenty-First Century*, edited by Marvin Sweeney and Ehud Ben Zvi, 32–45. Grand Rapids: Eerdmans, 2003.
Blum, Erhard. '"Formgeschichte" — Ein Irreführender Begirff?' In *Lesarten der Bibel: Untersuchungen zu Einer Theorie der Exegese des Alten Testaments*, edited by Helmut Utzschneider and Erhard Blum, 85–96. Stuttgaart: Kohlhammer, 2006.
Bøe, S. *Gog and Magog: Ezekiel 38-39 as Pre-Text for Revelation 19,17-21 and 20,7-10*. WUNT 2/135. Tübingen: Mohr Siebeck, 2001.
Böhl, Franz Marius Theodore. 'Wortspiele im Alten Testament'. *JPOS* 6 (1926): 196–212.
Borgen, Peder. *Philo of Alexandria: An Exegete for His Time*. SNT 86. Leiden: Brill, 1997.
Borgen, Peder. 'Philo—An Interpreter of the Laws of Moses'. In *Reading Philo: A Handbook of Philo of Alexandria*, edited by Torey Seland, 75–101. Grand Rapids: Eerdmans, 2014.
Boyarin, Daniel. 'Inner-Biblical Ambiguity, Intertextuality and the Dialectic of Midrash: The Waters of Marah'. *Prooftexts* 10 (1990): 29–48.
Boyarin, Daniel. *Intertextuality and the Reading of Midrash*. Bloomington; Indianapolis: Indiana University Press, 1990.
Brawley, Robert L. 'Nodes of Objective Socialization and Subjective Reflection in Identity: Galatian Identity in an Imperial Context'. In *T&T Clark Handbook to Social Identity in*

the New Testament, edited by J. Brian Tucker and Coleman A. Baker, 119–43. London: Bloomsbury, 2014.
Brawley, Robert L. *Text to Text Pours Forth Speech: Voices of Scripture in Luke-Acts.* ISBL. Bloomington: Indiana University Press, 1995.
Brickle, Jeffrey E. 'The Memory of the Beloved Disciple: A Poetics of Johannine Memory'. In *Memory and Identity in Ancient Judaism and Early Christianity: A Conversation with Barry Schwartz,* edited by Tom Thatcher, 187–208. Semeia Studies 78. Atlanta: SBL, 2014.
Brodie, Thomas L., Dennis R. MacDonald and Stanley E. Porter. 'Conclusion: Problems of Method—Suggested Guidelines'. In *The Intertextuality of the Epistles: Explorations of Theory and Practice,* edited by T. Brodie, D. MacDonald and S. E. Porter, 284–96. Sheffield: Sheffield Phoenix Press, 2006.
Brooke, George. *Exegesis at Qumran: 4QFlorilegium in Its Jewish Context.* JSOTSup 29. Sheffield: Sheffield University Press, 1985.
Brooke, George. 'Biblical Interpretation in the Qumran Scrolls and the New Testament'. In *The Dead Sea Scrolls Fifty Years after Their Discovery: Proceedings of the Jerusalem Congress, July 20-25, 1997,* edited by Lawrence Schiffman, Emanuel Tov and James Vanderkam, 60–73. Jerusalem: Israel Exploration Society, in collaboration with The Shrine of the Book, Israel Museum, 2000.
Brooke, George. '"The Canon within the Canon" at Qumran and in the New Testament'. In *The Scrolls and the Scriptures: Qumran Fifty Years After,* edited by Stanley E. Porter and Craig A. Evans, 242–66. Sheffield: Sheffield Academic Press, 1997.
Brooke, George J. 'Memory, Cultural Memory, and Rewriting Scripture'. In *Reading the Dead Sea Scrolls: Essays in Method,* edited by József Zsengellér, 51–65. EJIL, 39. Atlanta: SBL, 2013.
Brooke, George J. 'The Qumran Scrolls and the Demise of the Distinction between Higher and Lower Criticism'. In *Reading the Dead Sea Scrolls: Essays in Method,* edited by George J. Brooke, 1–17. SBLEJL, 39. Atlanta: SBL, 2013.
Brooke, George. 'Reading, Searching and Blessing: A Functional Approach to Scriptural Interpretation in the יחד'. In *The Temple in Text and Tradition: A Festschrift in Honour of Robert Hayward,* edited by R. Timothy McLay, 140–56. LSTS 83. London: Bloomsbury, 2015.
Brooke, George. 'Shared Intertextual Interpretations in the Dead Sea Scrolls and the New Testament'. In *Biblical Perspectives Early Use and Interpretation of the Bible in Light of the Dead Sea Scrolls Proceedings of the First International Symposium of the Orion Center, 12–14 May, 1996,* edited by Michael Stome and Esther Chazon, 35–57. STDJ 28. Leiden: Brill, 1998.
Brooke, George. 'Thematic Commentaries on Prophetic Scriptures'. In *Biblical Interpretation at Qumran,* edited by Matthias Henze, 134–57. Grand Rapids: Eerdmans, 2005.
Brown, Jeannine K. 'Genesis in Matthew's Gospel'. In *Genesis in the New Testament,* edited by Maarten J. J. Menken and Steve Moyise, 42–59. LNTS 466. London: Bloomsbury T&T Clark, 2012.
Brown, Jeannine K. 'Metalepsis'. In *Exploring Intertextuality: Diverse Strategies for New Testament Interpretation of Texts,* edited by B. J. Oropeza and Steve Moyise, 29–41. Eugene: Cascade, 2016.
Brueggemann, Walter. *The Bible and Postmodern Imagination.* London: SCM, 1993.
Cadbury, Henry J. 'The Titles of Jesus in Acts'. In *The Beginnings of Christianity, Part 1: The Acts of the Apostles, Vol. 5: Additional Notes to the Commentary,* edited by Kirsopp Lake and Henry J. Cadbury, 354–75. London: McMillian, 1933.
Carmignac, J. 'Le Document De Qumrân sur Melkisédeq'. *RevQ* 7 (1969–71): 343–78.

Carey, Holly J. *Jesus' Cry from the Cross: Towards a First-Century Understanding of the Intertextual Relationship between Psalm 22 and the Narrative of Mark's Gospel*. LNTS 398. London: T&T Clark, 2009.

Carr, David M. *The Formation of the Hebrew Bible: A New Reconstruction*. New York: Oxford University Press, 2011.

Carr, David M. 'Orality, Textuality, *and* Memory: The State of Biblical Studies'. In *Contextualizing Israel's Sacred Writings: Ancient Literacy, Orality, and Literary Production*, edited by Brian B. Schmidt, 161–73. Ancient Israel and its Literature, 22. Atlanta: SBL, 2015.

Carr, David M. *Writing on the Tablet of the Heart: Origins of Scripture and Literature*. New York: Oxford University Press, 2005.

Carter, Jonathan A. 'Telling Times: History, Emplotment, and Truth'. *History and Theory* 42 (2003): 1–27.

Casey, Jay S. 'Das Exodusthema im Buch der Offenbarung Vor Dem Hintergrund des Neuen Testaments'. *Concilium* 23 (1987): 22–8.

Cave, Terence. 'Towards a Passing Theory of Understanding'. In *Reading Beyond the Code: Literature and Relevance Theory*, edited by Terence Cave and Deirdre Wilson, 167–83. Oxford: Oxford University Press, 2018.

Cave, Terence, and Deirdre Wilson. 'Introduction'. In *Reading Beyond the Code: Literature and Relevance Theory*, edited by Terence Cave and Deirdre Wilson, 1–20. Oxford: Oxford University Press, 2018.

Cave, Terence, and Deirdre Wilson, eds. *Reading Beyond the Code: Literature and Relevance Theory*. Oxford: Oxford University Press, 2018.

Charles, R. H. *A Critical and Exegetical Commentary on the Revelation of St. John*. Edinburgh: T&T Clark, 1920.

Chester, Andrew. 'Resurrection and Transformation'. In *Auferstehung – Resurrection*, edited by H. Lichtenberger and F. Avemarie, 47–77. WUNT 135. Tübingen: Mohr Siebeck, 1999.

Cheung, Simon. *Wisdom Intoned: A Reappraisal of the Genre "Wisdom Psalms"*. LHBOTS 613. London: Bloomsbury T&T Clark, 2015.

Childs, Brevard. 'Psalm Titles and Midrashic Exegesis'. *JSS* 16 (1971): 137–50.

Chilton, Bruce D., ed. *The Isaiah Targum: Introduction, Translation, Apparatus and Notes* Vol. 11, ArB. Edinburgh: T&T Clark, 1987.

Ciampa, Roy E. *The Presence and Function of Scripture in Galatians 1 and 2*. WUNT 2/102. Tübingen: Mohr Siebeck, 1998.

Collingwood, Robin G. *The Idea of History*, edited by T. M. Knox. Oxford: Clarendon Press, 1967.

Collingwood, Robin G. *The Principles of History: And Other Writings in Philosophy of History*, edited by William H. Dray and W. J. van der Dussen. New York: Oxford University Press, 1999.

Crawford, Sidney White. 'Textual Growth and the Activity of Scribes'. *SEÅ* 82 (2017): 6–27.

Crenshaw, James L. 'The Influence of the Wise upon Amos: The "Doxologies of Amos" and Job 5.9-16; 9.5-10'. *ZAW* 79 (1967): 42–52.

Crenshaw, James L. 'Wisdom'. In *Old Testament Form Criticism*, edited by J. Hayes, 225–64. San Antonio: Trinity University Press, 1974.

Crites, Stephen. 'The Narrative Quality of Experience'. *JAAR* 39 (1971): 291–311.

Dell, Katharine J. 'All Is Decay: Intertextual Links between Lamentations 5 and Ecclesiastes 12:1-7'. In *Reading Lamentations Intertextually*, edited by Heath Thomas and Brittany Melton. LHBOTS. London: Bloomsbury, Forthcoming.

Dell, Katharine J. *The Book of Job as Sceptical Literature*. BZAW 197. Berlin: Walter de Gruyter, 1991.
Dell, Katharine J. 'Deciding the Boundaries of Wisdom: Applying the Concept of Family Resemblance'. In *Was There a Wisdom Tradition?: New Prospects in Israelite Wisdom Studies*, edited by Mark Sneed, 145–60. AIL. Atlanta: SBL Press, 2015.
Dell, Katharine J. 'Didactic Intertextuality: Proverbial Wisdom as Illustrated in Ruth'. In *Reading Proverbs Intertextuality*, edited by Katharine J. Dell and Will Kynes, 103–14. LHBOTS 634. London: Bloomsbury, 2019.
Dell, Katharine J. 'Ecclesiastes as Mainstream Wisdom (without Job)'. In *Goochem in Mokum/Wisdom in Amsterdam: Papers on Biblical and Related Wisdom Read at the Fifteenth Joint Meeting of the Society of Old Testament Study and the Oudtestamentisch Werkgezelschap, Amsterdam July 2012*, edited by George Brooke and Pierre Van Hecke, 43–52. OTS 68. Leiden: Brill, 2016.
Dell, Katharine J. 'Exploring Intertextual Links Between Ecclesiastes and Genesis 1–11'. In *Reading Ecclesiastes Intertextually*, edited by Katharine J. Dell and Will Kynes, 3–14. LHBOTS 587. London: Bloomsbury, 2014.
Dell, Katharine J. *Get Insight: An Introduction to Israel's Wisdom Literature*. London: Darton, Longman & Todd, 2000.
Dell, Katharine J. '"I Will Solve My Riddle to the Music of the Lyre" (Psalm Xlix 4 [5]): A Cultic Setting for Wisdom Psalms?' *VT* 54 (2003): 445–58.
Dell, Katharine J., and Will Kynes, eds. *Reading Job Intertextually*. LHBOTS 574. London: Bloomsbury, 2012.
Dell, Katharine J., and Will Kynes, eds. *Reading Proverbs Intertextually*, LHBOTS 634. London: Bloomsbury, 2018.
Dewey, Joanna. 'Textuality in an Oral Culture: A Survey of the Pauline Traditions'. In *Orality and Textuality in Early Christian Literature*, edited by Joanna Dewey, 37–65. Semeia, 65. Atlanta: SBL, 1995.
Doering, Lutz. 'Excerpted Texts in Second Temple Judaism: A Survey of the Evidence'. In *Selecta colligere, II: Beiträge zur Technik des Sammelns und Kompilierens griechischer Texte von der Antike bis zur Humanismus*, edited by Rosa M. Piccione and Matthias Perkams, 1–38. Hellenica, 18. Allesandria: Edizioni dell'Orso, 2005.
Dimant, Devorah. 'The Library of Qumran: Its Content and Character'. In *The Dead Sea Scrolls Fifty Years after Their Discovery*, edited by Lawrence Schiffman, Emanuel Tov and James Vanderkam, 170–6. Jerusalem: IES, 2000.
Dimant, Devorah. 'Use and Interpretation of Mikra in the Apocrypha and Pseudepigrapha'. In *Mikra: Text, Translation, Reading, and Interpretation of the Hebrew Bible in Ancient Judaism and Early Christianity*, edited by M. J. Mulder, 379–419. CRINT 2/1. Assen: Van Gorcum, 1988.
Docherty, Susan E. 'New Testament Scriptural Interpretation in Its Early Jewish Context'. *NovT* 57 (2015): 1–19.
Dodd, C. H. *According to the Scriptures: The Sub-Structure of New Testament Theology*. London: Nisbet, 1952.
Dray, William H. *History as Re-Enactment: R. G. Collingwood's Idea of History*. Oxford: Clarendon Press; Oxford University Press, 1995.
Dunn, James D. G. 'Jesus Tradition in Paul'. In *Studying the Historical Jesus: Evaluation of the State of Current Research*, edited by Bruce Chilton and Craig A. Evans, 155–78. Leiden: Brill, 1994.
Du Toit, Jaqueline. *Textual Memory: Archives, Libraries, and the Hebrew Bible*. SWBA 2/6. Sheffield: Phoenix, 2011.

Edenburg, Cynthia. 'Intertextuality, Literary Competence and the Question of Readership: Some Preliminary Observations'. *JSOT* 35 (2010): 131–48.

Elder, Nicholas A. 'New Testament Media Criticism'. *CBR* 15 (2017): 315–37.

Elledge, Casey D. 'Exegetical Styles at Qumran: A Cumulative Index and Commentary'. *RevQ* 21 (2003-4): 165–208.

Enns, Peter. *Inspiration and Incarnation: Evangelicals and the Problem of the Old Testament*. Grand Rapids: Baker Academic, 2005.

Eshel, Hanan. 'The Historical Background of the Pesher Interpreting Joshua's Curse on the Rebuilder of Jericho'. *RevQ* 15 (1992): 409–20.

Esler, Philip F. 'Collective Memory and Hebrews 11: Outlining a New Investigative Framework'. In *Memory, Tradition, and Text: Uses of the Past in Early Christianity*, edited by Alan Kirk and Tom Thatcher, 151–71. Semeia Studies, 52. Atlanta: SBL, 2005.

Esler, Philip F. 'Paul's Contestation of Israel's (Ethnic) Memory of Abraham in Galatians 3'. *BTB* 36 (2006): 23–34.

Evans, Craig A. 'The Function of the Old Testament in the New'. In *Introducing New Testament Interpretation*, edited by S. McKnight, 163–9. Grand Rapids: Baker Books, 1989.

Evans, Craig A. '"It Is Not as through the Word of God Had Failed": An Introduction to Paul and the Scriptures of Israel'. In *Paul and the Scriptures of Israel*, edited by Craig A. Evans and James A. Sanders, 13–17. JSNTSup 83. Sheffield: JSOT Press, 1992.

Evans, Craig A. 'Why Did the New Testament Writers Appeal to the Old Testament?' *JSNT* 38 (2015): 36–48.

Evans, Craig A., and James A. Sanders. *Paul and the Scriptures of Israel*. JSNTSup 83. Sheffield: JSOT Press, 1993.

Eve, Eric. *Behind the Gospels: Understanding the Oral Tradition*. London: SPCK, 2013.

Farber, Walter. 'Associative Magic: Some Rituals, Word Plays, and Philology'. *JAOS* 106 (1986): 447–9.

Fischer, David Hackett. *Historians' Fallacies: Towards a Logic of Historical Thought*. NewYork: Harper Torchbooks, 1970.

Fishbane, Michael. *Biblical Interpretation in Ancient Israel*. Oxford: Clarendon, 1985.

Fishbane, Michael. *Biblical Myth and Rabbinic Mythmaking*. Oxford and New York: Oxford University Press, 2003.

Fishbane, Michael. *The Garments of Torah: Essays in Biblical Hermeneutics*. ISBL. Bloomington: Indiana University Press, 1989.

Fishbane, Michael. 'The Qumran Pesher and Traits of Ancient Hermeneutics'. In *Proceedings of the Sixth World Congress of Jewish Studies: Hebrew University of Jerusalem, 13–19 August, 1973*, edited by Malka Jagendorf and Avigdor Shinan, 97–114. Jerusalem: World Union of Jewish Studies, 1977.

Fishbane, Michael. 'Use, Authority, and Interpretation of Mikra at Qumran'. In *Mikra: Text, Translation, Reading and Interpretation of the Hebrew Bible in Ancient Judaism and Early Christianity*, edited by Martin J. Mulder and Harry Sysling, 339–77. Assen: Van Gorcum, 1988.

Fitzmyer, Joseph A. *The Genesis Apocryphon of Qumran Cave I: A Commentary*. Rome: Pontifical Biblical Institute, 1966.

Fitzmyer, Joseph A. 'The Use of Explicit Old Testament Quotations in Qumran Literature and in the New Testament'. In *Essays on the Semitic Background of the New Testament*, 3–58. SBS 5. Atlanta: Scholars Press, 1974.

Fitzmyer, Joseph A. 'The Use of Explicit Old Testament Quotations in Qumran Literature and in the New Testament'. *NTS* 7 (1960-1): 297–333.

Fletcher, Michelle. *Reading Revelation as Pastiche: Imitating the Past.* LNTS 571. London: Bloomsbury T&T Clark, 2017.

Fohrer, G. *Introduction to the Old Testament.* Revised edn. Nashville: Abingdon Press, 1968.

Foley, John Miles. *Immanent Art: From Structure to Meaning in Traditional Oral Epic.* Bloomington: Indiana University Press, 1991.

Foley, John Miles. *The Singer of Tales in Performance.* Voices in Performance and Text; Bloomington: Indiana University Press, 1995.

Forman, Charles C. 'Qoheleth's Use of Genesis'. *JSS* 5 (1960): 256–63.

Foster, Paul. 'Echoes without Resonance: Critiquing Certain Aspects of Recent Scholarly Trends in the Study of the Jewish Scriptures in the New Testament'. *JSNT* 38 (2015): 96–111.

Foster, Robert B. *Renaming Abraham's Children: Election, Ethnicity, and the Interpretation of Scripture in Romans 9.* WUNT 2/421. Tübingen: Mohr Siebeck, 2016.

Fowl, Stephen. 'The Use of Scripture in Philippians'. In *Paul and Scripture: Extending the Conversation,* edited by Christopher D. Stanley. ECL 9, 163–84. Atlanta: Society of Biblical Literature, 2012.

Fraade, Steven. 'Response to Azzan Yadin-Israel on Rabbinic Polysemy: Do They "Preach" What They Practice?' *ASJR* 38 (2014): 339–61.

Frahm, Ellery. *Babylonian and Assyrian Text Commentaries: Origins of Interpretation.* Origins of Interpretation. Münster: Ugarit-Verlag, 2011.

Frei, Hans. *The Eclipse of Biblical Narrative: A Study in Eighteenth and Nineteenth Century Hermeneutics.* New Haven: Yale University Press, 1980.

Furlong, Anne. 'Relevance Theory and Literary Interpretation'. PhD diss., University College London, 1996.

Gabbay, Uri. 'Akkadian Commentaries from Ancient Mesopotamia and Their Relation to Early Hebrew Exegesis'. *DSD* 19 (2012): 267–312.

Gabbay, Uri. 'Levels of Meaning and Textual Polysemy in Akkadian and Hebrew Exegetical Texts'. In *Jewish Cultural Encounters in the Ancient Mediterranean and near Eastern World,* edited by M. Popović, M. Schoonover and M. Vandenberghe, 76–95. Leiden and Boston: Brill, 2017.

Gadamer, Hans-Georg. 'Truth and Method'. Translated by J. Weinsheimer and D. G. Marshall. New York: Bloomsbury, 1989.

Gallusz, Laslo. 'The Exodus Motif in Revelation 15-16: Its Background and Nature'. *AUSS* 46 (2008): 21–43.

Gallusz, Laslo. *The Throne Motif in the Book of Revelation.* LNTS 487. London: Bloomsbury, 2013.

Garsiel, Moshe. 'Punning upon the Names of the Letters of the Alphabet in Biblical Acrostics'. *Beth Miqra* 139 (1994): 313–34.

Gerber, Edward H. *The Scriptural Tale in the Fourth Gospel with Particular Reference to the Prologue and a Syncretic (Oral and Written) Poetics.* BIS 147. Leiden: Brill, 2017.

Gerstenberger, Erhard. 'Psalms'. In *Old Testament Form Criticism,* edited by J. H. Hayes, 179–221. San Antonio: Trinity University Press, 1974.

Gillmayer-Bucher, S. 'Intertextualität. Zwischen Literaturtheorie und Methodik'. *PzB* 8 (1999): 5–20.

Ginzberg, L. *Legends of the Jews.* Philadelphia: Jewish Publication Society, 1909.

Gladd, Benjamin L. *Revealing the Mysterion: The Use of Mystery in Daniel and Second Temple Judaism with Its Bearing on First Corinthians.* BZNW 160. Berlin: Walter de Gruyter, 2008.

Goldberg, A. 'Die Funktionale Form Midrasch'. *FJB* 10 (1982): 1–45.
Goldberg, A. 'Entwurf Einer Formanalytischen Method Für die Exegese der Rabbinischen Traditionsliteratur'. *FJB* 5 (1977): 1–14.
Goldingay, John. *Daniel*. WBC 50. Dallas: Word, 1989.
Goldingay, John. *Reading Jesus's Bible: How the New Testament Helps Us Understand the Old Testament*. Grand Rapids: Eerdmans, 2017.
Goldstein, Leon J. 'Dray on Re-Enactment and Constructionism: Review of William H. Dray, *History as Re-Enactment*'. *History and Theory* 37 (1998): 409–21.
Goppelt, Leonhard. *Typos: The Typological Interpretation of the Old Testament in the New*. Translated by Donald H. Madvig. Grand Rapids: Eerdmans, 1982.
Gordis, Robert. 'Studies in Hebrew Roots of Contrasted Meaning'. *JQR* 27 (1936–7): 33–58.
Goulder, Michael D. 'The Apocalypse as an Annual Cycle of Prophecies'. *NTS* 27 (1981): 342–67.
Grabbe, Lester L. *Etymology in Early Jewish Interpretation: The Hebrew Names in Philo*. BJS 115. Atlanta: Scholars, 1988.
Green, Keith. 'Relevance Theory and the Literary Text: Some Problems and Perspectives'. *JLS* 22 (1993): 207–17.
Green, T. M. *The Light in Troy: Imitation and Discovery in Renaissance Poetry*. New Haven: Yale University Press, 1982.
Greenspoon, Leonard. 'By the Letter? Word for Word? Scriptural Citation in Paul'. In *Paul and Scripture: Extending the Conversation*, edited by Christopher D. Stanley, 9–24. Atlanta: SBL, 2012.
Grossberg, Daniel. 'Pivotal Polysemy in Jeremiah XXV 10–11a'. *VT* 36 (1986): 481–5.
Gunkel, H. *The Psalms: A Form-Critical Introduction*. Translated by Thomas Horner. Philadelphia: Fortress, 1967.
Halbertal, Moshe. *Commentary Revolutions in the Making: Values as Interpretative Considerations in Midrashei Halakhah*. Jerusalem: Magnes Press, 2010.
Halbwachs, Maurice. *Les Cadres sociaux de la mémoire*. Paris: Alcan, 1925.
Halbwachs, Maurice. *La Mémoire collective*. Paris: Éditions Albin Michel, 1950/80.
Halbwachs, Maurice. *La Topographie légendaire des évangiles en terre sainte: Étude de mémoire collective*. Paris: Presses Universitaires de France, 1941.
Halivni, D. Weiss. *Peshat and Derash: Plain and Applied Meaning in Rabbinic Exegesis*. Oxford: Oxford University Press, 1998.
Halivni, David. 'Aspects of Classical Jewish Hermeneutic'. In *Holy Scriptures in Judaism, Christianity and Islam: Hermeneutics, Values and Society*, edited by Hendrik M. Vroom and Jerald D. Gort, 77–97. Amsterdam: Rodopi, 1997.
Hanson, Anthony Tyrrell. *The Living Utterances of God: The New Testament Exegesis of the Old*. London: Darton, Longman & Todd, 1983.
Hanson, Anthony Tyrrell. *The New Testament Interpretation of Scripture*. London: SPCK, 1980.
Harris, William V. *Ancient Literacy*. Cambridge: Harvard University Press, 1989.
Harrison, Carol. *The Art of Listening in the Early Church*. Oxford: Oxford University Press, 2013.
Hayes, Christine. *Gentile Impurities and Jewish Identities: Intermarriage and Conversion from the Bible to the Talmud*. Oxford: Oxford University Press, 2002.
Hayes, Katherine M. 'Metonymy'. In *The Dictionary of the Bible and Ancient Media*, edited by Tom Thatcher et al., 225–6. London: Bloomsbury, 2017.
Hays, Richard B. *The Conversion of the Imagination: Paul as Interpreter of Israel's Scripture*. Grand Rapids: Eerdmans, 2005.

Hays, Richard B. *Echoes of Scripture in the Gospels*. Waco: Baylor University Press, 2016.
Hays, Richard B. *Echoes of Scripture in the Letters of Paul*. New Haven; London: Yale University Press, 1989.
Hays, Richard B. 'Echoes of Scripture in the Letters of Paul: Abstract'. In *Paul and the Scriptures of Israel*, edited by Craig A. Evans and James A. Sanders, 42–6. JSNTSup 83. Sheffield: JSOT Press, 1993.
Hays, Richard B. *Reading Backwards: Figural Christology and the Fourfold Gospel Witness*. Waco: Baylor University Press, 2014.
Hays, Richard B. 'Who Has Believed Our Message: Paul's Reading of Isaiah'. In *New Testament Writers and the Old Testament: An Introduction*, edited by John Court, 46–70. London: SPCK, 2002.
Hays, Richard B., Stefan Alkier and Leroy Andrew Huizenga. *Reading the Bible Intertextually*. Waco: Baylor University Press, 2009.
Head, Peter M. 'Named Letter-Carriers among the Oxyrhynchus Papyri'. *JSNT* 31 (2009): 279–99.
Hearon, Holly E. 'The Implications of Orality for Studies of the Biblical Text'. In *Performing the Gospel: Orality, Memory, and Mark: Essays Dedicated to Werner Kelber*, edited by Richard A. Horsley, Jonathan A. Draper and John Miles Foley, 3–20. Minneapolis: Fortress Press, 2006.
Hearon, Holly E. 'Mapping Written and Spoken Word in the Gospel of Mark'. In *The Interface of Orality and Writing: Speaking, Seeing, Writing in the Shaping of New Genres*, edited by Annette Weissenrieder and Robert B. Coote, 379–92. Biblical Performance Criticism, 11. Eugene: Cascade Books, 2015.
Heaton, Eric W. *The School Tradition in the Old Testament*. Oxford: Oxford University Press, 1994.
Heaton, E. W. *Solomon's New Men*. London; New York: Pica Press, 1974.
Heckl, Raik. 'Inside the Canon and Out: The Relationship Between Psalm 20 and Papyrus Amherst 63'. *Sem* 56 (2014): 359–7.
Heil, John Paul. *The Rhetorical Role of Scripture in 1 Corinthians*. SBLMS 15. Atlanta: Society of Biblical Literature, 2005.
Heinemann, Isaac. *Darkhe Ha-Aggadah*. Jerusalem: Magnes, 1948.
Heltzer, Michael. 'Epigraphic Evidence Concerning a Jewish Settlement in Kition (Larnaca, Cyprus) in the Achaemenid Period (IV Cent. BCE)'. *Aula Orientalis* 7 (1989): 133–71.
Hengel, Martin. *Judaism and Hellenism*. Translated by John Bowden. 2nd edn. Philadelphia: Fortress Press, 1981.
Herzberg, Walter. 'Polysemy in the Hebrew Bible'. PhD diss., New York University, 1979.
Hezser, Catherine. *Jewish Literacy in Roman Palestine*. TSAJ, 81. Tübingen: Mohr Siebeck, 2001.
Hibbard, J. Todd. *Intertextuality in Isaiah: The Ruse and Evocation of Earlier Texts and Traditions*. FAT II 16. Tübingen: Mohr Siebeck, 2006.
Hoffman, Yair. 'The Technique of Quotation and Citation as an Interpretive Device'. In *Creative Biblical Exegesis: Christian and Jewish Hermeneutics through the Centuries*, edited by Benjamin Uffenheimer and Henning Graf Reventlow. JSOTSup 59. Sheffield: JSOT Press, 1988.
Hollander, John. *Figure of Echo: A Mode of Allusion in Milton and After*. Berkeley: University of California Press, 1981.
Holm-Nielsen, Svend. *Hodayot: Psalms from Qumran*. Aarhus: Universitets-forlaget I Aarhus, 1960.
Hooker, Morna D. 'Review of Christopher D. Stanley, Arguing with Scripture: The Rhetoric of Quotations in the Letters of Paul'. *JTS* 57 (2006): 270.

Horrell, David. 'The Label Christianos: 1 Peter 4:16 and the Formation of Christian Identity'. *JBL* 126 (2007): 361–81.

Horsley, Richard A. *Hearing the Whole Story: The Politics of Plot in Mark's Gospel*. Louisville: Westminster John Knox Press, 2001.

Horsley, Richard A. 'Oral Performance and Mark: Some Implications of *The Oral and the Written Gospel*, Twenty-Five Years Later'. In *Jesus, the Voice, and the Text: Beyond The Oral and the Written Gospel*, edited by Tom Thatcher, 45–70. Waco: Baylor University Press, 2008.

Horsley, Richard A. 'A Prophet Like Moses and Elijah: Popular Memory and Cultural Patterns in Mark'. In *Performing the Gospel: Orality, Memory, and Mark: Essays Dedicated to Werner Kelber*, edited by Richard A. Horsley, Jonathan A. Draper and John Miles Foley, 166–90. Minneapolis: Fortress Press, 2006.

Horsley, Richard A. with Jonathan A. Draper. *Whoever Hears You Hears Me: Prophets, Performance, and Tradition in Q*. Harrisburg: Trinity Press International, 1999.

Hubbard, David A. 'The Wisdom Movement and Israel's Covenant Faith'. *TynBul* 17 (1966): 3–33.

Hughes, Julie A. *Scriptural Allusions and Exegesis in the Hodayot*. Leiden: Brill, 2006.

Humphreys, W. Lee. 'The Motif of the Wise Courtier in the Book of Proverbs'. In *Israelite Wisdom: Theological and Literary Essays in Honour of Samuel Terrien*, edited by J. G. Gammie, 177–90. Missoula: Scholars Press, 1978.

Hurtado, Larry W. 'Correcting Iverson's "Correction"'. *NTS* 62 (2016): 201–6.

Hurtado, Larry W. *Destroyer of the Gods: Early Christian Distinctiveness in the Roman World*. Waco: Baylor University Press, 2016.

Hurtado, Larry W. 'Oral Fixation and New Testament Studies? "Orality", "Performance" and Reading Texts in Early Christianity'. *NTS* 60 (2014): 321–40.

Instone-Brewer, David. *Techniques and Assumptions in Jewish Exegesis before 70 CE*. TSAJ 30. Tübingen: Mohr, 1992.

Iverson, Kelly R. 'An Enemy of the Gospel? Anti-Paulinisms and Intertextuality in the Gospel of Matthew'. In *Unity and Diversity in the Gospels and Paul: Essays in Honor of Frank J. Matera*, edited by Christopher W. Skinner and Kelly R. Iverson, 7–32. Atlanta: SBL, 2012.

Iverson, Kelly R. 'Oral Fixation or Oral Corrective? A Response to Larry Hurtado'. *NTS* 62 (2016): 183–200.

Iverson, Kelly R. 'Orality and the Gospels: A Survey of Recent Research'. *CBR* 8 (2009): 71–106.

Jaffee, Martin S. *Torah in the Mouth: Writing and Oral Tradition in Palestinian Judaism, 200 BCE – 400 CE*. New York; Oxford: Oxford University Press, 2001.

Jauhiainen, M. *The Use of Zechariah in Revelation*. WUNT 2/199. Tübingen: Mohr, 2005.

Johnson, Peter. *R. G. Collingwood: An Introduction*. Bristol Introductions. Bristol; Dulles: Thoemmes, 1998.

Johnson, William A. *Readers and Reading Culture in the High Roman Empire: A Study of Elite Communities*. Classical Culture and Society. New York: Oxford University Press, 2010.

Judge, Edwin A. 'Higher Education in the Pauline Churches'. In *Learning and Teaching Theology: Some Ways Ahead*, edited by Les Ball and James Harrison, 23–31. Eugene: Wipf and Stock, 2015.

Judge, Edwin A. 'St Paul and Classical Society'. *JAC* 15 (1972): 16–36.

Judge, Edwin A., and David M. Scholer. *Social Distinctives of the Christians in the First Century : Pivotal Essays*. Peabody: Hendrickson Publishers, 2008.

Juel, Donald. *Messianic Exegesis: Christological Interpretation of the Old Testament in Early Christianity*. Philadelphia: Fortress Press, 1988.

Kaiser, Walter C. *The Uses of the Old Testament in the New*. Chicago: Moody Press, 1985.

Kamesar, Adam. 'Biblical Interpretation in Philo'. In *The Cambridge Companion to Philo*, edited by Adam Kamesar, 65–92. Cambridge: Cambridge University, 2009.

Kaufman, S. 'The Temple Scroll and Higher Criticism'. *HUCA* 53 (1982): 29–43.

Katz, Peter. *Philo's Bible: The Aberrant Text of Bible Quotations in Some Philonic Writings and Its Place in the Textual History of the Greek Bible*. Cambridge: Cambridge University, 1950.

Kayatz, C. *Studien zu Proverbien 1-9: Eine Form- und Motivgeschichtliche Untersuchung Unter Einbeziehung Ägyptischen Vergleichmaterials*. WMANT 22. Neukirchen-Vluyn: Neukirchener Verlag, 1966.

Keesmaat, Sylvia C. 'Exodus and the Intertextual Transformation of Tradition in Romans 8.14-30'. *JSNT* 16 (1994): 29–56.

Keith, Chris. 'Literacy'. In *The Dictionary of the Bible and Ancient Media*, edited by Tom Thatcher et al., 206–10. London: Bloomsbury, 2017.

Keith, Chris, and Anthony Le Donne. *Jesus, Criteria, and the Demise of Authenticity*. London: T&T Clark, 2012.

Keith, Chris, and Tom Thatcher. 'The Scar of the Cross: The Violence Ratio and the Earliest Christian Memories of Jesus'. In *Jesus, the Voice, and the Text: Beyond The Oral and the Written Gospel*, edited by Tom Thatcher, 197–214. Waco: Baylor University Press, 2008.

Kelber, Werner H. 'Jesus and Tradition: Words in Time, Words in Space'. In *Orality and Textuality in Early Christian Literature*, edited by Joanna Dewey, 139–67. Semeia, 65. Atlanta: SBL, 1995.

Kelber, Werner H. *The Oral and the Written Gospel: The Hermeneutics of Speaking and Writing in the Synoptic Tradition, Mark, Paul, and Q*. Philadelphia: Fortress Press, 1983.

Kelber, Werner H. 'The Works of Memory: Christian Origins as Mnemohistory – A Response'. In *Memory, Tradition, and Text: Uses of the Past in Early Christianity*, edited by Alan Kirk and Tom Thatcher, 221–48. Semeia Studies, 52. Atlanta: SBL, 2005

Kellermann, Ulrich. 'Erwägungen zum Esragesetz'. *ZAW* 80 (1968): 373–85.

Konstan, David. 'Excerpting as a Reading Practice'. In *Thinking Through Excerpts: Studies on Stobaeus*, edited by Gretchen Reydams-Schils, 9–22. Turnhout: Brepols, 2011.

Kirk, Alan. 'Manuscript Tradition as a *Tertium Quid*: Orality and Memory in Scribal Practices'. In *Jesus, the Voice, and the Text: Beyond The Oral and the Written Gospel*, edited by Tom Thatcher, 215–34. Waco: Baylor University Press, 2008.

Kirk, Alan. 'The Memory of Violence and the Death of Jesus in Q'. In *Memory, Tradition, and Text: Uses of the Past in Early Christianity*, edited by Alan Kirk and Tom Thatcher, 191–206. Semeia Studies, 52. Atlanta: SBL, 2005.

Kister, Menahem. 'Wisdom Literature and Its Relation to Other Genres: From Ben Sira to Mysteries'. In *Sapiential Perspectives: Wisdom Literature in Light of the Dead Sea Scrolls: Proceedings of the Sixth International Symposium of the Orion Center for the Study of the Dead Sea Scrolls and Associated Literature, 20–22 May, 2001*, edited by John J. Collins, Gregory E. Sterling and Ruth A. Clements, 13–47. STDJ 51. Leiden; Boston: Brill, 2004.

Kister, Menahem, and Elisha Qimron. 'Observations on 4QSecond Ezekiel'. *RevQ* 15 (1992): 595–602.

Klawans, Jonathan. *Impurity and Sin in Ancient Judaism*. Oxford: Oxford University Press, 2004.

Koskenniemi, Erkki. 'Philo and Classical Education'. In *Reading Philo: A Handbook of Philo of Alexandria*, edited by Torey Seland. Grand Rapids: Eerdmans, 2014.

Kostenberger, Andreas J. 'Hearing the Old Testament in the New Testament: A Response'. In *Hearing the Old Testament in the New Testament*, edited by Stanley E. Porter, 255-94. MNTS. Grand Rapids: Eerdmans, 2006.

Kowalski, Beate. *Die Rezeption des Propheten Ezechiel in der Offenbarung des Johannes*. SBS 31. Stuttgart: Verlag Katholisches Bibelwerk, 1996.

Kowalski, Beate '"Let My People Go, That They May Serve Me". (Exod. 10:3). Exodus Motifs in the Revelation of John'. *Henoch* 38 (2016): 32-53.

Kratz, Reinhard G. '"Denn Dein Ist Das Reich": Das Judentum in Persischer und Hellenistisch-JüDischer Zeit'. In *Götterbilder-Gottesbilder-Weltbilder. Polytheismus und Monotheismus in der Welt der Antike*, edited by R. G. Kratz and H. H. Spieckermann, 347-74. Tübingen: Mohr Siebeck, 2006.

Kratz, Reinhard G. 'Die Redaktion der Prophetenbücher'. In *Rezeption und Auslegung im Alten Testament und in Seinem Umfeld: Ein Symposion Aus Anlass des 60. Geburts- Tags von Odil Hannes Steck*, edited by Reinhard G. Kratz and Thomas Krüger, 9-27. OBO 153. Göttingen: Vandenhoeck & Ruprecht, 1997.

Kratz, Reinhard G. 'Innerbiblische Exegese und Redaktionsgeschichte im Lichte Empirischer Evidenz'. In *Das Judentum im Zeitalter des Zweiten Tempels*, 126-56. FAT 42. Tübingen: Mohr Siebeck, 2013.

Kristeva, Julia. 'Word, Dialogue and Novel'. In *Desire in Language: A Semiotic Approach to Literature and Art*, edited by Leon S. Roudiez, 64-91. Oxford: Basil Blackwell, 1980.

Kugel, James. 'The Beginnings of Biblical Interpretation'. In *A Companion to Biblical Interpretation in Early Judaism*, edited by Matthias Henze, 3-26. Grand Rapids: Eerdmans, 2012.

Kugel, James. *In Potiphar's House: The Interpretive Life of Biblical Texts*. San Francisco: Harper, 1990.

Kugel, James. *Traditions of the Bible: A Guide to the Bible as It Was at the Start of the Common Era*. Cambridge: Harvard University Press, 1998.

Kugel, James L. *The Bible as It Was*. Cambridge: Belknap Press of Harvard University Press, 1997.

Kugel, James L., and Rowan A. Greer. *Early Biblical Interpretation*. 1st edn. Philadelphia: Westminster Press, 1986.

Kynes, Will. *My Psalm Has Turned into Weeping: Job's Dialogue with the Psalms*. BZAW 437. Berlin: Walter de Gruyter, 2012.

Kynes, Will. 'The Wisdom Literature Category: An Obituary'. *JTS* 69 (2018): 1-24.

Labahn, Michael. 'Scripture *Talks* Because Jesus *Talks*: The Narrative Rhetoric of Persuading and Creativity in John's Use of Scripture'. In *The Fourth Gospel and First-Century Media Culture*, edited by Anthony Le Donne and Tom Thatcher, 133-54. LNTS 426. London; New York: T&T Clark Continuum, 2011.

Lange, Armin. 'Pre-Macabean Literature Form the Qumran Linrary and the Hebrew Bible'. *DSD* 14 (2006): 277-305.

Lange, Armin, and Matthias Weigold. *Biblical Quotations and Allusions in Second Temple Jewish Literature*. Göttingen; Oakville: VandenHoeck & Ruprecht, 2011.

Le Donne, Anthony. *The Historiographical Jesus: Memory, Typology, and the Son of David*. Waco: Baylor University Press, 2009.

Le Donne, Anthony, and Tom Thatcher, eds. *The Fourth Gospel in First-Century Media Culture*. LNTS 426. London: T&T Clark, 2011.

Leonard, Jeffery M. 'Identifying Inner-Biblical Allusions: Psalm 78 as a Test Case'. *JBL* 127 (2008): 241-65.

Levenson, Jon. '1 Samuel 25 as Literature and as History'. *CBQ* 10 (1978): 12-28.

Levinson, B. *Deuteronomy and the Hermeneutics of Legal Innovation*. New York: Oxford University Press, 1997.
Lewis, Michael. *The Undoing Project: A Friendship That Changed Our Minds*. New York: W.W. Norton & Company, 2017.
Liebengood, Kelly D. *The Eschatology of 1 Peter: Considering the Influence of Zechariah 9-14*. SNTSMS 157. Cambridge: Cambridge University Press, 2013.
Lieberman, Stephen J. 'A Mesopotamian Background for the So-Called Aggadic "Measures" of Biblical Hermeneutics?' *HUCA* 58 (1987): 157–225.
Lim, Timothy H. *Holy Scripture in the Qumran Commentaries and Pauline Letters*. Oxford: Clarendon Press, 1997.
Lim, Timothy H. 'Qumran Scholarship and the Study of the Old Testament in the New Testament'. *JSNT* 38 (2015): 68–80.
Lincicum, David. *Paul and the Early Jewish Encounter with Deuteronomy*. WUNT 2/284. Tübingen: Mohr Siebeck, 2010.
Lincicum, David. 'Review of Christopher D. Stanley, Arguing with Scripture: The Rhetoric of Quotations in the Letters of Paul'. *JETS* 49 (2006): 430.
Lindars, Barnabas. *New Testament Apologetic*. London: SCM, 1961.
Lindblom, J. 'Wisdom in the Old Testament Prophets'. In *Wisdom in Israel and in the Ancient near East*, edited by Martin Noth and D. Winton Thomas. VTSup 3. Leiden: Brill, 1995.
Litwak, Kenneth D. 'Echoes of Scripture? A Critical Survey on Paul's Use of the Old Testament'. *CurBS* 6 (1998): 260–88.
Litwak, Kenneth D. *Echoes of Scripture in Luke-Acts: Telling the History of God's People Intertextually*. JSNTSup 282. London: T&T Clark International, 2005.
Lonergan, Bernard. *Method in Theology*. New York: Herder and Herder, 1972.
Lucas, Alec J. 'Assessing Stanley E Porter's Objections to Richard B Hays's Notion of Metalepsis'. *CBQ* 76 (2014): 93–111.
Lyons, Michael A. *From Law to Prophecy: Ezekiel's Use of the Holiness Code*. New York and London: T&T Clark, 2009.
Lyons, Michael A. 'How Have We Changed? Older and Newer Arguments About the Relationship of Ezekiel and the Holiness Code'. In *The Formation of the Pentateuch: Bridging the Academic Cultures of Israel, Europe, and North America*, edited by Jan C. Gertz, Bernard M. Levinson, Dalit Rom-Shiloni and Konrad Schmid, 1055–74. FAT 111. Tübingen: Mohr Siebeck, 2016.
Lyons, Michael A. 'Psalm 22 and the "Servants" of Isaiah 54; 56-66'. *CBQ* 77 (2015): 640–56.
Lyons, Michael A. 'Transformation of Law: Ezekiel's Use of the Holiness Code (Leviticus 17-26)'. In *Transforming Visions: Transformations of Text, Tradition, and Theology in Ezekiel*, edited by William A. Tooman and Michael A. Lyons, 1–32. PTMS 127. Eugene: Wipf and Stock, 2010.
Macmurray, John. *The Clue to History*. London: Faber and Faber, 1981.
Macmurray, John. *The Self as Agent (Gifford Lectures 1953)*. London: Faber and Faber, 1957.
Maier, Johann. *Die Qumran-Essener: Die Texte vom Toten Meer, Vol. 3: Einführung, Zeitrechnung, Register und Bibliographie*. UTB.W 1916. München: Reinhardt, 1996.
Mandel, Paul D. *The Origins of Midrash: From Teaching to Text*. Leiden; Boston: Brill, 2017.
Mason, R. 'The Use of Earlier Biblical Material in Zechariah 9-14: A Study in Inner-Biblical Exegesis'. In *Bringing Out the Treasure: Inner-Biblical Allusion in Zechariah 9-14*, edited by Mark J. Boda and Michael Floyd, 3–207. JSOTSup 203. Sheffield: Sheffield Academic Press, 2003.

Mattingly, Harold B. 'The Origin of the Name "Christiani"'. *JTS* 9 (1956): 26–37.
Maxwell, Kathy Reiko. *Hearing Between the Lines: The Audience as Fellow-Workers in Luke-Acts and Its Literary Milieu*. LNTS 425. London: T&T Clark, 2010.
McGrath, James F. 'Orality and Intertextuality'. In *Exploring Intertextuality: Diverse Strategies for New Testament Interpretation of Texts*, edited by B. J. Oropeza and Steve Moyise, 176–86. Eugene: Cascade Books, 2016.
McKane, William. *Prophets and Wise Men*. SBT 44. London: SCM Press, 1965.
McKane, William. *Proverbs: A New Approach*. OTL. London: SCM Press, 1970.
Meek, Russell. 'Intertextuality, Inner-Biblical Exegesis, and Inner-Biblical Allusion: The Ethics of a Methodology'. *Bib* 95 (2014): 280–91.
Menken, Maarten J. J. *Old Testament Quotations in the Fourth Gospel: Studies in Textual Form*. CBET 15. Kampen: Kok Pharos, 1996.
Menken, Maarten J. J., and Steve Moyise, eds. *Deuteronomy in the New Testament*. London: T&T Clark, 2007.
Menken, Maarten J. J., and Steve Moyise, eds. *Genesis in the New Testament*. LNTS 466. London: Bloomsbury T&T Clark, 2012.
Menken, Maarten J. J., and Steve Moyise, eds. *The Minor Prophets in the New Testament*. Vol. 377. LNTS. London; New York: T&T Clark, 2009.
Mettinger, Tryggve N. D. 'The Enigma of Job: The Deconstruction of God in Intertextual Perspective'. *JNSL* 23 (1997): 1–19.
Meyer, Ben F. The *Aims of Jesus*. London: SCM Press, 1979.
Milgrom, Jacob. *Leviticus 1-16*. AB 3. New York: Doubleday, 1991.
Miller, Geoffrey D. 'Intertextuality in Old Testament Research'. *CBR* 9 (2011): 283–309.
Misztal, Barbara A. *Theories of Social Remembering*. Philadelphia: Open University Press, 2003.
Montanaro, Andrew. 'The Use of Memory in the Old Testament Quotations in John's Gospel'. *NovT* 59 (2017): 147–70.
Moore, George F. *Judaism of the First Centuries of the Christian Era: The Age of the Tannaim*. 3 Vols. Cambridge: Harvard University Press, 1927–30.
Morales, Nelson R. *Poor and Rich in James: A Relevance Theory Approach to James's Use of the Old Testament*. BBRSup 20. University Park: Eisenbrauns, 2018.
Morawski, S. 'The Basic Functions of Quotation'. In *Sign, Language, Culture*, edited by Algirdas Julien Greimas, 690–705. The Hague: Mouton, 1970.
Morgan, Donn F. *Wisdom in the Old Testament Traditions*. Atlanta: John Knox, 1981.
Moyise, Steve. 'Does Paul Respect the Context of His Quotations'. In *Paul and Scripture: Extending the Conversation*, edited by Christopher D. Stanley, 97–114. ECL 9. Atlanta: SBL, 2012.
Moyise, Steve. 'Dialogical Intertextuality'. In *Exploring Intertextuality. Diverse Strategies for New Testament Interpretation of Texts*, edited by B. J. Oropeza and Steve Moyise. Eugene: Wipf and Stock, 2016.
Moyise, Steve. *Evoking Scripture: Seeing the Old Testament in the New*. London: T&T Clark, 2008.
Moyise, Steve. 'Intertextuality and Historical Approaches to the Use of Scripture in the New Testament'. In *Reading the Bible Intertextually*, edited by Richard B. Hays, S. Alkier and L. Huizenga, 23–32. Waco: Baylor University Press, 2009.
Moyise, Steve. 'Intertextuality and the Study of the Old Testament in the New'. In *The Old Testament in the New: Essays in Honour of J. L. North*, 14–41. JSNTSup 189. Sheffield: Sheffield Academic Press, 2000.
Moyise, Steve. *The Old Testament in the Book of Revelation*. JSNTSup 115. Sheffield: JSOT Press, 1995.

Moyise, Steve, ed. *The Old Testament in the New Testament*. London: T&T Clark, 2000.
Moyise, Steve. 'Scripture in the New Testament: Literary and Theological Perspectives'. *Neot* 42 (2008): 305–26.
Moyise, Steve, and Menken Maarten J. J. eds. *Isaiah in the New Testament*. London; New York: T&T Clark, 2005.
Moyise, Steve, and Menken Maarten J. J. eds. *The Psalms in the New Testament*. London; New York: T&T Clark International, 2004.
Murphy, Roland E. 'A Consideration of the Classification "Wisdom Psalms"'. *VTSup* 9 (1962): 156–67.
Murphy, Roland E. *Wisdom Literature, the Forms of the Old Testament Literature, Volume XIII*, edited by Rolf P. Knierim and Gene M. Tucker. Grand Rapids: Eerdmans, 1981.
Najman, Hindy. *Seconding Sinai: The Development of Mosaic Discourse in Second Temple Judaism*. JSJSup 77. Leiden: Brill, 2003.
Neilson, K. *Yahweh as Prosecutor and Judge: An Investigation of the Prophetic Lawsuit (Rib Pattern)*. JSOTSup 9. Sheffield: JSOT Press, 1978.
Neusner, Jacob. *Midrash as Literature*. Philadelphia: University Press of America, 1987.
Neusner, Jacob. *What Is Midrash?* Philadelphia: Fortress, 1987.
Nickelsburg, George W. E. 'The Bible Rewritten and Expanded'. In *Jewish Writings of the Second Temple Period*, edited by Michael Stone, 89–156. Assen: Van Gorcum, 1984.
Nickelsburg, George W. E. 'The Search for Tobit's Mixed Ancestry: A Historical and Hermeneutical Odyssey'. *RevQ* 17 (1996): 339–49.
Nielsen, Margut Hurup. 'Re-Enactment and Reconstruction in Collingwood's Philosophy of History'. *History and Theory* 20 (1981): 1–31.
Nihan, Christophe. 'Ezekiel 34–37 and Leviticus 26: A Reevaluation'. In *Ezekiel: Current Debates and Future Directions*, edited by William Tooman and Penelope Barter, 153–78. FAT 112. Tübingen: Mohr Siebeck, 2017.
Nihan, Christophe. 'Ezekiel and the Holiness Legislation – a Plea for Nonlinear Models'. In *The Formation of the Pentateuch: Bridging the Academic Cultures of Israel, Europe, and North America*, edited by Jan C. Gertz, Bernard M. Levinson, Dalit Rom-Shiloni and Konrad Schmid, *FAT 111*, 1015–40. Tübingen: Mohr Siebeck, 2016.
Noegel, Scott. 'Polysemy'. In *Encyclopedia of Hebrew Language and Linguistics, Vol. 3: P–Z*, edited by Geoffrey Kahn, 178–86. Leiden: Brill, 2013.
Noegel, Scott. "Sign, Sign, Everywhere a Sign": Script, Power, and Interpretation in the Ancient near East'. In *Science and Superstition: Interpretation of Signs in the Ancient World: The Fifth Annual University of Chicago Oriental Institute Seminar*, edited by Amar Annus, 143–62. Chicago: Oriental Institute of the University of Chicago, 2010.
Nongbri, Brent. *Before Religion: A History of a Modern Concept*. New Haven: Yale University Press, 2013.
North, J. Lionel. 'ΚΑΙΝΑ ΚΑΙ ΠΑΛΑΙΑ: An Account of the British Seminar on the Use of the Old Testament in the New Testament'. In *The Old Testament in the New Testament: Essays in Honour of J. L. North*, edited by Steve Moyise. JSNTSup 189. Sheffield: Sheffield Academic Press, 2000.
Novakic, Lidija. 'Matthew's Atomistic Use of Scripture: Messianic Interpretation of Isaiah 53.4 in Matthew 8.17'. In *Biblical Interpretation in Early Christian Gospels, Vol. 2: The Gospel of Matthew*, edited by Thomas Hatina, 147–62. LNTS 310. London: T&T Clark, 2008.
Novick, Tzvi. 'Biblicized Narrative: On Tobit and Genesis 22'. *JBL* 127 (2007): 755–64.
Nowell, Irene. 'The Book of Tobit: An Ancestral Story'. In *Intertextual Studies in Ben Sira and Tobit: Essays in Honor of Alexander A. Di Leila, O. F. M.*, edited by Jeremy Corley

and Vincent Skemp. CBQMS, 3–13. Washington: Catholic Biblical Association of America, 2005.
O'Brien, Kelli S. *The Use of Scripture in the Markan Passion Narrative*. LNTS 384. London: T&T Clark, 2010.
Olick, Jeffrey K. 'Products, Processes, and Practices: A Non-Reificatory Approach to Collective Memory'. *BTB* 36 (2006): 5–14.
Olyan, Saul. 'Purity Ideology in Ezra-Nehemiah as a Tool to Reconstitute the Community'. *JSJ* 35 (2004): 1–16.
Oropeza, B. J., and Steve Moyise. *Exploring Intertextuality: Diverse Strategies for New Testament Interpretation of Texts*. Eugene: Cascade, 2016.
Ostmeyer, Karl-Heinrich. 'Dabeisein Ist Alles (Der Verlorene Sohn)–Lk15,11-32'. In *Kompendium der Gleichnisse Jesu*, edited by R. Zimmermann, 618–33. Gütersloh: Gütersloher Verlagshaus, 2007.
Pakkala, Juha. 'The Quotations and References of the Pentateuchal Laws in Ezra-Nehemiah'. In *Changes in Scripture: Rewriting and Interpreting Authoritative Traditions in the Second Temple Period*, edited by H. von Weissenberg, Juha Pakkala and M. Marttila, 193–221. BZAW 419. Berlin and New York: De Gruyter, 2011.
Pao, David W., and Eckhard J. Schnabel. 'Luke'. In *Commentary on the New Testament Use of the Old Testament*, edited by G. K. Beale and D. A. Carson, 251–414. Grand Rapids: Baker Academic, 2007.
Pattemore, Stephen W. *The People of God in the Apocalypse: Discourse, Structure and Exegesis*. SNTSMS 128. Cambridge: Cambridge University Press, 2004.
Paulien, J. *Decoding Revelation's Trumpets: Literary Allusions and the Interpretation of Revelation 8:7-12*. AUSDDS 11. Berrien Springs: Andrews University Press, 1988.
Paulien, J. 'Elusive Allusions. The Problematic Use of the Old Testament in Revelation'. *BiR* 33 (1988): 37–53.
Perdue, Leo G. *Wisdom in Revolt*. Sheffield: Almond Press, 1991.
Perdue, Leo G. 'The Wisdom Sayings of Jesus'. *Forum* 2 (1986): 3–35.
Perrot, Charles. 'The Reading of the Bible in the Ancient Synagogue'. In *Mikra: Text, Translation, Reading, and Interpretation of the Hebrew Bible in Ancient Judaism and Early Christianity*, edited by Martin J. Mulder and Harry Sysling, 137–59. Philadelphia: Fortress, 1988.
Perry, Peter S. 'Relevance Theory and Intertextuality'. In *Exploring Intertextuality: Diverse Strategies for New Testament Interpretation of Texts*, edited by B. J. Oropeza and Steve Moyise, 207–21. Eugene: Cascade Books, 2016.
Pilkington, Adrian. *Poetic Effects: A Relevance Theory Perspective*. PBNS 75. Amsterdam: John Benjamins Publishing Company, 2000.
Popović, Mladen. 'Prophet, Books and Texts: Pseudo-Ezekiel and the Authoritativeness of Ezekiel Traditions in Early Judaism'. In *Authoritative Scriptures in Ancient Judaism*, edited by Mladen Popović, 227–51. SJSJ 141. Leiden: Brill, 2010.
Popović, Mladen. 'Reading, Writing, and Memorizing Together: Reading Culture in Ancient Judaism and the Dead Sea Scrolls in a Mediterranean Context'. *DSD* 24 (2017): 447–70.
Porter, Stanley E. 'Allusions and Echoes'. In *As It Is Written: Studying Paul's Use of Scripture*, edited by Stanley E. Porter and Christopher D. Stanley, 29–40. SBLSS 50. Leiden: Brill, 2008.
Porter, Stanley E. *Sacred Tradition in the New Testament: Tracing Old Testament Themes in the Gospels and Epistles*. Grand Rapids: Baker Academic, 2016.
Porter, Stanley E. 'The Use of the Old Testament in the New Testament: A Brief Comment on Method and Terminology'. In *Early Christian Interpretation of the Scriptures of*

Israel: Investigations and Proposals, edited by C. A. Evans and J. A. Sanders, 79–96. JSNTSup 148. Sheffield: JSOT Press, 1997.
Powell, Mark Allan. *Chasing the Eastern Star: Adventures in Biblical Reader-Response Criticism.* Louisville: Westminster John Knox, 2001.
Powell, Mark Allan. *What Is Narrative Criticism.* Minneapolis: Fortress, 1991.
Punt, Jeremy. 'Identity, Memory, and Scriptural Warrant: Arguing Paul's Case'. In *Paul and Scripture: Extending the Conversation*, edited by Christopher D. Stanley, 25–53. Atlanta: SBL, 2012.
Qimron, Elisha. מגילות מדבר יהודה. החיבורים העבריים / *the Dead Sea Scrolls: The Hebrew Writings, Volume Two*. Jerusalem: Yad Ben-Zvi Press, 2013.
Radner, Ephraim. *Time and the Word: Figural Reading of the Christian Scriptures.* Grand Rapids: Eerdmans, 2016.
Rainbow, Jesse. 'Male Μαστοί in Revelation 1.13'. *JSNT* 30 (2007): 249–53.
Rawidowicz, Simon. 'On Interpretation'. *PAAJR* 26 (1957): 83–126.
Redditt, Paul. 'Daniel 9: Its Structure and Meaning'. *CBQ* 62 (2000): 236–49.
Ricoeur, Paul. *Interpretation Theory: Discourse and the Surplus of Meaning.* Fort Worth: Texas Christian University, 1976.
Ringgren, Helmer. 'Oral and Written Transmission in the OT: Some Observations'. *ST* 3 (1949): 34–59.
Rodríguez, Rafael. '"According to the Scriptures": Suffering and the Psalms in the Speeches of Acts'. In *Memory and Identity in Ancient Judaism and Early Christianity: A Conversation with Barry Schwartz*, edited by Tom Thatcher, 241–62. Semeia Studies, 78. Atlanta: SBL, 2014.
Rodríguez, Rafael. *Oral Tradition and the New Testament: A Guide for the Perplexed.* London: Bloomsbury, 2014.
Rodríguez, Rafael. 'Reading and Hearing in Ancient Contexts'. *JSNT* 32 (2009): 151–78.
Rodríguez, Rafael. *Structuring Early Christian Memory: Jesus in Tradition, Performance and Text.* LNTS 407. London: T&T Clark, 2010.
Rodríguez, Rafael. 'Textual Orientations: Jesus, Written Texts, and the Social Construction of Identity in the Gospel of Luke'. In *T&T Clark Handbook to Social Identity in the New Testament*, edited by J. Brian Tucker and Coleman A. Baker, 191–210. London: Bloomsbury, 2014.
Rösel, Martin. 'Israels Psalmen in Ägypten? Papyrus Amherst 63 und die Psalmen XX und LXXV'. *VT* 50 (2000): 81–99.
Rosner, Brian S. *Paul, Scripture and Ethics: A Study of 1 Corinthians 5-7.* Leiden: Brill, 1994.
Rowe, C. Kavin. *One True Life: The Stoics and Early Christians as Rival Traditions.* New Haven: Yale University Press, 2016.
Rowland, Christopher. 'Imagining the Apocalypse'. *NTS* 51 (2005): 303–27.
Ruppert, Lothar. 'Das Buch Tobias – Ein Modellfall Nachgestaltender Erzählung'. In *Wort, Lied und Gottesspruch: Beiträge zur Septuaginta Festschrift Für Joseph Ziegler*, edited by Josef Schreiner, 109–19. Fb 1. Würsburg: Echter Verlag, 1972.
Samely, Alexander. *The Interpretation of Speech in the Pentateuch Targums: A Study of Method and Presentation in Targumic Exegesis.* Tübingen: Mohr Siebeck, 1992.
Samely, Alexander. *Profiling Jewish Literature in Antiquity: An Inventory, from Second Temple Texts to the Talmuds.* Oxford: Oxford University Press, 2013.
Samely, Alexander. *Rabbinic Interpretation of Scripture in the Mishna.* Oxford: Oxford University Press, 2002.
Sandmel, Samuel. 'Parallelomania'. *JBL* 81 (1962): 1–13.

Savran, George W. *Telling and Retelling: Quotation in Biblical Narrative*. Bloomington and Indianapolis: Indiana University Press, 1988.

Schaper, Joachim. 'Hebrew Culture at the "Interface Between Written and the Oral"'. In *Contextualizing Israel's Sacred Writings: Ancient Literacy, Orality, and Literary Production*, edited by Brian B. Schmidt, 323–40. AIL 22. Atlanta: SBL, 2015.

Schenck, Kenneth. *A Brief Guide to Philo*. Louisville: Westminster John Knox, 2005.

Schorch, Stefan. 'Between Science and Magic: The Function and Roots of Paronomasia in the Prophetic Books of the Hebrew Bible'. In *Puns and Pundits: Wordplay in the Hebrew Bible and Ancient near Eastern Literature*, edited by Scott Noegel, 205–22. Bethesda: CDL, 2000.

Schultz, R. *Search for Quotation: Verbal Parallels in the Prophets*. JSOTSup 180. Sheffield: Sheffield Academic Press, 1999.

Schwartz, Barry. *Abraham Lincoln and the Forge of National Memory*. Chicago: University of Chicago Press, 2000.

Schwartz, Daniel R. 'Special People or Special Books?: On Qumran and New Testament Notions of Canon'. In *Text, Thought, and Practice in Qumran and Early Christianity*, edited by Daniel R. Schwartz and Ruth A. Clements, 49–60. Leiden: Brill, 2009.

Scott, Bernard Brandon. 'Jesus as Sage: An Innovating Voice in Common Wisdom'. In *The Sage in Israel and the Ancient near East*, edited by John G. Gammie and Leo G. Perdue, 319–416. Winona Lake: Eisenbrauns, 1990.

Scott, Ian W. *Implicit Epistemology in the Letters of Paul: Story, Experience and the Spirit*. WUNT 205. Tübingen: Mohr Siebeck, 2006.

Scott, James M. 'The Use of Scripture in 2 Corinthians 6.16c-18 and Paul's Restoration Theology'. *JSNT* 56 (1994): 73–99.

Scott, Matthew, *The Hermeneutics of Christological Psalmody in Paul: An Intertextual Enquiry*. SNTSMS 158. New York: Cambridge University Press, 2014.

Segal, Michael. 'Between Bible and Rewritten Bible'. In *Biblical Interpretation at Qumran*, edited by Matthias Henze, 10–28. Cambridge: Eerdmans, 2005.

Segal, Michael. *Dreams, Riddles, and Visions: Textual, Contextual, and Intertextual Approaches to the Book of Daniel*. BZAW 455. Berlin: de Gruyter, 2016.

Segal, Michael. 'Identifying Biblical Interpretation in Parabiblical Texts'. In *The Dead Sea Scrolls in Context: Integrating the Dead Sea Scrolls in the Study of Ancient Texts, Languages, and Cultures*, edited by Armin Lange, Emmanuel Tov and Matthias Weigold, 295–308. Leiden; Boston: Brill, 2011.

Seidel, Moshe. 'Parallels between Isaiah and Psalms'. *Sinai* 38 (1955-6): 149–72, 229–40, 271–80, 335–55.

Shemesh, Aharon, and Cana Werman. 'Hidden Things and Their Revelation'. *RevQ* 18 (1998): 409–27.

Shepherd, Michael B. *The Twelve Prophets in the New Testament*. SBL 140. New York; Oxford: Peter Lang, 2011.

Shroyer, Montgomery J. 'Alexandrian Jewish Literalists'. *JBL* 55 (1936): 261–84.

Shum, Shiu-Lun. *Paul's Use of Isaiah in Romans: A Comparative Study of Paul's Letter to the Romans and the Sibylline and Qumran Sectarian Texts*. Wissenschaftliche Untersuchungen Zum Neuen Testament 2 Reihe 2/156. Tübingen: Mohr Siebeck, 2002.

Smith, Steve. *The Fate of the Jerusalem Temple in Luke-Acts: An Intertextual Approach to Jesus' Laments over Jerusalem and Stephen's Speech*. LNTS 553. London: Bloomsbury T&T Clark, 2017.

Sneed, Mark. 'Is the "Wisdom Tradition" a Tradition?' *CBQ* 73 (2011): 50–71.

Snodgrass, K. 'The Use of the Old Testament in the New'. In *Interpreting the New Testament: Essays on Methods and Issues*, edited by David Alan Black and David S. Dockery, 209–29. Nashville: Broadman & Holman, 2001.

Sommer, Michael. *Der Tag der Plagen. Studien zur Verbindung der Rezeption von Ex 7-11 in Den Posaunen- und Schalenvisionen der Johannesoffenbarung und der Tag des Herrn-Tradition.* WUNT 2/287. Mohr: Tübingen, 2015.

Sommer, Benjamin D. *A Prophet Reads Scripture: Allusion in Isaiah 40-66.* Contraversions. Stanford: Stanford University Press, 1998.

Spellman, Ched. *Toward a Canon-Conscious Reading of the Bible: Exploring the History and Hermeneutics of the Canon.* NTM 34. Sheffield: Sheffield Phoenix Press, 2014.

Sperber, Dan, and Deirdre Wilson. *Relevance: Communication and Cognition.* 2nd edn. Oxford: Blackwell, 1995.

Stackert, Jeffrey. *Rewriting the Torah: Literary Revision in Deuteronomy and the Holiness Legislation.* FAT 52. Tübingen: Mohr Siebeck, 2007.

Stamps, Dennis L. 'The Use of the Old Testament in the New Testament as a Rhetorical Device: A Methodological Proposal'. In *Hearing the Old Testament in the New Testament*, edited by Stanley E. Porter, 9–37. MNTS. Grand Rapids: Eerdmans, 2006.

Stanley, Christopher D. *Arguing with Scripture: The Rhetoric of Quotations in the Letters of Paul.* New York; London: T&T Clark International, 2004.

Stanley, Christopher D. *Paul and the Language of Scripture: Citation Technique in the Pauline Epistles and Contemporary Literature.* SNTMS 69. Cambridge: Cambridge University Press, 1992.

Stanley, Christopher D. *Paul and Scripture: Extending the Conversation.* Atlanta: SBL, 2012.

Stanley, Christopher D. 'Paul's "Use" of Scripture: Why the Audience Matters'. In *As It Is Written: Studying Paul's Use of Scripture*, edited by Stanley E. Porter and Christopher D. Stanley, 125–55. SBLSS 50. Leiden: Brill, 2008.

Stanley, Christopher D. 'The Rhetoric of Quotations: An Essay on Method'. In *Early Christian Interpretation of the Scriptures of Israel: Investigations and Proposals*, edited by C. A. Evans and J. A. Sanders, 44–58. JSNTSup 148. Sheffield: Sheffield Academic Press, 1997.

Stead, Michael. *The Intertextuality of Zechariah 1-8.* LHBOTS 506. New York: T&T Clark, 2009.

Steinmetz, Devorah. 'Beyond the Verse: Midrash Aggada as Interpretation of Biblical Narrative'. *ASJR* 30 (2006): 325–45.

Sterling, Gregory E. 'The Interpreter of Moses: Philo of Alexandria and the Biblical Text'. In *A Companion to Biblical Interpretation in Early Judaism*, edited by Matthias Henze. Grand Rapids: Eerdmans, 2012.

Sterling, Gregory E. 'Jeremiah as Mystagogue: Jeremiah in Philo of Alexandria'. In *Jeremiah's Scriptures: Production, Reception, Interaction, and Transformation*, edited by Hindy Najman and Konrad Schmid. Brill: Leiden, 2016.

Sternberg, Meir. 'Proteus in Quotation-Land: Mimesis and the Forms of Reported Discourse'. *Poetics Today* 3 (1982): 107.

Stone, Michael, and Esther Chazon, eds. *Biblical Perspectives Early Use and Interpretation of the Bible in Light of the Dead Sea Scrolls Proceedings of the First International Symposium of the Orion Center, 12–14 May, 1996.* STDJ 28. Leiden: Brill, 1998.

Stromberg, Jake. *Isaiah after Exile the Author of Third Isaiah as Reader and Redactor of the Book.* Oxford: Oxford University Press, 2011.

Sweeney, Marvin. 'Textual Citations in Isaiah 24-27: Rhetoric and Redaction in Trito-Isaiah: The Structure, Growth, and Authorship of Isaiah 56-66'. *JBL* 107 (1988): 39–52.

Talmon, S. *Text and Canon of the Hebrew Bible: Collected Studies*. Winona Lake: Eisenbrauns, 2010.
Tanner, Beth. *The Book of Psalms through the Lens of Intertextuality*. SBL 26. New York: Lang, 2001.
Teeter, Andrew. 'The Hebrew Bible and/as Second Temple Literature'. *DSD* 20 (2013): 349–77.
Teeter, Andrew. 'Isaiah and the King of as/Syria in Daniel's Final Vision: On the Rhetoric of Inner-Scriptural Allusion and the Hermeneutics of 'Mantological Exegesis'. In *A Teacher for All Generations: Essays in Honor of James C. Vanderkam*, edited by Eric Mason and Samuel Thomas, 169–99. JSJSup 153/1. Leiden: Brill.
Teeter, Andrew. *Scribal Laws: Exegetical Variation in the Textual Transmission of Biblical Law in the Late Second Temple Period*. FAT 92. Tübingen: Mohr Siebeck, 2014.
Teugels, Lieve M. *Bible and Midrash: The Story of 'the Wooing of Rebekah' (Gen. 24)*. Leuven: Peeters, 2004.
Thatcher, Tom. 'Cain and Abel in Early Christian Memory: A Case Study in "the Use of the Old Testament in the New"'. *CBQ* 72 (2010): 732–51.
Thatcher, Tom. 'John's Memory Theatre: A Study of Composition in Performance'. In *The Fourth Gospel and First-Century Media Culture*, edited by Anthony Le Donne and Tom Thatcher, 73–91. LNTS 296. London; New York: T&T Clark Continuum, 2011.
Thompson, Michael B. *Clothed with Christ: The Example and Teaching of Jesus in Romans 12.1 - 15.13*. Sheffield: Sheffield Academic Press, 1991.
Tigay, Jeffery. 'An Early Technique of Aggadic Exegesis'. In *History, Historiography, and Interpretation: Studies in Biblical and Cuneiform Literatures*, edited by H. Tadmor and M. Weinfeld, 169–89. Jerusalem: Magnes Press, 1983.
Tobin, Thomas H. *The Creation of Man: Philo and the History of Interpretation*. CBQMS 14. Washington DC: Catholic Biblical Association, 1983.
Todorov, Tzvetan. *Genres in Discourse*. Translated by Catherine Porter. Cambridge: Cambridge University Press, 1990.
Tõniste, Külli. *The Ending of the Canon: A Canonical and Intertextual Reading of Revelation 21-22*. LNTS 526. London: Bloomsbury T&T Clark.
Tooman, William. 'Authenticating Oral and Memory Variants in Ancient Hebrew Literature'. *JSS* 64 (2019): 91–114.
Tooman, William. 'Between Imitation and Interpretation: Reuse of Scripture and Composition in Hodayot (1QHa) 11.6-19'. *DSD* 18 (2011): 54–73.
Tooman, William. *Gog of Magog: Reuse of Scripture and Compositional Technique in Ezekiel 38-39*. FAT II/52. Tübingen: Mohr Siebeck 2011.
Torrey, Charles Cutter. *Pseudo-Ezekiel and the Original Prophecy*. New York: KTAV, 1970.
Trotter, David. 'Analysing Literary Prose: The Relevance of Relevance Theory'. *Lingua* 87 (1992): 11–27.
Tzoref, Shani. 'Qumran Pesharim and the Pentateuch: Explicit Citation, Overt Typologies, and Implicit Interpretive Traditions'. DSD 16 (2009): 190–220.
Ulrich, Eugene. 'The Qumran Biblical Scrolls'. In *The Dead Sea Scrolls in Their Historical Context*, edited by Timothy Lim, 67–87. Edinburgh: T&T Clark, 2000.
van der Dussen, W. Johannis. *History as a Science: The Philosophy of R. G. Collingwood*. Dordrecht: Springer, 2012.
Vanderkam, James, and Peter Flint. *The Meaning of the Dead Sea Scrolls: Their Significance for Understanding the Bible, Judaism, Jesus, and Christianity*. San Francisco: HarperSanFrancisco, 2002.
Veeser, Harold A., ed. *The New Historicism*. London: Routledge, 1989.
Venter, Pieter M. 'Intertekstualiteit, Kontekstualiteit en Daniël 9'. IDS 31 (1997): 327–46.

Vermes, Geza. 'Bible and Midrash: Early Old Testament Exegesis'. In *The Cambridge History of the Bible Vol. 1: From the Beginnings to Rome*, edited by Peter R. Ackroyd and Christopher F. Evans, 199–231. Cambridge: Cambridge University Press, 1970.

Vermes, Geza. *Scripture and Tradition in Judaism; Haggadic Studies*. Studia Post-Biblica; Leiden: E. J. Brill, 1961.

Vleeming, Sven P., and Jan W. Wesselius. *Studies in Papyrus Amherst 63: Essays on the Aramaic/Demotic Papyrus Amherst 63*. Vol. 1. Amsterdam: Juda Palache Instituut, 1985.

Von Rad, Gerhard. 'The Joseph Narrative and Ancient Wisdom'. Translated by E. W. Trueman Dicken. In *The Problem of the Hexateuch and Other Essays*, 292–300. Edinburgh: Oliver & Boyd, 1966.

Wagner, J. Ross. *Heralds of the Good News: Isaiah and Paul 'in Concert' in the Letter to the Romans*. NovTSup, 101. Leiden: Brill, 2002.

Wall, Robert W. *Community of the Wise: The Letter of James*. NTC. Valley Forge: Trinity Press International, 1997.

Watson, Francis. *Paul and the Hermeneutics of Faith*. London: T&T Clark, 2004.

Watson, Francis. 'Paul the Reader: An Authorial Apologia'. *JSNT* 28 (2006): 363–73.

Watts, Rikk. 'Christianity and the Ancient World'. *Crux* 53 (2017): 2–26.

Watts, Rikk. 'Echoes from the Past: Israel's Ancient Traditions and the Role of the Nations in Isa 40-55'. *JSOT* 28 (2004): 481–504.

Watts, Rikk. '"For I Am Not Ashamed of the Gospel": Romans 1:16-17 and Habakkuk 2:4'. In *Romans and the People of God*, edited by Sven K. Soderlund and N. T. Wright. Grand Rapids: Eedrmans, 1999.

Watts, Rikk. 'How Do You Read? God's Faithful Character as the Primary Lens for the NT Use of the OT'. In *Essays in Honor of Greg Beale: From Creation to New Creation – Biblical Theology and Exegesis*, edited by Daniel M. Gurtner and Benjamin L. Gladd, 199–220. Peabody: Hendrickson, 2013.

Watts, Rikk. *Israel's Scriptures and the Character of God—an Initial Exploration of Romans 9-11*. https://www.academia.edu/13778590/Israels_Scripture_and_the_Character_of_God_an_Exploration.

Watts, Rikk. 'Messianic Servant or End of Israel's Exilic Curses? Isaiah 53.4 in Matthew 8.17'. *JSNT* 38 (2015): 81–95.

Watts, Rikki E. *Isaiah's New Exodus and Mark*. Tübingen: Mohr Siebeck, 1997.

Weber, M. *The Theory of Social and Economic Organization*. Translated by A.M. Henderson and Calcott Parsons. Glencoe: Free Press, 1947.

Weeks, Stuart. *An Introduction to Wisdom Literature*. ABS. London: T&T Clark, 2010.

Weinryb, Elazar. 'Re-Enactment in Retrospect'. *The Monist* 72 (1989): 568–80.

Weitzman, Steven. 'Allusion, Artifice, and Exile in the Hymn of Tobit'. *JBL* 115 (1996): 49–61.

Whedbee, J. William. *Isaiah and Wisdom*. Nashville: Abingdon, 1971.

Whitenton, Michael R. *Hearing Kyriotic Sonship: A Cognitive and Rhetorical Approach to the Characterization of Mark's Jesus*. BIS, 148. Leiden: Brill, 2017.

Whybray, R. Norman. *The Second Isaiah*. OTG. Sheffield: Sheffield Academic Press, 1983.

Whybray, R. Norman. *The Succession Narrative*. SBT Second Series 9. London: SCM, 1968.

Willi, Thomas. *Die Chronik Als Auslegung: Untersuchungen zur Literarischen Gestaltung der Historischen ÜBerlieferung Israels*. FRLANT 106. Gottingen: Vandenhoeck & Ruprecht, 1972.

Williams, Catrin H. 'First-Century Media Culture and Abraham as a Figure of Memory in John 8:31-59'. In *The Fourth Gospel and First-Century Media Culture*, edited by

Anthony Le Donne and Tom Thatcher, 205–22. LNTS 426. London; New York: T&T Clark Continuum, 2011.

Williams, Catrin H. 'Patriarchs and Prophets Remembered: Framing Israel's Past in the Gospel of John'. In *Abiding Words: The Use of Scripture in the Gospel of John*, edited by Alicia D. Myers and Bruce G. Schuchard, 187–212. SBLRBS 81. Atlanta: SBL Publications, 2015.

Williams, Catrin H. 'Persuasion through Allusion: Evocations of Shepherd(s) and their Rhetorical Impact in John 10'. In *Come and Read: Interpretive Approaches to the Gospel of John*, edited by Alicia Myers and Lindsey Trozzo. Lanham: Lexington Books/Fortress Academic, forthcoming.

Williamson, Hugh G. M. *The Book Called Isaiah: Deutero-Isaiah's Role in Composition and Redaction*. Oxford: Oxford University Press, 1994.

Wilson, Deirdre. 'Metarepresentation in Linguistic Communication'. In *Meaning and Relevance*, edited by Deirdre Wilson and Dan Sperber, 230–58. Cambridge: Cambridge University Press, 2012.

Wilson, Deirdre. 'Relevance Theory and Literary Interpretation'. In *Reading Beyond the Code: Literature and Relevance Theory*, edited by Terence Cave and Deirdre Wilson, 185–204. Oxford: Oxford University Press, 2018.

Wilson, Deirdre. 'Relevance and Understanding'. In *Language and Understanding*, edited by Gillian Brown, 37–58. Oxford: Oxford University Press, 1994.

Wilson, Deirdre, and Dan Sperber, eds. *Meaning and Relevance*. Cambridge: Cambridge University Press, 2012.

Wilson, Deirdre, and Dan Sperber. 'Relevance Theory'. In *Handbook of Pragmatics*, edited by Laurence Horn and Gregory Ward, 607–32. Oxford: Blackwell, 2003.

Wilson, Gerald. 'The Prayer of Daniel: Reflection on Jeremiah 29'. *JSOT* 48 (1990): 91–9.

Wimsatt, William K., and Monroe C. Beardsley. 'The Intentional Fallacy'. *Sewanee Review* 54 (1946): 468–88.

Winston, David. 'Philo's Mysticism'. *SPhA* 8 (1996): 74–82.

Winter, Bruce W. 'Revelation Versus Rhetoric: Paul and First-Century Corinthian Fad'. In *Translating Truth: The Case for Essentially Literal Bible Translation*, edited by Wayne A. Grudem, 135–50. Wheaton: Crossway, 2005.

Witherington III, Ben. *Jesus the Sage: The Pilgrimage of Wisdom*. Edinburgh: T&T Clark, 1984.

Wolff, Hans Walter. *Joel and Amos*. Translated by W. Janzen. Philadelphia: Fortress Press, 1977.

Wolfson, Harry A. *Philo: Foundations of Religious Philosophy in Judaism, Christianity, and Islam*. Cambridge: Harvard University Press, 1947.

Wright, N. T. *The New Testament and the People of God*. Christian Origins and the Question of God 1. London: SPCK, 1992.

Yadin, Yigael. *The Temple Scroll* [in Text in English and Hebrew; notes in English.]. 3 Vols. Jerusalem: Israel Exploration Society, The Institute of Archaeology of the Hebrew University and The Shrine of the Book, 1983.

Yadin-Israel, Azzan. *Scripture as Logos: Rabbi Ishmael and the Origins of Midrash*. Philadelphia: University of Pennsylvania Press, 2011.

Yadin-Israel, Azzan. *Scripture and Tradition: Rabbi Akiva and the Triumph of Midrash*. Philadelphia: University of Pennsylvania Press, 2014.

Yamasaki, Gary. *Perspective Criticism: Point of View and Evaluative Guidance in Biblical Narrative*. Eugene: Cascade, 2012.

Young, Kay, and Jeffrey L. Saver. 'The Neurology of Narrative'. *SubStance* 30 (2001): 72–84.

Zakovitch, Yair. 'Assimilation in Biblical Narratives'. In *Empirical Models for Biblical Criticism*, edited by Jeffery Tigay, 175–96. Philadelphia: University of Philadelphia Press, 1985.

Zerubavel, Eviatar. *Time Maps: Collective Memory and the Social Shape of the Past*. Chicago: University of Chicago Press, 2003.

Zerubavel, Yael. *Recovered Roots: Collective Memory and the Making of Israeli National Tradition*. Chicago: University of Chicago Press, 1995.

Zevit, Ziony. 'Echoes of Texts Past'. In *Subtle Citation, Allusion, and Translation in the Hebrew Bible*, edited by Ziony Zevit, 1–21. Sheffield: Equinox Publishing Ltd., 2017.

Zevit, Ziony, ed. *Subtle Citation, Allusion, and Translation in the Hebrew Bible*. Sheffield: Equinox Publishing Ltd., 2017.

Author Index

Abasciano, B. J.   134, 136, 137, 142
Achtemeier, P. J.   54
Ackroyd, P.   13, 16
Adams, S. V.   168
Adamsen, G. S.   98, 99
Aitken, E. B.   56
Albl, M. C.   148
Alexander, P.   14, 24, 29, 33, 35, 37, 111, 116, 179
Alkier, S.   93
Allen, D. M.   3, 6, 11, 73, 134, 143, 158, 161, 170, 179, 183
Allen, G.   20, 89, 91, 102
Allison, D. C.   54, 62
Anderson, W. H.   43
Avioz, M.   30
Avrahami, Y.   160, 169

Barbour, J.   47
Bartholomew, C.   50–2, 179
Barton, J.   26, 27, 31–3, 43
Barton, S. C.   66
Bates, M. W.   137, 172, 173
Bauckham, R.   50, 151, 178
Beale, G. K.   15, 74–7, 84, 85, 87, 88, 95, 102, 129, 130, 131, 134, 137, 138, 148, 183, 184
Beardsley, M. C.   170
Beentjes, P. C.   19
Beetham, C. A.   134, 135
Beker, J. C.   140
Ben-Porat, Z.   46, 91, 146
Bernstein, M.   24, 28, 115
Bertholet, K.   23
Bertrand, D. A.   29
Blomberg, C.   180
Bloomquist, L. G.   90
Blum, E.   25, 41
Bøe, S.   87, 90
Böhl, F. M. T.   36
Borgen, P.   108, 111
Boyarin, D.   14, 24, 33, 139, 179
Brawley, R. L.   67, 135

Brickle, J. E.   68
Brodie, T. L.   77
Brooke, G.   vii, viii, 13, 25, 28, 57, 58, 64, 120, 181
Brown, J. K.   135, 136, 142
Brueggemann, W.   183

Cadbury, H. J.   31
Carey, H. J.   136
Carmignac, J.   28
Carr, D. M.   12, 19, 64
Carter, J. A.   170
Casey, J. S.   98, 99
Casey, M.   viii
Cave, T.   144, 145, 153
Charles, R. H.   184
Chazon, E.   24
Chester, A.   124
Cheung, S.   42
Childs, B.   24
Chilton, B. D.   166
Ciampa, R. E.   134, 142
Collingwood, R. G.   157, 162, 163, 168, 173, 177
Crawford, S. W.   19
Crenshaw, J. L.   40, 44
Crites, S.   170

Dell, K. J.   3, 41–4, 46, 47, 179
Dewey, J.   54
Dimant, D.   116, 124
Docherty, S. E.   1, 2, 13, 14, 51, 158, 179, 186
Dodd, C. H.   3, 4, 74, 129, 166
Doering, L.   65
Dray, W. H.   162, 163, 170
Dunn, J. D. G.   140
Du Toit, J.   26

Edenburg, C.   61
Elder, N. A.   55
Elledge, C. D.   116

Enns, P.   82, 83, 158
Eshel, H.   121
Esler, P. F.   56, 66, 67
Evans, C. A.   13, 74–7, 80, 81, 84, 87, 89, 137, 165, 181
Eve, E.   59

Farber, W.   36
Fischer, D. H.   162
Fishbane, M.   1, 2, 12–15, 20, 23, 24, 26, 30, 31, 36, 116, 129, 131, 179
Fitzmyer, J. A.   13, 17, 28, 116–20, 122, 125, 181
Fletcher, M.   7, 20, 183–5
Flint, P.   117, 118
Fohrer, G.   44
Foley, J. M.   53, 56, 59, 60
Forman, C. C.   47
Foster, P.   16, 17, 85, 130, 131, 143, 153, 154, 167, 179, 184
Foster, R. B.   31
Fowl, S.   130
Fraade, S.   37
Frahm, E.   32
Frei, H.   114
Furlong, A.   145

Gabbay, U.   32, 37
Gadamer, H-G.   87
Gallusz, L.   99
Garsiel, M.   36
Gerber, E. H.   60, 66
Gerstenberger, E.   40
Gillmayer-Bucher, S.   90
Ginzberg, L.   13
Gladd, B. L.   134, 172
Goldberg, A.   29, 37
Goldingay, J.   44, 131
Goldstein, L. J.   163
Goppelt, L.   99, 130
Gordis, R.   36
Goulder, M. D.   viii, 89
Grabbe, L. L.   viii, 103
Green, K.   144
Green, T. M.   179
Greenspoon, L.   63, 65
Grossberg, D.   36
Gunkel, H.   40–2

Halbertal, M.   37
Halbwachs, M.   65
Halivni, D.   24, 37
Hanson, A. T.   vii, viii, 4, 74, 77, 84, 129
Harris, W. V.   53
Harrison, C.   54, 62
Hayes, C.   30
Hayes, K. M.   59, 62
Hays, R. B.   viii, 1, 5, 6, 15, 16, 43, 45, 60, 77–9, 129–42, 147–50, 152, 165–7, 172, 179, 184–6
Head, P. M.   170
Hearon, H. E.   56, 59
Heaton, E. W.   40, 43
Heckl, R.   26
Heil, J. P.   21
Heinemann, I.   32
Heltzer, M.   26
Hengel, M.   158
Herzberg, W.   36
Hezser, C.   53, 57, 60
Hibbard, T.   31
Hieke T.   93
Hoffman, Y.   42
Hollander, J.   1, 131
Holm-Nielsen, S.   29
Hooker, M. D.   166
Horrell, D.   158
Horsley, R. A.   56, 59, 60
Hubbard, D. A.   51
Hughes, J. A.   29
Humphreys, W. L.   40
Hurtado, L. W.   54, 158, 160

Instone-Brewer, D.   174
Iverson, K. R.   54, 55, 61

Jaffee, M. S.   54, 57, 58
Jauhiainen, M.   91
Johnson, P.   162
Johnson, W. A.   151
Judge, E. A.   158, 160, 164, 171
Juel, D.   31, 129, 174

Kaiser, W. C.   80, 81, 181
Kamesar, A.   105
Katz, P.   104
Kaufman, S.   20
Kayatz, C.   45

Keesmaat, S. C.   134, 135, 139
Keith, C.   55, 68, 141
Kelber, W. H.   55, 57, 66
Kellermann, U.   30
Kirk, A.   54, 68
Kister, M.   28, 124
Klawans, J.   30
Konstan, D.   65
Koskenniemi, E.   109
Kostenberger, A. J.   138
Kowalski, B.   4, 5, 86, 90, 92, 102, 182
Kratz, R. G.   25, 26, 28, 33
Kristeva, J.   42, 131
Kugel, J.   13, 25, 26, 32, 33, 37
Kynes, W.   43, 47

Labahn, M.   56
Lange, A.   23, 117
Le Donne, A.   2, 53, 66, 141
Leonard, J. M.   147
Levenson, J.   30
Levinson, B.   13, 14, 19, 20, 27
Lewis, M.   161
Liebengood, K. D.   134
Lieberman, S. J.   31, 37
Lim, T. H.   13, 14, 23
Lincicum, D.   165, 169, 176, 185
Lindars, B.   viii, 4, 74, 129
Lindblom, J.   45
Litwak, K. D.   131, 134–6, 140, 142
Lonergan, B.   162, 163, 167
Lucas, A. J.   130, 137, 150
Lyons, M. A.   16, 20, 27, 33, 180

McGrath, J. F.   60, 61
McKane, W.   40, 45
Macmurray, J.   157, 170
Maier, J.   117
Mandel, Paul D.   24, 37
Mason, R.   18
Mattingly, H. B.   158
Maxwell, K. R.   62
Meek, R.   139
Menken, M. J. J.   vii, ix, 64, 178
Mettinger, T. N. D.   47
Meyer, B. F.   163
Milgrom, J.   30
Miller, G. D.   43, 45
Misztal, B. A.   66

Montanaro, A.   64
Moore, G. F.   31
Morales, N. R.   145, 149, 152
Morawski, S.   16
Morgan, D. F.   44
Moyise, S.   vii–ix, 7, 14, 15, 78, 79, 81,
   84, 87, 89, 90, 138, 139, 143, 171,
   178, 179, 183
Murphy, R. E.   40, 42

Najman, H.   24, 117
Neilson, K.   171
Neusner, J.   33
Nickelsburg, G. W. E.   29, 116
Nicklas, T.   93
Nielsen, M. H.   29, 162
Nihan, C.   27
Noegel, S.   36
Nongbri, B.   160
North, J. L.   vii
Novakic, L.   31
Novick, T.   29
Nowell, I.   29

O'Brien, K. S.   129, 132, 135
Olick, J. K.   66
Olyan, S.   30
Oropeza, B. J.   138, 139
Ostmeyer, K-H.   95, 96

Pakkala, J.   17, 18
Pao, D. W.   82, 83, 148
Pattemore, S. W.   145, 149, 184
Paulien, J.   46, 87–9, 99
Perdue, L. G.   41, 48–50, 204
Perrot, C.   165
Perry, P. S.   145
Pilkington, A.   152, 153
Popavic, M.   124
Porter S. E.   77, 87, 89, 133, 137–40
Powell, M. A.   111, 135, 136
Punt, J.   67

Qimron, E.   123, 124

Radner, E.   173
Rainbow, J.   183, 184
Rawidowicz, S.   32
Redditt, P.   31

Ricoeur, P. 111
Ringgren, H. 12
Rodríguez, R. 55, 56, 58–60, 68
Rösel, M. 26
Rosner, B. S. 142
Rowe, C. K. 167
Rowland, C. viii, 65
Ruppert, L. 29

Samely, A. 14, 24, 29, 32, 35, 179
Sanders J. A. 137
Sandmel, S. 86, 129, 160
Saver, J. L. 170
Savran, G. W. 18
Schaper, J. 54, 61
Schenck, K. 5, 105
Schnabel E. J. 82, 83, 148
Schorch, S. 36
Schultz, R. 12, 15–17, 19, 20
Schwartz, B. 67, 180
Schwartz, D. R. 23
Scott, B. B. 50
Scott, I. W. 160
Scott, J. M. 159
Scott, M. 140
Segal, M. 26, 28, 31, 33, 117
Seidel, M. 19
Shemesh, A. 37
Shepherd, M. B. 79
Shroyer, M. J. 105
Shum, S-L. 132, 136
Smith, S. 6, 135, 144, 145, 148, 149, 185
Sneed, M. 41
Snodgrass, K. 74–7, 84
Sommer, B. D. 1, 12, 15, 16, 20, 42, 146
Sommer, M. 91, 92–3
Spellman, C. 46
Sperber, D. 6, 143–5, 185
Stackert, J. 14
Stamps, D. L. 130
Stanley, C. D. 21, 60, 130, 135, 137, 148, 166, 169, 180, 183–5
Stead, M. 42
Steinmetz, D. 33
Sterling, G. E. 28, 103, 104
Sternberg, M. 39, 182
Stone, M. 24
Stromberg, J. 27
Sweeney, M. 31

Talmon, S. 19
Tanner, B. 42
Teeter, A. 25, 33, 37, 180
Teugels, L. M. 24, 37
Thatcher, T. 2, 6, 53, 65–8, 141
Thompson, M. B. 129, 134, 140, 142
Tigay, J. 32, 37
Tobin, T. H. 106, 112
Todorov, T. 144
Tõniste, K. 134–5
Tooman, W. 2, 12, 16, 19, 20, 29, 30, 35, 178–80
Torrey, C. C. 25
Trotter, D. 144
Tzoref, S. 23, 33

Ulrich, E. 23

van der Dussen, W. 162
Vanderkam, J. 25, 117, 118
Veeser, H. A. 163
Venter, P. M. 31
Vermes, G. 13, 24, 25, 33
Vleeming, S. P. 26
Von Rad, G. 44

Wagner, J. R. 133, 134, 142
Wall, R. W. 50
Watson, F. 78, 79, 130, 133, 165, 166
Watts, R. 6, 7, 78, 79, 165, 169, 172, 183, 185
Weber, M. 162
Weeks, S. 43
Weigold M. 117
Weinryb, E. 162
Weitzman, S. 29
Werman, C. 37
Wesselius, J. W. 26
Whedbee, J. W. 44
Whitenton, M. R. 62
Whybray, R. N. 42, 44
Willi, T. 24
Williams, C. H. viii, 3, 63, 67, 68, 180
Williamson, H. G. M. 27
Wilson, D. 6, 143–6, 149, 151, 185
Wilson, G. 31
Wimsatt, W. K. 170
Winston, D. 108
Winter, B. W. 168

Witherington III, B. 48, 49, 51, 52
Wolff, H. W. 44
Wolfson, H. A. 103
Wright, N. T. 78, 163, 168

Yadin, Y. 28
Yadin-Israel, A. 37

Yamasaki, G. 111
Young, K. 170

Zakovitch, Y. 27, 28, 38
Zerubavel, E. 66
Zerubavel, Y. 66
Zevit, Z. 1, 147

Index of References

1. OLD TESTAMENT

Genesis
1	110, 112, 124
1–2	112
1–11	34
1.1–2.24	34
1.26-27	160
1.27	110, 112
1.27-28	110
2	112
2–3	123
2.1–6.4	34
2.4	34
2.7	112
2.9b	29
2.18-24	123
2.23b-24	123 n.23
2.24	97 n.47, 123
3	34
3.1-23	34
3.8	106
3.16	123
3.20	112
3.24	108
4.1-2	34
4.3-16	34
4.17-26	34
5.1-32	34
6.1-4	34
6.5–9.17	34
6.5–11.9	34
6.6	106
6.9-10	34
7–9	31 n.26
9.18-19	34
9.20-27	34
9.28	34
10.1-32	34
10.12-20	37
11.1-9	34
11.10-30	34
12	28, 37–8, 112
12.1	4, 97–8
12.10-20	180
14.18-20	107
15.2	112–13
15.6	78, 185
17.19	146
18.27	112
19.19	97 n.47
19.26	147
20	28, 37–8, 112, 180
22.12	112
24.6-8	18
24.40-41	18
26	28
27.8	34
27.10	34
27.12	34
27.16	34
27.30-41	34
27.42–28.5	34
28.10-22	34
29.31	112
31.13	109
31.14-15	112
31.23	97 n.47
31.28	112
33.5	112
34.3	97 n.47
39.12	174
50.24	174
50.24a	175
50.24-25	174
50.25	174–5

Exodus
1–13	38
3–4	111
3.2	111
3.4	100, 111
3.6	4, 74, 78, 82–3, 100, 174
3.7	100

3.8	100	26.5	16
3.8-10	174	26.15	29
3.9	100	26.44	122
3.10-14	100		
3.12	100	*Numbers*	
3.13	100	5.18	108
3.13-14	169	14.24	14
3.14	91, 99–100	14.30	14
3.15	100	24.8	80
3.20	100	24.15-17	121
4.12	112	36.7	97 n.47
4.22	168, 175	36.9	97 n.47
6.2	169		
7–10	91–3	*Deuteronomy*	
7–11	92–3	4.4	97 n.47
8.10	168	5–6	122
10.3	100	5.12	118
12.10	64	5.12-14	13, 20
13	122	5.28-29	121
13.19	175	6.5	29
14.15	174	6.13	96 n.45
15.11	168	7	30
15.17	175	7.1-3	29, 30
15.17-18	120	7.8	159
16.2	68	9.5	159
18.4	112	10.20	96 n.45, 97 n.47
18.7	112	11	122
19	99 n.53	11.22	97 n.47
20	112, 122	13.5	97 n.47
20.21	121	13.18	97 n.47
23	30	18.18-19	121
23.20	159 n.6	21.15-17	112–13
24	31 n.26	23	30
28	108	23.7	29
33.15-16	175	23.3-5	18
33.17–34.9	168	23.6-7	30
33.18	68	25.4	171 n.58
33.22	68	25.5	14
34	30	28	31 n.26
34.6	68	28.21	97 n.47
		28.60	96 n.45, 97 n.47
Leviticus		29–30	176
13.45-46	122	29.19	96 n.45
17.11	112	30.11-14	172
18.5	78	30.20	97 n.47
18.19-30	30	31–32	29
25.18	16	32.5	161
25.19	16	33	120
26	29, 31 n.26	33.8-11	121

Joshua

6.26	121
22.5	97 n.47
23.8	97 n.47
24.32	175

Judges

5.31	184
18.22	97 n.47
20.42	97 n.47
20.45	97 n.47

Ruth

1.14	95, 97
1.16	95–7
2.8	95–7
2.9	96
2.11	97–8
2.14-18	96
2.21	97 n.47
2.23	97 n.47
3.15	96

1 Samuel

2.2	168
14.22	97 n.47
25	30
31.2	97 n.47

2 Samuel

1.6	97 n.47
7	120
7.10-11a	175
7.11b	175
7.11c	175
7.12b	175
7.13b-14a	175
20.2	96 n.45, 97 n.47
23.10	97 n.47

1 Kings

11.2	96 n.45, 97 n.47

2 Kings

1.18	96 n.45
3.3	96 n.45, 97 n.47
5.27	96 n.45, 97 n.47
14.6	17
18.6	96 n.45, 97 n.47

1 Chronicles

17.20	168
10.2	97 n.47

2 Chronicles

3.12	97 n.47
6.14	168

Ezra

9	30, 30 n.24
9.1-2	30
9.4-15	30
9.10	17
9.11b-12	29

Nehemiah

13.1-2	18
13.15-16	20

Job

7	46
11.7-9	47
14	46
19.20	97 n.47
23.8-9	47
26	31 n.26
29.10	96 n.45, 97 n.47
31.7	97 n.47
38.38	96 n.45, 97 n.47
41.16	96 n.45, 97 n.47
41.23	96 n.45, 97 n.47

Psalms

1	41
1.1	41
1.1a	175
1.4-6	41
2	120
2.1-2	120, 176
2.7	29, 175
8	171 n.57
8.4	46–7
19.1	42
19.4	42, 179
22	33, 94, 180
22.1	87
22.15	96 n.45, 97 n.47
23	47
25.21	96 n.45

33.6	42	10.31	48
33.21 LXX	64	10.32	51 n.59
35.10	168	15.11	48
36.6	168	15.20	51 n.59
36.6 LXX	148	15.31	48
44.25	96 n.45, 97 n.47	16.8	49
47	41	16.24	51 n.59
51	123	18.8	51 n.59
63.8	96 n.45, 97 n.47	21.21	46
69	33	24.5	48
74	31 n.26	26.11	48
86.8	168	30	44 n.33
89	31 n.26		
95.11	14	*Ecclesiastes*	
101.4	96 n.45, 97 n.47	1	51
102	33	7	49
102.5	96 n.45, 97 n.47	7.20	50
102.25	42	11	47
110.1	14, 159–60	12.5	48
114.3	174	12.13	51
117	31 n.26		
118	31 n.26	*Song of Songs*	
119.25	96 n.45, 97 n.47	1.2	183–4
119.31	96 n.45, 97 n.47	1.4	183
119.133	123	4.10	183
135	41	5.2	184
137.6	96 n.45, 97 n.47	7.12	183
139	47	*Isaiah*	
139.5	47	1.4	112
139.7-10	47	2	31 n.26
139.7-12	47	2.22	119
146	41	5	31 n.26
146.5-8	122	6.3	100
		7.14	180
Proverbs		8.11	175
1.3	45	11	31 n.26
3.13-20	42, 45	16.11-14	13
6.2	51 n.59	17	31 n.26
6.6	46	21	31 n.26
7.6	51	22.21	182
7.8	51	22.22	182
7.27	51	22.25	182
8	42, 45	24	31 n.26
8.2-3	45	24–27	30, 31 n.26
8.7	51 n.59	24.17	119
9	51	28.29	45
9.1	51	29.13	160
9.14	51	31.2	45

33.5	45	48	31 n.26
34	93	50–51	92–3
40–55	33		
40.3	168 n.45	*Lamentations*	
40.10	88 n.6	2.2	96 n.45
42.1	29	4.4	96 n.45, 97 n.47
42.4	42	5	47
45.12	42	5.15	48
45.23	60 n.46, 160	*Ezekiel*	
50	93	1.26-27	19
52	31 n.26	1.26-28	19
52.5	180	3.26	97 n.47
52.10	146	8.2	19
53	33	18.2-3	44
53.7-8	14	18.2a	44
54	31 n.26, 33	23.3	183
54.14-17	33	23.8	183
56–66	33	23.21	183
56.7	159	29.4	97 n.47
57.1	33	37	123–4
58.6	58, 148	37.4	123
60	31 n.26	37.4-10	124 n.30
61.1	58, 122	37.9	124
61.1-2	146, 148	37.11-12	124 n.26
61.2	58	37.23	175
65	174	38	93
65–66	33	38–39	19, 30, 90
65.1	173		
65.1-2	172	*Daniel*	
65.2	173	1–7	44
66	31 n.26	7	183, 185
66.5-6	33	7.13	159
		9	31, 185
Jeremiah		9.2	13
7.11	159	9.4b-19	20 n.34
9.24	45	9.24-27	13
10.12	45	10	183
13.11	96 n.45, 97 n.47	12.3	161
17.21-22	13, 20	12.10	176
18.18	45	*Hosea*	
22.3	45	3.4	119
22.15	45	4	31 n.26
23.5	45	6.1-3	80
25.11-14	13	11.1	4, 74, 78–81, 83, 181–2
26	25	11.1-11	80
31.29-30	44	13–14	31 n.26
33.15	45	14.1-9	80

Joel
3	93
3.1-5	116 n.6

Amos
1–2	44 n.33
3.2	173
3.3-8	44
5	31 n.26
9.11	175

Micah
1	31 n.26

Habbakuk
2.4	4, 73–4, 78–9, 83
2.8	119

Zechariah
11.12-13	17

Malachi
3.1	17, 159 n.6, 168 n.45

2. QUMRAN

1QH
11.6-19	20 n.34

1QpHab
7.1-5	119 n.15
7.3	57 n.29
7.7-8	119 n.15
9.3-5	119

1QM
10.6	23 n.2

1QS
5.17-18	119
6.6-8	57–8, 61 n.54
6.8	57
7.1	57 n.29
8.14-15	57 n.29

1QSa
1.4	57 n.29

4Q174
1–2 i 16	23 n.2
i 6	120
i 8	120
i 17	120
i 19	120

4Q274
1 i 3-4	122

4Q379
22 ii 7-14	121

4Q385
2 3	124
2 5	123–4
2 6	124
2 7	124
2 8	124
2 9	124
4	124 n.29

4Q416
2 ii 21	123
2 iii-iv	123
2 iii 20	123
2 iii 21	123
2 iii 21-2 iv 1	123
2 iv 2-7	123
2 iv 4	123
2 iv 5	123
2 iv 13	123

4Q463
1 2-3	122

4Q521
ii 8-13	122

4QD
5.8	23 n.2
7.10	23 n.2
8.14-15	23 n.2

4QDb
19.7	23 n.2

11Q13
2.10	23 n.2

11QPsa
19.15-16	123
27.11	23 n.2

CD
4.12-18	119
5.2	57 n.29

5.15-17	159	*Cher.*	
7.8-9	118	11	108
8.14-15	159	12	108
9.2	118	17	108
9.5	118	27–28	108
9.7-8	118	35	106
10.16-17	118	49	104
11.7-9	20		
16.6-7	118	*Creation (Opif.)*	
20.15-17	119	1–2	105
		13	106

3. APOCRYPHA/PSEUDEPIGRAPHA

		77	110, 180
		78	110
Baruch		83	110
1.20	96 n.45	134–135	112
3.4	96 n.45		
		Conf.	
1 Esdras		2–3	105 n.8
4.20	96 n.45	146	106 n.15
		190	105
1 Enoch			
14.8-25	20 n.34	*Cong.*	
		11	109
2 Enoch		15	109
30.15	29		
		Contempl.	
Jubilees		28–29	105
2.29-30	20		
3.6b-7	123 n.23	*Dec.*	
50.8	20	36	109
		37–43	109
1 Maccabees		121–131	113
3.2	96 n.45	126	113
6.21	96 n.45	127	113
2 Maccabees		*Deus*	
15.9	94	22	106
		29	106
Sirach		32	106
2.3	96 n.45		
19.2	96 n.45	*Fug.*	
49.10	94	108	106
Tobit			
6.19	96 n.45	*Her.*	

4. PHILO

		22–62	112
Abr.		201	106
3	112		
52	106	*Leg.*	
82	107	3.4	106
103	112		

3.79	107	7.21-29	52
3.96	106	7.24-27	51
		8.20	48
Migr.		10.24	48
89	103–4	10.39	49
91	105	11.16-19	51
92	105	11.19	51
102	106	15.32	48
		15.34	48, 87
Mos.		17.2	184
1.63-84	111, 180	19.5	96 n.45, 97 n.46
1.67	111	19.24	49
2.46-47	105 n.10	23.35	67
		27.9-10	17
Praem.			
1–2	105 n.10	*Mark*	
2	112	1.2	17
		1.2-3	56, 158, 168, 168 n.45
QG		2.27-28	49
4.61	112	7.1-13	159, 169
		7.13	166
Somn.		7.14	165
1.227-230	109	8.35	49
		10.2-9	159
Spec.		10.25	49
1.1	112	10.45	33
1.66	106	11.17	159
1.67	105	12.24-27	14
1.82-97	108	12.27	166
1.85	108	12.28-33	169
1.86	108	12.35-37	14
1.87	108	14.62	159

5. NEW TESTAMENT

		Luke	
		1.13	146
Matthew		1.70	17
1.22	180	2.30	146
2.5	17	2.30-32	33
2.15	4, 74, 78–81, 83, 181–2	2.46	50
2.23	17	3.22	29
5.17	166	4	147
5.21-48	165	4.4	146
5.43-48	84	4.8	146
6.22-23	51	4.10	146
6.25	51	4.12	146
6.25-32	51	4.16-20	58
7	51	4.16-21	54
7.2	48	4.17	58
7.12	169	4.18-19	146, 148

4.21	58	19.36	63
4.25-27	58, 147	19.37	56
5.1	166		
6.2b	49	*Acts*	
6.38	48	2.14	116 n.6
6.40a	48	2.43-47	111 n.24
7.22	58	3.22	17
9.59	48	4.31	166
10.11	96 n.45, 97 n.46	5.13	96 n.45, 97 n.46
11.51	67	7.38	164
13.34	148	8.28	54
15	4	8.29	96 n.45, 97 n.46
15.11-32	97	8.30	54
15.13	96	8.34	14
15.15	95–6, 97 n.46	9.2	158
15.16	95	9.26	96 n.45, 97 n.46
16.10	48	10.28	96 n.45, 97 n.46
17.26	147	11.26	158
17.32	147	15.21	54
17.37	49	17.11	160
18.25	49	17.34	96 n.45, 97 n.46
19.41-44	149	19.9	158
20.37	4, 74, 78, 82–3	19.23	158
22.20	165 n.33	22.3	164
22.37	33	24.14	158
23.46	148	24.22	158
24.27	56	26.23	33
24.32	56	26.28	158
24.44-45	56		
24.44-47	147	*Romans*	
24.46	56	1.17	4, 73–4, 78, 83
		2.24	180
John		3.2	164
1.14-16	68	3.10	51
1.23	56 n.21	3.10-18	146, 159
5.29	58	4.3	56
6.41	68	4.6	56 n.21
6.43	68	7.12	165
7.38	56, 184	7.14	165
7.42	56	8	51
8.39	63	9–11	164, 169, 173
8.56	63	9.6	164, 166
10	63	9.17	56
10.35	164, 166	10	174
12.25	49	10.18	179
12.38-39	56 n.21	10.19	56 n.21
13.16	48	10.20	56 n.21
15.20	48	10.20-21	172
19.24	56	11.2	56

11.9	56 n.21	3.1	160
12.9	96 n.45, 97 n.46	3.10	160
12.15	17	4.16	54

1 Corinthians   *1 Thessalonians*

4.6	160, 169	1.1	169
5.3-5	166	1.9	166
6.16-17	96 n.45, 97 n.46	2.7-8	169
		2.13	166
8.6	159, 168, 168 n.45	5.27	54

                                        1 Timothy

9.8-10	179	5.18	56
9.9	171 n.58		
9.26	166	*Hebrews*	
11.17-34	54	1.5-14	56
14.1-40	54	1.6	172
14.36	166	1.7	172
		1.8	172
2 Corinthians		2.6	17
1.12-14	169	2.12-13	56
1.24	169	3–4	14
6.16	166	3.7-9	56
6.16-18	159	4.1-11	110 n.22
9.6	17	4.9	14
9.7	17	4.12-13	108
		5.6	172
Galatians		5.12	164
3.8	56	7.1-2	107
3.15	164 n.29	8.8	172
3.17a	164 n.29	8.8-12	56
3.17b	164 n.29	8.13	165 n.33
3.19a	164 n.29	9.14	166
3.19b	164 n.29	10.1	105
3.21	164 n.29	10.31	166
3.23-24	164 n.29	11	67
4.30	56	11.4	67
5.16-26	169	12.24	67
		13.15	17
Ephesians		*James*	
5.19-20	54	1.5-6	50
		2.23	58
Philippians			
2	60 n.46	*1 John*	
2.10	161	1.1-3	169
2.15	161	3.12	67
Colossians		*Jude*	
2.17	105	11	67
2.22	160		

Revelation

1.1	100
1.3	54
1.4	100–1
1.5	99
1.5b-6	99
1.8	100–1
1.9	100
1.12-18	183–5
1.13	184
1.16	183
2.9	100
2.10	100
2.12-17	99
2.22	100
3.7	182
3.8	183
3.12	100
3.20	184
4–5	100
4.8	100–1
5.9	99
6.1-2	93
6.12-17	92–3
7.1-17	99
7.9-17	99
7.14	100
8–9	99
8.6–11.19	99
11.1-14	99
11.15-19	99
11.17	100–1
12–13	99
12.1	100
12.3	100
13.13	100
13.14	100
14.1-5	99
15–16	99
15.1	100
15.1-5	99
15.2-4	99
15.3	87
15.5–16.21	99
16.5	100–1
16.14	92, 100
17.1–21.8	99
17.8	100–1
18.4	93, 99–100
18.5	96 n.45, 97 n.46
19–22	184
19.20	100
20.1-6	99
21.2	100
21.1-8	99
21.4	100
21.6	100
21.9–22.5	99
21.10	100
21.22–22.5	99
22.4	100
22.12	88 n.6

www.ingramcontent.com/pod-product-compliance
Lightning Source LLC
Chambersburg PA
CBHW052035300426
44117CB00012B/1839